DESIRE AND THE ASCETIC IDEAL

STUDIES IN RELIGION AND CULTURE

John D. Barbour and Gary L. Ebersole, Editors

DESIRE AND THE ASCETIC IDEAL

Buddhism and Hinduism in the
Works of T. S. Eliot

EDWARD UPTON

UNIVERSITY OF VIRGINIA PRESS
Charlottesville and London

University of Virginia Press
© 2023 by the Rector and Visitors of the University of Virginia
All rights reserved
Printed in the United States of America on acid-free paper

First published 2023

9 8 7 6 5 4 3 2 1

Library of Congress Cataloging-in-Publication Data

Names: Upton, Edward, author.
Title: Desire and the ascetic ideal : Buddhism and Hinduism in the works of
    T. S. Eliot / Edward Upton.
Description: Charlottesville : University of Virginia Press, 2023. |
    Series: Studies in religion and culture | Includes bibliographical
    references and index.
Identifiers: LCCN 2023011332 (print) | LCCN 2023011333 (ebook) |
    ISBN 9780813949987 (hardcover) | ISBN 9780813949994 (paperback) |
    ISBN 9780813950501 (ebook)
Subjects: LCSH: Eliot, T. S. (Thomas Stearns), 1888–1965—Religion. | Eliot,
    T. S. (Thomas Stearns), 1888–1965—Criticism and interpretation. |
    Buddhism in literature. | Hinduism in literature.
Classification: LCC PS3509.L43 Z885 2023 (print) | LCC PS3509.L43 (ebook) |
    DDC 821/.912—dc23/eng/20230607
LC record available at https://lccn.loc.gov/2023011332
LC ebook record available at https://lccn.loc.gov/2023011333

Cover art: Thomas Stearns Eliot, portrait by Wyndham Lewis, 1930. (National
Gallery of Victoria, Melbourne / © Wyndham Lewis Memorial Trust. All
rights reserved 2023 / Bridgeman Images)

To my entire family, especially to my wife, Nicole,
and
in memory of my grandfather, William Phillips

CONTENTS

Acknowledgments — ix

Introduction: Eliot and Skillful Means — 1

1. Skillful Means and Asceticism in T. S. Eliot's
    Critique of Schopenhauer — 35

2. T. S. Eliot's *Ars Religiosa:* Transmigration and
    Faith in *Knowledge and Experience* — 63

3. India among the Fragments: Pessimism and Desire in
    The Waste Land — 80

4. Language and the Cultivation of Desire in
    "The Fire Sermon" — 107

5. Transcendence Revisited: Hallucination and
    Literary Asceticism — 152

6. Language in the Middle Way: T. S. Eliot's Engagement
    with Madhyamaka Buddhism in *Four Quartets* — 180

7. Performing the Divine Illusion: Memory, Desire, and
    the Performance of Form in "Burnt Norton" — 210

Notes — 241
Bibliography — 283
Index — 297

ACKNOWLEDGMENTS

This book was written over many years, beginning as a dissertation at the University of Chicago but growing into something very different from that original document. I therefore have friends and colleagues from several different institutions to thank for encouragement and support. It is a pleasure to remember with gratitude the generosity of all of them. Whatever good appears here is no doubt due to them; whatever is erroneous is completely my own.

First and foremost, I must thank Wendy Doniger, my adviser at the University of Chicago. This book would not have been written without her encouragement, wisdom, and advice over many years. Her intellect, strength, and good will are a model for me, and I am amazed at her abiding generosity and relentless curiosity. Likewise, many thanks to Richard Rosengarten, a mentor and friend whose grace, optimism, intelligence, and humor kept this project on course. Wendy and Rick believed in this project from early on. I would not have been able to bring it to a conclusion without their support. Thanks also to faculty at Chicago while I was there who encouraged this project in its earlier stages: Dan Arnold, Robert Bird, Arnold Davidson, Mark Krupnick Shiro Matsumoto, Paul Mendes-Flohr, James E. Miller Jr., Margaret M. Mitchell, Teresa Hord Owens, Stephanie Paulsell, Winnifred Fallers Sullivan, Kathryn Tanner, David Tracy. This project began under the mentorship of the late Anthony C. Yu, from whom I learned greatly. Thanks also to Nathelda McGee, Sandy Norbeck, and Sandra Peppers. The project benefited from the conversation, wit, and generosity of good friends. Thanks especially to Kristen Bloomer, Katie Brink, Elizabeth Bucar, Geoff Chaplin, David Clairmont, Brian Collins, Courtney Fitzsimmons, M. Cooper Harriss, Joel Harter, John Howell, Michael Johnson, Sonam Kachru, Meira Kensky, Karen Meyers, Jay Munsch, Jennifer Muslin, Joanna Nemeh, Robert Saler, Lea Schweitz, Marsaura Shukla, Michael Skerker, William Wood.

At Christ College, the Honors College of Valparaiso University, the project benefited from the support of several distinguished deans:

Mel Piehl, Panayiotis (Peter) Kanelos, Susan VanZanten, and Jennifer Prough. I also owe a debt of gratitude to the solidarity and support of the wonderful colleagues I have had there, including Dorothy Bass, Gretchen Buggeln, Joseph Creech, Margaret Franson, Joseph Goss, Samuel Graber, Carter Hanson, Agnes Howard, Tal Howard, Slavica Jakelic, Stephanie Johnson, Jon MacFarlane, George Pati, Matthew Puffer, Mark Schwehn, Julien Smith, Garry Sparks, Anna Stewart, David Western. Likewise, I could not have completed this without the patience and guidance of our wonderful administrative staff, including Katie Bringman-Baxter, Brett Calland, Sharon Dybel, Kristin Nygaard, Patrice Weil, and Jo Ellen Zromkoski. Hearty thanks to my two unstoppable research assistants, Elizabeth Park and Jeremy Reed. Randall Zromkoski provided constant good humor and perspective. My deep thanks to David Kenis, Anand Popli, and Teresa Young, without whose help this book would not have been written. Finally, my abiding gratitude to all of my students at Christ College; their hope, optimism, intelligence, and dedication inspire me every day to continue our communal pursuit of truth.

I have also appreciated conversation, support, and practical wisdom from members of the International T. S. Eliot Society, especially Jewel Spears Brooker, Tom Brous, Sara Fitzgerald, Deborah Leiter, Kinereth Meyer, Patrick Query, Kevin Rulo, Ronald Schuchard, Jayme Stayer, Aakanksha Virkar-Yates.

Very, very early on, this project was given support by figures who probably wouldn't even remember giving such support. I name them nevertheless with abiding gratitude: Brian Daley, SJ, Daniel Donoghue, J. Bryan Hehir, Harbour Hodder, Robert Kiely, Anthony Kubiak. Very special thanks to Larry Lowe, a mentor and friend, the first to teach me that poetry was to be performed.

Sincere thanks for the patience and practical wisdom of Eric Arthur Brandt at the University of Virginia Press and to all members of the production staff, especially J. Andrew Edwards, and copyeditor Jane M. Curran. Also, deep thanks to the anonymous reviewers for the press. They truly showed me what the peer review process should be: critical, constructive, and collegial.

My deep gratitude to the Estate of T. S. Eliot along with Faber and Faber, Ltd., which has given kind permission to quote from Eliot's unpublished notes on Masaharu Anesaki's course, housed at Harvard's Houghton Library. Likewise, many thanks to the professional and courteous staff at Harvard's Houghton Library, where it was a pleasure to do research.

Earlier versions of some chapters appeared in the following publications. All have my thanks for the permission to work with the material again:

Chapter 1: "Approaching Nirvana: Skillful Means and Asceticism in T. S. Eliot's Critique of Schopenhauer." Reprint permission granted by the University of Notre Dame, *Religion & Literature* 48, no. 1 (Spring 2016).

Chapter 2: "T. S. Eliot's *Ars Religiosa*: Transmigration and Faith in *Knowledge and Experience*." *Journal of Religion* 100, no. 1 (January 2020). (University of Chicago)

Chapter 5: "Translation, Comparison, and the Hermeneutics of the Fragment in *The Waste Land*." *Journal of Religion* 96, no. 1 (January 2016). (University of Chicago)

Chapter 6: "Language in the Middle Way: T. S. Eliot's Engagement with Madhyamaka Buddhism in *Four Quartets*." *Journal of the American Academy of Religion* 86, no. 3 (March 2018).

Finally, this book is dedicated to my entire family, every last one of them (parents, in-laws, brothers, sister, brother- and sisters-in-law, nieces, aunts, uncles, cousins, etc.), and especially to my beautiful wife, Nicole, upon whose love, constant support, and sense of humor I always depend. I give thanks for her every single day. Most of my family have never read anything by T. S. Eliot and may not even read this book much past the acknowledgments page. No matter. I love them, and this book is for them. The book is also in memory of my grandfather, William Phillips, who died in the initial wave of the pandemic.

DESIRE AND THE ASCETIC IDEAL

INTRODUCTION

ELIOT AND SKILLFUL MEANS

Long before I was a Christian, I was a student of Indian philosophy, and of the Buddhist scriptures in Pali: both from study of some original texts, under teachers of Indic philology and philosophy at Harvard, and from an early interest in Schopenhauer and Deussen in connexion with Sanskrit. I have thought that as the scholastics notably St. Thomas, incorporated Aristotelianism into Christian thought, so the task remains for some still more encyclopedic scholar (who would need also an encyclopedic imagination) to reconcile and incorporate Eastern religious thought into that of Christianity. So far, most students of the East have known little, and cared less about their own western tradition of thought; or else have started from the assumption that the East has nothing to teach us. The result is, that we have largely learned the wrong things. . . . This is outside of my competence, and I have little learning; but I do think that some of my poetry is peculiar in a kind of poetic fusion of Eastern and Western currents of feeling.

—T. S. ELIOT TO EGON VIETTA, February 23, 1947, *The Poems of T. S. Eliot*

I have never known a desire to be expelled by anything but another desire. And psychology seems to me for the most part to ignore the more intense, profound and satisfying emotions of religion. It must ignore their value, because its function is merely to describe and not to express preference. But if this is true, it can never take the place of religion, though it can be an important accessory.

—T. S. ELIOT, "The Search for Moral Sanction"

As the sense of sin depends upon the supernatural, so from the sense of sin issues the ascetic life.

　　—T. S. ELIOT, "The Modern Dilemma"

The field of T. S. Eliot studies is currently undergoing a major transformation. We are witnessing the publication of new, critical, annotated editions of his poetry, his complete correspondence, and all of his prose works in a new critical edition. This latter project in particular is impressive, since it brings together so much of Eliot's unpublished materials. The release of such new material is leading to a renaissance of Eliot studies and is prompting literary critics into a new assessment of Eliot's work. We are currently only at the beginning of this critical reappraisal.

This book seeks to draw from this newly released material as well as material not yet released in an attempt to reread Eliot's interest in material from ancient India. There has not been a major book-length study on Eliot and Indian sources since Cleo McNelly Kearns's seminal book, *T. S. Eliot and Indic Traditions*, in 1995.[1] Kearns did the necessary groundbreaking research in tracking down the Indian sources to which Eliot had access. She also connected Eliot's interest in Indian materials to his concomitant interest in Western mysticism, showing how both of these informed the dialectic of "surrender and recovery" we find in Eliot's poetry and criticism.[2] Kearns, following A. David Moody, also perceptively demonstrated how the engagement with Indian sources led to Eliot's later interest in poetry's ability to give voice to a wisdom that spans discursive traditions.[3] In its wide-ranging scope, Kearns's valuable work placed Eliot's interest in India in terms of different discourse communities of which he was a part (philosophical, literary, and religious) and initiated a truly interdisciplinary inquiry.[4]

Kearns's book should have led to a realigning of Eliot studies, looking at Eliot's careful and sustained negotiations of religious difference. Indeed, her work has been well received and often admired as a central contribution to Eliot studies. The present book would not have been possible without Kearns's pioneering research, and I see it as pursuing possibilities opened up by that research. The reader can discern my debt throughout. Nevertheless, her work has, in my estimation, become largely ignored in favor of a renewed interest in Eliot's "Anglo-Catholicism." Hence, we see the efforts of scholars such as Barry Spurr to downplay the influence of Indian materials on Eliot's work, centering his approach instead on unfolding the ritual texture of the Anglo-Catholic communities of which Eliot would eventually become a part.[5] Indeed, in a recent essay on *The Waste Land*, Spurr gently dismisses the importance of Indian sources, writing that "Eliot's allusions in his poetry to Eastern philosophy and religion are striking because of their rarity, providing different perspectives, or a brief widening of vision, when they do appear, in relation to the Western philosophical, spiritual and religious sources and ideas."[6] Spurr's approach in fact echoes some of the early dismissals of the appearance of Indian materials in *The Waste Land*, such as that of F. R. Leavis, who claimed that these materials only served to provide an "appropriate portentousness" to the poem.[7] Spurr's work in its own right is excellent and a real contribution to our understanding of Eliot's proclaimed religious affiliation. However, it merely raises the question of Eliot's interest in India more insistently: how do we understand Eliot's abiding interest in these materials, even long after his conversion to a rigorous and ritually ornate Anglo-Catholicism? *Four Quartets*, after all, represents one of Eliot's most sophisticated engagements with these sources.

On the other hand, the study of Orientalism, as well as of colonialism and its aftermath, has opened up new ways of thinking about literary negotiations of religious difference. As a result, it offers us an opportunity to revisit Kearns's project in a different key. Postcolonial criticism has gradually moved away from a too-simplistic reliance on Edward Said's orientalist binaries, opting instead for a more nuanced view of intercultural negotiation, in both colonies and imperial centers alike.[8] In Eliot studies, such an approach has been adapted by Jahan Ramazani, who has suggested that Eliot's poetry is best understood as hybrid, attempting to negotiate the various religious and cultural fragments in which he is situated. In writing about *The Waste Land*, Ramazani suggests, "*The Waste Land*, while not escaping the Orientalism of modern Western representations of the East, also sets Eastern and Western texts in dialogic relation with one another, and in this double-voicedness, in the seams between the pieces of the transhemispheric collage, in the cross-cultural slippage between text and embedded text, the Eastern quotations retain at least some capacity to make themselves heard."[9] Ramazani does not deny Eliot's conservative cultural politics, or his later endorsements of empire. Nevertheless, despite Eliot's own claims, Ramazani insists that

Eliot's poetry bears the traces of the cultural other despite Eliot's later nostalgic demands for cultural homogeneity. In effect, Ramazani is reading Eliot against Eliot. His work, looking at the interactions of culture in a more nuanced way, opens up a whole new range of ways of seeing Eliot's corpus. Indeed, this book suggests that it may in fact be Eliot's dialogical engagement with and study of Indian materials that eventually leads him to a more conservative view of Christianity. At the very least, Ramazani's approach suggests that we cannot consider Eliot's religious views outside of the context of nineteenth- and twentieth-century colonialism, orientalism, and interreligious encounter. This makes Eliot into a far more interesting figure than simply a straightforward early century Anglo-Catholic. In fact, even later in his life Eliot would claim the importance of Indian texts on his work, suggesting that theologians ought to attempt a synthesis of Christian revelation with Indian philosophy.[10] In the letter to Egon Vietta from 1947, quoted at the outset of this introduction, Eliot suggested, "I have thought that as the scholastics notably St. Thomas, incorporated Aristotelianism into Christian thought, so the task remains for some more still encyclopedic scholar . . . to reconcile and incorporate Eastern religious thought into that of Christianity."[11]

This book accepts Ramazani's invitation to see Eliot as a hybrid literary figure, influenced crucially by his early engagement with Indian texts in graduate school. It takes as its point of departure Eliot's criticisms of Arthur Schopenhauer's interpretation of Indian materials in lectures and correspondence. The book also draws its analysis from Eliot's graduate school notebooks on Indian philosophy (not yet published) and explores his connection with Japanese Buddhist scholar Masaharu Anesaki, from whom he learned about Buddhist thought, especially from Mahayana Buddhism. Eliot studied Indian texts at a time when they were largely interpreted in philosophy departments through the lens of Arthur Schopenhauer. Schopenhauer depicted these texts as refusing desire in the same way as he refused the blindly striving will. The Indian texts were therefore pessimistic, counseling a withdrawal from the world that negated the possibility of any kind of ascetic self-cultivation. However, Eliot's teacher Anesaki resisted this interpretation, describing Buddhism as a path of cultivation toward an impossible end, where desire is channeled toward its own eradication.

In this book, I argue that Eliot also resisted it, and in a similar way as Anesaki. This can be seen most clearly in the later Clark Lectures, but also, I argue, in hints and guesses raised from *Knowledge and Experience,* fragments of *The Waste Land,* and *Four Quartets.* In this sense, my argument grows more persuasive the more these fragments interact in the book. Eliot's poetry in part posits a possible transition from a pessimistic, Schopenhauerian world to one that is informed by premodern ascetic religious traditions. This idea gains a paradigmatic form, for example, in section III of *The Waste Land,* where Eliot brings together a "collocation" of ascetic fragments from the Buddha's Fire Sermon and Augustine's *Confessions.* If one understands the Fire Sermon in its ancient philosophical and textual context, one finds that it not only criticizes the attachments of human desire but also represents an early form of the later Mahayana Buddhist concept of *upaya,* or skillful means. This doctrine insists on the Buddha's ability to use a variety of means, including aesthetic display, praxis, and verbal representation, to move practitioners to higher levels of truth. Realizing this adds a new dimension to the dissonance at the end of section III of Eliot's poem and echoes with other fragments that raise ascetic possibilities. *The Waste Land,* while presenting the problem of human desire, also presents, through its references to asceticism, the possibility—but just the possibility—that desire can be cultivated toward a metaphysical Absolute (in the poem represented in terms of an Indian text). If Eliot's next move is a conversion to a very ascetic version of Christianity, then we could see *The Waste Land* as a pre-conversion poem, dramatizing the difficulty and promise of religious conversion in the modern world. We could also see Eliot's later religiosity, in contrast to Spurr, as hybrid, influenced in a deep way by his engagement and negotiation with non-Christian religious texts. In fact, we see the influence of these non-Christian texts emerge again later in Eliot's corpus. This book therefore concludes with a reading of *Four Quartets* that finds the influence of the *Lotus Sutra* and the *upaya* doctrine informing a theological inclusivism that seeks to negotiate the fragments of otherness from a rooted position within the modern flux.

My argument in this book is that Eliot exhibits a marked interest in the concept of *upaya,* a concept that plays a large part in Mahayana Buddhism but finds its roots deep in the Buddhist tradition. The concept is usually translated as "skillful means" and refers to the Buddha's ability to teach different people differently. This means the Buddha meets human beings where they are and, using all of his resources, including affective and aesthetic measures, moves the human being closer to an embrace of the full Buddhist truth. Lying implicit in the concept is the idea of levels of truth, to which one only has access after one has performed the stage before. I argue that in *Knowledge and Experience* Eliot invokes this idea obliquely at the conclusion to gesture toward an ascetic element in the movement from one perspective to another. In *The Waste Land*, the *upaya* idea takes on a heightened significance. The Fire Sermon itself represents an early assertion of a proto-*upaya* narrative. The liberation of the priests of Agni in that sermon only comes about after a long period of aesthetic cultivation by the Buddha. The sermon itself can be seen as an aesthetic artifact in a similar process of cultivation. Further, it echoes in the poem's concluding Indian references to the *Brhadaranyaka Upanishad*, bringing out the ascetic dimensions of that text as well. The dialogical dimension of this text is explicit, and the poem raises the possibility that translated fragments from an Indian other could challenge Europe to set its own fragmented lands in order.

Finally, in *Four Quartets*, I suggest that the *upaya* doctrine, represented by allusions to the *Lotus Sutra*, helps Eliot develop an inclusivism that finds its basis in a dynamic view of the common logos. Eliot's theological vision, rather than closing off comparison, becomes the basis of opening it up. In and through a comparison with the Buddha's aesthetic powers in the *Lotus Sutra*, Eliot depicts divinity as endlessly active and calling, leading the poet and readers through a sifting of the fragments. In these exquisite poems, Eliot uses a musical model to explore sameness in difference. Despite the more philosophically flowing passages of the poem, it is still a poem of fragments, in which resonances are significant and dissonances are apparent. These resonances are explored from an explicitly committed position, not from a detached, rational one. At the same time, the philosophical resources that Eliot uses in that exploration are in part inspired and taken from the Indian sources to which he had access. The end result is, as A. D. Moody observes, that Eliot's Christianity in *Four Quartets* looks different because of his engagement with the Indian sources.[12] Christianity itself is not reified as a single thought-system. Eliot's Christianity looks, in part, Buddhist. In this, *Four Quartets* as a theological statement looks like an incipient comparative theology, a step toward Eliot's vision in the letter to Vietta, where the home tradition is reformed in light of recognitions from engaging with a cultural other.[13] The poems, though metaphysically dialectical, open up comparatively a space of hybrid analogical thinking supported by a theory of language and aesthetics that itself is influenced by Indian sources.

Eliot and Schopenhauer

When Eliot discusses Indian texts in essays, lectures, or correspondence, he often mentions Arthur Schopenhauer, grouping him with those who have misunderstood the Indian traditions through romantic bias. To be sure, Arthur Schopenhauer was one of the most influential interpreters of Indian texts, at least in philosophical and literary circles. Schopenhauer was explicit in identifying his entire project with "Brahmanism" and Buddhism. He associated the Indian notion of *maya* with his own brand of radicalized Kantian phenomenalism and asserted the identity of his depiction of the will's self-negation with the Buddhist *nirvana,* the final soteriological state of selflessness (in Pali, *nibbana*). The Buddhist *nirvana* was, according to Schopenhauer, the same as his (Schopenhauer's) *Nichts,* and the Buddhists consequently were "worshiping nothingness."[14] Alternately, the Upanishadic idea of the identity of *atman* (the believer's "self") and *brahman* (the ultimate reality behind the phenomenal world) became, in Schopenhauer's eyes, the realization of blindly striving will, the true essence of the world that united subject and object.

Schopenhauer saw the phenomenal world, in fact, as an illusory projection of this blind will. The will was behind consciousness's individuation of objects in the world and, consequently, behind our knowledge of them. Once one realized this fundamental truth, the will could turn against itself and withdraw from worldly concerns. For Schopenhauer, the ancient Indian traditions realized, as he did, the illusory nature of the world; they were among the earliest instances of ascetic traditions that turned their back on the will, thought, and ultimately the worldly existence of blind striving. Incidentally, Eliot places Schopenhauer's condemnation of the will as a breaking point of idealism in the later nineteenth century. In the Clark Lectures (1926), Eliot claims that Jules Laforgue had made the most heroic attempt to live out Schopenhauer's ideology and his "Kantian pseudo-Buddhism," and that, of course, he failed. He failed because Schopenhauer's philosophy criticized desire as blindly striving and causing great suffering; it could find no legitimation for it, while Laforgue, in his poetry, kept constantly seeking for one.[15] To a certain extent, I believe Eliot's poetry recapitulates Laforgue's project (as he perceives it) and attempts to resolve it. As I argue in what follows, the epiphanic moments of *The Waste Land* evoke ascetic texts that do in fact operate with sophisticated understandings of the engagement and transformation of desire.

I argue that, against Schopenhauer and following Anesaki, Eliot depicts the Indian traditions, along with their Western analogues, as ascetic paths that engage human desire and draw the self to a self-cultivation that engages with language, memory, and desire in the paradoxical attempt to transcend them. For Schopenhauer, the will cannot be trained or educated. It cannot be mobilized toward a telos beyond it. Eliot's evocation of Indian texts, however, evokes the ascetic cultivation of desire, the attempt to overcome desire paradoxically through a process that involves desire. Cleo McNelly Kearns indeed recognizes that Eliot, by the time of the Clark Lectures, was explicitly comparing Indian traditions to the Christian mystical figures interested, like Dante, in "transforming the nature of desire itself."[16] In this, Eliot's interpretation of Indian texts stands in stark contrast to those that would see them as "quietist" and simply given over to nihilistic withdrawal from the world. As Kearns observes in her description of the Fire Sermon, these texts depict and incite "the willed and deliberate burning of purification."[17]

Eliot's initial diagnosis of the problem of desire emerges in his early concerns with solipsism in his graduate student work.[18] I suggest that Eliot is drawing on texts from India and Europe that describe the solipsism of the self and the cycle of memory and desire in similar ways. Both depict suffering as resulting from the reiteration of the harmful desires, enshrined in language, that drive the dialectic of memory and desire. The harmful desires of the self lead to engagements with the world that are likewise destructive. These experiences in turn impress themselves on the memory and lead to future experiences of sinful desire. The self therefore becomes mired in repetition.

However, the ascetic texts to which Eliot points in the texts I examine share an assumption that the analysis of the round of suffering does not lead to a retreat from the difficulties of the world. Rather, the experience, depiction, and consideration of suffering disclose a *potential* liberation from it. A teleology of sorts is opened up when a source outside of the self (God, the Buddha) prompts the desire for a better state of affairs. The world then becomes a soteriological clinic; an end state is imagined for which one endures the sufferings of the moment. One engages in the process of ascetic cultivation, in an attempt to follow the intuitions of a more wholesome and whole state beyond solipsism. This enables human activity by placing the individual in a lived path toward a transcendent end.

Jewel Spears Brooker has observed that Eliot's early engagement with religion was thoroughly practical. She writes that Eliot initially saw religion as a "scheme or system" and claims that the "object of such a scheme or system is, first, to enable one to make sense out of experience, and second, to enable one to live and to act."[19] Part of this understanding can even be seen in his later work. In his 1929 essay on Dante, Eliot describes this in terms of the souls in Purgatory, who suffer the consequences of their sins but also seek to cultivate themselves to prepare for the *visio Dei*. Eliot claims that they "*wish to suffer*, for purgation. And observe that they suffer more actively and keenly, being souls preparing for blessedness, than Virgil suffers in eternal limbo. In their suffering is hope, in the anaesthesia of Virgil is hopelessness; that is the difference."[20] In *The Waste Land*, it is in Schopenhauer's Nothingness and boredom, and in Baudelaire's *Ennui*, that hopelessness manifests itself. The imagination of suffering, however, leads to intuitions of that which lies beyond it. It presents the option of suffering in hope. In *Four Quartets*, the experience of time itself includes an awareness of alienation, from others and from God. The timeless moment becomes an intuition of communion pursued through the fragments.

The ascetic paths described by Eliot shape this desire for liberation, transforming it from within rather than repressing it in a violent manner. They engage desire through aesthetic representations, the creations of the imagination, and through praxis. When Eliot speaks of the dissociation of sensibility, he is in part responding to a situation in modernity in which, in the search for truth, artistic artifacts, including poetry, are divorced from the proper work of reason. The aesthetic is distanced from truthful intellectual practices and relegated to the category of "mere" art.[21] Kearns traces something like this conception in Deussen's distinction between exoteric and esoteric religion in the Vedanta.[22] In resistance to this, Eliot attempts to merge premodern modes of self-cultivation, modes that move to higher levels of abstraction only after sensibility and affectivity are engaged. I believe Eliot wants to see the exoteric and esoteric as part of a continuum of ascent. For Eliot, this model emerges in the Western context in certain types of monastic mysticism that find their definitive expression for Eliot in Dante; in the Indian context this means engaging with theories of *upaya,* or skillful means.

The Indian traditions in their classical forms built ascetic paths that must be performed at various levels of sophistication and truth. Affectivity and reason were both parts of this performance. In this, the Buddhist theory has definite analogues with the Brahmanical tradition. Jonardon Ganeri has noted that ancient Indian texts, both Brahmanical and Buddhist, are "protreptic," aiming for a fundamental change in the orientation of the one who engages with them:

> The *protreptic* nature of the Buddha's reported discourse is unmistakable. I mean by this not merely that the dialogues are hortative, encouraging the interlocutor to take up and pursue the Buddhist way; I mean more specifically that the teachings are explicitly directed toward a 'turn' or transformation or reorientation in the mind of the listener. . . . The proper grasp and reflective acceptance of the truths taught by the Buddha *upturns* the mind of the student, and transforms their vision. As a genre, the recorded dialogues of the Buddha are closer to the meditation or soliloquy than to the summa or disputation.[23]

The ancient ascetic texts seek to shape the self, then, by enabling the self to perform certain operations in order to provoke a transformative recognition that moves it to a higher level and a more profound truth. Likewise, Ganeri speaks of both the Buddhist Nikaya and the Brahmanical Upanishads as "trojan texts": they burrow into the brain, indirectly provoke a recognition, and then self-destruct. He writes, "they self-detonate: . . . they detonate the self of the reader and they detonate themselves as part of the same process."[24] The text incites a transformation in the mind of the listener in and through the listener's engagement with the text itself. The text then shows itself to be only a provisional moment in a larger process.

These texts accomplish this transformation by inciting the listener to engage actively with the text. This occurs most often as part of a path of graduated teaching, in which the listener moves through various levels of understanding, some of which might be rudimentary or even false. The texts "do not simply announce; they find subtle strategies and indirect methods to help the reader undercut their false sense of self: techniques of graded instruction, embedded and contextualized description, literary devices of disguise and deceit, the use of figures and characterizations."[25] The aesthetic here has a place in taking part in a performative ascent. The listener meditates, or wrestles with the matter of the text, or occupies false perspectives in order to learn that they are false. In this, Ganeri likens these texts to Kierkegaard's "indirect communication"; they require the reader's engagement in order to learn something only obliquely referenced.[26] Ultimately, as the text transforms the self, the text itself "self-destructs" in the wake of the recognition. I suggest that this process of engagement and transcendence in the Indian texts is one way Eliot envisions the work of poetry vis-à-vis a religious tradition.[27]

Eliot, Modernity, and the Disciplining of Religion

Eliot's religiosity should be read against a history of secularism that sees religion as more and more private and disembodied. In a sense, it should be seen as a reaction against all three forms of Charles Taylor's secularisms: a reduction of the world to empirical causality, the privatization of religion and removal of it from politics, and the vastly expanded intellectual marketplace that makes religion optional.[28] Ronald Schuchard has shown that Eliot's interest in religious ideas goes all the way back to his graduate studies at Harvard.[29] Schuchard notes that the basic components of Eliot's "classical" and conservative positions were all in place by 1916.[30] He bases his argument on the influence of T. E. Hulme, whose reaction against romanticism Eliot had already adopted by the time of his Oxford class on modern French literature in 1916. Thus, in Eliot's syllabus for the class (provided by Schuchard), we find: "The beginning of the twentieth century has witnessed a return to the ideals of classicism. These may roughly be characterized as *form* and *restraint* in art, *discipline* and *authority* in religion, *centralization* in government (either as socialism or monarchy). The classicist point of view has been defined as essentially a belief in Original Sin—the necessity for austere discipline."[31] In commenting on this syllabus, Schuchard goes on to explain the epistemological bases of Hulme's concept of "Original Sin," developed against Romantic interiority. According to Hulme, romanticism describes an intellectual trend to see the human person as the center of all things; concomitant with this is the inability to see the real failings and limitations of human beings. As Schuchard describes,

> When the romantic becomes blind to the fact of his limited and imperfect nature, he turns inward to establish and glorify a hierarchy of values originating within himself and based on the fact of his own "unlimited" existence. This error falsifies the true nature of both the human and the divine; consequently, it "creates the bastard conception of *Personality*" and "distorts the real nature of ethical values by deriving them out of essentially subjective things, like human desires and feelings."[32]

Schuchard acknowledges that this notion of Original Sin is distinct from theological conceptions.[33] Nevertheless, the fact remains that the seeds of Eliot's conversion, the setting of the parameters for his later thought, must be pushed back. Eliot's conversion was not a "road to Damascus" moment, but a gradual process. As Schuchard concludes, "Though Eliot's formal conversion to Anglo-Catholicism was eleven years away, his sensibility was religious and Catholic, and his primary concerns were moral in 1916."[34]

Beyond this crucial research is the fact that Eliot's student notes betray an intense interest in mysticism; Donald Childs has noted that Eliot may even have had a mystical experience of his own.[35] Eliot's indebtedness to Evelyn Underhill's book on mysticism is well known, and his graduate student notes demonstrate an intense interest in Indian religious traditions. We also know, from Manju Jain's excellent work on Eliot's graduate papers, that Eliot criticized the scientific study of religion as found in Frazer, Müller, and Durkheim as incapable of providing an account of intentionality and meaning in religious discourse and practice. In Royce's seminar, Eliot argued vociferously against a reductive interpretation of religion, vigorously insisting in class presentations that a science of religion was not possible per se because it was always based on interpretation and preconceptions.[36] Brooker argues that F. H. Bradley's philosophy provided Eliot already with a quasi-religious thought world that lent itself well to the young Eliot's searching.[37] But ultimately one could also look to Eliot's first set of essays, *The Sacred Wood*, for an interest in religious ideas. Those ideas are wedded with elements of Eliot's own "classical" critical project. The essays there, especially "Tradition and the Individual Talent," clearly show an interest in mysticism (though a particular kind of mysticism, as we will see later). Further, his early essay on Dante shows a concerted effort to demonstrate how Dante's "philosophical" discourse provided the basis for a poetic praxis and a mystical vision.

Discussions of religion in Eliot often flounder on one of two dangers: either a too narrow view of religion or of Eliot's modernism. For many, "religion" refers to Eliot's moment of conversion, that moment when he took on belief in certain orthodox dogmas or doctrines that seem regressive to contemporary scholars. When I first encountered Eliot as an undergraduate, I remember a professor proclaiming that T. S. Eliot was a great poet until he converted to Christianity, at which point he became a religious poet and wrote poetry not worth reading. (We subsequently read *Four Quartets*.) Such scholars missed the detail that Schuchard uncovered, and they unwittingly take part in the reification of the term "religion" as an entity marked solely by belief.[38] To be fair, Eliot's own early critical method seems to support this. Eliot has often been characterized as marking the boundaries between areas of thought, strictly drawing the border between, for example, religion and literature. Under this understanding, Eliot's move at the end of "Tradition and the Individual Talent" becomes a policing of boundaries. There he writes, "This essay proposes to halt at the frontier of metaphysics or mysticism, and confine itself to such practical conclusions as can be applied by the responsible person interested in poetry."[39] It is certainly possible to see Eliot's move here as reifying the boundaries and telling the critic to mind his or her own business.

However, I believe this interpretation misses Eliot's sensibility and critical tendencies, nourished by both the modernist context and his studies in Aristotle. Michael Levenson has suggested that, though the modernists were certainly interested in defining aesthetic activity as distinct, they were also interested in how that activity interacted with others, especially politics. He writes: "The growth of art as a self-conscious practice rarely implied indifference to the social realm. Rather, it suggested that aesthetic labor had a distinctive, not an autonomous, character. Its formal features aside, what gave it distinctiveness . . . was the presence of the artworld as complex as the political culture with which it vied."[40] Levenson persuasively argues that the emergence of this artworld prompted modernist artists to more pressingly ask about the relation of that specific activity to that which existed seemingly outside of it. In terms of politics, Levenson remarks that this led, on the whole, to an experience

14 DESIRE AND THE ASCETIC IDEAL

of "radical undecidability."[41] In Eliot's quote, the undecidability may only be apparent. The reader senses that the author knows precisely what the relation is and has decided to explain it with a suitably obscure passage from Aristotle (in Greek no less).

Eliot's move at the end of "Tradition" is also more Aristotelian in that it attempts to firmly place that which it defines in relation to something else to which it is crucially connected. Aristotle claims that to know the boundary between two relative things means clearly to know those two things:

> From this it is plain that, if a man definitely apprehends a relative thing, he will also definitely apprehend that to which it is relative. Indeed this is self-evident: for if a man knows that some particular thing is relative, assuming that we call that a relative in the case of which relation to something is a necessary condition of existence, he knows that also to which it is related. For if he does not know at all that to which it is related, he will not know whether or not it is relative.[42]

Eliot's move assumes a knowledge both of poetics and of metaphysics or mysticism and professes to know how they are related. The fact that they are related at all is, of course, highly significant. As Joshua Richards points out, this move at the end of tradition is most likely due to Eliot's reading in the work of Evelyn Underhill, who clearly placed the role of the poet at the limit of mysticism, given over potentially to mystical visions.[43]

By the 1928 preface to *The Sacred Wood*, influenced by the concerns of his conversion, Eliot is explicitly making the point that thought cannot in reality stop anywhere. The fragments of the whole are always already related:

> And certainly poetry is not the inculcation of morals, or the direction of politics; and no more is it religion or an equivalent of religion, except by some monstrous abuse of words. And certainly poetry is something over and above, and something quite different from, a collection of psychological data about the minds of poets, or about the history of an epoch. . . . On the other hand, poetry as certainly has something to do with morals, and with religion, and even with politics perhaps, though we cannot say what. If I ask myself . . . why I prefer the poetry of Dante to that of Shakespeare,

I should have to say, because it seems to me to illustrate a saner attitude towards the mystery of life. And in these questions, and others which we cannot avoid, we appear already to be leaving the domain of criticism of "poetry." So we cannot stop at any point. The best that we can hope to do is to agree upon a point from which to start.[44]

The aesthetic realm has by this time become the starting point for exploration, but seen against a web of relations. Eliot expresses here a sensibility that, according to Brooker, was informed by nineteenth-century idealism and specifically the work of Bradley. In that sensibility, "since everything is ultimately part of one thing, everything is connected to everything else in the system. All relations are internal, for all things are within systems, and given an ultimate perspective, within a single system."[45] Hence, we should see Eliot's definitions as relational and perspectival, demarcating areas of distinct activity but always with a sense of holistic relationality.

Eliot's engagement with religion and religious practice takes place against the historical background of the reduction of religion to belief. This reduction has been the overwhelming contemporary critical preoccupation of religious studies. The historian of religion Jonathan Z. Smith has noted that prior to the eighteenth century, the term "religion" tended to be associated with ritual practice. It is after the Reformation and in the wake of Enlightenment rationalism that religion becomes associated purely with belief. He writes:

> This shift to belief as the defining characteristic of religion (stressed in the German preference for the term *Glaube* over *Religion,* and in the increasing English usage of "faiths" as a synonym for "religions") raised a host of interrelated questions as to credibility and truth. These issues were exacerbated by the schismatic tendencies of the various Protestantisms, with their rival claims to authority, as well as by the growing awareness of the existence of a multitude of articulate, non-Christian traditions.[46]

Smith's point is not that "belief" suddenly becomes important to Christianity in the eighteenth century. This would be ludicrous. Rather, he argues that the term "religion" takes on a different valence in the modern period, one that removes this term from the sphere of ritual cultivation.

This removal was entailed in part by Luther and Calvin's insistence on the primacy of faith over works in salvation. The crisis in authority in the wake of the Reformation then led to a contestation of theologies and positions of "faith." Religions were characterized by the "faith" that they articulated rather than the practices they embodied. Finally, and most importantly for our purposes, the modern understanding of "religion" according to Smith is already forged in the encounter, through exploration and colonization, with other traditions that become characterized as "religion" with their own "faiths." In other words, the modern use of the term "religion" takes place in a comparative and dialogical context that has its roots in the Reformation.

This characterization of religion as belief would, in the colonial context, lead to a difficult set of negotiations in which Christianity viewed itself as a more "rational" and ethical faith than those of other religious traditions. Wilhelm Halbfass has exhaustively shown that such a move excluded for a long time the consideration of Indian thought as rational and "philosophical." If Western thought was rational, Indian thought was "other," "traditional" rather than rational, and inferior to progressive Western thought.[47] Halbfass, importantly for our purposes, notes the tension in this problem. In point of fact, Indian thought both does and does not fit the standards of Western thought. On one hand, classic Indian thought is as rigorous, reasoned, and logical as any example of Western theology or philosophy. On the other hand, and as nineteenth-century thinkers perhaps sensed obliquely, classical Indian thought was pursued always within a soteriological framework that presupposed practical techniques. Halbfass writes:

> Indian as well as Western authors have emphasized that the philosophical views or systems which are the subject-matter of the Sanskrit doxographies should not be interpreted as systems of "pure theory" in the Greek-European sense. Indeed, the soteriological and practical perspective is as obvious in the basic texts of the systems (*darśana*) as in their doxographic recapitulations. . . . Indian philosophers usually take it for granted, or even postulate explicitly, that the desire to know has to be motivated and guided by a goal or purpose (*prayojana*). For the majority of philosophical systems (*darśana*), the ultimate purpose is final liberation (*mokṣa, mukti,*

apavarga) from the cycle of rebirth and its inherent deficiency and distress.[48]

Halbfass's account of this soteriological dimension of Indian thought is nuanced. He asserts that Indian thought insists that thought must be directed, most often to a goal of liberation. However, he also notes that many of these thinkers hold the *end* result to be a state that passes *beyond* goal-oriented thinking to a "pure, free, disinterested contemplation in which all causal and instrumental relations, and with them the world itself, become transparent and irrelevant."[49] Thought must be goal-directed, but the goal itself is one that exists beyond such goal-related thinking and acting. The goal generates the desire, and the end state is beyond this desire.

At this point, we would do well to recall Edward Said's analysis of Orientalism, in which the West is defined as everything the East is not: "The Oriental is irrational, depraved (fallen), childlike, 'different'; thus the European is rational, virtuous, mature, 'normal.'"[50] This orientalist dialectic leads, in some quarters, to the characterization of Indian culture as more "poetic," and in others as more "mystical." Richard King has importantly noted that the reduction of Indian religions to "mysticism" is doubly unfortunate. It first equates the Indian traditions with a purely Christian phenomenon of seeking union with God. Second, it denigrates both Christian mysticism and Indian traditions in light of mature, rational Western philosophy.[51] The "mystical" into which Indian traditions were being assimilated was, in his estimation, already a site of contestation in the West, with a visionary, embodied, and gendered model placed in tension with a more exegetical, apophatic one at the conclusion of the middle ages.[52] In modernity, mysticism was characterized broadly as experiential, inner, and private, divorced from communal life, ethics, or politics.[53]

T. S. Eliot's characterization of religion militates against the depiction of religion in terms of belief and privacy, and he seeks to recast mysticism as embedded in social, intellectual, and embodied practice. He seeks to insert the life of embodied feeling back into the religious sphere, and that means insisting on habituation, ritual, and ascetic practices on one hand and putting poetry—the genre of thought and feeling—into relation with religious practices on the other. This places Eliot also in the position of frankly identifying discipline and authority as part of premodern religious practices. It is striking that Eliot's embrace of this element of religious practice, in resistance to modern Enlightenment rationality, foreshadows the anti-humanist philosophers and theorists of ascetic self-formation such as Michel Foucault and theorists of discipline in premodern religion such as Talal Asad.[54]

As Jewel Spears Brooker has insisted, Eliot first and foremost, and from his earliest thinking, considers religion to be a framework for living. She writes, "The object of such a scheme or system is, first, to enable one to make sense out of experience, and second, to enable one to live and to act."[55] Brooker goes on to note that the "pragmatic" function of this scheme is essential to Eliot.[56] The religious system is something to be lived, and that makes possible different experiences in the world; it enables one to see things that one might not otherwise see, including visions of the highest contemplation. The locus classicus for this idea in Eliot is in the early "Dante" essay, in which Eliot claims that Dante—the mystic poet—achieves his masterpiece because his theological system enables vision: "We are not here studying philosophy, we *see* it, as part of the ordered world. The aim of the poet is to state a vision, and no vision of life can be complete which does not include the articulate formulation of life which human minds make."[57] Such vision takes place in a system that has been created by many minds. Dante's vision is particular to him and yet is enabled by and utilizes the system that has been forged by others in relation.

Eliot also, in building on the practical dimension of religion, tends to present religion in terms of what Joshua Richards, following Eliot himself in "The Modern Dilemma," has called Eliot's "ascetic ideal."[58] Richards has done comprehensive work in tracing exactly what Eliot meant by this term as well as the sources to which he had access. He boils it down to three fundamental tenets that develop over Eliot's career: an insistence that discipline is required in approaching an apprehended Divine Beauty, a belief in the alienating influence of sin, and an increasing acceptance of the idea of a common logos.[59] As Schuchard noted, the first two of these tenets are present in Eliot's early admiration for T. E. Hulme.[60] It is also, he notes, influenced by the "neoclassicism of Babbitt" and the "royalist-Catholic authoritarianism of Maurras."[61]

To this picture I would add the theological issue of the practical cultivation of desire. I see Eliot's focus on discipline and asceticism as not simply a repression of desire, but a cultivation of it. In the speech cited by Richards, "The Modern Dilemma," Eliot wrote at length about asceticism, placing it at the heart of Christian religious experience. Indeed, the religious life here is nothing but asceticism, though asceticism defined in terms both of discipline and desire:

> As the sense of sin depends upon the supernatural, so from the sense of sin issues the ascetic life. The ascetic ideal is essential to Christianity. The modern world suffers from two great disasters: the decay of the study of Latin and Greek and the dissolution of the monasteries. These defects can be supplied. The benefit of monasticism is not only for those individuals who have the vocation for that life; it is also in the ideal of life that it sets before those whose lives are in the world. For Christian asceticism is a matter of degree; and every life, in so far as it is Christian, is ascetic: in self-abnegation, self-discipline, and the love of God. Exceptional austerities are for exceptional men; for ordinary men, the practice of prayer and meditation and the daily battle against distractions which the world offers to the mind and the spirit. The ascetic ideal—and asceticism is of course far more than a mere *doing without*—seems to me implied in the Summary of the Law.
>
> We like to interpret the love of our neighbors as ourselves as a vague benevolence, or as practical charity alone. We like to think that as we want to be happy, and have some "right" to be happy, so we must remember that our neighbors have rights too and that we should try to make them happy: the love of our neighbors becomes fair play, and doing the decent thing. But the real love of our neighbor, in and for God, means transcending the bounds of love and benevolence as we know them, and reaching a plane at which what is given is not as the world gives.[62]

This passage shows first of all the degree to which Eliot's early interest in Hulme easily became translated into a Christian idiom. Here Eliot couches his "classical" concerns about sin and discipline in the language of Christian asceticism. Eliot primarily characterizes the religious life as one of shaping the self through both inner and outer practices of self-denial and attention. The self keeps itself away from the distractions of the world and undertakes practices of prayer and meditation. Eliot also says, however, that for the Christian, the love of God itself is ascetic. The idea of love provides the line of continuity between the first paragraph and the second. Christian love is not a mere assessment of "rights" and fair play. It is ascetic. It is shaped through practice, and it is directed toward a telos beyond this world. Indeed, true Christian love is not only directed to this telos, it is given *by* this telos. In other words, the self must prepare itself for a gift, but one that is only given in and through the shaping. Implicit here is a paradox, in which human effort must be exerted in order to receive something that human effort cannot possibly give.

At the same time, there is an insistence that human desire must be transformed, not refused or rejected. Affective training exists in order to effect this transformation. Richards notes that Eliot insists on maintaining the "relational connection between the higher and lower forms of love," thus recovering the Platonic dimension of premodern Christian philosophy and theology.[63] Eliot's most explicit and persuasive statement of this comes in the Clark Lectures, where he writes:

> Dante and his contemporaries were quite aware that human love and divine love were different, and that one could not be substituted for the other without distortion of the human nature. Their effort was to enlarge the boundary of human love so as to make it a stage in the progress of the divine. Dante's words before Beatrice appears to him in the Paradiso leave no doubt that his feeling toward Beatrice in heaven, an exalted feeling toward an exalted being, differs in kind from his feeling on the revelation of the godhead.[64]

It is the love directly for Beatrice and indirectly for God that drives Dante down through the Inferno and up Mount Purgatory. This desire is gradually purified or, as Eliot terms it, enlarged. To see the divine love as different would lead to "distortion of human nature," a repression of desire so severe as to harm human nature. The love of the human being becomes a stage in the ascent to the divine, a stage that must be accepted, engaged, pursued, and purified. Note also that Eliot describes this, even at the highest levels of contemplation, as a matter of feeling. The ultimate vision of the Godhead, a vision beyond vision and a desire in which Dante's will is being turned by the divine itself, is still characterized as a moment of feeling. It is a feeling, however, that has been taken up into intellectual vision, "the development and subsumption of emotion and feeling through intellect into the vision of God."[65] It is this model, incidentally, that Brooker uses to describe Eliot's overall intellectual trajectory.[66]

I believe it is the desire to reconcile affectivity and intellect, discipline and human nature, and desire and its consummation that lead Eliot to compare Western asceticisms with the Buddhist *upaya* texts in *The Waste Land* and *Four Quartets* and to criticize Schopenhauer's view of these texts as rejecting human desire in an unsophisticated, harsh manner. Eliot himself observed that he found himself torn between two poles that Christianity brought together: "I am one whom this sense of void tends to drive towards asceticism or sensuality, and only Christianity helps to reconcile me to life, which is otherwise disgusting."[67] Religion here walks a "middle way" between the ascetic and the sensual. These are, in fact, precisely the terms that Buddhists would use to describe their own path, a path that is ascetic, but in a particular manner that seeks to avoid harsh self-punishment.[68]

I have found Gavin Flood's definition of asceticism to be extremely helpful in coming to terms with Eliot's invocations, both explicit and implicit. In his book *The Ascetic Self: Subjectivity, Memory and Tradition*, Flood argues that asceticism is the performance of both "the memory of tradition" and the "ambiguity of the self."[69] He writes:

> Asceticism entails subjectivity, it entails a self who renounces, but a self that is always expressed through the structures of tradition. Rather than being subjected to individual desire as the person's predominant driving force, asceticism advocates the subjection of oneself to tradition, to a master, in order to undergo a transformation. The ascetic submits her life to a form that transforms it, to a training that changes a person's orientation from the fulfillment of desire to a narrative greater than the self. The ascetic self shapes the narrative of her life to the narrative of tradition. There is a deep ambiguity here. On the one hand, asceticism entails the assertion of the individual will, a kind of purified intentionality, yet on the other it wishes to wholly form itself in the shape of tradition and in terms of the tradition's goals. The goals of ascetic traditions are so often the eradication of subjectivity through the self becoming wholly passive (as in Christianity), through the self realizing its non-agency (as in Advaita Vedānta) or through the self understanding its non-essential nature (as in Buddhism). Yet the eradication of subjectivity in ascetic pursuit entails the assertion of subjectivity in voluntary acts of will. Asceticism, then, is the performance of this ambiguity.[70]

22   DESIRE AND THE ASCETIC IDEAL

The ascetic both renounces the self and asserts the desires of the self. The goal of the ascetic is a transformation of one's individual desire in and through the texts and practices of a tradition; the ascetic attempts to allow the memory enshrined in the tradition to reshape individual desire. Yet Flood highlights the paradox of the self who desires to give up desire, who submits herself to the authority embedded in a tradition in the hopes of conforming herself to the goal of that tradition. Such cultivation occurs through individual acts of will, even while the goal of the path is the renunciation of that will and the transcendence of the self. According to Flood, the presupposition for all such paths is that ascetic discourse contains the influence of "others" on the self: other human beings with whom the ascetic converses, and the "Other," that which lies at the end of the path, which will "replace the ascetic volition."[71]

In the Buddhist concept of *upaya*, the monk engages with affective language, artistic artifacts, and ritual practices before moving to higher levels of meditation in which desire is finally eradicated. As we will see with certain Buddhist narratives, the primary desires of the initiate can be evoked as a way into the practices and texts of the path, though those practices will themselves transform the desire of the initiate, bringing him or her to an awareness of the insufficiency of the initial desire. I suggest that Eliot invokes asceticism to describe the engagement with a broad tradition of writings, both Eastern and Western, about the problems with and the transformation of desire. I believe that Eliot sees the broad cultural tradition as a repository of memory traces that can be retrieved in cultivating and transforming desire. Further, Eliot's poetry suggests the radical ambiguity of which Flood writes, of desiring to give up desire, of desiring to die to the self in order to live more fully. But most especially, Eliot's poetry dwells on the notion that the ascetic paths to which he refers do not simply renounce desire; they engage and cultivate it through affective means. Ultimately, the poetry attempts to show that poetry itself can have an ascetic function, by engaging desire in the search for a transcendence of the solipsism of the self. Eliot reminds readers that ascetic paths often begin with aesthetics and affective praxis. In fact, as I discuss in chapter 1 in examining the Clark Lectures, Eliot wants to co-opt the initial stages of ascetic paths in order to suggest that poetry can fulfill the function of describing and diagnosing suffering and following the intuitions of transcendence through the cultivation of memory

Eliot's Religion in Dialogical Relation

We have seen that Eliot's view of religion and asceticism is shaped in reaction to the disembodiment of religion in modernity. Eliot's embrace of Buddhist *upaya* is meant to push back against this by insisting on the merging of thought and feeling in ascesis. I suggest that Eliot's notion of religion is dialogically shaped; in fact, I argue that Eliot's conservative cultural criticism is itself the result of an explicit engagement with Indian sources and the perceived difficulties of intercultural hermeneutics. I am mindful of the insight of Jessica Berman that the presence of the influence of the cultural other can be felt at times when it is not explicitly present.[72] I would like to see the formation of Eliot's conservative Christianity similarly, though I think Eliot gives us some moments that reveal this influence openly, giving us a hermeneutical key.

Further, I suggest that Eliot's engagement with Buddhism, an engagement that included a consideration of the affective dimensions of the tradition, influenced the kind of ascetic Christianity he would later adopt. In other words, Eliot's conversion to Christianity, rather than being a wholesale repudiation of the Indian sources, was perhaps aided by an engagement with those sources and a doubt about the ability to engage with fragments of those traditions in a meaningful way. Part of that consideration was also a relatively explicit consideration on how to think about intercultural comparison and linguistic signification. In order to get at this, I discuss one of Eliot's post-conversion critical works, *After Strange Gods*. Though this series of lectures is infamous for its insistence on the necessity of a homogenous culture, it expresses a crisis in signification that itself emerges from an engagement with religious others by Eliot and other intellectual figures he knew. This is a crisis he would move beyond, but at the time of the lectures, Eliot's sensibility has turned away from comparison.

Earlier in his critical life, Eliot tended to represent the relationship between feeling and thought in two distinct ways. The ideal way for thought and feeling to be related was for the poet to be able to inhabit a system of thought, as was the case, according to Eliot, for Dante. Dante was able to use the intellectual framework of his time to pursue a vision. In Eliot's words, "But the true mystic is not satisfied merely by feeling, he must pretend at least that he sees, and the absorption into the divine is only the necessary, if paradoxical, limit of this contemplation."[73] In "The Metaphysical Poets," on the other hand, Eliot depicts the process of the poet in the modern world as attempting to create new wholes from his experiences of thought and feeling. In Eliot's words, "a degree of heterogeneity of material compelled into unity by the operation of the poet's mind is omnipresent in poetry."[74] The metaphysical poet in this essay is the poet of hybridity and diversity, who seeks new unions of thought and feeling in and through the process of writing poetry. The term Eliot uses, a term that reappears in *After Strange Gods*, is the term "amalgamating." The poet's mind "is constantly amalgamating disparate experience."[75] This process in poetry leads not only into a unifying of the disparate experiences of modern life, but also into a testing of philosophical theories. True, the poet did not have the metaphysical system of Dante, but the poet could attempt to see fragments of philosophy, embodying them in moments of clarity. He writes, "A philosophical theory which has entered into poetry is established, for its truth or falsity in one sense ceases to matter, and its truth in another sense is proved."[76] Their truth and falsity cease to matter since they do the work of the poem itself, and the poem is to some extent detached from reality. The truth is proven, however, in that the poet has used it for a new merging of thought and feeling.

In *After Strange Gods*, we find a repudiation of the model represented in "The Metaphysical Poets" and a nostalgic lament for the loss of the situation open to Dante. This model of the hybrid poet is rejected in part due to considerations of intercultural and broadly interreligious understanding. I take as my inspiration here the work of Anita Patterson, who has noted that the explicit hybridity of Eliot's poetry and the implicit dialogical exchange that helped form it made Eliot's poetry so attractive to poets from colonial and marginalized backgrounds.[77] Patterson argues that Eliot both explicitly acknowledges and laments this hybridity.[78] She notes that Eliot's background, like that of many modernist writers,[79] was one of migration and placelessness. In this, Eliot shares in a "hemispheric memory of dislocation" that yields a "creative practice of allusion" in his work.[80] Indeed, this hybridity seems to be painfully at odds with Eliot's cultural theory, which often argued for the ideal of a cultural homogeneity.

Nowhere is this more startlingly presented than in *After Strange Gods.* These lectures on the whole are, in my estimation, lamentable. Eliot's anti-Semitism is fully on display, and he mercilessly criticizes people who were critical to his success, such as Irving Babbitt and Ezra Pound. Nevertheless, it is in *After Strange Gods* that Eliot exhibits the anxiety about hybridity that Patterson notes, but also reflects on his own cultural and religious identity. These reflections show clearly a consideration of implicit dialogical exchange, as Eliot considers the possibility of becoming a member of a foreign tradition and then rejects this for principled reasons.

Eliot asserts that he seeks to expand on the notion of tradition that he articulated in "Tradition and the Individual Talent." In doing so he develops the conception of a dialectic between thought and feeling that becomes, in these lectures, a dialectic between tradition and orthodoxy. Tradition, it seems, is a matter of culture, practice, and habit, while orthodoxy becomes a kind of higher-level intellectual conversation both in the present and between the present and the sources of the past:

> A *tradition* is rather a way of feeling and acting which characterizes a group throughout generations . . . the maintenance of *orthodoxy* is a matter which calls for the exercise of all our conscious intelligence. The two will therefore considerably complement each other. Not only is it possible to conceive of a tradition being definitely bad; a good tradition might, in changing circumstances, become out of date. Tradition has not the means to criticize itself; it may perpetuate much that is trivial or of transient significance as well as what is vital and permanent. And while tradition, being a matter of good habits, is necessarily real only in a social group, orthodoxy exists whether realized in anyone's thought or not. Orthodoxy also, of course represents a consensus between the living and the dead: but a whole generation might conceivably pass without any orthodox thought. . . . Tradition may be conceived as a by-product of right living, not to be aimed at directly. It is of the blood, so to speak, rather than of the brain: it is the means by which the vitality of the past enriches the life of the present. In the co-operation of both is the reconciliation of thought and feeling. The concepts of *romantic* and *classic* are both more limited in scope and less definite in meaning.[81]

This is a development of Eliot's notion of tradition, and it should be noted that this is not what Eliot means by the term in the earlier essay. Here, Eliot establishes an Aristotelian model based in *phronesis*, the interplay of habit and intellect in the *Nicomachean Ethics*. Tradition becomes a matter of habit and the shaping of the affects, while orthodoxy becomes a reflective understanding that shapes and potentially transcends the common life. Eliot imagines this relation as mutually informing and at least hypothesizes that cultures can be a repository for error and regressive habits. Orthodoxy here becomes a potential way of criticizing habituation, though presumably if thought strays too far from life as lived, it could also be criticized in the opposite direction. The reconciliation of thought and feeling is, of course, the role Eliot envisions for poetry. Eliot sees this mutual cooperation and critique as something that happens in and through poetry. Poetry points back both to the affective dimension of life and to the highest levels of intellectual reflection.

Interestingly, Eliot comes at this definition shortly after noting Paul Elmore More's exasperation, one shared no doubt by many, with a perceived incongruity in Eliot's work. Eliot notes that one "cannot treat on the same footing the maintenance of religious and literary principles."[82] After clearly asserting that religious faith must take precedence over all other values, he addresses More's criticism of Eliot's apparently different sensibilities as a cultural critic and as a poet. As noted by the editors of *The Complete Prose of T. S. Eliot*,[83] More had written that the poet Eliot was a "lyric prophet of chaos," against which "must be set the critic who will judge the world from the creed of the classicist, the royalist, and the anglo-catholic, who will see behind the clouds of illusion the steady decrees of a divine purpose."[84] Elsewhere, More was more specific about the "poetic" Eliot, describing Eliot's depiction of life in the poetry: "the disorganized flux of images; its lack of clear meaning in the obscurity of language; its defiance of authoritative creeds in a license of metrical form; its dislocated connection with the past in the floating debris of allusion; while its flattened emotions will be reproduced realistically, without comment."[85]

In response, Eliot importantly does not dispute it; rather, he claims that poetry and prose must begin from different circumstances. He claims that "in one's prose reflexions one may be legitimately occupied with ideals, whereas in the writing of verse one can only deal with actuality. Why, I ask, is most religious verse so bad; and why does so little religious verse reach the highest levels of poetry? Largely, I think, because of a pious insincerity. . . . People who write devotional verse are usually writing as they want to feel, rather than as they do feel."[86] By implication, if the situation in which the poet finds himself is one of chaos, multiplicity, and doubt, then this will be reflected in his verse. Then as now, pious cliche makes for bad poetry. Eliot's response to More suggests that the conflict and "chaos" in his verse reflect a conflict and chaos in the culture, and by extension in the mind of the poet.

It is against this backdrop that, in the next lecture, Eliot unloads a vast criticism against Irving Babbitt and, in passing, Ezra Pound. Given Eliot's observations above, one wonders whether the broadside is aimed at Eliot's own tortured life. At any rate, Babbitt becomes the example of decaying Protestant culture, a culture that had lost any sense of a singular tradition, but that has, paradoxically, become more "provincial and crude in the major intellectual centres of Europe."[87] Babbitt's problem, according to Eliot, was that he knew too much. Eliot writes that "the very width of his culture, his intelligent eclecticism, are themselves symptoms of a narrowness of tradition, in their extreme reaction against that narrowness. His attitude towards Christianity seems to me that of a man who had had no *emotional* acquaintance with any but some debased and cultural form."[88] Eliot's logic here is reactionary, but for our purposes it is worth getting right. Note that Babbitt's problem is that, since he emerged in a Protestant culture, he had no emotional connection to the Christianity of his time. Protestant Christianity is represented as emotionally weak; it is reduced to a "debased and cultural form." Without the affective connection to a strong cultural form, Babbitt attempted to compensate through eclecticism, and it is this eclecticism that led him to an interest in other religious traditions or systems of thought.

The problem is twofold. First, Babbitt cannot fully commit to any single tradition of thought. Second, the traditions he will entertain cannot be understood from the outside, without the practices associated with them. To read these texts torn from their contexts risks severe misunderstanding. Eliot claims that one who does not belong to a certain culture cannot possibly understand, at least with any significant comprehension, the texts from that culture. On Babbitt's interest in Confucianism, Eliot writes: "Just as I do not see how anyone can expect really to understand Kant and Hegel without knowing the German language and without such an understanding of the German mind as can only

28   DESIRE AND THE ASCETIC IDEAL

be acquired in the society of living Germans, so a fortiori I do not see how anyone can understand Confucius without some knowledge of Chinese and a long frequentation of the best Chinese society."[89] Not only can, for example, an American or English scholar not understand Confucius, but the same scholar outside of Germany could not truly understand Kant and Hegel. Eliot argues that in order to understand Confucius's texts and ideas, one would really have to immerse oneself in the language and the culture of China and converse with Chinese elites. Linguistic knowledge is part of the attempt, but linguistic knowledge is not enough. One would have to know how the language operates in a specific cultural location. The problem with intellectual figures such as Babbitt is that they accumulate knowledge of many different sources without immersing themselves in the cultures from which they have emerged. This argument assumes, it would seem, a kind of homogeneity in the culture of the other. Eliot cannot countenance at this point the possibility that the ideas of Confucius could very well have been part of a cultural contestation in his own time, and in the history of China, not part of a consistent "mind," or that cross-cultural understanding could occur between diverse strands of thought of different cultures that approach the world with similar concerns. The border, in other words, is drawn as absolute.

At any rate, it is this same tendency to accumulate ideas that Eliot claims to have avoided by not pursuing further an interest in Indian materials. In a famous passage, Eliot claims that he ultimately found it impossible to think and feel as anything other than an "American and European."[90] I quote the passage in full:

> Two years spent in the study of Sanskrit under Charles Lanman, and a year in the mazes of Patanjali's metaphysics under the guidance of James Woods, left me in a state of enlightened mystification. A good half of the effort of understanding what the Indian philosophers were after—and their subtleties make most of the great European philosophers look like schoolboys—lay in trying to erase from my mind all the categories and kinds of distinction common to European philosophy from the time of the Greeks. My previous and concomitant study of European philosophy was hardly better than an obstacle. And I came to the conclusion—seeing also that the "influence" of Brahmin and Buddhist thought upon Europe, as in

Schopenhauer, Hartmann, and Deussen, had largely been through romantic misunderstanding—that my only hope of really penetrating to the heart of that mystery would lie in forgetting how to think and feel as an American or a European: which, for practical as well as sentimental reasons, I did not wish to do. And I should imagine that the same choice would hold good for Chinese thought: though I believe that the Chinese mind is very much nearer to the Anglo-Saxon than is the Indian. China is—or was until the missionaries initiated her into Western thought, and so blazed a path for John Dewey—a country of tradition; Confucius was not born into a vacuum; and a network of rites or customs, even if regarded by philosophers in a spirit of benignant skepticism, makes a world of difference. But Confucius has become the philosopher of the rebellious Protestant.[91]

I have more to say about this passage's reference to Schopenhauer's intellectual lineage later in this book, since I think that Eliot is insightful in his criticism of the philosopher. I merely note for now that Eliot places himself in an interpretive position opposed to that of Schopenhauer. Eliot's analysis here is, of course, self-contradictory. The European or American mind is not able to understand the texts and ideas of India, and yet he, Eliot, is able to understand them enough to condemn Schopenhauer for approaching them through romantic misunderstanding. Nevertheless, Eliot's main argument, it seems, is that to really learn the Indian texts and philosophies, he would have to leave behind his own habituation as an "American or a European." He would have to learn how to "think and feel" differently. Eliot's coy statement that, for "practical and sentimental reasons," he did not wish to do this masks a very real difficulty, that for someone like him to understand, he would have to essentially give up his emotional attachments and habits to relearn how to live.

Part of the issue, it seems, is that he would have to undertake the "rites and customs" of another place; in other words, those things that the philosophical traditions would consider properly "religious." Eliot portrays the philosophical field in Europe as having drifted apart from the sphere of religious ritual cultivation. Philosophers are likely to regard the rites of China (or India) with "benignant scepticism," and the rites of its own European past with skepticism less benignant. Given Eliot's Aristotelianism from the first lecture, his portrait of the poet here seems to be as one who takes part in a line of habit, ritual, and thought in which the poet is constantly attempting to mediate and balance the habitual and the intellectual. The unspoken influence lying behind these reflections is Eliot's Dante, who viewed his own poetry as partaking in the cultivation of the ascending soul. The dissociation of sensibility here is a dissociation of thought from not just emotion but all of the affective and practical means of shaping individuals.

The very real consequence of all of these arguments is that comparison between cultures would seem to be virtually impossible. The comparing intellect would have to belong to two cultures or traditions simultaneously. Eliot's homogenizing or totalizing view of culture seems to cut off this possibility. One cannot know the other except from within the cultural practices of the other. This is surprising from the earlier Eliot, or even the Eliot as late as *The Waste Land,* who allowed himself to think comparatively, at least to some extent. It is also surprising from the eventual poet of *Four Quartets,* who once again carefully engaged in intercultural and interreligious comparison.

Eliot is no doubt concerned about the hybridity that he sees in Babbitt and Pound, and more broadly in that portion of modernism that Marjory Perloff has described as the "other tradition" of modernist indeterminacy, initiated by Rimbaud.[92] Patterson has clearly demonstrated Eliot's ambivalence about such hybridity,[93] and this set of lectures surely represents an extreme of Eliot's view of such cultural diversity. There is also a racism implicated in this view as well, indicated in Eliot's view that cultural tradition is a matter of the "blood" of a particular people. Finally, Eliot's identification of Confucianism as significant for modern intellectuals surely reflects a negative evaluation of Ezra Pound's own Orientalism and a disagreement with his friend over the role of the poet vis-à-vis intercultural fragments.[94]

At the same time, Eliot does reflect a significant intellectual concern, one that would be shared by disciples of Edward Said. Said's critique posits the Western gaze as constructing its object of study in and through its epistemological institutions in a vision that cares little for the actual lives of those it purports to study.[95] Such a construction is actually a reduction of the other to the same, to the cultural projects of the same. The other exists only insofar as it fulfills a role in the home culture's view of itself and its activities. The danger in this critique is that we might end up reifying cultures in the same way as Eliot does. The more one sees the cultural life of both poles of a comparison as internally consistent with itself and containing strict ontological and epistemic borders, the more one sees only misrepresentations projected onto the cultural other. Indeed, Said himself nuances his claims toward the end of *Orientalism,* claiming that it is possible for more responsible scholars to see beyond the ontological binaries he describes earlier.[96] This nuancing no doubt led Said to defend his "humanism" in his 1994 afterword to the book.[97]

Eliot also potentially reinforces the modern Enlightenment prejudices he is out to criticize by insisting on pursuing his "ideal" of a homogenous society in the absence of the other side of the dialectic. It is one thing to mediate between thought and feeling. If the ideal is not tied firmly to the emotional currents of the time, however, the "ideal" of thought maintains its own domineering autonomy. It floats away from the actual circumstances from which it issues, and it becomes a purely rational sphere that disciplines the affective with all the repression of the most violent ascetic. This is, in fact, decidedly *not* the ideal of asceticism I explore in this book. Eliot's asceticism generally seeks a cultivation of desire rather than a violent repression of it. The ascetic impulse proceeds in and through the affective to higher levels of contemplation. It is not an imposition of a detached rational order upon the messiness of life. In *After Strange Gods,* Eliot places his reified view of culture as an autonomous substitute here for the modern subject. It is the source by which all is judged and brought into order. The Indian materials do not challenge this order; they simply represent one of its mute borders.

After the pessimism of *After Strange Gods,* it is surprising that, later in his career, Eliot returns to interreligious comparison in *Four Quartets.* The impact of Indian materials on Eliot can be clearly seen in his early philosophy and philosophical notebooks and can be seen in the verse as late as *The Waste Land.* After this, however, they subtly fall away. In *Four Quartets,* the engagement with these texts is back, I argue, in a very sophisticated and sustained way that points the poet back to his earlier studies. I cannot claim to understand how the change in negotiation takes place, but it is worth noting that, as Patterson decisively recognizes, by the time Eliot writes "The Music of Poetry" in 1942, he is thinking concretely about the diversity contained within language itself.[98] Instead of viewing language as embedded within a homogenous culture, Eliot acknowledges that language, especially the English language, bears the traces of the diversity of cultures with which it has come into contact.

32   DESIRE AND THE ASCETIC IDEAL

Instead of language forming a consistent linguistic system that enables poetic vision, as in the "Dante" essay of 1920, Eliot acknowledges that English bears traces of many different systems:

> What I think we have, in English poetry, is a kind of amalgam of systems of divers sources (though I do not like to use the word "system," for it has a suggestion of conscious invention rather than growth): an amalgam like the amalgam of races, and indeed partly due to racial origins. The rhythms of Anglo-Saxon, Celtic, Norman French, of Middle English and Scots, have all made their mark upon English poetry, together with the rhythms of Latin, and, at various periods, of French, Italian and Spanish. As with human beings in a composite race, different strains may be dominant in different individuals, even in members of the same family, so one or another element in the poetic compound may be more congenial to one or another poet or to one or another period. The kind of poetry we get is determined from time to time, by the influence of one or another contemporary literature in a foreign language; or by circumstances which make one period of our own past more sympathetic than another; or by the prevailing emphasis in education. But there is one law of nature more powerful than any of these various currents, or influences from abroad or from the past: the law that poetry must not stray too far from the ordinary everyday language which we use and hear. Whether poetry is accentual or syllabic, rhymed or rhymeless, formal or free, it cannot afford to lose its contact with the changing language of common intercourse.[99]

Here poetry does not feed on a unified system of thought; rather, poetry feeds on a variety of different sources that have informed the language. English itself is an amalgam of different sources, and any poem written in the language is inherently hybrid. English partakes of the immediate cultural resources and also influences from Europe and from further abroad. The poet's task—indeed, the task of any speaker—is to inhabit the interstices of these various sources and systems. The implicit point is that there is no single system that England or America embodies. One might add that there never was, though it seems Eliot is not willing to go this far. There is still a nostalgia here for an imagined time where such composite races did not exist, or where the jumble of systems was not as pronounced. Nevertheless, he is thinking about language and culture in more dynamic terms. Language here is constantly in motion, based on the "common intercourse," the back and forth of conversation in common speech. Eliot is reinforcing the dialogical interplay of language. As he claims later, poetry is still, at its most basic level, "one person talking to another."[100]

Indeed, Eliot goes on later in the essay to defend, as Mikhail Bakhtin might say, the "internal dialogism of the word."[101] One element of poetry's music, according to Eliot, is the resonance that a word possesses from its immediate context and its use in a wide array of context:

> The music of a word is, so to speak, at a point of intersection: it arises from its relation first to the words immediately preceding and following it, and indefinitely to the rest of its context; and from another relation, that of its immediate meaning in that context to all the other meanings which it has had in other contexts, to its greater or less wealth of association. . . . This is an "allusiveness" which is not the fashion or eccentricity of a peculiar type of poetry; but an allusiveness which is in the nature of words, and which is equally the concern of every kind of poet.[102]

The resonance of meaning resulting from all of the contexts in which a word is used is not simply a modernist invention, but constitutive of the music of poetry. Eliot acknowledges that words carry with them an internal set of resonances, based on the diverse circumstances in which the word has been dialogically deployed. Music in this sense is the polyvalent nature of language. In this view, language can never purely belong to one context. One is always already working with tools that are "co-owned," that exist at the interstices of different linguistic speakers, and by extension the different cultural spheres and "systems" that they occupy. Words are not tied down in signification to one specific context, and the current moment of speech always adds to the resonance the word potentially carries. Here the boundaries between contexts of usage breaks down, since words themselves breach the boundaries and demand negotiation of those boundaries. Indeed, the portable nature of the text breaks these barriers down; as Patterson notes, Eliot later in life acknowledged that reading literature in foreign languages provided a key creative impulse in his early development.[103] We are back to Eliot's earlier observation that the task of the soul "does not consist in the contemplation of one consistent world but in the painful task of unifying (to a greater or less extent) jarring and incompatible ones and passing, when possible, from two or more discordant viewpoints to a higher which shall somehow include and transmute them."[104]

I suggest in this book that when it comes to an engagement with religious difference, Eliot's sensibility develops dialectically in three movements, for which the conversion acts as a pivot point. This conception is inspired by, but is different from, the dialectic described by Jewel Spears Brooker in her magisterial book, *T. S. Eliot's Dialectical Imagination.* I believe that the Eliot of the philosophical studies, and up through *The Waste Land,* is willing to attempt to approach a mystical endpoint in and through the play of hybrid fragments. At the very least he is willing to entertain that this may be possible. This position is haunted by nostalgic longing for a Europe united by a single thought system, as Eliot thought Dante enjoyed. *The Waste Land* brings this period to a decisive culmination, as Eliot seems to ask the question of whether such an approach to a metaphysical absolute is at all possible. Eliot then enters, after the conversion, into a period of time in which Indian materials do not figure explicitly in the poetry. This is the period marked by the lamentation of *After Strange Gods.* By the time of *Four Quartets,* Eliot is willing to attempt to reconcile both a religious belonging and an assessment of hybrid fragments, in what I describe as a theological inclusivism. The dialectic might be described as an initial searching among the fragments, followed by an embrace of rootedness, and a subsequent comparative dialogism from a rooted position within a single religious tradition whose boundaries are inherently porous due to the dialogism of language.

1

SKILLFUL MEANS AND ASCETICISM IN T. S. ELIOT'S CRITIQUE OF SCHOPENHAUER

In 1933 T. S. Eliot gave his Page-Barbour lectures at the University of Virginia, published later as *After Strange Gods*. Despite the problematic material of these texts, they are valuable in revealing something of the poet's retrospective assessment of his interest in Indian materials. At the end of the second lecture, Eliot takes a moment to reflect back on his study of Indian texts and culture. He focuses on the problems of looking into a tradition from outside of it:

> Two years spent in the study of Sanskrit under Charles Lanman, and a year in the mazes of Patanjali's metaphysics under the guidance of James Woods, left me in a state of enlightened mystification. A good half of the effort of understanding what the Indian philosophers were after—and their subtleties make most of the great European philosophers look like schoolboys—lay in trying to erase from my mind all the categories and kinds of distinction common to European philosophy from the time of the Greeks. My previous and concomitant study of European philosophy was hardly better than an obstacle. And I came to the conclusion—seeing also that the influence of Brahmin and Buddhist thought upon Europe, as in Schopenhauer, Hartmann, and Deussen, had largely been through romantic misunderstanding—that my only hope of really penetrating to the heart of that mystery would lie in forgetting how to think and feel as an American or European: which, for practical as well as sentimental reasons, I did not wish to do.[1]

DESIRE AND THE ASCETIC IDEAL

This passage holds great interest for assessing Eliot's changing views of intercultural understanding, especially given the fact that Eliot claims to at one time have considered converting to Buddhism.[2] What is more interesting for my purposes here, however, is Eliot's evaluation of the "misunderstandings" to which the religious traditions of India, specifically Hinduism and especially Buddhism, had been subjected. In characteristic fashion, he singles out Schopenhauer and his disciples for particular criticism. In fact, when Eliot explicitly discusses his interest in Indian religious traditions, he often discusses the negative example of Schopenhauer and his supposed "romantic misunderstanding." In the Clark Lectures (which I examine in detail later), Eliot makes the same criticism, there in the context of a discussion of Jules Laforgue's interest in Buddhism.[3] Eliot calls Laforgue's Buddhism "the Kantian pseudo-Buddhism of Schopenhauer and Hartmann."[4] Further, Manju Jain describes a letter from Eliot to I. A. Richards, in which Eliot reiterates both his concern with the "translation" of traditions as well as his criticism of Schopenhauer: "Even Deussen, whom Eliot supposed to be the very best interpreter of the Upanishads, had merely translated Indian thought into Schopenhauerian, and the orientalism of Schopenhauer was as superficial as superficial could be."[5] Eliot's negative evaluations of Schopenhauer's orientalism, however, should be considered alongside his acknowledgment that early in his studies he was interested in Schopenhauer's interpretation of the Indian traditions. In a retrospective moment in a letter to Egon Vietta from 1947, Eliot writes, "Long before I was a Christian, I was a student of Indian philosophy, and of the Buddhist scriptures in Pali: both from study of some original texts, under teachers of Indic philology and philosophy at Harvard, and from an early interest in Schopenhauer and Deussen in connexion with Sanskrit."[6]

This chapter seeks to provide some explanation for Eliot's consistent references to Schopenhauer's Kantian and "romantic" interpretation of Indian materials and attempts to provide precedents for Eliot's own presentation of mysticism and asceticism later in his career, notably in the Clark Lectures of 1926. Eliot's references to Schopenhauer's interpretation of Indian materials place him in a particularly influential Orientalist historical trajectory; Schopenhauer's presentation of these materials was a prominent one in late nineteenth- and early twentieth-century philosophy and literature. I argue that Eliot's own interpretation of the Indian materials occurs in reaction to Schopenhauer's orientalism. Eliot's criticism of Schopenhauer, in fact, took place as part of his broader "classical" polemic against romanticism. That polemic itself, however, was partially informed by Eliot's reading of the Indian materials in distinction to Schopenhauer. Eliot read the Indian traditions in a manner that emphasized their ascetic aspects, drawing inspiration from the idea of *upaya,* or skillful means, in the Buddhist tradition. This idea was a central one in the presentations and writings of Masaharu Anesaki, one of Eliot's professors in his graduate studies, who himself was a critic of Schopenhauer's interpretation of Buddhism.

Whereas Schopenhauer views religious liberation as simply withdrawal and renunciation, Eliot knew that Indian Buddhism depicted the religious path as a "middle way" between ascetic self-punishment and hedonistic indulgence. This overriding priority finds expression in the concept of *upaya,* or "skillful means," in which the Buddha engages students in and through their desires, meeting them in their cultural and linguistic embeddedness and bringing them closer and closer to the ultimate truth through various "ruses," disguises, practices, and metaphors. *Upaya* therefore provides for a way of utilizing poesis in the progress of a mystical ascent that mobilizes language, thought, and desire in the attempt to overcome them. Though it is true that Buddhist texts utilize a rhetoric of renunciation and detachment, in fact they were pragmatic about the effort to approach the final detachment in and through various modes of attachment.

I show that Eliot was clearly exposed to the idea of *upaya,* especially in the class he took at Harvard with a visiting Japanese scholar, Masaharu Anesaki in 1913–14. Though it is hard to judge precisely how influential Schopenhauer's representations were at Harvard while Eliot was attending, nevertheless key figures there clearly engaged with his ideas in studies of Indian philosophy. James Woods was certainly intrigued by them, and Anesaki, who had translated Schopenhauer's works into Japanese, jousted with Schopenhauer both in lectures and in print. A look at Anesaki's work, rooted in Tiantai Mahayana Buddhism, shows also a subtle resistance to Schopenhauer that provides a crucial precedent for Eliot's critique. For this reason, I suggest that Eliot was more open to the Mahayana than Kearns allows.[7] Kearns thinks that Eliot was primarily influenced early on by the Theravada texts, especially in the collection by Henry Clarke Warren. I believe Eliot's interest in Dante made him more open to the aesthetic dimensions of the Mahayana as described by Anesaki.

Anesaki suggests that Schopenhauer takes Indian traditions—and indeed religious traditions in general—out of a true ascetic context, thereby jettisoning ritual, text, poesis, and praxis as means to enlightenment or release. The moment when the will turns against itself, for Schopenhauer, happens without explanation (though occasionally he suggests that profound suffering can lead to the result). Indeed, his metaphysics demands such an inexplicable turning, for in his philosophical vision the will cannot be taught. Schopenhauer's will is an erotic, self-perpetuating, blindly striving force that manifests itself throughout reality most paradigmatically in desire, sexual drive, and affective experience. Desire and affectivity are to be rejected, not engaged. Both Eliot and Anesaki, however, are concerned to maintain a focus on the ability of ascetic traditions to shape the self in soteriologically beneficial ways. They therefore attempt to reinsert praxis and poesis back into the assessment of Indian traditions. In this, they also react against a tradition of Orientalist representations of India (of which Schopenhauer's is a descendent) that viewed these traditions as quietistic, renouncing meaningful, significant, and ethical activity in the world. Eliot's concern with Schopenhauer's philosophy, and his subsumption of Indian materials into it, is its focus on withdrawal from the world of action, its elimination of the active capacities of human beings in the approach to the *summum bonum*.[8]

Schopenhauer's Veneration of India

The engagement with Indian texts in the latter half of the nineteenth century would not be as ecstatic as that of the Romantics earlier in the century, for a number of reasons. Thrown into the midst of a series of intellectual and political crises was an anxiety created by the emergence in the European milieu of translations of texts from a "new" and very different religious source, Buddhism. Raymond Schwab characterizes the years of 1830–50 as a period of increased "spiritual instability."[9] Thomas Tweed characterizes the culmination of this crisis in the 1870s as a multifaceted anxiety over Christian orthodoxy: "What was going on? A confluence of social and intellectual forces was shaking the foundations of 'orthodox' Christian faith . . . the foundations were being dissolved by the acids of biblical criticism, the new geology, the new biology, anthropology, and comparative religion."[10] Suddenly, biblical accounts could not be taken historically anymore as a sufficient account of the age of the world or the development of human beings, nor was it clear what role the divinity could possibly play in the physical development of the world.[11] Further, the engagement with texts from diverse (and divergent) religious traditions opened the eyes of Europe and America to traditions that were of comparable antiquity to Christianity, indeed often even older than it or than even the oldest origins of the Hebrew Bible. Though some Romantics earlier in the century could see this as an exciting return to origins, others of a more mainline Christian faith could not but see all of these developments as radically decentering and distressing.

It was in the midst of this developing crisis, in 1844, that Eugène Burnouf's extremely influential study *Introduction à l'histoire du Buddhisme indien* would appear, a work that clearly set the tone for subsequent European discussions of Buddhism. Burnouf set Buddhism apart from the "Brahmanical tradition" in his characterizations of the Buddhist *nirvana* not as union with the divine, or absorption into the divine essence, but as complete extinction or "annihilation," "the absorption or dissipation of the individual into nothing."[12] In this volatile period, Buddhism, with its reaction against the Vedic tradition that had enjoyed great popularity among the Romantics, its denial of the essential self, its anti-metaphysical bent, and its affirmation of the un-providential nature of dependent origination, seemed one of the greatest religious and philosophical threats.[13] The course of the Oriental Renaissance would henceforth take on a far more antagonistic tone: "The newly acquired understanding of Buddhist beliefs brought to light a danger which, until then, only Anglicanism had feared. In France, where it was particularly studied, positions on Buddhism were hardening in a way they had not hardened regarding Hinduism."[14]

The force of this debate would be felt not only in France but across the continent and in England and America as well. Following on characterizations of Buddhism formed, it should be noted, solely from the small number of texts available in Europe at the time, a polemic was being launched by scholars and Christian apologists against a perceived Buddhist nihilism and rejection of lived existence. Tweed notes that "mid-century European scholars were increasingly inclined to employ a language of otherness and a rhetoric of negation to describe many of its most basic beliefs. Buddhism was 'strange' and 'singular.' Its doctrines were not only 'atheistic' and 'nihilistic' but also 'quietistic' and 'pessimistic.'"[15] The Buddhist doctrine of no-self, its focus on meditation and detachment, and its seeming rejection of providential theism challenged the perceived necessity of theism as the proper grounds for ethics. The denial of the essential self took away the individualism necessary for considering the self as a moral agent, and the doctrine of dependent origination and karma seemed to refuse the possibility of any providential plan of creation of which human beings could be a part.[16]

These facets of Buddhism made the tradition seem the epitome of Indic irrationality and childishness, a syndrome that, by the latter half of the nineteenth century, was not on the whole valued as it had been with the Romantics. Thus, the polemic against Buddhism, though more pronounced, carried with it elements of the broader polemic against the "oriental mind." As Philip C. Almond observes, "Indolence, laziness, inactivity had therefore their spiritual counterparts—Nirvana, mysticism, contemplation. *The Christian Remembrancer* stressed the necessity for its readers to 'ever bear in mind the distinction between the keen, subtle, logical, discriminating intellect of the West, and the vague, thoughtful, comprehensive, mystical turn of mind that prevails among the nations of the East.'"[17] Almond describes a very familiar kind of Orientalism, in which the cultural "other" is described in nonrational terms vis-à-vis Europe. Whereas the first wave of Indic texts emerged in Europe with the blossoming of Romanticism, Buddhist texts appeared in Europe as the reaction against Romanticism was well under way. As a consequence, the negative reaction was not limited to Buddhism; Buddhism, rather, was seen as exemplary of the quietism and anti-humanistic bent of the East.[18] Indian religions in general were criticized as failing to conform to European Enlightenment rationality, considered the final arbiter of civilization and proper ethical religion.

Arthur Schopenhauer was a key figure in the appropriation of Indic texts in Europe, and he was largely responsible for the association of Buddhism with philosophical pessimism. Schopenhauer's influence in the interpretation of Indian texts has been explored well by figures such as Wilhelm Halbfass, Raymond Schwab, Guy Welbon, and Roger-Pol Droit.[19] In particular, Halbfass, in *India and Europe: An Essay in Understanding,* has done seminal work in documenting European philosophy's sustained interest in Indian thought, even while its restrictive, modern understanding of "philosophy" would often denigrate that thought.[20] According to Halbfass, Schopenhauer represents both an illustrative and exceptional chapter in that history. Schopenhauer viewed his own philosophy as the more systematic "fulfillment" of the Indian philosophies he admired.[21] In this sense, he represents a common European supercessionist model that sees European philosophy as the only lens through which to complete or correct non-Western philosophies and traditions.[22] Nevertheless, Halbfass sees Schopenhauer as a figure who "showed an unprecedented readiness to integrate Indian ideas into his own, European thinking and self-understanding, and to utilize them for the illustration, articulation and clarification of his own teachings and problems."[23] Schopenhauer's thought would therefore come to be associated with Indian thought in a powerful way, even though he did not know much about Buddhism or Indic thought in general when he published the first edition of *The World as Will and Representation*. Indeed, he began to make comparisons between his thought and Indic texts only in the appendixes of subsequent editions of the work.[24] He would later bequeath this fascination with Indian materials to his disciples, including both Nietzsche and Wagner, both of whom also took a strong interest in them.[25]

Raymond Schwab has noted the "anti-occidental" and "anti-biblical" tenor of Schopenhauer's arguments.[26] In a move analogous to the Romantics, though much more renunciatory and pessimistic in nature, Schopenhauer reacted against European modernity by valuing Indian texts for precisely those things for which they were most criticized. If Indian texts were criticized in some quarters for abandoning ethical agency in favor of renunciatory mysticism, this was, for Schopenhauer, precisely their deepest wisdom. The comparisons come mainly in the second (1844) and third (1859) editions of *The World as Will and Representation,* as Schopenhauer became more acquainted with the Indian materials.[27] It is also with these later editions that Schopenhauer vaulted into prominence in both literary and philosophical circles.[28] His work was therefore reappraised during the time period in which the estimation of the Indian traditions was changing, especially with the "discovery" of the supposedly nihilistic religion of Buddhism.[29]

Schopenhauer's interest in Indian texts centered around his attempt to support two key elements of his system, his metaphysics of the will and his depiction of the final escape from the world into "nothingness." Though he often joins the two traditions together, broadly speaking he utilizes Hinduism most often in support of the former, and Buddhism generally in support of the latter. The Upanishadic doctrine of the identity of the individual soul (*atman*) with the world soul (*brahman*) becomes, for Schopenhauer, a depiction of the metaphysical unity of all existence as blindly striving will.[30] This identification turned upon the philosopher's interpretation of Kantian metaphysics. Schopenhauer argues that the Vedas (broadly conceived as including the Upanishads) expressed Kant's distinction between noumena and phenomena in mythical form:

> The same truth . . . is also a principal teaching of the *Vedas* and *Puranas*, namely the doctrine of Maya, by which is understood nothing but what Kant calls the phenomenon as opposed to the thing-in-itself. For the work of Maya is stated to be precisely this visible world in which we are, a magic effect called into being, an unstable and inconstant illusion without substance, comparable to the optical illusion and the dream, a veil enveloping human consciousness, a something of which it is equally false and equally true to say that it is and that it is not. Now Kant not only expressed the same doctrine in an entirely new and original way, but made of it a proved and incontestable truth through the most calm and dispassionate presentation.[31]

Schopenhauer views the concept of *maya*, illusion, as the heart of the Upanishads. Indeed, he builds on this notion of "cosmic illusion;" for him, *maya* becomes Kant's world of phenomena, though now conceived as an illusory projection of the blindly striving will pervading the universe. He claims that the Indian traditions provide mythological support to Kant's argument that the human mind structures experience through the forms of space and time and the concepts of the understanding. In Schopenhauer's hands, phenomena become merely illusory, like dreams, mere representations. In reality, the one thing-in-itself, behind all phenomena in the world, is the blindly striving, erotic will. The world itself is nothing other than a projection of this will in and through the representations of the human mind. The Upanishadic identification of the *atman*, the individual self, with *brahman*, the universal principle of reality, becomes, therefore, the expression of the singular reality of the will.[32]

On the other hand, Schopenhauer claims that the release from suffering is the realization of the nothingness of the world. This is alternately explained as absorption into *brahman*, or a realization of Buddhist nothingness. For Schopenhauer, the Buddha realized, as he did, that the world as human beings experience it is nothing other than the sum of all the reifications of the will.[33] The life of the will then is a round of constant desiring, a game in which the attainment of the object of desire inevitably leads one to further desiring. The happiness gained in the attainment is fleeting, and the eventual loss of it causes intense suffering. Once one has realized this, the only thing one can do is to renounce the world and its false promises of abiding happiness. As Guy Welbon notes, the failure to do this is its own punishment: to embrace the cycle of willing is to suffer its inevitable punishments. It is this "system" of justice that Schopenhauer likens to Indian karmic retribution[34] and the round of desire and suffering, *samsara*.[35] To renounce the world, however, entails the will's self-renunciation and the embrace of the "nothingness" with which one is left when one has abandoned all of the phenomena of the world. One is left in a state beyond all reifications.[36] Further, our fear of this nothingness serves to diagnose the depth of our illness: "That the prospect repels us is merely the mark of our unregeneracy, our clinging to life, our affirmation of the will to live."[37]

Thus, Schopenhauer associates his notion of the world of representation in which the human being is engaged with Buddhist notions of attachment,[38] and he compares *nirvana* with his self-denial of the will.[39] Once one has realized that all of reality is in fact only such a projection of the will, one will naturally want to escape such an empty existence and renounce such projections. The self thus renounces its reifications and its "claim of theoretical, representational mastery and domination."[40] It seems that there are two major ways to make the great escape: one can have an unexplained, sudden, transformative intuition of the reality of things, or one can grasp the reality of the world through a moment of intense personal suffering. In either case, the moment of intuitive knowledge leads first to virtue and then to the will turning against itself and leading to withdrawal and resignation.[41] Such knowledge "is a direct and intuitive knowledge that cannot be reasoned away or arrived at by reasoning; a knowledge that, just because it is not abstract, cannot be communicated, but must dawn on each of us."[42]

The moment must be direct and intuitive because Schopenhauer argues that the will itself, if it acts for motives, is always acting selfishly. For this reason, the will cannot be trained. It has to wait for a conversion of some sort. It is here that Schopenhauer breaks with a conception of

DESIRE AND THE ASCETIC IDEAL

ascetic self-cultivation in favor of a mystical moment of intuition. And it is precisely against this move that Eliot and his teacher Anesaki would react. Schopenhauer argues:

> Dogmas can of course have a powerful influence on conduct, on outward actions, and so can custom and example . . . but the disposition is not altered in this way. All abstract knowledge gives only motives, but, as was shown above, motives can alter only the direction of the will, never the will itself. But all communicable knowledge can affect the will as motive only; therefore, however the will is guided by dogmas, what a person really and generally wills still always remains the same. He has obtained different ideas merely of the ways in which it is to be attained, and imaginary motives guide him like real ones. . . . As we have already said, the will can be reached from outside only through motives; but these alter merely the way in which it manifests itself, never the will itself. *Velle non discitur* (Willing cannot be taught).[43]

Schopenhauer specifically targets the discursive teachings of religious traditions here, though in the process makes a broader point about all "communicable knowledge." The teachings of a religious tradition, its "dogmas" or "doctrines," cannot shape the will or change someone's "disposition." There can be no gradual turning or training of the will. To be sure, Schopenhauer seems here to be referring mostly to belief, though he also discusses "custom" and "example." None of these can "alter" substantially the will. The fact that he categorizes such traditions mainly by their "dogmas" is also itself significant. He either does not see or cannot conceptualize a religious tradition as a unified whole of discourse and practice. Asceticism, for Schopenhauer, is not a gradual refining of the will; rather, asceticism only comes after the moment of intuitive knowledge and can only take the form of a renunciation. A religious tradition quite simply cannot communicate in a meaningful way the kind of knowledge that is necessary for an escape from willing. If it redirects the will, it redirects it merely from one self-serving motive to another.

Eliot and Anesaki

By the time Eliot attended graduate school, beginning in 1911, Schopenhauer was very much in the air in the analysis of Indian texts.[44] As mentioned above, Eliot claims in the Egon Vietta letter that he himself was interested in Schopenhauer and Deussen in his early studies of Sanskrit texts. Recall again his assertion, "Long before I was a Christian, I was a student of Indian philosophy, and of the Buddhist scriptures in Pali: both from study of some original texts, under teachers of Indic philology and philosophy at Harvard, and from an early interest in Schopenhauer and Deussen in connexion with Sanskrit."[45] In addition, James Woods, one of Eliot's teachers of Sanskrit, was a student of Paul Deussen, who himself was a devotee of Schopenhauer.[46] Woods taught courses in Indian philosophy both in the 1910–11 and 1912–13 academic years. The course description for the 1912 course, Philosophy 11, reads as follows:

> The object of this course will be to read selections from the classical Upanishads in their relation to the various later philosophical systems, monistic and theistic and pluralistic. Special attention is given to psychological analysis of the different ideal states and to the epistemological assumptions and discussions. The original philosophical texts in translation, other translations in the Sacred Books of the East, and modern handbooks will be in constant use. The different systems will also be considered from the point of view of Schopenhauer's philosophy.[47]

The course description of the earlier course, Philosophy 18, "Philosophical Systems of India, with special reference to Vedanta, Sankhya, and Yoga," also pairs the systems of Indian philosophy with the philosophy of Schopenhauer. The course description reads as follows: "The object of this course will be to read and discuss the original texts of the classical Upanishads in their relation to the system of Shankara, to the pluralistic systems, and to the philosophy of Schopenhauer. The translations of the Sacred Books of the East, and modern handbooks will be in constant use."[48]

More concretely, however, the work of Masaharu Anesaki shows both a debt and a subtle criticism of Schopenhauer's interpretation of Indian traditions. Eliot took Anesaki's course on Eastern Philosophy in 1914. A follower of Tiantai Buddhism, Anesaki was, in fact, quite an important figure in the development of religious studies in Japan in the early twentieth century, occupying the first chair in religious studies at Tokyo University in 1898.[49] Most importantly for our purposes, Anesaki translated into Japanese Schopenhauer's *The World as Will and Representation* in

46 DESIRE AND THE ASCETIC IDEAL

1912 and von Hartmann's *Religious Philosophy* in 1899.[50] Eliot took Ane-saki's course, Philosophy 24A, "Schools of Religious and Philosophical Thought in Japan." The course's focus was on Japanese religion, though Anesaki ranged quite broadly through foundational Indian Buddhist fig-ures, especially Vasubandhu and Nagarjuna, the founder of the Mad-hyamaka. He also spent a great deal of time on the *Lotus Sutra,* a locus classicus for Mahayana doctrine on *upaya,* or skillful means (more on this below).

Anesaki mentions Schopenhauer in passing several times in his lectures. Eliot's lecture notes record that in a discussion of the *prajna-paramita* texts on October 21, Anesaki compares the Buddhist *shunyata,* or "emptiness," with Schopenhauer's *Nichts*:

> Especially in the larger texts of this group the various conditions of B-hood manifestation described, but only to emphasize the ulti-mate emptiness of the world of things. Every conception contains an inconsistency. "Come" + "go" are negative and positive, and op-pose each other. Buddha is neither being nor non-being, neither non-nonbeing nor non non non being. This sort of analysis for 100000 shlokas . . . SBE v.49.p.140 "Those who saw and heard me in the form (*rupena*) have not seen me. One must see the *dharma-tas.* But dharmata cannot be conceived, for conception supposes an antithesis. Shunyata = *Schopenhauer's* 'nichts.' The person of the Buddha consists in the dharmakaya and not in the rupakaya."[51]

In a discussion of Mahayana prajna texts, Anesaki observes the dis-tinction between *rupakaya,* the physical body of the Buddha, and *dharmakaya,* the higher reality of the Buddha. The latter is a complex term, but in the *prajnaparamita* texts it refers not only to the truth of the Buddha's instruction but to the "pure mental *dharmas* [i.e., constituents or elements] cognizing emptiness."[52] The enlightened one sees beyond the things of the world as they really are; he sees the "*dharmata*," the "true nature of things . . . emptiness."[53] The comparison in Anesaki's lecture is consistent with what we have seen in Schopenhauer's own analysis of the similarity between his philosophy and that of the Buddhists. The reali-zation of the emptiness of the world is a realization of its "nothingness," *Nichts.* The true reality, Nothingness (*Nichts*), lies beyond the dualities with which the mind works. However, it should be noted that whereas Schopenhauer's *Nichts* is a negation of the world, a negative designation, here Anesaki discusses how the Buddha nature, or Buddhahood, exists beyond distinctions and dualities. What lies beyond the dualisms of the world is the Buddha's *dharmakaya,* not merely "nothing." In this, Anesaki represents traditional Tiantai Buddhist thinking.[54]

Likewise, in the January 9 lecture, Anesaki mentions the German philosopher in comparison with the Chittamatra texts. According to Eliot's notes of the lecture, Anesaki compares the Indian idealism of these texts with Schopenhauer's description of the will's constitution of the world:

> The mind organizes not only itself but also the environment (dhatu) acc. to its own tendencies; responds only to the dhatu wh. it wishes to have and not to others. Similar minds group together to produce the world common to them. The world in which we live (lokadhatu) is the result of our commonalities and efforts. (This is neglected in Western philosophy). Citta provides the common environment of similar minds. Lokadhatu is product of citta, because samkhara has control over external world as well as internal. When the world is made our will is no longer free but is controlled by the dhatus. In this respect agrees with Schopenhauer. Will itself is free until it is an individual existence.[55]

Anesaki compares the world's creation by *chitta* (mind) with the world as will. Just as the will constitutes the world of objects and phenomena, so too here does *chitta* produce the world. However, Anesaki also notes a communal and active dimension to these texts, a dimension he also discusses in his text on ethics (see below). Eliot's notes contain a parenthesis critical of Western philosophy, citing the intersubjective nature of the world created by common effort. It is unclear whether this represents the thoughts of Anesaki or Eliot, though it is clearly a prominent idea in Tiantai Buddhism.[56] Nevertheless, according to Anesaki, both the *chitta* texts and Schopenhauer's philosophy are in agreement that once the mind or will produces the world, then the will is not free; the individual's attachments to external objects in the world traps him or her within existence. The will that has not individuated itself into a person freely acts, and it is only when it becomes objectified in an actual human person that it becomes limited.

These references to Schopenhauer in the lecture notes, and in the course description for Woods's class, are suggestive and show that at the very least Woods and Anesaki were making running comparisons

48   DESIRE AND THE ASCETIC IDEAL

with Schopenhauer in their discussions of Indian materials. More suggestive, however, is the pamphlet by Anesaki entitled "Buddhist Ethics and Morality" from 1912. Kearns observes that the text was "an offprint of an article Anesaki had written on Buddhist ethics for the *Encyclopaedia of Religion and Ethics.*"[57] It is unclear whether the text itself was required reading for the course, and whether Anesaki provided it to the class.

Anesaki's text is notable not only for the running comparison with Schopenhauer but also for its implied criticism of the philosopher. In this text, there seems to be an implicit acknowledgment that Schopenhauer has provided a basis for discussing mystical and ascetic texts in a philosophically rigorous way, while also a criticism that Schopenhauer leaves behind in his analysis the practical, communal, and ascetic portions of the tradition. In answer, Anesaki relentlessly focuses on both the communal aspect of the Buddhist tradition and the element of training, especially mental cultivation, *bhavana*, necessary for the attainment of the goal of the Buddhist path. Thus early in the text, we find the following in a discussion of *nirvana*:

> There are perplexing questions as to the real meaning of the term, and its negative aspect has led not only many European scholars but a section of Buddhist thinkers to a thoroughly negative view. Not entering into these discussions, we shall content ourselves with noting that Buddhism here faced the same problem as Schopenhauer did as to the ultimate nature of nothingness (*Nichts*), especially in its relation with the mystic experiences of saints, both Buddhist and Christian. But the difference between the Buddha and Schopenhauer consists in this, that the former was not content with the merely theoretical attitude of the latter, but, having himself realized the experience of transcending the phenomenal and of entering into the height of mystical illumination, tried to lead his followers to the same attainment. This ideal of the same attainment is expressed in the term "One Way" or "Sole Road" (*eka-yāna*), treading in which is the very essence of Buddhist morality, and the basis of which is found in the stability of truths. . . . In summarizing positively the highest aim of Buddhist morality, we might say it consists in entering into the communion of all the Buddhas and Saints, through

realizing the oneness and eternity of truths in one's own person. Not only insight and wisdom . . . but morality and mental training are possible on the ground of this assumption, and all virtuous acts flow from this metaphysical source.[58]

Anesaki alludes precisely to the questions that would make Buddhism seem a religion of "nothingness" to many late nineteenth-century thinkers.[59] He points to the negative way in which the concept of *nirvana* has been interpreted in Europe, though wisely maintaining that the European scholars have their Indian counterparts. According to Anesaki, Schopenhauer and the Buddhists, and Christian mystics for that matter, face the same problem in referring to a "summum bonum" that lies beyond language. Nevertheless, the key difference between the German philosophers and the Buddha is the latter's insistence on the ability to bring others to the same enlightenment. The necessity to pass along the enlightenment of the path, to communicate with and train others, leads the Buddhist beyond a merely theoretical pose and into theorizing about the efficacy of the Buddhist path. The path is efficacious because of the stability of the truths of the path, and because of the constant example of Buddhas and "saints" who have come before. Granted, Anesaki's Japanese Buddhism is not the same as early Indian Buddhism; the early Indian texts would almost certainly not describe the attaining of *nirvana* as "realizing the oneness and eternity in one's own personality."[60] Nevertheless, the distinction holds; the entire Buddhist path depends not only on the end state to be reattained, but also on the continuity of the path with its ability to communicate and train future generations.

In fact, Anesaki opens the entire text with precisely this concern. He not only depicts Buddhism as a path attempting to fuse the theoretical and the practical; he claims that this is a characteristic shared by both Buddhism and Hinduism:

> Starting with an eager yearning for emancipation from sorrows and pains, the Buddha attained the solution of his mental struggles in the enlightenment of the Four Noble Truths. The infusion of practical needs with theoretical knowledge, on the one hand, and the stress laid upon the ascetic life as against the worldly, on the other, make up the key-note of Buddhist morality. As its religion is inseparably connected with its philosophy, its morality is based upon its ethical

theories, which, again, are the outcome of practical demands and training. In the close connexion between, or identification of, the practical and the theoretical sides, Buddhist ethics betrays clearly its inheritance from the ordinary Hindu mental disposition, and in its ascetic aspects it differs little from the other religious orders of India.[61]

Anesaki engages in a defense of Buddhism against those who accuse it of being a quietist religion. He also makes a point of bringing Hinduism into his defense. Buddhism and Hinduism do not have a separate "ethics" apart from a religion, but rather the close intertwining of ritual practice, ethical behavior, and abstract thought. Anesaki's move here is very similar to that of Eliot in his literary criticism, the attempt to fuse thought and feeling, theory and praxis (see below). In opposition to the tendency in the nineteenth century to view religion in terms either of metaphysics on the one hand or simply as a system of moral precepts on the other, both figures insist that the intellectual formulation of religious truth and the lived practice of a tradition are inherently connected. This is, further, precisely what Eliot admired in Dante.

What's more, Anesaki suggests that religious praxis itself awakens moral activity, that praxis awakens the Buddha nature within and leads to greater and greater ethical freedom:

> The religious acts for the entrance to moral life awaken the manifestation of the radical good; and the continual efficacy of faith and sacraments causes the *bodhichitta* to manifest itself more and more, and leads finally to its full realization—the enlightenment. Thus, when the *bodhichitta* is once awakened, its essence . . . is manifested in life, and, because the essence in itself is unmade, is of non-action . . . the moral life of the initiated needs less and less exertion, and so much the more partakes in the communion of the saints.[62]

Here, the religious acts themselves, based on the truth of the Buddha's teachings, awaken the good through habituation. This sense of the good, a sign of the *bodhichitta*, the Buddha's awakening mind, grows as the individual engages with the "sacraments" of the path and as his "faith" improves. The *bodhichitta* expands to such an extent that, eventually, it takes over the activities of the believer. The adherent does less and less, and the *bodhichitta* does more and more. It is the presence of the *bodhichitta* in all people that enables this activity and also enables the "community of saints." Others have achieved this high level of moral activity, and the novice can too. The "saints" stand as proof of a different, enlightened way of life. Anesaki's soteriology is therefore broadly universalistic and grounded in ethics.

Most significantly for our purposes, Anesaki places aesthetics firmly within the purview of the training necessary for the individual to awaken this *bodhichitta* and to make progress in the Buddhist path. He asserts that the Buddhist theory of morality that he describes aided in the spread of Buddhism in East Asia, making Buddhist morality "capable of being applied to various conditions of life."[63] He then provides a crucial footnote: "It is in this way that Buddhist morality in China, and more in Japan, has become connected with poetry and plastic arts. Aesthetic sense among them is derived from the source of mental training, and it is manifested in their daily life. An art for art's sake used to be an inconceivable thing among them."[64] Thus poetry and sculpture take their place within the context of the religious path as part and parcel of the "mental training" necessary for higher levels of enlightenment. Indeed, it is no coincidence that the very next section of Anesaki's text deals with "Mental Training and Spiritual Attainments."[65] There, he claims that Buddhists associated moral development with "spiritual exercises."[66] Thus, poetry and sculpture become elements of those "spiritual exercises," meant to incite believers to morality and bring them to a point where they can make a bid for enlightenment.

Anesaki is referring to the Mahayana Buddhist concept of *upaya,* or "skillful means." *Upaya* refers to the Buddha's ability to teach people at different levels of the religious path.[67] The Buddha speaks differently to different people and engages them through the most expedient means possible. The Buddha, then, engages listeners through the concepts, categories, practices, and texts with which they are familiar. Because the Buddha meets potential adherents in such a manner, it is possible that his teaching at that particular moment does not represent the fullness of Buddhist teaching. In fact, occasionally the Buddha's teaching seems to be at odds with a full Buddhist understanding. Nevertheless, the Buddha uses any means at his disposal, including figurative language, discursive

52   DESIRE AND THE ASCETIC IDEAL

reasoning, and grand aesthetic displays, to situate the individual in such a way as to make her or him more disposed to accept a fuller explication of the truth later on.

There is a hierarchical understanding of the tradition embedded in this model; those who are further along the path have a higher understanding of the truth. Nevertheless, the provisionality of lower levels of the path highlights the provisionality of the entire path; compared to *nirvana,* every stage of the path must be provisional. The *upaya* doctrine also explains how the Buddhist path, which counsels detachment, could counsel monks to become attached to the practices of the Path. It is necessary first to become attached to various positive practices and texts before one can be in the position to become completely detached. Detachment comes in and through the prior process of becoming attached to the proper things.

One locus classicus of the *upaya* doctrine for the Mahayana is the *Lotus Sutra,* a text upon which Anesaki lavished a good deal of attention in the class that Eliot took. The discussion commenced on November 14, and the text remains a touchstone in the lectures that follow, though some have a tangential relationship with the sutra. Anesaki titled part IV of the syllabus, "THE LOTUS OF THE LAW; ITS CIRCULATION AND INFLUENCE, ITS EXEGESIS."[68] In the December 16 lecture, the subject of *upaya* emerges clearly through a discussion of several crucial parables in the *Lotus Sutra* that give imaginative form to the idea of skillful means. Eliot writes there, "The method of teaching inferior men consisted in the upaya. Temporary consolation."[69]

Anesaki presents *upaya* as the mark of the Buddha's quasi-theological powers in the *Lotus Sutra.* The Buddha has taken on finite form specifically to lead all human beings to enlightenment. Eliot's notes read:

> In the 2nd chap. The purpose of B. app. is given. The nirmanakaya is insisted on. But it is not a mere human existence: it was taken up for a special purpose, that of leading all men to B.hood by upaya-kausalya (S (2)II)[?]. In the exercise of upaya-kausalya his personality is manifested as a sambhogakaya: the adaptation of B. to the capacities of various beings is upaya-kausalya. And this is possible through, by virtue of, dharmakaya. So various aspects of dharma are explained in this chapter. . . . These manifestations appear for the future security of the dharma. The necessary

connection of these manifestations with the final dharma. So in sambhogakaya the other two aspects are never lost sight of. XVI. Is meant to affirm the eternity of Buddha's life (past and future) in spite of his physical death. Dharmakaya is his real entity. The dharmakaya is not here a mere dharma; but his eternal life is devoted to the education of men. B. *Kern* misses the connection of the whole of the Sadd-pund.[70]

The Buddha in some sense exists eternally and because of this can take on an infinite number of shapes in finite existence. As Eliot notes, this "eternal life is devoted to the education of men." *Upaya-kausalya* then refers to the means by which the Buddha leads human beings in ways specific to each toward a final union in the dharma. These skillful means have as their final goal this ultimate liberation.

The *Lotus Sutra* describes these means through a series of famous parables. Anesaki discusses the parable of the house on fire, the parable of the "prodigal son," and the parable of the watered plants. Eliot's notes on the parables read as follows:

The parables are told for the sake of those of middle capacity. The house of fire. Children in the house. The father tries to entice them out by toys, etc. finally succeeds by showing them an oxencart. This is explained minutely in the commentary. The oxencart represents the Buddhayana.

The second parable is the prodigal son. Returning, he is gradually elevated to his son and heirship again. All men are Buddhaputras.

3rd parable. [*sic*] This is the most beautiful in expression. There are innumerable plants of all sorts. When a rain comes, all the plants are nourished by the same rain water, and grow according to their respective capacities. This parable has greatly influenced Japanese literature, and gave impetus to the Love for Nature [*sic*] (naturgefuhl). Statement of B.'s power as the dharmaswami. Anguttara v. I p. 110.[71]

Each of these three parables presents a different facet of the *upaya* doctrine. I focus on the first of them, since it employs burning imagery similar to that found later in "The Fire Sermon." In chapter 3 of the *Lotus Sutra,* the Buddha uses the image of a burning house to explain to Sariputra how there can be both many Buddha paths and one Buddha path.

54 DESIRE AND THE ASCETIC IDEAL

In the process, he asserts the ability of the Buddha to teach differently based on the dispositions of those who listen to him.

The fable presents the listener with the image of a decaying house on fire. There is only one door out of the house. Inside the house, children play, unaware of the fire burning all around them. Their father escapes the burning house, only to realize that his sons still play inside, ignorant of the danger in which they live, and slow to heed the father's warnings. Ironically, though they dwell in the middle of a massive conflagration, they are in need of someone to describe to them the situation and the danger:

> My children, those young boys, are staying in the burning house, playing, amusing, and diverting themselves with all sorts of sports. They do not perceive, nor know, nor understand, nor mind that the house is on fire, and do not get afraid. Though scorched by that great mass of fire, and affected with such a mass of pain, they do not mind the pain, nor do they conceive the idea of escaping.[72]

The father attempts to shout into the house from outside of it, warning the children to escape the flames. However, they do not heed the warning; indeed, they cannot even understand the basic vocabulary the father uses. They neither "know nor understand the purport of the word 'burning.'"[73] Those metaphorically caught in the flames of lust and infatuation cannot even understand the Buddha's language when they first encounter it. They have no context from which to understand it. Since they do not recognize the need for deliverance, the vocabulary of deliverance is meaningless. The man outside of the house therefore attempts a ruse: since his sons are given over to playing with toys (bullock carts, goat carts, and deer carts), he decides to lure them outside with the promise of more such toys outside. When they emerge, they find instead richly decorated bullock carts (oxen carts), far more beautiful than anything they could have imagined.

The implied tension beneath this story is the existence of different Buddhist approaches to *nirvana*. The *Lotus Sutra* attempts to co-opt competing models of practice (those of the *arhats*, or enlightened monks, and *pratyekabuddhas*, or solitary Buddhas)[74] by claiming that they are lesser "devices" meant to address people of a certain disposition. Nevertheless, in reality there is only one authentic Buddha "vehicle," that of the bodhisattva. Still, these lesser vehicles, along with all the inferior modes of representation and practice at early stages of the path, are ruses whereby the Buddha places his followers in a position to learn higher truths. He utilizes the desire for amusement and pleasure in order to reveal a more splendid truth when escape has been secured. Allegorically speaking, the father/Buddha uses attachment to bring his suffering followers to a different kind of attachment, a better kind of attachment:

> Without availing myself of some device, these beings will not escape. For they are attached to the pleasures of the five senses, to worldly pleasures; they will not be freed from birth, old age, disease, death, grief, wailing, pain, melancholy, despondency, by which they are burnt, tormented, vexed, distressed. Unless they are forced to leave the triple world which is like a house the shelter and roof whereof is in a blaze, how are they to get acquainted with Buddha-knowledge?[75]

The Buddha uses a "device" precisely to engage with human beings through "worldly pleasures." Because they are immersed in pleasures, human beings cannot receive the Buddha's teaching. Therefore, the Buddha must reach them first through the promise of pleasures in his "device." The desires of his followers become transformed once they have reached the prize outside of the house. What they had once wanted now recedes with the prize that lies in front of them. Still, the desire of the followers must first be engaged in order to persuade them to leave their life of suffering.

Anesaki invokes *upaya*, both in his text on ethics and in his lectures, to stand against Schopenhauer's depiction of Buddhism as quietist and nihilistic. Rather than a tradition that embraces nothingness and annihilation, Anesaki depicts Buddhism in terms of communal activity and training that is both mental and ethical. His Buddhism combines both theoretical knowledge and praxis. Far from dismissing aesthetic experience, Anesaki places it firmly within the process of training and does not divorce it from the work of abstract thought. Aesthetic experience takes its place in the ascetic path as a mode of engaging and transforming desire. I suggest in the next section of this chapter that Eliot has a very similar criticism of Schopenhauer and, in the final section of this chapter, that Eliot also comes to a similar estimation of Schopenhauer's interpretation of Indian traditions.

The Clark Lectures

The Clark Lectures, given by Eliot at Trinity College, Cambridge, in 1926, combine Eliot's analysis of Schopenhauer with a criticism of Schopenhauer's Orientalism, culminating in a criticism of Schopenhauer's "Kantian pseudo-Buddhism."[76] I suggest that Eliot's characterization of the Indian traditions (and especially Buddhism) as allied with the "classical" traditions of mysticism in part reflect Anesaki's earlier characterization of Buddhism as an engaged, praxis-oriented tradition.[77] Eliot's polemic also ultimately continues the criticism of Schopenhauer, that the German philosopher had abandoned praxis and activity in favor of withdrawal. This latter model is, in fact, precisely how Eliot characterizes the "romantic" mystical traditions.[78] Eliot sees Indian ascetic traditions as operating in a similar way to some medieval Western contemplative texts that begin with the merging of thought and affect and proceed on an ascetic path that trains the self for higher levels of transcendence.

Eliot's chief concern in the Clark Lectures is to show how "metaphysical poetry," the poetry that attempts to merge thought and feeling into an expanded sensibility, changed after the breakup of the medieval *sensus communis*. Eliot's definition of metaphysical poetry builds on Santayana's definition of "philosophical poetry" but makes one crucial departure. He claims that Santayana's definition restricts itself to poets attempting to envision a philosophical system. According to Eliot, if one grants Santayana his definition, then only Santayana's three figures (Lucretius, Dante, Goethe) would be included.[79] Hence, Eliot's own definition is a bit broader: "It is a function of poetry both to fix and make more conscious and precise emotions and feelings in which most people participate in their own experience, and to draw within the orbit of feeling and sense what had existed only in thought. It creates a unity of feeling out of various parts . . . the union of [things] hitherto unconnected in experience."[80] Here, Eliot describes the job of metaphysical poetry as providing more precise formulations to common "emotions and feelings," and also as attempting to bring thought into affective experience. Poetry becomes the locus for a negotiation and correlation between the realm of sense and affectivity and the abstract realm of thought. By attempting to merge thought and feeling in this way, the poet enlarges the experience both of himself and of his readers: he or she creates "the union of [things] hitherto unconnected in experience."

It is interesting to observe that this merging of thought and feeling, the abstract and the sensuous, emerges again in the Clark Lectures when Eliot discusses the kind of mysticism that finds expression in Dante's *Commedia*, a mysticism that owes much, according to Eliot, to Aristotle's ethical philosophy. Though acknowledging a wide range of mysticisms, Eliot delineates two different types to highlight what he takes to be a fundamental change in modernity. He characterizes the Spanish mysticism of the sixteenth century, exemplified by St. Teresa of Ávila and St. John of the Cross, as "romantic" and "psychological" and, astoundingly, compares them with Descartes and Rousseau.[81] When Eliot describes the "psychological" trend of modernity, he characterizes it as a belief, of which Descartes is the chief representative: "Instead of ideas as meanings, as references to an outside world, you have suddenly a new world coming into existence, inside your own mind and therefore by the usual implication inside your own head."[82] In this context all of the Spanish figures come to represent a kind of mysticism that focuses more on "psychology" than on "ontology," more on exploring the human mind rather than directing the human mind beyond itself to something outside of it which can be perceived in greater and lesser degrees.[83] This mysticism concerns itself with a turn within rather than a progression toward an external, ontological telos.[84]

In distinction to this "romantic" type of mysticism, Eliot posits one that is "in the direct classical, Aristotelian tradition, and which is the mysticism of Dante."[85] It is crucial to realize here that this romantic/classical distinction is not new in Eliot's thought: he is continuing to pursue a distinction he made as early as 1916, influenced by the writings of T. E. Hulme.[86] When it comes time to describe this type of mysticism, Eliot does so in detail:

> There is a type of religious mysticism which found expression in the twelfth century, and which is taken up into the system of Aquinas. Its origin is in the *Metaphysics* of Aristotle 1072b and elsewhere, and in the *Nichomachean Ethics*, and it is the opposite of Bergsonism. You know how the Absolute of Bergson is arrived at: by a turning back on the path of thought, by divesting one's mind of the apparatus of distinction and analysis, by plunging into the flow of immediate experience. For the twelfth century, the divine vision or enjoyment of God could only be attained by a process in which

the analytic intellect took part; it was through and by and beyond discursive thought that man could arrive at beatitude. This was the form of mysticism consummated in Dante's time. It is very different from the mysticism of Ignatius, Theresa and St. John of the Cross, who were romantics, and from that of Eckhardt [sic], who was a heretic. In its own way it was perfect. But the human mind, when it comes to a terminus, hastens to look up the next train to almost anywhere. In the fourteenth century Meister Eckhardt and his followers—appropriately in Germany—reasserted the God of the Abyss; the God, in short, of Mr. D.H. Lawrence.[87]

Eliot begins by using Bergson as an example—but just one—of romantic mysticism.[88] On the other hand, the passage of the *Metaphysics* that Eliot mentions provides a brief summation of Aristotle's teleology: "The final cause, then, produces motion as being loved, but all other things by being moved."[89] Eliot's "classical" mysticism operates not by turning one's back on the realm of thought and intellect, but by an ascent that operates in and through the operations of the intellect. This is not a mysticism that proceeds by immediate divestment, as with the romantic mystics, but one that operates with a paradox: thought is engaged in order to move beyond it: "it was through and by and beyond discursive thought that man could arrive at beatitude."

Eliot explains what he means here by referring to the mysticism of Richard of St. Victor, a mysticism that, he asserts in several places, lies behind Dante's own mysticism. Indeed, he states this rather starkly: "This mysticism of Richard of St. Victor, which is the mysticism also of St. Thomas Aquinas and of Dante. . . . The Aristotelian-Victorine-Dantesque mysticism is ontological."[90] It is also significant for our purposes that Richard's text is provocatively compared with "some Indian mystical systems."[91] So what is it about Richard's mysticism that Eliot takes to be Aristotelian? First and foremost, Eliot discusses Richard's portrayal of the mystical path, one that proceeds through "*cogitation, meditation* and *contemplation.*"[92] Eliot provides a lengthy quotation from Richard's *Benjamin Major,* which not only describes the various stages of the ascent, but discusses the role of the imagination in this process: "Thus, it is evident that all things that are grasped by the imagination, as well as many other things that are above it, are grasped by reason. Similarly, those things which imagination and reason grasp, as well as things which they are not able to grasp, are perceived by the understanding."[93] The ascent begins with the imagination and then proceeds through higher levels of understanding to that point where the mind is lifted beyond itself in ecstatic contemplation. Eliot explains the path in this way: "The method and the goal seem to me essentially the same as with Aquinas and Dante: the divine contemplation, and the development and subsumption of emotion and feeling through intellect into the vision of God."[94] Whether or not Eliot is right about the similarities between Aquinas and Richard need not detain us here. What is interesting, however, is Eliot's choice of a model of mystical ascent in which emotion and feeling are first developed and then subsumed into the path, merged with thought and channeled toward the ultimate telos. These forms of mystical ascent become counterexamples for Eliot; they represent a crucial moment prior to the deterioration of the medieval sensus communis in which affect, imagination, and activity were not divorced from the work of the mind.

Later in the nineteenth century, Laforgue embodies, for Eliot, the tensions that result from a slow, modern retreat into the mind.[95] The intellectual truth he attempts to hold is found in Schopenhauer's system of philosophy. Eliot's analysis of Laforgue seeks to make sense of the poet's lacerating irony. According to Eliot, modern irony emerges from the need for a philosophical system that provides a fulfillment, rather than a rejection, of human desires.[96] He writes of Laforgue:

> He had an innate craving for order: that is, that every feeling should have its intellectual equivalent, its philosophical justification, and that every idea should have its emotional equivalent, its sentimental justification . . . for Laforgue, life was *consciously* divided into thought and feeling; but his feelings were such as required an intellectual completion, a *beatitude* and the philosophical systems which he embraced were so much *felt* as to require a sensuous completion. They did not fit. Hence the metaphysicality of Laforgue reaches in two directions: the intellectualising of the feeling and the emotionalising of the idea. Where they meet, they come into conflict, and Laforgue's irony, an irony always employed against himself, ensues.[97]

The poet requires a dual justification: feelings require philosophical justifications, and ideas require "sentimental justification," a justification of affectivity. Laforgue's problem is that he cannot find a proper coalescence of thought and "feeling." The philosophy he attempts to "feel" does not "fit" with the emotions he attempts to understand. Laforgue's emotions require a "beatitude," an end state or telos in which desire comes to fulfillment. Laforgue's problem becomes emblematic of a much broader one, since Laforgue already lived in a world in which the division between thought and feeling had decisively occurred, and both halves worked at cross-purposes.

Schopenhauer's philosophy represents the abstract system that cannot metaphysically situate Laforgue's desires. In this, Schopenhauer represents simply a late stage of the dissociation of sensibility. Nevertheless, according to Eliot, he is one of the decisive influences on Laforgue's predicament:

> It is noticeable how often the words "inconscient," "néant," and "L'absolu" and such philosophical terms from the vocabulary of Schopenhauer and Hartmann, the Valkyrie, and such properties from the dramas of Wagner, recur. Laforgue is the nearest verse equivalent to the philosophies of Schopenhauer and Hartmann, the philosophy of the unconscious and of annihilation, just as Wagner is the nearest music equivalent to the same philosophies . . . in Laforgue there is continuous war between the feelings implied by his ideas, and the ideas implied by his feelings. The system of Schopenhauer collapses, but in a different ruin from that of *Tristan und Isolde*.[98]

Instead of collapsing in a glorious *Liebestod*, in which Isolde welcomes death as the path toward unification with Tristan, for Laforgue Schopenhauer's system collapses into a loss of agency: Eliot cites a passage from the "Grande complainte de la Ville de Paris," in which Laforgue's poetic speaker, after a string of advertisements, cries, "Oh the rapidity of life also sole agency."[99] The self is annihilated by the rapidity of modern life and its material enticements. The erotic desires of the self are taken up in commercialism and become the sole source of agency. At the same time, Laforgue attempts to turn an analytic gaze on his own desires, treating them with the utmost suspicion. Here we have the emergence of Schopenhauer's will as blind, erotic force and also Schopenhauer's attempt to view the world of will from a neutral, philosophical position.

Nevertheless, Laforgue seems unable to rest in this depiction of eros. Schopenhauer's philosophy can neither be lived out nor validate affect as pointing to a higher, intelligible reality. Eliot validates Laforgue's sentimentalism, while also criticizing Schopenhauer and his interpretation of Buddhism:

> Laforgue is in revolt, not in acceptance; he is at once the sentimentalist day-dreaming over the *jeune fille* at the piano with her geraniums, and the behaviourist inspecting her reflexes. (p. 216) What he wants, you see, is either a *Vita Nuova* to justify, dignify and integrate his sentiments toward the *jeune fille* in a system of the universe, or else some system of thought which shall keep a place [for and] even enhance these feelings and at the same time enable him to *feel* as intensely an abstract world. On the one hand he was fascinated by Miss Leah Lee, the English governess, and on the other hand by the Kantian pseudo-Buddhism of Schopenhauer and Hartmann.[100]

Laforgue's affective experience continues unabated, as it must, but he operates with a metaphysics that can only approach that experience through scientific rationalization, a rationalization that identifies the world with will. Laforgue explains away his love with a thoroughgoing pessimism, a pessimism influenced by Schopenhauer in general as well as Schopenhauer's interpretation of Buddhism more specifically. Schopenhauer's "Kantian pseudo-Buddhism" in this instance is a detachment from the world based on the identification of the world with will, with blindly striving desire. According to Eliot, both Schopenhauer and Laforgue after him associate Buddhism with a metaphysical system that simply denies desire, that fails to provide any sort of fulfillment to desire.

In the process of showing the clash of intellect and sensibility in Laforgue's work, Eliot critiques Schopenhauer's interpretation of Indian materials. In this, he mirrors the earlier critique of Anesaki and demonstrates that he operated with a clear knowledge of contemporary Indological debates. Eliot sees Indian religious texts not as Schopenhauer did, as dedicated purely to the renunciation of affect, desire, and thought. To do this would be to see them as allied with a "romantic" turn within, concerned only with the "world inside one's head" instead of an engagement with an external path. Eliot's characterization, similar to Anesaki's, envisions Buddhism as more similar to the "classical" traditions, engaging and subsuming affect, desire, and thought in the process of transcending those things. In this regard, Eliot also resembles his friend and mentor Irving Babbitt, who also saw the Buddhist path as one of discipline.[101] What is at stake for both Eliot and Anesaki is the path of ascetic cultivation and the place of the affective in those paths. The approach to *nirvana*, for Anesaki, was one that passed through ritual, affect, and theoretical cultivation; for Eliot, it was through the merging of thought and feeling and the transcending of those things en route to a metaphysical Absolute.

For Schopenhauer, there was no such path; the will could not be taught. Eliot describes Schopenhauer's philosophy as "pseudo-Buddhism" because it splits thought and feeling and attempts to operate only within the sphere of the mind, without engaging first with lived, affective experience. Indeed, it denies the efficacy of externality to move one to that Absolute. In doing this, Schopenhauer denies ritual, practice, and language itself. Eliot recognizes, however, that though traditions such as Buddhism and Hinduism might operate with a rhetoric of the denial of the world and of desire, in reality they mobilize the world and desire in order to transcend those things. This view resembles very closely then Anesaki's view of Buddhism and resonates strongly with the Buddhist *upaya* doctrine, which tried to explain how the Buddha could use various practices and figures in order to move his followers ever closer to the point at which they could understand the Buddhist path in higher and higher levels of comprehension, up to the point where such comprehension itself ceased.

Ultimately, the examination of Anesaki's critique of Schopenhauer provides us with a closer look at an important influence on Eliot's understanding of Indian materials. As Cleo Kearns has shown, these materials had an impact on Eliot throughout his life and appear in significant places throughout his poetry and plays. I do not mean to argue that Anesaki was the only interpreter of Buddhism for Eliot. Kearns has done the most definitive work in exploring the many mediators of Indic traditions to Eliot.[102] I do wish to suggest that an examination of Anesaki's work brings to light an important Indological debate of which Eliot was a part, and that Eliot's classicism is, to some extent, both informed by and responding to that debate. The fault lines for this Indological debate were issues of the practices and discipline, both intellectual and aesthetic, of the Buddhist tradition. To this extent, it represents a crucial precursor to Eliot's later understanding of classicism and, ultimately, religion. Finally, an understanding of Eliot's engagement with Anesaki places Eliot's thought in an intercultural context, a perspective that is still, despite Kearns's groundbreaking work, urgently needed in Eliot studies.

2

T. S. ELIOT'S *ARS RELIGIOSA*

Transmigration and Faith in *Knowledge and Experience*

In *Eliot's Dark Angel: Intersections of Life and Art,* Ronald Schuchard dispelled the myth that Eliot's religious conversion came suddenly in 1927, changing him from a darling of the avant-garde into a reactionary Anglo-Catholic in a matter of mere moments.[1] By examining Eliot's Extension School syllabi and tracing Eliot's early debts to T. E. Hulme, Schuchard concluded that "by 1916 Eliot's classical, royalist, and religious point of view was already formulated."[2] Schuchard's work has made it possible to discern a more nuanced picture of Eliot's religious trajectory, pointing critics to Eliot's early interest in mysticism, Indian religious traditions, and various surrogates for religious belief and practice.[3] Indeed, critical work on this has been done by Jewel Spears Brooker who, in an important essay, documents Eliot's early interest in religion as a "scheme" for living in the world and engaging in experience: "The object of such a scheme or system is, first, to enable one to make sense out of experience, and second, to enable one to live and to act."[4] According to Brooker, Eliot viewed religion in his early essays and letters as a way of organizing and viewing the world that could enable one to act with purpose in it. It provided an order from which to begin action and a motivation to enable it.

In pursuing Eliot's early religious interests, Brooker insightfully notes that a religious sensibility is already present in the work of F. H. Bradley, whose work would form the basis for Eliot's doctoral dissertation, "Knowledge and Experience in the Philosophy of F. H. Bradley," completed in 1916.[5] She insightfully shows that Bradley's work pits the

64 DESIRE AND THE ASCETIC IDEAL

fragmentation of the world against the alienated unity of immediate experience.[6] Thus, human beings, mired in consciousness and thought, always attempt to reapproach that immediate unity in and through their consciousness and thought.

In this chapter, I suggest that Eliot uses this religious dimension to Bradley's thought, while ultimately criticizing Bradley's use of religious and philosophical language. Eliot subtly suggests that Bradley's project is unable to provide the all-encompassing "scheme" for life that religious paths do. Indeed, I argue that the conclusion of *Knowledge and Experience* reveals several religious influences to the text whose importance and impact have not been sufficiently recognized. They reveal that what Eliot has done in this text, among many other things, is to provide a description of conversion, of the movement from one view of the world to another, of transformation and self-transcendence. This becomes abundantly clear in Eliot's evocation and unique combination of two distinct religious concepts, "transmigration" and "faith," at the text's conclusion.

Transmigration, or the reincarnation of the self in another body, would have been familiar to Eliot in and through the Indian religious texts with which he had extensive contact in his graduate studies.[7] In the dissertation, Eliot uses this concept to describe the passage of the self from one point of view and one version of the self to a higher one. The self is, in a sense, reincarnated into different ways of being situated in the world. In this, I suggest that Eliot evokes the Buddhist notion of *upaya*, or skillful means, to describe how one passes from one set of truths to another higher set. In this Buddhist teaching, the Buddha uses different means to teach different types of human beings, even if the means the Buddha uses do not represent the fullness of the Buddhist truth. In this way, the Buddha is able to put the cycle of reincarnation to work, marshaling it toward an ascetic telos. This teaching implies then that the movement from one version of the self to another can become the movement between different degrees of truth, and one degree of truth could prepare for a higher degree. In this approach, I am building on the suggestion from Cleo McNelly Kearns that Eliot's philosophical "thought itself profited at several points from immersion in Indic philosophy."[8]

On the other hand, Eliot's invocation of the leap of faith represents a disguised quarrel with how Bradley himself uses this Christian term at the conclusion of *Ethical Studies*. There, Bradley denies that faith is a qualitative leap between perspectives. His "faith" is an identification with the Absolute, followed by a voluntaristic persistence in moral activity. Eliot, however, insists that faith is part of the temporal becoming of a finite center, enabling it to move from one point of view to another in and through the engagement with practice. This hidden polemic, taken together with the evocation of Indian transmigration, reveals Eliot's text to be not only a covert *Ars Poetica,* as A. David Moody and Kearns suggest,[9] but also an incipient *ars religiosa,* where Eliot insists on the modification of the self toward a virtually impossible goal through a process that develops both thought and feeling, higher thought and aesthetics.

In many ways, Eliot's syncretistic yoking of these distinct religious terms would be problematic for adherents of either tradition. This move, however, enables a complex comparison; when considered in the context of his argument, it suggests that the religious traditions Eliot invokes provide a language and practical context for describing the transformation of the self that metaphysical philosophy by itself lacks. This is not to say that Eliot has converted to any specific religious tradition, nor is it to claim that his dissertation describes any religious doctrinal position. It is to suggest that Eliot recognizes that philosophical conceptions alone cannot provide the finite center with a sufficient praxis-based schema for living. The text implies that there is something that religious language and praxis provides that Bradley's metaphysics does not. The "religious" here includes the recognition that thought and practice, intellect and feeling, can cultivate the self and move the self to higher levels of understanding, and that this ascent is composed of real changes to the self. In this, Eliot produces a view that strongly resonates with Dante's view of his own ascent in *The Divine Comedy.* Eliot's move implicitly criticizes the reduction of religion to moral philosophy on one hand and the primacy of metaphysics divorced from practice on the other. At the same time, it provides a religious sensibility to aesthetics that will bear fruit in his later poetry and criticism.

Ultimately, I suggest that the conclusion of Eliot's text demonstrates its own insufficiency by invoking the religious traditions. For this reason, I disagree with Kearns that this moment is "not some foreshadowing of his later beliefs."[10] Given Schuchard's demonstration that by 1916, Eliot's "*sensibility* was religious and Catholic, and his primary critical concerns were moral,"[11] I think we have warrant enough for considering it so. Eliot posits an advantage of having a religious sensibility in making sense of the movement from one self to another, from one set of objects to another.

66   DESIRE AND THE ASCETIC IDEAL

His philosophy, however, cannot provide an appropriate scheme to generate desire, hope, and confidence that this movement actually heads toward its formal epistemological limit. Eliot's text therefore implies that traditions that unite theory and praxis toward an unthinkable limit provide a "scheme" for action and living that his philosophy cannot.

Faith and Transmigration in *Knowledge and Experience*

In a bizarre and provocative move at the end of *Knowledge and Experience*, Eliot explains the process of moving from one set of object types to another in terms of religious ideas taken from both Western and Eastern religious traditions. In the process of going back through the various types of objects that he has described over the course of the text, Eliot uses the following astounding language:

> But every transformation of type [i.e., object type] involves a leap which science cannot take, and which metaphysics must take. It involves an *interpretation,* a transmigration from one world to another, and such a pilgrimage involves an act of faith. In a transformation of object-type there is a change of point of view; in a metaphysical theory there is an attempt to bind together all points of view in one. . . . A philosophy can and must be worked out with the greatest rigour and discipline in the details, but can ultimately be founded on nothing but faith.[12]

The movement from one point of view to another, from one set of related objects to another, and from one version of the self to another is likened to transmigration, the reincarnation of a self in a different life. Further, this movement is given a sense of purpose by being described in terms of pilgrimage, a movement toward a final place of meaning or significance. But this movement comes about only through interpretation, and interpretation implies an "act of faith." By interpretation, Eliot means "a valuation and an assignment of meaning,"[13] but also the broader process of selection by which the subject comes to accept some objects as true and others as not. These assignments of meaning are based on a felt rightness, the "felt identity between appearance and reality,"[14] that then provides a new foundation for metaphysical speculation. Eliot uses the term "faith," I believe, to mark the movement from one point of view to another as a moment of conversion, when one gives oneself over to a new perspective, a new way of seeing the world, a new set of objects and relations. It marks a trust in the reliability and truth of the new way of seeing. If this is the case, though, Eliot sees life as a never-ending series of conversions.

The foundation of Eliot's depiction of interpretation is the idea that experiences of feeling have continuity with the Feeling that is immediate experience. Eliot holds that human beings are united with their objects of study through an immediate experience prior to the self-object relation. The necessity for holding this can be found through inference.[15] Individual feelings are different sorts of objects for us because they participate in the Feeling that is immediate experience.[16] There is no experience or knowledge without Feeling. Feeling provides the initial impulse behind the drive to knowledge and the ultimate goal toward which knowers move. Eliot writes:

> And although immediate experience is the foundation and goal of our knowing, yet no experience is only immediate. There is no absolute point of view from which real and ideal can be finally separated and labeled. All of our terms turn out to be unreal abstractions; but we can defend them, and give them a kind of reality and validity (the only validity which they can express or can need) by showing that they express the theory of knowledge which is implicit in all our practical activity. And therefore we allow ourselves to hold both that a lower stage of mere feeling is irrelevant and that knowledge is based upon and developed out of feeling.[17]

Immediate experience provides the beginning of all knowing and the end of all knowing. The objects of our experience emerge from the primacy of feeling, and along with those objects comes the emergence of subjects. Once this subject/object relation emerges, we become alienated from that primacy of feeling. The process of knowing, however, attempts to reapproach that primacy, to describe it in more concrete terms in and through conscious thought.[18]

What Eliot ends up giving us then is a picture of human activity that begins with immediate experience and ends with a complete knowing of that initial experience as the formal limit of our knowing. Jewel Spears Brooker has shown how this picture gives a quasi-religious element to both Bradley's philosophy and Eliot's use of it.[19] Eliot provides us with a kind of teleology, between immediacy and the complete knowing of that immediacy in and through thought. Brooker crucially notes that

DESIRE AND THE ASCETIC IDEAL

the reapproach to that immediacy, the striving after "transcendent experience," must always come in and through the combination of thought and feeling.[20]

Eliot's telos is the Absolute, but conceived as a formal limit to knowing rather than Bradley's ultimate metaphysical unity:

> We are led to the conception of an all-inclusive experience outside of which nothing shall fall. If anyone object that mere experience at the beginning and complete experience at the end are hypothetical limits, I can say not a word of refutation for this would be just the reverse side of what opinions I hold. And if anyone assert that immediate experience, at either the beginning or the end of our journey, is annihilation and utter night, I cordially agree. That Mr. Bradley himself would accept this interpretation of his "positive non-distinguished non-relational whole" is not to be presumed (ETR 188). But the ultimate nature of the Absolute does not come within the scope of the present paper.[21]

Eliot gently sets aside Bradley's notion of the Absolute here, though elsewhere he is more critical of it.[22] The scientific assertion of the Absolute would imply an ability to distance oneself from the whole of reality and objectively characterize the metaphysical whole, and this is precisely what Eliot, in the dissertation, claims is impossible.[23] Nevertheless, Eliot does adopt the idea of the Absolute, as a formal, hypothetical limit to knowing.[24] It provides a virtually impossible limit of human knowing, in which the mind would have complete knowledge of all of reality, a point at which the self would cease to exist in any meaningful sense. Selves are dependent upon discreet objects in the world. Complete experience would be a complete encompassing of experience, in and through the merging of thought and feeling. Any self that could possibly accomplish that would cease to be a discreet self with discreet objects. Therefore at each limit of knowing we find "annihilation and utter night."

In describing these limits, Eliot places the interpreting and transmigrating self between a primal origin and a hypothetical, ultimate telos. It is undertaking a "pilgrimage." Indeed, by the end of the text, Eliot is describing this process of interpretation, change, and faith as a movement toward the Absolute (though this is not "God" in Bradley's thought), and one that potentially passes through various "degrees of truth."[25] One makes this "pilgrimage," according to Eliot, chiefly through the experience of error, incited by decisive modifications of feeling or the experience of other people.[26] These moments cast one's own understanding into question, prompting one to doubt the reality of one's objects of experience. In these instances of development and transformation, the self within the finite center[27] comes to see the potential new objects as "half-objects," or possible objects.[28] In reality, then, the consideration of a different point of view also prompts one to doubt the point of view currently held.[29] One is poised between the old and the new, holding them in tension, pausing in judgment on the "real."

The self discovers the reality or illusion of a point of view gradually through the test of practice. As practice changes, so too do the objects that appear to the self and consequently the self itself. Likewise, new theory must always pass the test of praxis. Eliot writes:

> An account of reality, or any field of it, which has the appearance of going to the point of substituting a new type of objects for the old will be a true theory and not merely a new world, if it is capable of making an actual practical difference in our attitude toward the old, or toward some already accepted object . . . it is this felt identity between appearance and reality that will constitute explanation, and that the identity is a fragile and insecure thing.[30]

Eliot implies then that the validation of a particular point of view is a feeling of rightness, and this feeling becomes strengthened or diminished in and through the crucible of practice. Any adoption of the new (or readoption of the old) presupposes then a "leap" to a new perspective, but that perspective then needs to be lived out. Eliot therefore describes a path of consistent leaps of faith, rooted in feeling and marking degrees of truth, that are undertaken along the path to the Absolute, described as a formal limit to human experience of the world.[31] Each of these leaps represents a transmigration, a qualitative transformation into a new self and a new world: a rebirth.

Buddhism in *Knowledge and Experience*

I suggest that Eliot's invocation of transmigration and degrees of reality demonstrates the partial influence of Indian texts on his philosophy, particularly through the concept of *upaya* discussed in the previous chapter. This concept in an early form (as we will see below) can be

70   DESIRE AND THE ASCETIC IDEAL

found in many of the Buddhist texts Eliot read. *Upaya* finds a classical expression, though, in Mahayana Buddhism, and especially in the *Lotus Sutra*. As discussed in chapter 1, this was a text explicated in detail by Masaharu Anesaki in the course that Eliot took at Harvard in 1914, entitled "Schools of Religious and Philosophical Thought in Japan."[32] Recall that *upaya* refers to the Buddha's ability to teach people at different levels of practice and understanding of the religious path.[33] The Buddha speaks differently to different people and engages them through the most expedient means possible. The Buddha, then, engages listeners through the concepts, categories, rituals, practices, and texts with which they are familiar. Because the Buddha meets potential adherents in such a manner, it is possible that his teaching at that particular moment does not represent the fullness of Buddhist teaching. In fact, occasionally the Buddha's teaching seems to be at odds with a full Buddhist understanding. Nevertheless, the Buddha uses any means at his disposal, including practice, figurative language, discursive reasoning, and grand aesthetic displays, to situate the individual in such a way as to make her or him more disposed to accept a fuller explication of the truth later on. The doctrine of *upaya* allows Buddhists to imagine the cultivation of the practitioner over the course of many lives, through many transmigrations. The practice and process of discovery in one life allows for a transformation to a different kind of life later. It is this movement through different levels of practice and different levels of understanding in an ascetic path toward *nirvana* that in part informs Eliot's allusion to transmigration and "degrees of reality" in *Knowledge and Experience.*

Kearns identifies this element of the early Eliot's thought as she assesses his potential engagement with the *Lotus Sutra*. She admits that Eliot might have been drawn to the use of literary or mythical tropes in the text: "it is possible that a growing acceptance of the need for a religion replete with myth and symbolism and adapted to the psychological and spiritual needs of lay devotional life would have rendered Eliot, as time went on, more sympathetic to later Buddhism."[34] Kearns recognizes here that elements of Buddhism lend themselves well to Eliot's gradual interest in an embodied religiosity, one that embraced ritual and aesthetics.[35] I suggest that Eliot's exposure to later Buddhism alerts him to an aesthetic dimension of the tradition as a whole. I defend this at length in chapter 4. It is precisely this aesthetic dimension of religion that Eliot would later embrace in his conversion to Anglo-Catholicism. Barry Spurr notes that Eliot's early religious searching was for a view of life that would satisfy the need for emotional fulfillment. On discussing Eliot's depiction of Paul Elmer More, Spurr writes that "Eliot noted that his friend had journeyed from 'a form of worship from which the office of the imagination and the aesthetic emotions had . . . been so ruthlessly evicted' to one where they were satisfied. This too was Eliot's journey."[36]

To understand the Buddhist conceptualization of the "degrees of reality" within the path, it is first necessary to understand the tradition's general teaching on the abilities of the Buddha. These abilities are later used to characterize the stages along the path that the practitioner performs in leading up to its highest levels. The Buddha's "skillful means" give him the ability to communicate to every listener in the manner most appropriate to that person's ideological, intellectual, and affective situation. Indeed, skillful means often entails not directly confronting the listener with Buddhist truths, but rather bringing them a certain way toward the ultimate truths through various practices, ruses, and fictions. Michael Pye has noted that the Buddha's teaching takes form in many different discursive genres:

> This fundamental conception of the manner of the Buddha's beginning to teach has far-reaching implications. A teaching which relates to diverse needs in a differentiated world clearly requires a great flexibility and this was legitimated by the way in which the Buddha's own activity is understood. . . . A great variety of literary forms is accepted as appropriate in all schools of Buddhism, and it has been seen that in The Lotus Sutra the various genres of Buddhist teaching are all conceived in terms of the Buddha's skillful means. Even the rules of religious practice submit to many re-adjustments. The laxity of the Mahasanghikas and the Mahayanists has found its way into the histories of Buddhism, but the analogous flexibility of Theravada discipline is often overlooked. In general it is fair to say that the idea of a differentiated yet consistent teaching was the basic style of pre-Mahayana Buddhism anyway, presumed to stem from the Buddha himself. Skillful means is the Mahayana name for this style.[37]

The truth of the Buddhist path is, in one sense, absolute. In another sense, however, it can be differentiated for practical purposes. In fact, it does not depend on any single formulation of the doctrine. The Buddhist doctrine is based on strategy, on how to bring any particular individual to the highest goal, though this goal may be many rebirths away. The Buddhist path may lead to a single truth, that of *nirvana*, but this path and this goal can be represented in a myriad of ways, in a myriad of genres.[38] Also note that Pye reminds us that such a "differentiated" path is characteristic of both Mahayana and earlier Theravada Buddhism.

In a very real way, because the ultimate meaning of the path is always deferred, every stage along the path becomes an instance of skillful means. The Buddhist tradition holds that a monk usually cannot immediately enter *nirvana* but must move through many different levels of desire, understanding, and insight. At each moment, the discourse used is provisional, meant to move the monk to a different level of understanding. After the teaching has been used, it is seen as imperfect or illusory and laid aside for a higher teaching. The canonical image for this is the raft that takes the monk across the river to the farther shore and then is discarded as he moves onto land.[39] The path is, then, self-destructing; each teaching or doctrine is used and then discarded.[40]

In *Knowledge and Experience*, Eliot does not, of course, posit any sort of privileged, external teacher like the Buddha, positioning his monks for higher levels of learning. He does, however, present the process of reincarnation or transmigration as part of a path of aesthetic, practical engagement with the world that can lead to higher and higher levels of knowledge. He does this while also placing the self within a "pilgrimage" between immediate experience and the Absolute, invoked not as Bradley's metaphysical reality but as the limit of human experience. Eliot raises the concept of transmigration through an interreligious comparison that implies a teleology of sorts. The self moves through different versions of itself, on the way to the Absolute, in faith (which is, of course, not a Buddhist concept). This faith is a trust that the next version of the self will be somehow a higher version of the self with a more effective vision of the world. In reality, this may or may not be true, but this faith is the only way for the self to make the "leap" from one life to the next. Eliot's text then does not invoke any sort of supernatural teacher or force guiding the self through life. Rather, Eliot invokes this view of transmigration in order both to describe the provisionality of knowledge and to insist that such provisionality need not be crippling but can be part of a process of development and an approach to higher levels of truth for a self. Eliot himself, however, cannot provide confidence that that will be the case. This seems to be a confidence that philosophy cannot provide, but perhaps the religious traditions could. We see this emerge clearly in Eliot's use of the term "faith," a use of the term at odds with that of Bradley.

Contesting Bradley's Faith

Eliot uses the term "faith" in describing the movement, based in feeling, from one point of view to the next, and one self to the next, in the moment when one hovers on the edge between two different points of view and then enters the new point of view.[41] In other words, Eliot is offering not just a theory of the degrees of truth, but a theory of conversion. With his use of the term "leap,"[42] Eliot's view of faith superficially resembles Kierkegaard's conception of this term, though Eliot would come to read Kierkegaard's work only later in life. Eliot's theory of faith also bears some similarity to the classic conception of faith in the Letter to the Hebrews: "Now faith is the assurance of things hoped for, the conviction of things not seen."[43] The author of the letter represents his readership as having on one hand moved from the position of nonbelieving to believing in Christ. On the other hand, their faith is not just believing that Christ is who he said he is, but also a trusting in Christ's promises for the future.

Perhaps more to the point, Eliot's invocation of faith as a "leap" seems to echo and criticize F. H. Bradley's own use of "leap" language at the conclusion of *Ethical Studies* (1876).[44] There, Bradley attempts to interpret elements of his own system through a Christian theological lens (though this does not entail a serious commitment to Christian theology). Bradley initially delves into the question of religion as he meditates on the paradox of morality: morality demands pure action and does not discover it in this world. Therefore, morality must posit a religious end state in which such perfection is achieved.[45] Over the course of the concluding remarks, he builds an understanding of religious faith that moves from a consideration of the belief in the object of faith, an object representing the whole of reality, to a mode of moral action. Thus Bradley first states, "Faith is both the belief in the reality of an object, and the will that that object be real; and where either of these elements fails, there is not faith."[46] Bradley claims that faith pertains not to objects in the world that one experiences in life, but to an object that lies beyond immediate

74   DESIRE AND THE ASCETIC IDEAL

knowing. Further, faith includes will, the desire for that super-sensuous object to be real. In fact, this object becomes symbolic for the unity of all things in the Absolute.

But for Bradley, this implies at first a sense of distinction or separation from the religious object. The self desires what it does not yet attain. It is this sense of distance that faith seeks to eradicate:

> I must perceive the chasm between myself, as this or that unreal part of the unreal finite world, and at the same time must perceive the ideal-real object, which is all reality, and my true reality. . . . Faith then is the recognition of my true self in the religious object, and the identification of myself with that both by judgment and will; the determination to negate the self opposed to the object by making the whole self one with what it really is. It is, in a word, of the heart. It is the belief that only the ideal is real, and the will to realize therefore nothing but the ideal, the theoretical and practical assertion that only as ideal is the self real.[47]

Bradley describes the religious life then as a raising of both mind and heart to the religious object. In the context of this discussion, one would say this is the approach to God.[48] But Bradley's God is, of course, his metaphysical Absolute. We are divided from the Absolute through our conscious existence, embroiled within our subject/object relations. In faith, however, we desire to be one with the Absolute through that religious object, and we understand that we are *in fact* united with it. Faith therefore sees beyond the subject/object dualism to perceive the united nature of all things in the Absolute. This depiction of religious life leads to a view of moral action in the world as a uniting of the will with the one divine reality. If one wills along with the will of the whole, then one wills morally. Religion provides the ideal toward which one moves, in this case the full merging of one's will with the will of the whole.[49]

This brings us then to Bradley's use of "leap" language in reference to faith. Bradley claims that faith should in no way be seen as a leap, a qualitative change from one view of things to another. This is because faith should be considered in terms of the constant willing of the ideal, the uniting of one's will with the will of the whole:

> In faith we do not rise by the intellect to an idea, and leave our will somewhere else behind us. Where there is no will to realize

the object, there is no faith; and where there are no works, there is no will. If works cease, will has ceased; if will has ceased, faith has ceased. Faith is not the desperate leap of the moment; in true religion there is no one washing which makes clean. In Pauline language, that "I have died," have in idea and by will anticipated the end, proves itself a reality only by the fact that "I die daily," do perpetually in my particular acts will the realization of the end which is anticipated.[50]

Faith for Bradley is a unity of purpose born out of an identity of one's self with the ideal whole. It becomes intentional and voluntaristic; faith is a matter both of intending the object, and as a matter of willing the object, and willing it consistently, over time. In this way, it's not a "leap" per se. We have to "will the realization of the end which is anticipated." Faith cannot be seen simply as the sudden acceptance of an object of faith. Real faith, according to Bradley, includes the constant willing of that object, and the constant moral striving toward a divine end. It means uniting our will, however imperfectly, with the will of the whole, regardless of how successful we are. Therefore, ultimately, faith provides us with a divine end and also with the consistent willing to attain that end.

Though Bradley is at pains to claim that religion and morality are distinct, yet related, it is difficult to see how the religious life for Bradley is anything but morality enacted in the world, in light of the unity of all in the Absolute. When one has understood the oneness of self with the whole, one's will still must act in the world itself. And those actions must be moral. Bradley asserts that the "practical content which religion carries out comes from the state, society, art, and science. But the whole of this sphere is the world of morality, and all our duties there are moral duties."[51] This reduction of a great deal of the religious life to morality allows Bradley to unify his own ethics and metaphysics with a Christian theological language, but it also leaves behind much of Christian ritual or devotional practice:

The true doctrine is, that devotional exercises, and sacraments, and church-goings, not only should not and ought not to go by themselves, but that by themselves they simply are not religious at all. They are isolating a sphere of religion which, so isolated, loses the character of religion, and is often even positively sinful, a hollow mockery of the divine, which takes the enjoyment without giving the activity, and degenerates into what may be well enough aesthetic or contemplative, but, for all that, is both irreligious and immoral.[52]

Religious practices as such must be the handmaidens to morality; they can further estrange the individual and draw the believer away from their duty. In fact, it is especially the "aesthetic" and the "contemplative" that act as villains here. Bradley's model emphasizes the persistence of an intellectual belief and will over the life of the self but does not admit the shaping influence of practice and aesthetics in forming that will. This is, I suppose, because the religious subject doesn't really need to be shaped in this way on his account. The soteriological goal is to desire oneness, to realize oneness. In fact, Bradley himself seems to see faith as a moment that issues in moral action, imperfect though it be. The religious life is a persistence in this moral action, more or less perfectly united with the will of the whole.

Conclusion

In contrast to Bradley's denial of the "leap," I suggest that Eliot uses this concept at the end of *Knowledge and Experience* to gesture toward a more ascetic way of thinking about the change and potential development of the self. This gesture relies on a practical shaping of the self toward a telos, though a telos that is more like a formal limit to human experience. It is just such a cultivation that Bradley overlooks or dismisses. Indeed, Eliot uses all of his religious language to highlight the embodied, practical dimension to all experience. Eliot ends his entire text by claiming, "If I have insisted on the practical (pragmatic?) in the constitution and meaning of objects, it is because the practical is a practical metaphysic. And this emphasis upon practice—upon the relativity and the instrumentality of knowledge—impels us towards the Absolute."[53] Eliot's description of knowledge, though not Eliot's philosophical practice, points in the direction of the "protreptic" nature of early Indian discourse described by Jonardon Ganeri, a view of discourse "directed towards a 'turn' or transformation or reorientation in the mind of the listener."[54] Eliot's position here resonates with the Buddhist theories of *upaya*; knowledge is valuable because it moves you closer to the end stage of the path. Knowledge is relative and instrumental; once one inhabits one stage, one leaves it behind in favor of another. As one progresses along the way, one's practices and one's objects change, until one approaches the impossible conclusion of the path. At the same time, Eliot posits a "faith" that is necessary in giving oneself over to a new set of objects and a new life, a conversion of sorts. It is a faith rooted in modifications of feeling, not in a voluntaristic willing.

Given these invocations, however, Eliot's ultimate descriptions of this process ring a bit hollow, and perhaps intentionally so. Eliot's true "protreptic" discourse emerges in poetry, the genre that combines thought and feeling. It is not a philosophical "emphasis" on anything that impels us toward the Absolute. Practice, not philosophy, does this. Further, if knowledge is instrumental and always implicitly aimed at the limit, the reader might, within the bounds of Eliot's text, ask whether the movement from one perspective to another might merely be a fluctuation between perspectives, moving neither toward nor away from any particular end. What is it that ensures that our practical efforts are part of a "pilgrimage" and not a senseless series of object-moments? Given the unmistakable fact of error, what is it that provides the confidence that practices will not ultimately be fruitless? It is, merely, feeling and faith.

Eliot concludes with the presupposition that the natural desire for knowledge simply requires a formal limit to impel it. Nevertheless, the end of Eliot's argument opens out his reflection toward gradual religious paths, not as systems of discipline per se, but as paths that incorporate traditions of practice in the movement toward an impossible telos, at the limit of human experience. The religious paths that Eliot invokes not only describe an ascent to truth but also cultivate a hope and desire for that truth in and through practice. They provide assurance or "faith" that the next stage will be an effective stage along the way. Nothing in the dissertation prior to the final chapter explains how one is to move from one world to another "with faith," or how one is to be confident in the moving from one level of truth to another.

In other words, the dissertation gestures in the direction of religious paths that provide a sense of purpose in moving toward the Absolute with the confidence that each "leap" will be a step toward the limits of human experience, another step along the pilgrimage. But Eliot's philosophy itself doesn't provide any basis for this. It reduces human knowing to practice and aesthetics, but it does not itself provide any basis for such confidence. Most of Eliot's philosophy then is critical, dismantling the dualities of epistemology and metaphysics, but only gesturing towards a model of knowing based in practice.

78   DESIRE AND THE ASCETIC IDEAL

I believe that Eliot is gesturing toward the possibility that religion could provide a precondition for action in the world. Jewel Spears Brooker has made precisely this point in describing Eliot's early thoughts on religion: "Eliot's early references to religion, found principally in book reviews, indicate that he thought of religion not in terms of a god, or even a primary allegiance, but in terms of a scheme, a system of ideas. The object of such a scheme or system is, first, to enable one to make sense out of experience, and second, to enable one to act."[55] Brooker goes on to note specifically that Eliot's early interest in Buddhism was ultimately an interest in the "scheme" that it offered for living.[56] The scheme that these traditions provide is an explanation for the world, a plan for inhabiting that world, and a telos toward which to direct one's desire. They offer a network of objects through which the individual can approach the world and attempt to move to higher levels of understanding. Eliot himself described such a scheme in his letter to Herbert Read in December of 1925, in which he observes, "Meanwhile—to make possible the required patience, attentiveness and anonymity—one needs of course some tentative scheme which shall simply go far enough to make action possible, and give to action a kind of moral and liturgical dignity."[57] Such a scheme provides a ritual dimension to ordinary human life, clothing human action with ultimate practical significance.

It is possible that Eliot's comparison is meant to be a syncretistic move, as if a combination of religious traditions could perhaps provide such a scheme. In that sense, Eliot would be seen as combining points of view in an attempt at representing a new view of the world that transcends them. This is arguably part of the experiment of *The Waste Land,* but with the crucial exception that the latter is a poem to be performed by poet and reader and not a philosophy to be thought. If this is true, though, Eliot would not rest in such an explicitly syncretistic vision, though even his mature work, I argue, is inherently hybrid. Eventually, he would adopt the strategy of explicitly burrowing more deeply into one tradition of practice, prior to attempting to assess another. The problem is that the religious ideas used in *Knowledge and Experience* in an abstract way cannot provide what he wants them to provide, which is ultimately a reason to act and a confidence in the process of practice. In the dissertation, Eliot's attempt to gesture toward religion is really a gesture toward a practical process that incorporates both thought and aesthetics, something the writing of philosophy itself cannot do.

Examining Eliot's earlier religious negotiations becomes increasingly important in evaluating his later conversion as more of the poet's prose and correspondence is made public. Indeed, these earlier engagements could provide a critical lens for evaluating some of this later work, bringing light to the dialogical nature of Eliot's religious identity. For example, it is difficult not to see the religious language in *Knowledge and Experience* as a predecessor to Eliot's thoughts on mysticism in the Clark Lectures of 1926, where he valorizes Dante's mysticism as one that is based on "the development and subsumption of emotion and feeling through intellect into the vision of God."[58] The pursuit of God represented in this latter text begins, as does the pursuit of the Absolute in *Knowledge and Experience,* with an engagement with and attentiveness to feeling, leading to higher systems of thought and speculation, and potentially higher insights. Eliot's "classical" mysticism represents religion as a tradition of forms to be performed, and not a philosophy to be thought.

3

INDIA AMONG THE FRAGMENTS

Pessimism and Desire in *The Waste Land*

Interpreting *The Waste Land* is always a dangerous endeavor. I have never seen a work of literature provoke such strong criticism bordering on street brawl. Present a conference paper on *The Waste Land,* and one will see a crowd of otherwise genial literary critics suddenly draw hidden daggers, their smiles hiding the battle to come in the later "conversation." Such strong reaction is not, mind you, simply among modernists. No. Medievalists, Renaissance historians, romanticists, it makes no difference. Mention the poem, and views harden; there is always a read. I therefore undertake the next three chapters with considerable fear and trembling. Because of the complex history of interpretation of this poem, I think it is important to articulate an overall approach to the poem informed by previous scholarly work. Others will strongly disagree with my approach, but at least they will understand why I approach the text as I do. I will also criticize others who have come before me in order to clarify my approach. I hope to do this not with a drawn dagger, but with respect, gratitude, and a chastened view of how difficult it is to say anything simply or without controversy about this poem.

Many critics reading *The Waste Land* after the emergence of critical theory in the 1960s insisted that it was simply a collection of fragments, a collage of sorts that represented perhaps the mental breakdown Eliot experienced as he was writing the poem, or, more theoretically, perhaps the resistance of writing to epistemic closure. As Nancy Gish notes, this latter option was especially enabled by the publication of the facsimile edition of the original manuscript of the poem.[1] An extreme version of such an interpretive outlook can be seen in the work of critics such as Ronald Bush and Harriet Davidson. These critics see no narrative, no progression, and no unity of consciousness in the poem. So, for example, Bush argues that what unites the poem is a "dominant tone,"[2] while Davidson argues that the poem conveys only absence, especially the absence of a "persona."[3] Because of this, analysis is "wisely" reduced to "technique" and not "theme."[4] These critics have given due weight to the fragmentary nature of the text, the absences and the gaps, and to that extent provided the necessary corrective to the approach of the New Critics.

One shortcoming of work such as this is the refusal to consider that Eliot himself theorized about fragments and the fragmentary nature of poetic composition. Perhaps such theorizing will not aid in an understanding of the poem, but it would seem to be at least worthy of consideration in a poem of fragments. More seriously, their protestations to the contrary, neither of these critics can actually abide by their claims that no unity exists between the fragments. In fact, as their analyses proceed, they cannot help drawing connections and positing some other sort of unity to the poem than simply that of "tone" or "technique." Davidson is instructive in this, for she has written a whole book about *The Waste Land* with very little close reading. This is, of course, perfectly consistent with her presupposition that such reading would be beside the point, and she relentlessly asserts the lack of a center in the poem. That is, until she finds one in and through a Lacanian analysis. The poem apparently has a psychic center: "This enactment of the trauma of the child is the psychic center of the poem, imaging the cosmic bonding between death and desire."[5] Suddenly, with the help of Lacan, we can indeed explain the movements of the poem. Its oscillation between love and loss enacts the anxiety over the primal separation of the child from his mother. The poem may lack a consciousness, but it inexplicably now contains a subconsciousness. The same could be said for Ronald Bush's interpretation, which criticizes the unity of consciousness and yet claims subconscious psychological processes at work in the poem.[6] In other words, it is very difficult to read and write about this poem without drawing the kinds of connections that these critics do. One can do this either self-consciously (which I believe is what the poem invites) or without conscious reflection. The poem forces and eludes interpretation, putting that interpretation on display for all to see.

In response to the unsatisfactory conclusions of this critical trend, the alternative approaches to the poem have attempted to find points of

82   DESIRE AND THE ASCETIC IDEAL

continuity within it, even while acknowledging its fragmentary nature.[7] They do not see a consistent questing narrative as some of the earlier critics did, nor are they liable to identify a protagonist of the poem with a single character of the poem (though even here there are variations). Nevertheless, through their chastened view, they attempt to draw modest connections across the poem through close reading. My research on Indian sources in the poem places me in a tradition of reading that places the poem within a broadly mystical context, even while I understand the danger of using this label to characterize Indian sources. My own reading lies closest to critics such as Moody,[8] Childs,[9] Kearns, Gish,[10] Bedient[11] and, to some extent, Brooker and Bentley.[12] Many of these critics see the poem through the lens of mysticism or asceticism, as the pursuit of a metaphysical absolute beyond language, or love, or a deeper communion, or a mythic consciousness, in and through the fragments.

Calvin Bedient's work is perhaps the most provocative and controversial of these attempts at interpretation, since he strongly argues for a single protagonist in the poem. This thesis is related to one originally put forth by F. R. Leavis, who thought the poem presented "an effort to focus an inclusive human consciousness."[13] Cleo McNelly Kearns modified this approach in light of research into Eliot's interest in mysticism and Indian religions, claiming that the poem presents a mind in the early stages of meditation struggling for contemplative focus.[14] Bedient takes Leavis's argument and combines it with Bakhtin's theories of heteroglossia and the carnivalesque. His argument is that the poem represents a consciousness that "performs" various voices in the hopes of approaching the Absolute:

> In the protagonist, both a psychoanalytic and a historical straying . . . come to crisis over against, and finally begin to find redemption in, an experience and cultivation of a metaphysical reality: a One transpychic, transhistorical, and thus literally beyond words, though it may be the ultimate happiness of words to die into it. . . . The mercurial theatricality of the protagonist performs the illusion of 'being someone,' indeed many, in a void in which identity is a fiction. But what might at least approach purity is the right performance, a properly chastened one. In any case, the eternal silence cannot be conceived except in relation to temporal language, which, though always based in abjection, can counter it through original disciplines of form.[15]

Such a performance, for Bedient, amounts to "*doing* a voice of conversion, and then a voice of (allegorical) highest pilgrimage."[16] With this approach, I am in substantial agreement, for the idea of *upaya* is, in a sense, a process of higher and higher performances. Conversion must be performed, enacted, and desired. In fact, Bedient latches onto the ascetic aspect of the poem, calling *The Waste Land* "ascetic art" that "both courts and forestalls, or displaces, 'the silence.' . . . In order to perceive silence, we must retain an acute sense of the speech (or music) that marks it off. Ascetic art thus not only displaces the silence, but empowers it."[17]

Bedient's premise implies a single consciousness that performs various fragments in the hopes of performing the right combination to enact transcendence. Without the soteriological valence, Nancy Gish agrees with the assertion that the poem represents the motion of a single consciousness, arguing that the continuity of imagery, allusions, and thematic tropes from one section to another clearly signals a single continuum.[18] Bedient's reasons for positing a single consciousness are twofold: first, the weight he gives to the original title of the poem as a whole and, second, his attempt to make sense of the quasi-allegorical nature of the final section of the poem. As he reminds us, the original title of the poem was "He Do the Police in Different Voices."[19] The title refers to Charles Dickens's novel *Our Mutual Friend,* in which one of the characters, Sloppy, reads through the newspaper out loud, performing the stories in different voices.[20] Further, Bedient feels that the pilgrim character of the final section of the poem can only make sense if we see the poem as the mental wandering of a single consciousness:

> The hypothesis of an all-centering, autobiographical protagonist-narrator is not only consistent with the working title; it explains the confident surfacing, in the latter part of the poem, of an unmistakable religious pilgrim. Unless this pilgrim can be shown to develop—out of a waste land that is, or was, himself, the poem splits apart into two unequal sections, a long one constituted by what Lyndall Gordon calls 'the Voices of Society' and a shorter one on a lone pilgrim to elsewhere.[21]

Bedient thinks that he can, in certain circumstances, isolate the protagonist's voice among the other voices in the poem.[22] He asserts that only if we can identify an "autobiographical" voice in the poem can we make sense of the allegorical pilgrim at the end of the poem feeling the wreckage of modern culture.[23] Bedient does, however, insist that such a figure exceeds all of the allusions, although appearing in some.[24] There is, I think, no warrant for identifying any one voice as the definitive voice of the protagonist, and an Indian understanding of the shifting contents of consciousness can help us in modifying this. Bedient is correct, however, that the "protagonist" exceeds every particular allusion, even while he remains the necessary presupposition behind all of them. I argue that the poem presents us with a continuum of consciousness in which agency is ambiguous, in which fragments of memory, charged with desire, begin to coalesce around certain themes and images as they approach a few key moments of epiphanic imaginings. Fragments of Indian texts, both Buddhist and Hindu, play key roles in these latter decisive moments.

My engagement with *The Waste Land* itself is fragmentary, lifting out only one single action of the many actions embodied in the poem. It assumes, with Bedient and Kearns, that *The Waste Land* at least to some degree presents itself as a potentially ascetic text, as a series of performances with transcendence as the hoped-for end. With Joshua Richards, moreover, I assume that asceticism for Eliot represents an alternative to and liberation from solipsism.[25] I propose to show that the references to Indian thought in the poem both represent a Schopenhauerian pessimistic solipsism and a liberating alternative to it through poetic, ascetic performance. The poem leaves open the question of whether poet, reader, or poem itself actually reaches such a liberation. It repeatedly imagines possibilities for unifying the fragments, possibilities that either threaten to recede in the midst of the modern flux or hang in the air merely as hallucinations. Eliot's poem asks the question of whether the hybrid fragments can be mobilized ascetically to attain selflessness and self-surrender, or whether they merely cease in death.

To say that Eliot's engagement with and rejection of nineteenth-century pessimism is part of *The Waste Land* is not to say that the poem is only "about" this. It is, rather, to suggest that this is one action occurring in the poem, one action among many, many others. My interpretation is based on my reading of the Indian sources to which Eliot had access. Someone performing a biographical reading or a Marxist reading of Eliot would read and order the fragments differently. Perhaps such readings would suggest different structuring elements in the poem. My reading, I hope, illuminates one aspect of Eliot's poetry, even while it ignores details crucial to other readings of the poem. All I wish to show is that there is a criticism of pessimism presented in the poem, and that the Indian materials are marshaled as part—but only part—of that critique. In this way my reading contributes not only to debates about Eliot's interpretation of Indian sources but also to the history of Euro-American Orientalism.

The Waste Land invokes Schopenhauer's pessimism as one, but only one, strand of thought contributing to the malaise of modernity. Thus, Schopenhauer's ideas concerning desire, sexuality, and boredom find their way into the poem, and the term "nothing" emerges at key moments, with both positive and negative valences. In this respect, my reading of the poem reinforces an observation made by Cleanth Brooks in his seminal essay on *The Waste Land*: "The contrast is between two kinds of life and two kinds of death. Life devoid of meaning is death; sacrifice, even the sacrificial death, may be life giving, an awakening to life. The poem occupies itself to a great extent with this paradox, and with a number of variations upon it."[26] Just as it does with death, the poem presents a dual vision of nothingness, both positive and negative. On one hand, the perception of nothingness emerges from the profound disappointment and suffering entailed in the cycle of memory and desire. On the other hand, the poem presents a vision of nothingness that emerges from the loss of the self resulting from an encounter with something from outside the self. This latter nothingness enables the pragmatics of language, drawing the self outside of its solipsism. The former turns the self inward, away from meaningful interaction with the world. Thus, *The Waste Land* is significant for our appraisal of nineteenth- and twentieth-century Orientalism because it performs, through its comparisons with Indian texts, a reaction against and transformation of Schopenhauerian nihilism.

In what comes next, I aim to show, along with Kearns, the importance of Indian sources on the poem's initial, pessimistic characterization of desire, a characterization these sources problematize in later moments in the poem. I then leave the Indian sources temporarily to examine how the poem's initial, pessimistic lens leads to ethical consequences in part II of the poem. Still, one could see the figure alluding to Cleopatra there as representing an attempt to signify and control a sexual, divine, and cultural "other," and in this brings us back to the question of Orientalism. I return, with exhaustive detail, to a direct engagement with Indian texts in chapter 4. Later, it is the Indic "Orient" that, rather than being reduced to silence, speaks with the poem's most direct ethical and existential injunctions.

The Cycle of Memory and Desire

Like many of the Indian philosophical texts by which Eliot was influenced, *The Waste Land* uses the metaphor of water and growth in part to represent the problematic of desire. This problematic is introduced in the very opening lines of the poem, and sets one of the key symbolic parameters for the poem:

> April is the cruelest month, breeding
> Lilacs out of the dead land, mixing
> Memory and desire, stirring
> Dull roots with spring rain.
> Winter kept us warm, covering
> Earth in forgetful snow, feeding
> A little life with dried tubers.
> Summer surprised us, coming over the Starnbergersee
> With a shower of rain . . .[27]

Both Rainey and Southam point to the opening of Chaucer's *Canterbury Tales* as an obvious allusion.[28] There, April, with its "shoures soote,"[29] awakens all life and inspires human beings to begin their pilgrimages to Canterbury, to the shrine of St. Thomas Becket. Such a pilgrimage is teleological: the pilgrim sets off on the path and comes to the holy space of the martyr at the end of the journey. Here, however, April, the moment of regeneration and rejuvenation in nature, is "cruel"; it is so because it awakens, not a teleology, but a cycle of memory and desire. The puzzlement created in the first line by labeling April as the "cruelest month" is heightened by the negative term "breeding," a more bestial, disillusioned term for the growth of flowers in spring. Eliot's verse churns on its own, with the trochaic endings of the first three lines ("breeding," "mixing," and "stirring") forcing the reader to the next line in an incessant, almost mechanical, cyclical fashion. These gerunds signal continuous action, undertaken not by any human being, but by nature itself, by the month of April (and by the winter). Human beings lose agency to the spring rain that stirs memory and desire. Whereas Chaucer's pilgrims travel to honor the martyr Becket, Eliot's poetic speaker walks toward his or her own end, haunted constantly by thoughts of death. Throughout the poem, the speaker asks whether the death of the self (both physical and contemplative) is to be seen as only regrettable and wasteful, or whether it carries with it the possibility of redemption. To this end, the fragment concerning the church of Magnus Martyr (l. 264) has special importance.[30]

It is important to realize exactly how the opening image works. The first two lines set up a parallel between two sets of terms, "Memory/desire" and "Dull roots/spring rain." The rain of desire nourishes the underground root of memory, which in turn gives rise to full-fledged vegetation, which in turn gives off further seeds to grow roots and be "watered." Together, the plant that rises from the ground and the rain that feeds it represent a human consciousness trapped solipsistically in its thoughts about death. But April is also cruel in that it offers the promise of a more profound rejuvenation, only to set the self off on its course of memory and desire that repeats the thoughts and attachments of the past. The spring's promise is cruelly deceptive, and the exhaustion the speaker expresses results from the frustration of all desires. The speaker would rather remain in the "forgetful snow" of winter, in the hopes that a burial of memory will lead to a ceasing of desire. And yet, the summer rains "coming over the Starnbergersee" launch the poem on a whirlwind chain of memories that ultimately comprise the entire poem.

Schopenhauer also uses similar imagery to describe the dialectic of desire and boredom. At the end of the second book of *The World as Will*, he describes the endless becoming of all matter—including human beings—as endless desiring with no telos and no final fulfillment:

> In fact, absence of all aim, of all limits, belongs to the essential nature of the will in itself, which is an endless striving . . . the striving of matter can always be impeded only, never fulfilled or satisfied. But this is precisely the case with the striving of all the will's phenomena. Every attained end is at the same time the beginning of a new course, and so on ad infinitum. The plant raises its phenomenon from the seed through stem and leaf to blossom and fruit, which is in turn only the beginning of a new seed, of a new individual, which once more runs through the old course, and so through endless time . . . the same thing is also seen in human endeavours and desires that buoy us up with the vain hope that their fulfillment is always the final goal of willing. But as soon as they are attained, they no longer look the same, and so are soon forgotten, become antiquated, and are really, although not admittedly, always laid aside as

88   DESIRE AND THE ASCETIC IDEAL

vanished illusions. It is fortunate enough when something to desire and to strive for still remains, so that the game may be kept up of the constant transition from desire to satisfaction, and from that to a fresh desire, the rapid course of which is called happiness, the slow course sorrow, and so that this game may not come to a standstill, showing itself as a fearful, life-destroying boredom, a lifeless longing without definite object, a deadening languor.[31]

We examined Schopenhauer's philosophy at length earlier. Here, I merely note the imagery he utilizes, along with its metaphysical presuppositions. At base, human beings share a crucial, underlying metaphysical reality with animals and the plant kingdom. All of the will's phenomena act in a similar fashion to the plant. Just as the plant develops from the seed and leads to the production of new seeds, so too does human willing contain within itself the seeds for future willing. Human beings would like to think that the next pleasurable object attained will be the one that endures. Attainment, however, simply leads to boredom, and then to another round of willing. One may see the attained object as a "vanished illusion," but this does not inhibit the generation of "fresh desire." The suffering of the human being, a slave to desire, continues.

The plant and water imagery at the outset of *The Waste Land* also crucially evoke the Indian traditions that Schopenhauer would co-opt as philosophical allies. In particular, such imagery came to represent the karmic cycle of death and rebirth, from the very earliest moments of the karma theory. Therefore, the *Brhadaranyaka Upanishad* (hereafter "BU"), a text to which Eliot turns at a crucial moment in the poem (fully discussed in chapter 5), presents the round of rebirth in one of its earliest forms.[32] It emerges in a speculative dialogue between a Kshatriya, King Pravahana of Panchala, and his unexpected Brahmin student, Gautama (BU 6.2). Pravahana describes two different paths taken by the dead. The first path is traveled by those who "have this knowledge and those there who practice (cherish) faith and truth."[33] The knowledge they have is the realization that the entire world is in some sense a "sacrificial fire."[34] Those who know this and practice faith travel through the smoke of their funeral pyre to the "world of the gods," the sun, and "the region of lightening."[35] There, "a Man or spirit of the nature of intelligence (purusho manasah) gets into contact with and leads them into the worlds of Brahman. There in the worlds of Brahman they reside in the parts of the highest distances. For such men there is no return to the world."[36] This myth uses similar terms in describing the moment of nonreturn as it elsewhere does to describe the height of contemplative absorption. Patrick Olivelle, in his notes on this passage, suggests that these people have practiced an inner cultivation that has allowed them to escape the world to be united with Brahman.[37] The terms here are inner terms: "knowledge," "faith," "truth." They contrast with those people whose activity is directed to the sphere of ritual activity:

> One the other hand, those, who gain the heavenly worlds through sacrifice, alms and penance, enter into the smoke (of the funeral fire), out of the smoke into the night ... out of the half-year into the world of the manes, out of the world of the manes into the moon. When they reach the moon, they become food: As food they are eaten by the gods, just as one consumes (drinks) the Soma with the words: 'O (Soma), swell forth (*āpyāyasva*) and disappear (*apakṣīyasva*).' After this has elapsed, they enter into the ether here, out of the ether into the wind, out of the wind into the rain, out of the rain, they come to the earth.
>
> After they have reached the earth, they become food and are again offered into the man considered to be the fire (*puruṣāgni*) and are afterwards reproduced in woman who is considered as the fire (*Yoṣāgni*) and they arise anew in the worlds. In this way they wander about round and round in a cycle.[38]

Those who direct their religious activities to the external actions of sacrifice, alms, and penance undertake a long journey of consumption in which they are ingested twice, first by the gods as a Soma-like liquid, then by human beings after they are rained down upon the earth. The human being rains down upon the earth, becomes a plant seed, and then grows out of the earth. A man eats the plant, and the human becomes another kind of seed, the semen, that then leads to a rebirth in a woman. The path of action leads to an implication in the cycle of existence; the individual is repeatedly consumed and reborn. Further, as a human being, the individual himself or herself becomes another such consumer, powering others also through the cycle. Though it is not fully clear in this passage, in the comparison made between the two paths, the first path (of "faith" and "truth") has a slightly more positive valence, though both are presented as legitimate.

90   DESIRE AND THE ASCETIC IDEAL

Here we have in broad strokes, however, a reflection of the *moksha* tradition in Indian thought, offering renunciation of ritual activity as a way of transcending the cycle of rebirth (later *samsara*). As Steven Collins has noted, this model of ritual, cyclical existence, often imagined through vegetation imagery of rain, seeds, and growth, came to be valued far more negatively in later Brahmanical and Buddhist thought and, in the growth of more systematic treatises, was internalized to reflect the implication of individual consciousness in suffering.[39] In the passages above from the BU, we find the authors of the Upanishad appropriating the flame imagery from the Vedic ritual to describe the cyclical processes of existence, just as the Buddha did in the Fire Sermon in a far more negative light. Whereas the Upanishadic myth envisages rain and seed as vehicles for the continuity of human identity through rebirths, something that perhaps is not so beneficial, later thought uses vegetation imagery to describe the budding of harmful constructions within consciousness, based on ignorance, attachment, and desire.[40] These constructions generate action and attachment, which in turn create memories and then seeds of further "vegetation." Thus memories and desires feed on themselves and continue human identity across rebirths.

As Kearns notes, a good example of this type of analysis comes in Patanjali's *Yoga Sutras*, a text Eliot knew quite well, having studied with one of its translators, James Woods. She persuasively associates Patanjali with the opening lines of the poem, though the basic imagery invokes the karma cycle in general.[41] The *Yoga Sutras*'s description of human consciousness resembles that of the Buddhists, though with a starkly different metaphysics: "ii.12 The latent-deposit of karma has its root in the hindrances and may be felt in a birth seen or in a birth unseen. ii.13 So long as the root exists, there will be fruition from it [that is] birth [and] length-of-life [and] kind of experience. ii.14 These [fruitions] have joy or extreme anguish as results in accordance with the quality of their causes whether merit or demerit."[42] In the case of Patanjali, the hindrances are "undifferentiated-consciousness (*avidya*) and the feeling-of-personality and passion and aversion and the will-to-live are the five hindrances."[43] As in much Buddhist argument, the prime cause of suffering here in *samsara* is ignorance (*avidya*) of reality, though in this case the ignorance is of the profound differentiation of *purusha*, the inner, transcendent consciousness, and *prakrti*, the realm of matter. All of the other hindrances flow from ignorance and prohibit the self from realizing this higher knowledge; all leave memory traces in consciousness that become "seeds" for new moments of desire and attachment. As Kearns notes, these traces, or *kleshas,* are vestiges of attachment, containing a "charge of desire or attachment" that could potentially lead to further such attachments.[44] Patanjali uses vegetation imagery to describe this process: these "latent deposits" that lead to rebirth are "roots" that will eventually come to "fruition." The latent impressions are elsewhere in the sutra called the "seeds [i.e., *bija*] of the defects."[45] The seeds of detrimental karma give rise to desires, actions, and attachments that in turn cause more detrimental seeds to be formed.[46] The self in essence waters its own seeds by desiring and creating more memories to "grow" in due season.

The solution for Patanjali and for the Buddhists is to cultivate the self with proper formations of consciousness, formations that will paradoxically lead to the end of continued consciousness. In other words, memory and desire can be mobilized to overcome memory and desire. The practitioner of yoga proceeds through a process of ethical practice, study, physical training, and meditation to form positive seeds.[47] Eventually, he or she will progress to "seedless concentration"[48] in which the consequences of all mental seeds disappear, and the "mind-stuff" is "borne down to discrimination, onward towards Isolation."[49] This meditative "concentration," in which even the residual impressions are destroyed, is called "Rain-cloud of [knowable] things," and once it is attained, "then follows the cessation of the hindrances and of karma" (xli).[50] The final "rain cloud" of Patanjali is a water that purifies the practitioner, clearing away defilements; it stands in opposition to the "rain" of desire that causes latent memories to grow into further desire. It is precisely this dual valence of water imagery that the poem utilizes ambivalently and ambiguously, especially in its final section.

Schopenhauer on Relationships

There is, however, no hint of any sort of redemption of desire at the outset of *The Waste Land.* Rather, there is merely the dread of repetition. Existence is mere mechanism. The poem explores the consequences of this view of life as it presents vignettes of human relationships. It benefits our discussion to turn away for the moment from the direct Indian references to discerning the depths of the poem's debt to Schopenhauer. Schopenhauer believed that the cycle of desire occurs hand in hand with bouts of boredom that themselves are moments of intense suffering. If the will possesses its object, or especially possesses it too easily, then boredom sets in, and the original object ceases to please. The pain of existence therefore fluctuates between the pain of willing, desiring, and attaining, and the moments of boredom that will inevitably lead to more futile willing.[51] It is interesting, however, that in Schopenhauer's essay, "On the Vanity of Existence," it is precisely the moment of boredom that proves to be the moment in which the emptiness and nothingness of the world reveals itself, to the horror of the one caught up in the will to life:

> That human existence must be a kind of error, is sufficiently clear from the simple observation that man is a concretion of needs and wants. Their satisfaction is hard to attain and yet affords him nothing but a painless state in which he is still abandoned to boredom. This, then, is a positive proof that, in itself, existence has no value; for boredom is just that feeling of its emptiness. Thus if life, in the craving for which our very essence and existence consists, had a positive value and in itself a real intrinsic worth, there could not possibly be any boredom. On the contrary, mere existence in itself would necessarily fill our hearts and satisfy us. Now we take no delight in our existence except in striving for something when the distance and obstacles make us think that the goal will be satisfactory, an illusion that vanishes when it is reached; or else in a purely intellectual occupation where we really step out of life in order to contemplate it from without, like spectators in boxes. Even sensual pleasure itself consists in a constant striving and ceases as soon as its goal is attained. Now whenever we are not striving for something or are not intellectually occupied, but are thrown back on existence itself, its worthlessness and vanity are brought home to us; and this is what is meant by boredom.[52]

Note first the depiction of human relationships this implies. Other human beings are objects of "sensual pleasure," and once attained, they are no longer pleasing. Boredom results. The inability to satisfy desire and the boredom that results when it is momentarily satisfied create the misery of human existence and, moreover, demonstrate to us the farcical nature of existence itself. The experience of boredom leads to a kind of horror, for it shows the "emptiness of existence." Boredom itself is the proof of the meaninglessness of existence; it is proof that our desires are never fully satisfied, even once they have achieved their object. Boredom is the reaction against existence itself, when "its worthlessness and vanity are brought home to us." The relationship between human beings cannot grow or be sustained; it merely consists of drive, attainment, and boredom.

The experience of the emptiness of life is also the experience of its nothingness. Schopenhauer later in the same essay asserts that the experience of boredom leads to a recognition that all things are phenomena and, as such, are really nothing:

> That we are *mere phenomena* as distinct from things-in-themselves, is illustrated and exemplified by the fact that the *conditio sine qua non* of our existence is the constant excretion and accretion of matter, as nourishment the need for which is always recurring. For in this respect, we resemble phenomena which are brought about through smoke, flame, or a jet of water and which fade away or stop as soon as the supply fails.
>
> It can also be said that the *will-to-live* manifests itself simply in phenomena that become absolutely *nothing.*[53]

Human existence can be reduced to the flux of matter, driven endlessly onward by blind will. We exist by "accretion" and "excretion," as mechanisms of will. We are always willing and always changing. Thus, human beings resemble other phenomena of nature in just this way, that they are empty, or nothing.

"Cleopatra" and the Reifications of Language

Section II first presents a scene in which a sensualized female other is reified as an object of potential sexual violation. The view of romance implied is strongly reminiscent of Schopenhauer's view of desire. Here, Schopenhauer's pessimism is implied in the reification of a sexual, religious, and cultural other who recedes from view in the poem. The ensuing dialogue then meditates on boredom and nothingness. I take the first scene first, leaving the dialogue for this chapter's conclusion. Section II demonstrates a view of language and culture that imprisons an "other," specifically a cultural and gendered other, a figure compared with Shakespeare's Cleopatra. It begins with this "Cleopatra" figure[54] hemmed into a boxlike room and ends with evocations of rape, violence, and

94   DESIRE AND THE ASCETIC IDEAL

violation. "A Game of Chess" begins with a reference not to *Women Beware Women* or *The Tempest*, but to Shakespeare's *Antony and Cleopatra*. Eliot himself points out the allusion in his endnotes: "cf. *Antony and Cleopatra*, II, ii, 190."[55] The lines in the poem are:

> The Chair she sat in, like a burnished throne,
> Glowed on the marble, where the glass
> Held up by standards wrought with fruited vines
> From which a golden Cupidon peeped out
> (Another hid his eyes behind his wing)
> Doubled the flames of sevenbranched candelabra
> Reflecting light upon the table as
> The glitter of her jewels rose to meet it,
> From satin cases poured in rich profusion;
> In vials of ivory and coloured glass
> Unstoppered, lurked her strange synthetic perfumes,
> Unguent, powdered, or liquid—troubled, confused
> And drowned the sense in odours; stirred by the air
> That freshened from the window, these ascended
> In fattening the prolonged candle-flames,
> Flung their smoke into the laquearia,
> Stirring the pattern on the coffered ceiling.[56]

The first line obviously echoes Enobarbus's description of Cleopatra in act 2 of Shakespeare's play: "The barge she sat in, like a burnished throne, / Burned on the water."[57] The iambic pentameter of the first line invites a comparison with the first lines of Enobarbus's speech. That speech presents Cleopatra as dynamic and supernatural. It describes her as "O'er-picturing that Venus where we see / The fancy outwork nature."[58] Cleopatra is a Venus who is more than Venus, and a picture that "o'er-pictures." She is an über-goddess and a superior work of art. Indeed, Cleopatra seems to outstrip both art and nature. Her beauty is more profound than the "fancy" with which an artist designs the perfect painting of Venus. She is, in a sense, a far more profound work of art, the most perfect. In Enobarbus's scene, Cleopatra uses her sexuality as a political weapon. The display of the barge clearly is meant to seduce Antony. It is a ploy that works. Antony orders Cleopatra to attend him; resisting, Cleopatra entreats him to come to her, which of course he does: "Our courteous Antony, / Whom ne'er the word of 'No' woman heard speak . . . goes to the feast, / And, for his ordinary, pays his heart / For what his eyes eat only."[59]

Eliot's poem also describes "Cleopatra" as a quasi-divine figure. The references here, however, are not to classical divinity but, in part, to the God of the Old Testament. When describing the "golden Cupidon," Eliot writes, "(Another hid his eyes behind his wing) / Doubled the flames of the sevenbranched candelabra." Both the "Cupidon" that hides his eyes behind his wing and the "sevenbranched candelabra" evoke images of the ark of the covenant with its winged cherubim and the Jewish temple, with its own sevenbranched candelabrum.[60]

Cleopatra appears first on a "barge" that "burnt" the water. Eliot however substitutes the term "Chair" for "barge." The term is a far more static image than is Shakespeare's. The barge moves along the currents of the water; the "Chair" remains still. The capitalization of the word increases this sense of motionlessness. This affect of stasis is heightened by comparison with the rough meter of the end of section I: "You! hypocrite lecteur!—mon semblable,—mon frère!"[61] Instead of the harsh stresses from this final line, the poem presents us with an elegant iambic rhythm, punctuated in the first line with an appoggiatura at the caesura ("sat in,") along with an elegant line of momentum, enabled by the middle anapest ("like a burnished throne") to the first word of the second line, "Glowed." Shakespeare's word is not "glowed," but "burned." In Shakespeare's play, Cleopatra's barge burns up the water; here, "Cleopatra's" chair merely reflects the light from elsewhere. It has no agency; it depends on another source of light for its illumination.

As the passage proceeds, other echoes of the Cleopatra scene emerge in various ways to heighten the irony: Cleopatra is fanned by boys who are "like smiling Cupids"[62] while "Cleopatra" sits by a glass table held up by a post with a "golden Cupidon"; the gold of the barge's hull becomes the gold of the artificial Cupidon; the "strange invisible perfume" that wafts from Cleopatra's barge becomes the "strange synthetic perfumes" of *The Waste Land;* the winds that are "love-sick" for Cleopatra's purple sails become the "air" that "stirs" the perfumes and "fattens" the flames of the candelabra.

When Cleopatra's perfumes hit the shores of the Nile, they inspire the people to rush out to see her. Enobarbus states, "From the barge / A strange invisible perfume hits the sense of the adjacent wharfs. The city cast / Her people out upon her."[63] Not only does Cleopatra possess

96 DESIRE AND THE ASCETIC IDEAL

an agency, but she quickens those around her to activity. Her perfumes inspire those in the city to rush out to see her. In *The Waste Land*, the perfumes confuse the self and lead it to a drugged oblivion. The man who approaches has his sense "troubled, confused / And drowned the sense in odours."[64] The senses of Cleopatra's people were quickened; here, the perfumes "drown" the sense in ennui. Cleopatra's perfumes were almost supernatural; they came out of nowhere to enchant the people on the shores. The perfumes in *The Waste Land* are "synthetic," made by human beings, created of mixtures of chemicals, precisely for the purpose of inducing intoxication. Eliot's "Cleopatra" wears perfumes designed for drugging the senses of those she encounters; instead of attentiveness, she invites confusion.

Indeed, these perfumes are so intoxicating they seem to make the pattern on the laquearia, the "paneled ceiling,"[65] come alive and swirl: "Stirring the pattern on the coffered ceiling." The poem's description of the room's ceiling here is highly suggestive. The term "laquearia," we are told by Eliot, comes from book 5 of the *Aeneid*, where the term refers to the ornate ceiling of Dido's dining hall. Rainey observes the tragedy of the moment; Dido falls in love with Aeneas at a dinner in this hall, thus setting this scene for his eventual betrayal.[66] The evocation of Dido also presents one more reference in *The Waste Land* to the conquering and violating power of ancient Rome, joining references to Cleopatra and the Punic Wars.

Cleopatra's room has a window that provides oxygen to feed the flames of the candelabra: "stirred by the air / That freshened from the window, these ascended / In fattening the prolonged candle-flames, / Flung their smoke into the laquearia." Even here, however, the window only serves to reinforce the static nature of the air. There is only so much air to feed the flames and to send the smoke of the flames straight into the air. The window does not disperse the perfumes or the smoke; it merely provides the air that keeps them aloft.

Further, the poem describes the ceiling as "coffered." This word is provocative, and Eliot invokes a large semantic range. First, the term refers to the influence of the perfumes on the perception of the ceiling; "to coffer" means "to curl up, twist, warp."[67] The perfume gives the ceiling a sense of motion that otherwise it does not have. The term also refers to the paneling of the room itself: "a sunk panel in a ceiling or soffit, of ornamental character, usually decorated in the centre with a flower or the like."[68] Thus our "Cleopatra" figure sits statically enthroned, amid perfumes that dull the senses, in a room with a paneled ceiling, one with a pattern that seems to move given the drugging potential of the perfumes. Beyond that, however, the resonances become even more interesting. A "coffer" can be a box for holding jewels and valuables: "a box, chest: *esp.* a strong box in which money or valuables are kept."[69] "Cleopatra" becomes one with her adornments, the "Chair," the ornate table, the candelabra, the jewels, the perfumes. She becomes reified into an object to be kept hidden in a box, rather than a figure to be attended to. In fact, this evokes another, older use of the term "coffer," to refer to a "coffin."[70] Brooker and Bentley make much the same point, as they note that the woman herself recedes from the view of the reader, while the objects and representations around her take the attention of the reader and point it away from her.[71] They write, "The woman in the poem is an absence manifested by her enclosing surfaces and by her voice."[72] In other words, the woman herself recedes from those things that enclose her, the materiality and representations that surround her. The woman here, reduced to materiality and to the body, occupies her coffered room as a body occupies a coffin, with that which marks her as human beyond that materiality hidden under coffered ceilings.

The imagery therefore resonates with the burial imagery from section I. There, the corpse represented the dangerous memory of human mortality and error, a memory the characters hoped to repress. Here, the "Cleopatra" figure represents in part an agency held in check, an otherness, sexual, theological, artistic, and cultural that human beings wish to bury, escaping a disruption to the ordinary round of memory, desire, and boredom. It is appropriate, therefore, that Eliot originally called this section "In The Cage," resonating with the image of the Sybil from the epigraph of the poem.[73] The character here also represents an otherness within the human being itself: another older use of the term associates "coffer" with the "pericardium."[74] In the final section of the poem the thunder's "DA" from the *Brhadaranyaka Upanishad* seems to suggest just such an otherness within. There, however, that otherness does not remain boxed; rather, it shakes the very blood of the poetic speaker.

Finally, reinforcing the religious imagery once again, the term "coffer" can refer to an "ark": "An ark. Applied to Noah's ark, the 'ark' of bulrushes in which Moses was laid, and the 'ark of God.'"[75] The "coffered" ceiling resonates with the previous references to the temple of Solomon

98   DESIRE AND THE ASCETIC IDEAL

and the ark of the covenant, while also adding a more explicitly religious reference to the barge of Cleopatra. Now the barge becomes an ark similar to Noah's ark. Indeed, the sea imagery here reinforces the boat imagery: "Huge sea-wood fed with copper / Burned green and orange, framed by coloured stone, / In which sad light a carved dolphin swam." The speaker now shows the coffered ceiling to be partly made of sea-wood, decorated with old, fading green-orange copper, and festooned with carved dolphins.

Ultimately what we see in these first ninety-six lines of section II is, in a sense, a meditation on idolatry, on the attempt to control the other through a kind of frozen signification. The sexual other, the divine other, the artistic other, the cultural other: all are controlled here and hidden amid endless ornament and almost hallucinogenic perfumes. Again, the contrast with Shakespeare's Cleopatra is instructive. Enobarbus confesses that, even given his attempts, Cleopatra "beggar'd all description."[76] It is as if the aesthetic assault Cleopatra unleashes on the world cannot be completely represented. Indeed, Cleopatra's divine presence is seemingly able to rip nature apart at the seams. Enobarbus writes that Antony was "Whistling to th' air; which, but for vacancy, / Had gone to gaze on Cleopatra too, / And made a gap in nature."[77] Cleopatra is beyond language and beyond nature, and when she appears she gathers those things to herself and yet eludes them.

No such eluding is suggested in the passage at hand. In fact, the passage goes on to describe a frozen scene of rape and mutation, one that reflects back on the static "Cleopatra" figure. Eliot writes:

> Above the antique mantel was displayed
> As though a window gave upon the sylvan scene
> The change of Philomel, by the barbarous king
> So rudely forced; yet there the nightingale
> Filled all the desert with inviolable voice
> And still she cried, and still the world pursues,
> 'Jug Jug' to dirty ears.
> And other withered stumps of time
> Were told upon the walls; staring forms
> Leaned out, leaning, hushing the room enclosed.[78]

The passage presents us with a supposedly naturalistic representation of the rape of Philomel, a naturalistic painting that represents "as though a window gave upon the sylvan scene." Eliot's note points us to Ovid's *Metamorphoses*: "V. Ovid, *Metamorphoses*, VI, Philomela."[79] The rape theme presented by this painting gets taken up later in the poem, especially in section III in Tiresias's vision and in the so-called "Song of the (three) Thames-daughters."[80] The story invoked by the painting, briefly, begins with Tereus setting out to bring Philomela to visit her sister Procne. Tereus falls madly in love with Philomela: "And Tereus looked at her, and in that moment / Took fire . . . He was a passionate man, and all the Thracians are all too quick at loving; a double fire / Burnt in him, his own passion and his nation's."[81] Consequently, upon arriving home, he brings her to a cottage in the woods and violates her. Further, he cuts out her tongue so she cannot tell her sister or her father that she's been violated. The sexually reified woman now literally becomes a woman without a voice. And yet Philomela finally does gain a voice, through art. She weaves her story into a tapestry: "her grief has taught her / Sharpness of wit, and cunning comes in trouble. / She had a loom to work with, and with purple / On a white background, wove her story in, / Her story in and out."[82] Her sister finally sees the work and interprets it, flying into a rage. Philomela and Procne then plan their horrifying revenge by killing Procne's son, Itys, and serving him to the king. As the king chases Procne and Philomela, the gods change them all to birds, and the "Jug Jug" becomes Philomela's nightingale song thereafter.

The poem ironically hints that naturalistic representation and poetic elegance may not be sufficient to portray humanity's potential for brutality. Here, the poem invokes a tale of incredible brutality and violation in a paradoxically elegant and calm way. Note the iambic rhythm in the first few lines, hardly interrupted at all, save by the anapests in "by the barbarous king." Further, anyone who has read Ovid's account of the rape of Philomela knows that the episode goes beyond mere "rudeness," as if Philomela's rape was somehow merely inconsiderate. This is a gory, vicious, visceral tale that seems to cry out for a more barbarous form. There is a sense here, though, that such a barbaric nature can still be sensed, even under the surface of the most elegant art.

Further, this painting reflects and develops the thematics of the depiction of Cleopatra. It sits right above her on the "antique mantel," and describes the physical manipulation and sexual reification of a woman by the "barbarous king" Tereus. Later we are told that other such paintings or perhaps even statues, as "staring forms / Leaned out, leaning, hushing the room enclosed." Notice the gentle trochaic rhythms to the line, beginning with the firm stress on "*staring*," followed by "*Leaned out* [a spondee] . . . *leaning* . . . *hushing*." It is as if the paintings on the wall are hemming the figure in on all sides, giving focus to her and yet making the imprisonment in the "coffered" box even more suffocating. On the other hand, the leaning forms seem to subsume the "Cleopatra" figure among them. Just as these artistic forms sit mute and staring, so too does she. They are all "withered stumps of time," seemingly unable to communicate to the present moment. They supposedly flowered at one point, and then receded, unable to speak to a contemporary audience. Donald Childs has noted the possible phallic imagery here as well, with the artistic works on the walls representing the "masculine sexual impulse so much a part of the stories told on the walls."[83]

The poem's meditation therefore engages the problem of the silencing of the sexual other and also the artistic other. Philomela has been denied a voice by the lust of Tereus; so too is the "Cleopatra" figure seemingly denied a voice here. The speaker tells us, "Under the firelight, under the brush, her hair / Spread out in fiery points / Glowed into words, then would be savagely still."[84] In this unusual image, the woman's hair catches on fire metaphorically and "glowed into words," and yet the poem does not give us any of those words. The reader gets a sense of the rage of the woman hemmed into a coffered room, but all that is left is the "savage stillness," now modifying the stasis noticed at the opening of the section. It might perhaps be argued that the dialogue in the middle of section II does present the words of "Cleopatra," but we presently see that though the woman in the dialogue speaks, she is not really heard or responded to in a meaningful way.

And yet, the poem does represent the possibility, just the possibility, that art can give voice to suffering. Philomela does, after all, use an artistic representation to express her violation to her sister. And further, Philomela continues to express that suffering in new form, finally with a voice, but a nonlinguistic voice, a voice of pure sound, "'Jug Jug' to dirty ears." It is an "inviolable" voice, always escaping the attempted violations of men like Tereus. Moody writes, "This is what has been missed: a natural music, expressing the reality of evil and suffering, the compelling need for a release from it, and a possible mode of transformation."[85] It is a voice that "the world pursues," presumably because the world is enamored of the sound, but also presumably to capture and imprison yet again. Indeed, such a pursuit presents a paradox of the engagement with works of art. On the one hand, human beings pursue the beauty of art because they are entranced and grasped by the beauty of sight or sound; on the other hand, the self grasps art, consuming it as soon as it begins to interpret.

In the same vein, the poem presents the paradox of representation. In both Cleopatra and Philomela, there is an attempted manipulation through reification. Representation is in itself a reification, a making static of that which has movement, and a reduction of that which is complex.[86] Here the poem presents this through the impossible task of representing metamorphosis. Change and metamorphosis are represented in a manner that freezes that change. In fact, one wonders how the "change" of Philomel could be represented at all. Perhaps Philomel is represented as half human–half bird, but the change itself cannot as such be represented.

With the awareness that the middle section of *The Waste Land* invokes the Buddha's Fire Sermon, it is difficult not to see the Buddhist theories of language echoed at this moment of the poem. I discuss this at length in the next chapter. For now, it is important to realize that, for the Buddhists, language itself instantiates desire, the desire to grasp, control, and possess. Language is an instrument of reification; it gathers sense data into objects of the understanding, suggesting essences where there are none. Thus the attempt to reify change in language is itself a source of suffering, if it is done without the transcendent perspective of the Buddha. If one has the good fortune to hear and understand the Buddha's teaching through his skillful means, if one has one's sufferings brought to reflection by the Buddha's discourse, then one can engage with the language of the path in the hopes that the Buddha's discourse can destroy language's reifications when it becomes necessary. Thus, language can present one with one's suffering and lead to its resolution, but only once its reifications have been laid bare.

On the other hand, unredeemed desire, desire that falls prey to "the fire of passion . . . hatred . . . infatuation" is self-perpetuating.[87] Not only is the "coffer" of "Cleopatra" lit with "flames of sevenbranched candelabra" that are "prolonged" by the perfumes surrounding her, but it also in and of itself burns. The "Huge sea-wood fed with copper / Burned green and orange." The copper of the coffer's wood sets it on fire. It burns with the green and orange of the partially oxidized copper. In Buddhist terms, the coffer box meant to control that which sits within is on fire

DESIRE AND THE ASCETIC IDEAL

with the attachment that the Buddha describes in the Fire Sermon. And as a result, that attachment and error reflect back on the passionate grip.[88] Just as words are instantiations of problematic desire, so too do the words that come from "Cleopatra" issue from a kind of hatred or resentment: "Under the firelight, under the brush, her hair / Spread out in fiery points / Glowed into words, then would be savagely still." The "brush" here is a comb but also conjures the idea of the "brush" of a fire. There is a sort of self-immolation here, but a self-immolation of hatred. The hair catches on fire, glows into words, and then burns out. As mentioned earlier, the speaker does not immediately provide the words; they are not heard, they simply drift off like burning embers. What is left behind is a savage stillness. In the Fire Sermon, fire can be seen as a liberating insight into the mutability of the human being, or it can be seen as an expression of human suffering and attachment. The extinguishing of the flames, of desires and attachments, can be a sign of *nibbana*. Here, however, there is no sense of liberation, only a sense that the hatred will continue. And indeed, lying in the background of this entire passage is the revenge taken upon King Tereus by his wife Procne and Philomela.

Finally, the myth of Philomela, seen in a different way, could be seen as a metaphor for the ascetic path itself. Philomela depicts her suffering and is eventually transformed through the agency of the gods. It is a myth of barbarity and revenge, but also a myth of metamorphosis and liberation, of achieving an "inviolable voice." There is a hint, just a hint, of the transcendence of desire's solipsism and repetition at this point in the poem. There are more substantial hints later in section III. Just as the self's tendency to reify and control is depicted most strongly in this portion of the poem, so too is the self's capacity to change form given as a potential release.

Nihilism and Dialogue

Section II begins with a scene that dramatizes the sexual reification implied in Schopenhauer's philosophy. It continues in a dialogue that depicts the boredom and recognition of nothingness that, according to Schopenhauer, emerges in those moments of comparative repose within the cycle of memory and desire. The dialogue portion of section II both is and is not connected to that which came before. The woman's opening statement ("'My nerves are bad tonight'") seems to follow upon the speaker's description of "Cleopatra's" hair glowing "into words." Still, it seems that the woman is a continuation of the previous scene and yet somehow distinct.[89] This fragment continues the notion of "voicelessness," though in a different mode. Here, the woman speaks to the man, but she is not heard. Much as "Cleopatra's" words flame out and yet are not heard, so too the woman in the dialogue speaks and is met with ennui, boredom. Indeed, all the figures in this section of the poem "are trapped in self and in loveless marriages."[90] The woman seeks a response, a conversation, a reassurance. All of the evidence suggests that she receives no response whatsoever. She speaks in quotation marks, while the man does not. Only her words flare out between them, while his remain within.[91]

The poem strongly suggests here that one of the sources of the pathology is the thought of death and nothingness. Here the Schopenhauerian pessimism shows itself to have ethical consequences. Note the number of times in this passage that the term "nothing" comes up. Earlier, in section I, the specter of "nothingness" emerged in a positive light, as a possibility of liberation. Here, the term emerges as a pessimistic mantra, as the speaker also seems to meditate on the word.

> 'What is that noise now? What is the wind doing?'
>> Nothing again nothing.
>>> 'Do
> You know nothing? Do you see nothing? Do you remember
> 'Nothing?'
>
>> I remember
> Those are pearls that were his eyes.
> 'Are you alive, or not? Is there nothing in your head?'[92]

The word "nothing" seems to jump back and forth between the two characters. The woman quite literally does not hear the man and yet responds as if she does. Both characters seem to be preoccupied with the specter of this nothingness. Speech occurs, but there is no communication.[93] The woman asks about noises outside and about natural processes. The man's answer to the range of phenomena outside of the room is "Nothing again nothing." The line has a temporal aspect to it; the phenomena of the world are a stream of "nothing" followed ("again") by nothing. Note also the isolation of the word in line 123, concluding the woman's question about memory. It comes at the conclusion of a string of epistemological questions, about knowing, seeing, and remembering.

What is remembered is death, a certain kind of "nothingness," though remembered through an allusion to *The Tempest*: "Those are pearls that were his eyes."[94] The reference to this particular moment in Shakespeare's play originates, in Eliot's poem, in Madame Sosostris's reading of the tarot, in which she describes the "drowned Phoenician Sailor, / (Those are pearls that were his eyes. Look!)"[95] Originally, the line provides part of Ariel's song to the shipwrecked Ferdinand, who mourns his father and yet finds solace in the music he hears coming over the waters. Here, however, the line provides no such solace. Rather, it emerges from memory as an overwhelming concern. The poem highlights the power of memory by isolating the man's first response, "I remember," as if the act of remembering suddenly has become the poem's sole focus. And the sole object of that memory at this moment is Ariel's line, "Those are pearls that were his eyes." The trochaic rhythm of the line, conditioned by the trochaic lines that preceded it ("Nothing? / I remember") provide an insistence to this memory; this memory pushes itself into consciousness, asserts itself into the midst of the relationship.

The shift to the music hall reference, then, with "O O O O that Shakespeherian rag" gives us the ultimate attempt to evade the thought of death, of nothingness.[96] Similarly, the man's response later shows the customs and rituals of everyday life as one long string of attempts at distraction: "The hot water at ten. / And if it rains, a closed car at four. / And we shall play a game of chess, / (The ivory men make company between us) / Pressing lidless eyes and waiting for a knock upon the door."[97] The reference to the game of chess comes, as Southam and Rainey note, from Thomas Middleton's *Women Beware Women*.[98] Grover Smith notes that the scene to which the poem alludes is one in which Bianca's mother-in-law is distracted by a game of chess while Bianca is violated upstairs.[99] In other words, the exigencies of the game, the attention given to its strategies, diverts attention away from the truly horrible acts taking place nearby, even as the game becomes a metaphor for those acts.[100] That episode echoes the diversions the man in the dialogue discusses, and also reflects back, as Smith realizes, on the Philomela scene from earlier.[101]

Smith also rightly notices the reference to chess playing in *The Tempest*, though he does not explore the dark shading of the passage. At the end of the play, Ferdinand plays chess with Miranda in a playful manner, and as Smith notes, the game "betokens amity and love."[102] On one level this is true; the two lovers certainly undertake the game in a spirit of levity and flirtatiousness. However, their conversation is disturbing. Miranda first accuses Ferdinand of cheating in the game, to which Ferdinand pleads his innocence. Miranda then posits the possibility that Ferdinand might cheat on her sexually for the purposes of imperial conquest: "Yes, for a score of kingdoms you should wrangle, / And I would call it fair play."[103] As Orgel observes in his annotation to the passage, the "wrangling" is clearly presented as the opposite of "fair play."[104] Ferdinand's "wrangling" becomes associated with "playing false," that is, sexual cheating, and fair play is its opposite. In other words, Ferdinand might conquer more land by conquering more women. And yet Miranda seems to be, jokingly, approving of such sexual politics.[105] The uneasy specter that is there conjured is of a man who collects lands and collects women, just as the "Cleopatra" figure earlier in the section is collected as a jewel in her "coffer." Ferdinand has gone through a process of purgation and trial prior to gaining the hand of Miranda; he supposedly has transcended this danger. I do not mean to suggest that the play means to cast doubt on Ferdinand in this regard. I merely suggest that the jesting does raise an uncomfortable thought that is passed over lightly in jest in Shakespeare's play. In the context of *The Waste Land*, the intertextual echo is ominous.

The crass and truly pessimistic vision *The Waste Land* leads us to in section II is that male desire possesses women as objects to satisfy sexual desire, and that, once that desire has been satisfied, the woman is stored away in a coffered box or coffin. As Brooker and Bentley note, the female characters in this section are "adjuncts to male power and . . . victims of it."[106] In the final pub scene we see that even Lil has lost favor with her husband because of the aging of her body; incredibly, he asks her to buy herself a new set of teeth. Lil's husband, Albert, a soldier demobilized, moves on to another conquest, just as Miranda playfully suggests that Ferdinand might do in their chess match. One could also say, however, that the religious and cultural other are also presented here as victims of power. The oriental "other" is reduced to silence, placed in a box as a museum piece rather than heard in an event of meaning. In chapter 5, I show that this situation is reversed in the poem's conclusion—the Indic other speaks in the most dramatic manner, demanding extended response.

The next section of the poem presents ascetic paths that follow an intuition of liberation that emerges from an analysis of suffering. These paths begin with the presupposition that one cannot reflect upon suffering without pursuing the potential solution to the suffering, imagining the improved state implied by the experience of suffering. Even the Buddhists, who agree with Schopenhauer on the transitory nature of the causal world, see the possibility that the world can still be mobilized for enlightenment, once the Buddha has preached the dharma through his skillful means. These paths presented by the poem are paths of cultivation that direct the individual not to ethical withdrawal but to an engagement with the world and an attitude of respect for the other.

4

LANGUAGE AND THE CULTIVATION OF DESIRE IN "THE FIRE SERMON"

To Carthage then I came
Burning burning burning burning
O Lord Thou pluckest me out
O Lord Thou pluckest
burning
　—T. S. ELIOT, *The Waste Land*

I propose to read the conclusion of section III of *The Waste Land* through the prism of the Buddha's Fire Sermon and the comparisons it makes possible in the poem. The Fire Sermon is first and foremost the exposition and elucidation of a metaphor, the metaphor of the world as being "on fire." It attempts to transform and move its readers by engaging them with this dominant metaphor. Cleo Kearns has rightly observed that "the point of the sermon lay not only in its metaphysical doctrine, but in its practical effect as a kind of active, communal meditation."[1] Any sermon seeks to move its hearers in a way that leads to their conversion; it does not seek simply to interest or titillate, but to find the most appropriate words to move others. Eliot calls the sermon, as a genre, "applied art, applied poetry."[2] The Buddha's sermon is an act of skillful means (*upaya*) that takes into consideration the proper depiction of human suffering and error, as well as the perception that can eradicate such error. The fire imagery in this sense is ingenious: it signifies both the flames of passion,

108   DESIRE AND THE ASCETIC IDEAL

infatuation, and so forth, but also the transience of the world in general that must be perceived in order for liberation to occur. The sermon in and of itself therefore embodies a contradiction; on the one hand it criticizes desire, attachment, and language, while on the other hand making an intellectual, imaginative, and affective appeal to the monks to which it is addressed. The sermon also reflects back on its own modus operandi: "'Perceiving this, O priests, the learned and noble disciple conceives an aversion for the eye."[3] If the Buddha can make the disciples see, make them perceive the errors of the world, and indeed realize them on a deep level, then they will imaginatively glimpse that which is beyond that suffering. They will begin to turn away from those errors, undertaking in a full sense the Buddhist path. This is the "protreptic" nature of the Buddhist text that Ganeri identifies in the tradition more broadly and that I discuss in the introduction.[4]

I suggest that a similar dynamic can be seen in elements of *The Waste Land*. Importantly, section III as a "Fire Sermon" moves from a romantic reiteration of the round of desire and the boredom that lies between cycles to a glimpse—just a hint—of a possibility of escape. The escape that the poem presents occurs through the juxtaposition of ascetic traditions at the end of section III. Suddenly, the possibility of a desire that is not merely solipsistic, that can receive a transcendence of that solipsism, is presented to the reader. The poem offers a glimpse of traditions of thought that engage affective experience and desire and transform them from within. The burning invoked at the end of section III is the burning of desire, a desire that can reflect the sins and errors of the world, or that can represent the very desire to transcend those things. The religious traditions that Eliot cites hold open the possibility that desire can be overcome through a transformed desire. And affective language, language that engages desire, by exploring suffering can hold open the hint of that which lies beyond it as well, strengthening the desire to transcend the self's fetters.

Such a view of literary language was not foreign to Eliot's critical writing and indeed forms part of an aesthetic that combined the pursuit of beatitude through an exploration of suffering and a questing among the shards and fragments of modern life. In his early essay on Dante, Eliot claims that the depiction of vice and sin is always the precedent to envisioning the positive state beyond it.[5] Similarly, in his essay on Baudelaire from 1930, Eliot provides a description of Baudelaire's aesthetics that could very easily be transferred to Eliot's own poetics in *The Waste Land*:

> He was one of those who have great strength, but strength merely to *suffer*. He could not escape suffering and could not transcend it, so he *attracted* pain to himself. But what he could do, with that immense passive strength and sensibilities which no pain could impair, was to study his suffering. And in this limitation he is wholly unlike Dante, not even like any character in Dante's Hell. But, on the other hand, such suffering as Baudelaire's implies the possibility of a positive state of beatitude. Indeed, in his way of suffering is already a kind of presence of the supernatural and of the superhuman ... His *ennui* may of course be explained, as everything can be explained in psychological or pathological terms; but it is also, from the opposite point of view, a true form of *acedia,* arising from the unsuccessful struggle towards the spiritual life.[6]

First note the dual vision of Baudelaire's ennui suggested in the passage. One could simply see it in terms of scientific causality, in terms of psychology. However, one could also see it as the necessary presupposition of spiritual renewal. There is a presence of the supernatural in suffering because only that which lies beyond the poet's experience, interrupting that experience, can show the poet that indeed he does suffer. Suffering can only be glimpsed as such by comparison with a better state. Only with the presence of beatitude does one realize one's infernal existence. It is certainly not by chance that Eliot compares Baudelaire's ennui with acedia, the monastic noontide demon. Both acedia and ennui inhibit the self from greater spiritual effort. Here, the effort lies in the suffering and striving to glimpse transcendence. And the poetic process of striving becomes likened to the ascetic spiritual striving.

The materials with which the poet must strive are the disparate materials of tradition, of that which is given. The poet is inescapably situated:

> He [i.e., Baudelaire] could, like any one else, only work with the materials which were there. It must not be forgotten that a poet in a romantic age cannot be a "classical" poet except in tendency. If he is sincere, he must express with individual differences the general state of mind—not as a *duty,* but simply because he cannot help participating in it. ... Furthermore, besides the stock of images which

> he used that seems already second-hand, he gave new possibilities
> to poetry in a new stock of imagery of contemporary life. . . . This
> introduces something new, and something universal in modern
> life. . . . It is not merely in the use of imagery of common life, not
> merely in the use of imagery of the sordid life of a great metropolis,
> but in the elevation of such imagery to the *first intensity*—presenting
> it as it is, and yet making it represent something much more than
> itself—that Baudelaire has created a mode of release and expression
> for other men.[7]

The classical poet is the ascetic poet, the poet whose aim is release, both for himself and for others. As in the Buddha's use of skillful means, however, such a release can only come when the teacher inhabits the images of contemporary life. The Buddha's first priority is to depict the "state of mind" of his audience, full of the desire and error to which it is given. The Buddha is both beyond that state of mind (because enlightened) and soteriologically occupying it. Likewise, only by exploring suffering can the poet potentially transform these images into something new, something that, like the Buddha's Fire Sermon, is a "mode of release and expression for other men."

The Buddhist depiction of suffering implies an end to that suffering that can be depicted in provisional ways. The realization that the entire world is characterized by the fires of desire and attachment finds its counterbalance in the notion that the believer can "conceive an aversion" to that destructive attachment. In other words, the Buddhists present, in answer to the problem of suffering, a technology of the self that is not arbitrary; it represents a path in which memory and desire are engaged, transformed, and transcended en route to the highest level of the path, *nirvana.* As Kearns observes, the Fire Sermon describes a soteriological path that includes "the willed and deliberate burning of purification."[8] Such a path, in which the practitioner transcends each particular stage, showing the previous to be conventional, finds its antecedents also in the Upanishads, as described in the next chapter.

In chapter 1, we saw Eliot's early criticism of Schopenhauer's pessimism and interpretation of Indian materials. We also saw Eliot's exposure to the *upaya* doctrine in and through Anesaki's presentations. Eliot also would have found similar ideas in the early Theravada Buddhist sources to which he had access in his studies. *Upaya* as an identifiable doctrine belongs to the Mahayana, though it clearly has its roots in earlier Buddhist material. I believe it is to such early instances of the idea that Eliot alludes in the decisive comparison of Eastern and Western asceticism at the end of section III of *The Waste Land*. There, Eliot juxtaposes fragments from Augustine's *Confessions* and the Buddha's Fire Sermon. This chapter unpacks the early version of the idea of skillful means as it appears in the Fire Sermon. I do this by relying on Richard Gombrich's illuminating insight of the place of the sermon in the *Mahavagga* and the broader tradition as a whole. I consider the sermon both as it appears in Henry Clarke Warren's collection of Buddhist texts (cited by Eliot in the poem's endnotes), and the *Mahavagga,* using a popular translation by T. W. Rhys Davids (from 1899), available to Eliot at the time of the poem's composition. I hope to show that our typical understanding of this textual allusion is short-sighted, and that having a fuller realization of the text's origins brings out a surprising parallel in the texts of Augustine with which it is "collocated."

Eliot's allusion to the Fire Sermon first and foremost evokes the "burning" of harmful desire and the "burning" or impermanence of the world and human selfhood. Further, it points to the negative role language plays when it reinforces and instantiates negative desire. However, Eliot realizes that language, for the early Buddhists, plays a positive role when it signals the absence within it, drawing attention to its own provisionality and pointing beyond itself. When language does signal such a provisionality, it can be put to use for the cultivation of the self—both intellectual and affective—through ascesis. Eliot approaches these issues through the questions of agency and epistemology discussed in the last chapter, especially through the problem of solipsism. Eliot's invocation of early Buddhism helps him formulate this problem in terms of repeated human erring and suffering. It locates this tendency on a phenomenological level in the dialectic of memory and desire: improper structures of thought, patterns of behavior, and modes of perception, engrained in the memory by desire, provide the basis for future experience. These structures are projected freely into the future and fuel the sinful desire of the individual in a never-ending process, in a "round," as the Buddhists would have it. This improper desire is one that reifies both things in the world and the self through improper attachments. The Fire Sermon depicts language as an instantiation and vehicle of attachment that provides a sense of identity, stability, and reality to things that lack all of these.

Language reifies both the self and objects in the world and creates discursive structures that perpetuate this reification. For the early Buddhists, this reification is expressed in consciousness's grasping of the self and objects in the world as "I" and "mine."

The dialectic of memory and desire determines the choices and activities of the individual who is doomed to repetition and suffering, unless he or she encounters the Buddha's enlightened teaching. Upon the intervention of the Buddha and the dharma, however, the entire cycle can be put to use for its own transcendence. Even language, which the Buddhists initially see as an instrument of desire and reification, can be used to bring the believer along to higher and higher levels of ascesis through, for example, the use of sermons. However, it is the experience of the unconditioned at the culmination of the path that definitively shows this language to be conventional; the proper use of language must be one in which it bears witness to the absence within it and the reality that lies beyond it. To guard against reification, language must point beyond itself, showing its ultimate referent to be absent. It must also enable the believer to see all of finite existence as pointing beyond itself. For the Buddhists, this means viewing language in the context of *upaya,* as providing way stations along the ascetic path, resting points that then dissolve once they have fulfilled their purpose. Language leads to the final realization that the world is "on fire," impermanent and without stable existence and yet, because of this, malleable. Once language is viewed as conventional, it can play a crucial role in a path of cultivation that, far from rejecting affective, aesthetic desire, engages and redirects it. The paradox is that desire is mobilized to transcend desire, language to transcend language, and time to transcend time. The Buddha therefore presents a path in which desire is redirected to its own impossible overcoming. The full integration of the aesthetic stage of the Buddhist path, in which the believer engaged with ritual, metaphor, and mimetic representations, was not well appreciated at the time of Eliot's writing (and is still being fully explored today). We will see later that the reference to aesthetics in the quotes from Augustine in *The Waste Land* brings out this dimension of the Buddhist texts and evokes the Buddhist notion of *upaya* embodied in the Fire Sermon in the *Mahavagga.*

Finally, an apologia for what is to come. It is my contention that Eliot scholars have not appreciated the full significance of the original Fire

Sermon and so have been deaf to the very real dissonance at the end of section III of the poem. I am trying to recover this music more fully. What follows is therefore an in-depth and lengthy treatment of the sermon and its epistemological and metaphysical presuppositions. If we as readers do not understand this significance, we risk underestimating the Buddhist fragments in section III, we miss the provocative comparison that Eliot makes at the conclusion of the section, and arguably we miss a poetic action in section III as a whole, which is, after all, named after the Buddhist text. After this thorough treatment, I return to the poem and its poetic comparison of asceticisms to show the very real, if enigmatic, ascetic possibilities it raises.

The Fire Sermon: Attachment and Suffering

The Fire Sermon can be found in the first *Khandakha* of the *Mahavagga,* which is itself the beginning of the *Vinaya Pitaka,*[9] the collection of texts providing rules for monastic discipline. Thus, the narrative of how the Buddha converts the "thousand priests" in the sermon is followed by narratives of the Buddha correcting the behavior of monks and setting the foundation for the monastic life. It should come as no surprise, therefore, that the Fire Sermon comes in the form of a sermon, an act of speech meant not only to describe the nature of reality, but to achieve an existential change in the priests who are listening. At stake is the ability of the Buddha's discourse both to reflect the truth experienced at first by the Buddha alone and to provoke a similar experience in his followers. One can also see the text's monastic nature through its repetitions, many of which Warren leaves out for the sake of space. Still, this is a text meant to be repeated, savored, tirelessly contemplated, and internalized. Its aim is to continue the process of cultivation culminating in complete liberation from the round of *samsara.*

The Buddha's Fire Sermon begins as he addresses a very large group of new converts on Gaya Head. His sermon focuses first on diagnosing human existential problems in terms of the six senses recognized by early Buddhism and then prescribing the solution. The text presents the Buddha's speech as so powerful that his new converts become instantly free of attachment and purified from the "depravities." For our purposes, the sermon needs to be presented as a whole:

"All things, O priests, are on fire. And what, O priests, are all these things which are on fire?

"The eye, O priests, is on fire; forms are on fire; eye-consciousness is on fire; impressions received by the eye are on fire; and whatever sensation, pleasant, unpleasant, or indifferent, originates in dependence on impressions received by the eye, that also is on fire.

"And with what are these in fire?

With the fire of passion, say I, with the fire of hatred, with the fire of infatuation; with birth, old age, death, sorrow, lamentation, misery, grief, and despair are they on fire.

"The ear is on fire; sounds are on fire; . . . the nose is on fire; odors are on fire; . . . the tongue is on fire; tastes are on fire; . . . the body is on fire; things tangible are on fire; . . . the mind is on fire; ideas are on fire; . . . mind-consciousness is on fire; impressions received by the mind are on fire; and whatever sensation, pleasant, unpleasant, or indifferent, originates in dependence on impressions received by the mind, that also is on fire.

"And with what are these on fire?

"With the fire of passion, say I, with the fire of hatred, with the fire of infatuation; with birth, old age, death, sorrow, lamentation, misery, grief, and despair are they on fire.

"Perceiving this, O priests, the learned and noble disciple conceives an aversion for the eye, conceives an aversion for forms, conceives an aversion for eye-consciousness, conceives an aversion for the impressions received by the eye; and whatever sensation, pleasant, unpleasant, or indifferent, originates in dependence on impressions received by the eye, for that also he conceives an aversion. Conceives an aversion for the ear, conceives an aversion for sounds, . . . conceives an aversion for the nose, conceives an aversion for odors, . . . conceives an aversion for the tongue, conceives an aversion for tastes, . . . conceives an aversion for the body, conceives an aversion for things tangible, . . . conceives an aversion for the mind, conceives an aversion for ideas, conceives an aversion for mind-consciousness, conceives an aversion for the impressions received by the mind; and whatever sensation, pleasant, unpleasant, or indifferent, originates in dependence on impressions received by the mind, for this also he conceives an aversion. And in conceiving this aversion, he becomes divested of passion,

LANGUAGE AND THE CULTIVATION OF DESIRE   115

and by the absence of passion he becomes free, and when he is
free he becomes aware that he is free; and he knows that rebirth
is exhausted, that he has lived the holy life, that he has done what it
behooved him to do, and that he is no more for this world."

Now while this exposition was being delivered, the minds of
the thousand priests became free from attachment and delivered
from the depravities.[10]

The Buddha's sermon utilizes one of the absolutely central images of
early Indian religion, the image of fire. The full significance of this imagery is discussed later, when we place the sermon in context of the *Mahavagga* in general. There, we will see that the men converted in the Fire
Sermon were once devotees of Agni, the Vedic fire god of the sacrifice.
For now, the basics will have to suffice, leaving a full contextualization
until a bit later. Steven Collins, in his excellent study of the imagery of
nirvana, has discussed how the Buddhists reappropriated and revalued
the image of the fire, an image originally of the power of the Vedic sacrifice to bestow rewards and benefits on both the priests and the patron of
the sacrifice, to diagnose the problem of attachment and suffering in the
world.[11] Richard Gombrich has similarly shown how this reappropriation
manifests itself specifically in the Fire Sermon (we will return later to
Gombrich's reading, which casts important light on Eliot's allusions in
The Waste Land). Gombrich notes the various types of fire in the traditional Vedic ritual sphere, all of which the Fire Sermon invokes and in-
verts. In the Vedic sacrifice, the Brahmin priests lit three major fires: the
garhapatya ("householder's fire"), the *dakshinagni* ("southern fire"), and
the *ahavaniya* ("the offertorial fire").[12] Likewise, they kept the domestic
fire for household rites. The Fire Sermon undoubtedly references, and
rejects, all of these fires, comprising a major portion of the social/ritual
complex.[13] As we can see in the passage above, the sermon, in appropriating this imagery, diagnosed the suffering of the world in terms of their
own "three fires," of "passion," "hatred," and "infatuation." Whereas the
flame of the sacrifice must burn in order for the cosmic order, or *Rta,* to
be upheld, and the benefits received, Buddhism's three flames must be
extinguished to attain the highest moments of the Buddhist path. Hence,
nibbana (Sanskrit: *nirvana*) itself is a "quenching of fire."[14]

The self's attachment both to itself and to objects in the world as ultimately existing fuels the three fires. It *is* such grasping, and the harmful

kammic activity engendered in it, that leads to the individual's entrapment in *kamma* (in Sanskrit *karma*), the round of rebirth and suffering. At the heart of this process is the tendency of human beings to take themselves as ultimately existing, eternal beings, rather than as causally conditioned through and through. In the Brahmanas and Upanishads, fire came to symbolize the *atman*, the point of identity within the individual that was identical with *brahman*, the eternal, originating power of the universe.[15] For the Buddhists, it was just such a conceptualization that leads to suffering, since it spurs on the grasping of the self as an entity, as an "I." In response to this, the Fire Sermon depicts the self's existence vis-à-vis its attachment to objects in the world in terms of the three flames. The Buddha thus extends the metaphor of fire both to the six senses of the human being and to their objects.[16] Aiming for comprehensiveness, he moves from sense to sense, showing that all senses and "all things . . . are on fire." He moves dialectically between the self and other, subject and object, interiority and exteriority. He begins with the "eye" and moves to "forms." Continuing the pattern, he moves from "eye-consciousness," the inner awareness of forms, to the "impressions received by the eye," the "touch" as it were of form with sense. The Buddha ends with "sensations," apparently the ultimate summation of the self's engagement with objects in the world. The Buddha lights the entire epistemic relation on fire; self and object exist only in dependence on one another, and both need to be viewed properly in order to attain *nibbana*.

The text's rhetorical efficacy depends on the juxtaposition of the idea of "things" in the world and the idea that these "things," solid or eternal though they may seem, are actually "on fire." The image of a fire, constantly flickering, always on the move, always changing by the minute, only existing as long as its fuel is replenished, seems at utter odds with the idea of an eternal "thing" or "form" or "essence." And yet, it is precisely grasping such impermanent forms that fuels the round of rebirth. Gombrich rightly notes that behind the *Mahavagga*'s flame imagery is the problem of grasping or attachment to elements of the 5 *khandhas*.[17] The "*khandhas*" in early Buddhism are "the 5 aspects in which the Buddha has summed up all the physical and mental phenomena of existence, and which appear to the ignorant man as his Ego, or personality, to wit: (1) the Corporeality group . . . (2) the Feeling . . . (3) the Perception . . . (4) the Mental-Formation . . . (5) the Consciousness-group."[18] These five groups provide the five bases for *upadana*, meaning "clinging" or "grasping."[19] Placed together as *upadana kkhandha*, they refer to the "5 groups of clinging," or the five elements of existence to which a human being could attach himself or herself.[20] Gombrich notes that the term *upadana* also properly means that which "fuels" the process of grasping. Citing the *Pali-English Dictionary*, he claims that the term means "(lit. that [material] substratum by means of which an active process is kept alive and going), fuel, supply, provision."[21] He therefore sees the fire metaphor reflected in the sermon implied in the very word used for those individual constituents that provide the necessary foundation for "grasping."[22] Thus returning to the rhetorical strategy of the sermon, those components of existence that the individual attempts to grasp in the world, those elements that "fuel" attachment, are not truly existing constituents; they are always changing, always developing, and to seize them as unchanging or stable is just as impossible as hugging flames to yourself.

For early Buddhist texts, such a grasping is ultimately a sign of harmful desire and powerful ignorance, an overwhelming unawareness of the conditioned nature of all things in the world, both self and objects. To describe this conditionality the Buddha preached the doctrine of dependent origination, or *paticcasamuppada* (Sanskrit: *pratityasamutpada*), a doctrine that, according to canonical texts, formed an integral part of the Buddha's enlightenment.[23] The "twelvefold chain" of dependent origination provides the Buddha with the explication of why human beings become entrapped in the round of *samsara*, the realm of repeated suffering and rebirth. Warren presents the twelvefold chain as is commonly found throughout the Pali canon in his section on the "Middle Doctrine":

> On ignorance depends karma; / On karma depends consciousness; / On consciousness depend name and form; / On name and form depend the six organs of sense; / On the six organs of sense depends contact; / On contact depends sensation; / On sensation depends desire; / On desire depends attachment; / On attachment depends existence; / On existence depends birth; / On birth depend old age and death, sorrow, lamentation, misery, grief, and despair. Thus does this entire aggregation of misery arise.[24]

The twelvefold chain supposedly explains how continued existence in the realm of rebirth is possible. Though the Buddhists give pride of place to ignorance at the head of the entire chain of causes, it is interesting to note, as Warren does in his "Introductory Discourse" to part II of

118 DESIRE AND THE ASCETIC IDEAL

his text, that there really are two starting points to the process, ignorance and desire: ignorance leads to the first appearance of a human being under the guise of consciousness and name/form, while desire leads to attachment and existence.[25] How exactly the sequence works is the subject of some debate within the tradition, and the details need not concern us here.[26] What is important, however, is the generative power of its two key terms, ignorance and desire.

By ignorance, the tradition usually means an unawareness of the Four Noble Truths, though often it comes to refer specifically to the second of the Truths, the origin of suffering. As Nyanatiloka observes: "[Ignorance] is the delusion tricking beings by making life appear to them as permanent, happy, substantial and beautiful and preventing them from seeing that everything in reality is impermanent, liable to suffering, void of I and Mine, and basically impure. . . . Ignorance is defined as 'not knowing the four Truths, namely suffering, its origin, its cessation, and the way to cessation."[27] The person plagued by ignorance does not realize the cause of suffering, the tendency to takes things in the world and oneself as permanent and abiding rather than as causally conditioned.

This entire analysis is presupposed in the Fire Sermon. The Buddha diagnoses the attachments of human beings as mired in "passion," "hatred," and "infatuation." His strategy for healing, on the other hand, is to rhetorically set the world on fire, to show its conditioned, impermanent nature. This strategy is meant to cure the assembled priests of their ignorant reifying of self and object and thereby free them of *kammic* repetition. For all the rhetorical repetitions that occur in the text, the Buddha's preaching is meant to put an end to *all* repetition. In Buddhist teaching, ignorance leads to improper activities in the world, which in turn generate further such activities. The individual will experience the results of these improper actions either in this life or the next, and these actions will determine the prospects for rebirth. The Buddhist metaphysics depends on the ancient Indian notion of *kamma* (Sanskrit *karma*), the idea that one will receive retribution for one's activities in the world: one will receive positive outcomes or beneficial rebirths if one performs moral deeds, and negative outcomes or poor rebirths if one performs immoral deeds. In many non-Buddhist texts, *kamma* works as an impersonal system of retribution: one need not actually know that one is performing an immoral action; sooner or later retribution to that action will come (usually in a deliciously ironic manner). Robert

Goldman describes the process as having two aspects: "One of these is the belief in transmigration of the animating principle, however defined, from one more or less physical, terrestrial body to another. A second fundamental belief is that all actions have at least the potential for future consequences quite different from those intended by their agents and that results of action rebound onto the agent itself."[28] Ultimately the individual who has performed such a transgression will be free of the effects of that transgression once he or she has suffered the appropriate punishment. Nevertheless, it is possible for someone who experiences a rebirth in a lower status to perform more immoral deeds, leading to even more deleterious consequences.

Buddhism is significant in the development of Indian religions for ethicizing the *kamma* system, making *kammic* retribution dependent on the intentions of the person committing the act.[29] The Buddhist term for intention or volition is *chetana*. Nyanatiloka cites the *Anguttara Nikaya* as describing its role in the *kammic* cycle: "Volition is action (Karma), thus I say, O monks; for as soon as volition arises, one does the action, be it by body, speech or mind."[30] In a more profound way, however, *chetana* refers to the activities of all of consciousness in its activities in the world. It refers to both the rational and affective elements of consciousness that drive human activity. Damien Keown provides an expansive definition; he states that *chetana*

> is best pictured as the matrix in which the push and pull of the rational and emotional aspects of the psyche are funneled in the direction of moral choice. It is therefore a function of the total personality and not merely its cognitive operations. This might be expected in view of its identification with *kamma*: if *cetana* was merely cognitive then all kammic evil would be intellectual (*moha*). We know, however, that it is not, since craving (*raga*) and hatred (*dosa*) also play an important role. Conversely, without the thrust of emotional commitment the appreciation of good ends remains static or takes the form of a vague and diffuse benevolence.[31]

Thus the ignorance that Buddhists place at the heart of the *kammic* cycle is in reality a part of a more fundamental, existential orientation, both intellectual and affective, that is flawed. It is this intellectual/emotional complex leading to moral activity in the world that determines, for the Buddha, the *kammic* consequences for the individual. When that intentionality is defiled, as the Fire Sermon asserts, by the three fires of "passion," "hatred," and "infatuation" (or "delusion"), then the individual becomes attached to objects in the world and to himself or herself in a complete way. It is this attachment that will lead, in subsequent lives, to continued attachment and defilement, to a repetition of harmful mental and emotional constructions.

The tradition describes these attachments as constructions of consciousness, or *samkhara*. On one level, these constructions are "wholesome or unwholesome volitions (cetanā) manifested as actions in body, speech or mind."[32] Even more strongly, the term can refer to "'inherited forces' . . . as it suggests both the dynamic, forward looking ideas of volition, desire, and so on, and also the fact that these samsaric phenomena are themselves held to be conditioned by and arise out of former karma."[33] Improper intention creates improper constructions within the consciousness that determine the future desires and conceptual apparatus of the individual. In other words, past attachments and mental constructions will influence future attachments and constructions, and it is just this type of repetition that drives the round of rebirth for Buddhism. This means that consciousness, in both its affective *and* intellectual portions, attach themselves to the world and generate the desire for a renewal of those attachments. The image generally used for this process is that of "seeds." Attachment creates "seeds" within consciousness that grow over time and come to fruition in some future state of the individual.[34] We have seen similar imagery and a similar analysis of consciousness in our discussion of Patanjali's influence on the opening passages of *The Waste Land*.

When intention is informed by an ignorant understanding of self and world that reifies both, the self not only maintains itself in the world of *kamma* but exacerbates its own suffering. The Pali term *dukkha* is usually translated as "suffering," and indeed it does mean this. However, the term also means a general sense that existence is unsatisfactory when desired for its stability;[35] the world has no such stability: "the term *dukkha* is not limited to painful experience . . . but refers to the unsatisfactory nature and the general insecurity of all conditioned phenomena which, on account of their impermanence, are all liable to suffering; and this includes also pleasurable experience."[36] In the terms of the Fire Sermon, things in the world have the stability of a flickering, ever-changing flame. Even pleasurable experience contributes to suffering, since the self desires to hold onto the experience, to think of it as abiding. When it does not abide, the self suffers its absence intensely. It is not simply pleasurable experience that causes suffering through its impermanence; all of conditioned phenomena, including the mental constructions that instantiate the individual's attachment to the world, also pass away and cause suffering to a self that would like to grasp itself as permanent. As Collins has noted, "Generally, the idea that what is 'constructed' or 'conditioned' is in itself a form of suffering depends on the whole of Buddhist doctrine, on the disjunction between what is causally conditioned and the unconditioned *nibbana,* and on the system of value-judgements which is entailed by it."[37] Whatever is temporally conditioned, whatever is constructed, must necessarily lead to the experience of suffering of dissatisfaction, since it will inevitably pass away. The only thing that does not pass away is *nibbana,* Buddhism's "other" to temporal, causal experience.

Buddhist Realism and Empiricism

Thus far we have seen that the Fire Sermon presupposes the Buddhist explanation of *kamma,* in which the self's attachment to the world and to itself, in and through its structures of intentionality, causes the repetition of thoughts, desires, and activities that lead to suffering. The Fire Sermon signaled this by the inner-outer dialectic, moving between the six senses and their objects. From this dialectic, it should also be clear that, despite our focus on intention, volition, and repetition, the Theravada Buddhists were not idealists. They did not hold that the mind itself is responsible for creating objects in the world, or that consciousness is all-determining. It is perhaps the realism and empiricism of the early Buddhist texts that ultimately drew Eliot to them. Collins explains the confusion that often arises in this regard:

> Theravada has not systematized this ethical and psychological metaphor into an epistemological and metaphysical "idealism," as did other Buddhist schools. For the *Vijnanavada* for instance, there was no difference between the fact of mental objects' existing at all, and the fact of mental defilement. It is only the ignorant, desiring, unenlightened mind which creates out of itself the separation between subject (grahaka, "grasper") and object (grahya, "grasped"). In Theravada, what we might call the "idealist tendency," which in

122 DESIRE AND THE ASCETIC IDEAL

some contexts is quite pronounced, is confined to the ethical sphere. That is to say, mind is regarded as creating the *desirability* of the objects of perception and thought, not their very existence. Thus there is a distinction to be drawn between the mere fact of mental objects existing, and their being occasions for moral defilement.[38]

The entire focus of the Buddhist analysis of suffering was on intention and attachment; when consciousness improperly desires objects in the world, or holds itself to be eternal, then the self adds to its mental defilements, increases its suffering, and binds itself to rebirth. But attachment implies something to which to be attached. We can see this clearly in the Fire Sermon's dialectical movement back and forth between human consciousness and outer forms (the distinction between "name" [*nama*] and "form" [*rupa*] in early Buddhism).[39] Such a realism provides the very foundation for the Fire Sermon's analysis. True, the distinction between name and form implies a kind of nominalism: in some very real way, consciousness and "naming" individuated the external world into objects of apprehension. At the same time, however, the early Buddhists never denied that there was an external world to be perceived and individuated. Reality was, to be sure, causally dependent and always impermanent. Nevertheless, it "existed" enough that one could become conscious of it and attached to it.

This empirical element of early Buddhist thought was ultimately amenable to Eliot's own reaction against nineteenth-century idealism. K. N. Jayatilleke has suggested that early Buddhism inherits its empiricism from the middle and later Upanishads (though I argue in the final chapter that Eliot finds foreshadowings of this in the early Upanishads). In a discussion of the epistemology of the *Kaushitaki Upanishad*, Jayatilleke states:

> Except for the fact that the "cognitive elements" are here metaphysically conceived as the agents of the sensory functions, there is a recognition of the mutual causal dependence of sensible objects and their respective cognitions. Likewise the importance of attention for sense cognition is recognized in the Upaniṣads where it is said, "my mind was elsewhere, I did not see; my mind was elsewhere, I did not hear, for with the mind does one see and with the mind hear."[40]

LANGUAGE AND THE CULTIVATION OF DESIRE   123

Jayatilleke's final passage here is from the *Brhadaranyaka Upanishad*, 1.5.3. As we will see later, this Upanishad is one of the key texts in Eliot's depiction of his speaker's inner, meditative ascent in the concluding passages of *The Waste Land*. Jayatilleke quickly makes the basic distinction between the Buddhists and the *Upanishads*, noting that in the latter, there is a metaphysical agent, the *atman*, behind cognition, whereas no such agent is posited in Buddhism. Nevertheless, subject and object are mutually dependent, and perception (and consequently grasping) are dependent on the individual's attentiveness to objects in the world. When this attentiveness is driven by impure desire, then the self perpetuates itself in the round of *samsara*.

The Middle Way and the Nominal Identity of the "I"

The Buddhist concept of the "middle way" embodied the tendency on the part of early Buddhism to maintain both poles of the epistemological relationship without reifying either; it was a concept that would be immensely important to Eliot's work even as late as *Four Quartets*, where it is a pivotal term (see especially chapter 6). In *The Waste Land*, its importance can be seen in and through the Fire Sermon. It is important to understand this concept in order to understand how Buddhists would consider the sermon as a linguistic artifact. The idea of the middle way operated on several different levels. On one hand, it was a refusal to categorize objects in terms of ontology; things could not be said either to exist or not to exist. Warren presents as paradigmatic a passage from the *Samyutta Nikaya*:

> The world, for the most part, O Kaccanā, holds either to a belief in being or to a belief in non-being. But for one who in the light of the highest knowledge, O Kaccanā, considers how the world arises, belief in the non-being of the world passes away. And for one who in the light of the highest knowledge, O Kaccanā, considers how the world ceases, belief in the being of the world passes away. The world, O Kaccanā, is for the most part bound up in a seeking, attachment, proclivity [for the groups], but a priest does not sympathize with this seeking and attachment, nor with the mental affirmation, proclivity and prejudice which affirms an Ego. He does

124   DESIRE AND THE ASCETIC IDEAL

> not doubt or question that it is only evil that springs into existence, and only evil that ceases from existence, and his conviction of this fact is dependent on no one besides himself. This, O Kaccanā, is what constitutes Right Belief.
>
> That things have being, O Kaccanā, constitutes one extreme of doctrine; that things have no being is the other extreme. These extremes, O Kaccanā, have been avoided by the Tathāgata, and it is a middle doctrine he teaches.[41]

The passage then launches into the presentation of the twelvefold-fold chain of dependent origination, *paticcasamuppada*, that I cite and discuss earlier. In this fascinating passage, the Buddha suggests that human beings can be improperly attached either to the belief in "being" or to the belief in "non-being:" the world "holds" these beliefs, it grasps them. However, one cannot say the world does not exist, when one sees that the world "arises" causally. On the other hand, the fact that things "pass away" precludes positing being of them. If something truly "exists" in this sense, it would be eternal and abiding, not subject to passing away. Nothing, save *nibbana*, fits this description. When one stands in "the light of the highest knowledge," the enlightenment of *nibbana*, one sees these truths clearly. The "experience" of that which is beyond conditionality (e.g., the Buddha's experience) allows one to see the truth of conditioned things. Thus the answer to both ontological positions seems to be in this passage the affirmation of the causally conditioned nature of all reality. As suggested earlier, in the Fire Sermon, this causality is expressed in terms of the constantly evolving nature of the flame itself. To see the objects in the world as on fire expresses this "middle way" of seeing objects: they exist as distinct from the senses, but they are impermanent. They exist, but they are dependent and causally changing. They exist, but they in part provide the "fuel" for human desire and attachment. Human conceptualization and "naming" attempts to provide them with a stability that they cannot possibly have. Such naming can only be seen as conventional.

At the same time, the passage suggests that one should consider "the self" in the same manner as objects in the world. It claims that the priest "does not sympathize with this seeking and attachment, nor with the mental affirmation, proclivity, and prejudice which affirms an Ego." One can neither say that the self exists or does not exist. Warren follows up the passage from *Samyutta Nikaya* with one from Buddhaghosa's *Visuddhimagga*, in clarification of the "middle way":

> By the complete phrase "Dependent Origination," inasmuch as such and such elements of being come into existence by means of an unbroken series of their full complement of dependence, the truth, or middle course, is shown. This rejects the heresy that he who experiences the fruit of the deed is the same as the one who performed the deed, and also rejects the converse one that he who experiences the fruit of the deed is different from the one who performed the deed, and leaning not to either of these popular hypotheses, holds fast by nominalism.[42]

Here, Buddhaghosa presents the causal analysis in terms of activity, of *kamma*. Such *kammic* activity is presented in terms of "fruit" and, by implication, seeds. When an individual performs an act, positive or negative, he or she plants a *kammic* seed within that eventually ripens into a "fruit" of benefit or suffering. Buddhaghosa presents two heresies, the first of which is that the individual does not change at all. If the individual did not change, then the very same entity could be said to act and experience the *kammic* consequences of that act. This would be an unchanging self, perhaps similar to the *atman* of the Upanishads; it is unclear whether such an unchanging individual could act in the first place or experience any *kammic* consequences whatsoever. Likewise, the second heresy states that a completely different individual experiences the consequences of an act from the one that did the original act. This heresy would posit a self that changes completely with each moment of time. It would be a complete determinism, in which each temporal moment was causally dependent on, but differed from, the previous one. This, again, would destroy the *kammic* metaphysics, since a completely different entity would reap the benefits or punishments of the act previously committed. At stake here is not only the conceptualization of personal continuity and change, but the entire ethical system of *kammic* consequences. In order for Buddhist ethics to be coherent, they must be able to affirm both that the individual changes, and that there is some form of continuity across which *kammic* "seeds" can ripen. Jayatilleke observes that such a teaching was meant to steer between the *atman*/agent of the Upanishads and the constantly changing self of the materialists. He writes that *paticcasamuppada*

126 DESIRE AND THE ASCETIC IDEAL

appears to have been used primarily to explain rebirth and karma without recourse to the metaphysical atman-hypothesis of the Eternalists and without falling into the other extreme of Materialism. The Eternalists of the Upaniṣads explained rebirth and karma by assuming a self-identical soul which passed on from existence to existence as the agent of all actions and the recipient of reactions. . . . As an Empiricist . . . the Buddha could not posit the existence of a soul. At the same time he could not, like the Materialists, deny the continuity of the individual after death and the responsibility of the individual for his actions. The *raison d'etre* of the "Chain of Causation" lies therefore mainly in the fact that it gives a causal account of the factors operating in maintaining the process of the individual and thereby of suffering.[43]

Not only are both of these options conceptually impossible, but they are also empirically invalid. Nowhere in causal experience is such an *atman* found; and to deny personal continuity would be to deny the reality of human acting, ethics, and suffering.

The Buddhists therefore constrain themselves to discussing the self only in nominalistic terms. One cannot speak of the "I" as an absolute essence, but one can speak of the self in a conventional sense. Indeed, normal, everyday speech would seem to demand this. Warren presents, again, Buddhaghosa, writing on a trope from the "Questions for King Milinda." In that text, the monk Nagasena asked the king to identify where, amid all the constituents of a chariot, the "chariot" in itself was to be found. Nagasena eventually tells Milinda that the term "chariot" simply designates the whole into which the parts are assembled. Likewise, Buddhaghosa writes:

Just as the word "chariot" is but a mode of expression for axle, wheels, chariot-body, pole, and other constituent members, placed in a certain relation to each other, but when we come to examine the members one by one, we discover that in the absolute sense there is no chariot . . . in exactly the same way the words "living entity" and "Ego" are but a mode of expression for the presence of the five attachment groups, but when we come to examine the elements of being one by one, we discover that in the absolute sense there is no living entity there to form a basis for such figments as "I am," or "I"; in other words, that in the absolute sense there is only name and form. The insight of him who perceives this is called knowledge of the truth.[44]

Words are mere "modes of expression" that conceptually unify the constituents of things in the world and give them a sense of continuity. They are conventional; they cannot signify in an "absolute" sense. And just as a chariot is but a "mode of expression," so too is the "I." The "I" is conventionally real, but ultimately dependent. In Collins's words, the Buddha "asserts the existence of an event described by the verbal notion, but denies that it is legitimate to infer the existence of a real subject from the verbal form."[45] In Buddhist philosophical analysis, especially in the *Abhidhamma*, the "self" would be subjected to a meticulous process of division into its constituent parts. It would be dismantled bit by bit, showing the absence of any persisting *atman* beyond the conventional name.

The Middle Way and the Paradoxes of the Path

The "middle way" doctrine provides a way for Buddhists to think about the conditioned self in a manner distinct to that of the Upanishads. However, it also provides them with a way of defending the efficacy of the Buddhist path. This dimension of the Fire Sermon is not immediately apparent, but is implicated in the evocation of the middle way. The path would be useless if the forms of the path, the rituals, practices, and texts, had no efficacy. The emphasis that the Buddhist causal analysis places on conventional reality and nominal utility provides the texts of the tradition with the ability to continue to signify as they must without reifying the self or its objects. Jayatilleke claims that the overriding purpose of the "middle way" was to preserve the conventional meaning of language, in the absence of direct metaphysical grounding. So, for example, when considering "Eternalism": "If Being = what exists, then only the specious present has being, for the past and future do not exist at the present moment. But when we talk of the concept 'Being' without a time reference, we violate convention and assume that the past as well as the future has existence in the sense in which the present has existence."[46] To use the term "Being" to refer to something beyond the realm of causality is to divorce it from any possible meaning. It attempts to stretch convention to that which can never be referred to conventionally. In a sense, the causal analysis plays a dual role: it banishes eternal essences

128   DESIRE AND THE ASCETIC IDEAL

from temporal becoming, but it also provides a critical mechanism to defend the conventional use of language.

If language and naming, however, have a tendency to reify the world, fueling *kamma* by enabling desire and grasping, then does not linguistic utterance, such as the Fire Sermon, for example, provide a danger for the aspiring monk? If naming implies intention, attention, and grasping, should the monk attempt to "grasp" the path? If the aim of the path is to overcome *kamma,* should not the monk attempt to refrain from all action, physical and conceptual? The Fire Sermon, as translated by Warren, would seem to suggest that the Path requires mental engagement, not retreat. Recall that the Buddha states, "Perceiving this, O priests, the learned and noble disciple conceives an aversion for the eye, conceives an aversion for forms." Again, the Buddha's inner/outer dialectic comes to the forefront. The monk perceives the reality of things, that all things are on fire. They are causally dependent and yet seized upon with desire by ignorant human beings. At this point in the sermon, however, the monk perceives the world, sees what is "out there," but sees it with new eyes, with a different lens. Further, the monk is asked to "conceive" an "aversion" to both self and other. In other words, the monk is being asked to do the paradoxical mental work of constructing or drawing into consciousness an aversion, or a turning away from the world. The Buddha provides a paradoxical medicine, in which the monk is asked to draw himself beyond conceptions by conceiving a way beyond conceptions.

We come quickly to the paradox of a path that demands that one use language to transcend language, that one mobilize desire in order not to desire, and that one act in order not to act. It is this paradox that Schopenhauer failed to appreciate in his orientalism, and it is this paradox that would fascinate Eliot so much. It is most easily seen in the distinction that some have used, following M. E. Spiro, between *kammic* and *nibbanic* Buddhism.[47] Briefly, the comparison suggests a distinction between the kind of Buddhism practiced by lay Buddhists, in which moral activity is performed in order to generate merit and enable positive rebirths, and the *nibbanic,* virtuoso Buddhism, in which monks undertake intense cultivating meditation in order to attain *nibbana.*[48] The reason the two types are generally seen as distinct is that the lay Buddhism seems to freely use the desire for a better rebirth as motivation enough for moral behavior (traditionally the first step of the Path). In other words, this type of Buddhism does not so much want to transcend *kamma* but to put it to use for one's own benefit. But doesn't the entire path also depend on this very principle: to put *kamma* to use in order to escape it? The tradition has always distinguished between good *kamma* and bad *kamma*, between improper desire and proper desire. A passage from the *Digha-Nikaya* (in Warren's text), for example, describes the sixth step:

> Whenever, O priests, a priest purposes, makes an effort, heroically endeavors, applies his mind, and exerts himself that evil and demeritorious qualities not yet arisen may not arise; purposes, makes an effort, heroically endeavors, applies his mind, and exerts himself that evil and demeritorious qualities already arisen may be abandoned; purposes, makes an effort, heroically endeavors, applies his mind, and exerts himself that meritorious qualities not yet arisen may arise; purposes, makes an effort, heroically endeavors, applies his mind, and exerts himself for the preservation, retention, growth, increase, development, and perfection of meritorious qualities already arisen, this, O priest, is called "right effort."[49]

The dutiful monk not only is to obey the moral precepts of the tradition but is to minimize the demeritorious qualities and maximize the meritorious qualities. This is the stage of the path right before right contemplation and right concentration.[50] As for the problem of desire, Warren also presents a passage from *Majjhima-Nikaya* discussing the "two cravings . . . the noble one, and the ignoble one."[51] The noble "craving" emerges once one has realized the suffering of the world:

> We may have, O priests, the case of one who, himself subject to birth, perceives the wretchedness of what is subject to birth, and craves the incomparable security of a Nirvana free from birth; himself subject to old age, . . . disease, . . . death, . . . sorrow, . . . corruption, perceives the wretchedness of what is subject to corruption, and craves the incomparable security of a Nirvana free from corruption.[52]

The realization of suffering gives birth to the proper kind of desire, a desire to transcend the realm of temporal becoming for liberation. It is that moment of insight that gives rise to the desire to undertake a path that will lead to the elimination of not only improper desire but all desire as such. But such an eradication is only the end point of a long path of cultivation, a cultivation that, as we have seen, requires strenuous effort, guided by

130   DESIRE AND THE ASCETIC IDEAL

a "craving" for *nibbana*. Collins acknowledges this as one of the central aporias of the early Buddhist tradition but notes that these two kinds of craving are not the same: "it would be better to talk of the aspiration to nirvana rather than the desire for it, of purposive action as intentionally oriented towards its goal rather than as desiring it. Less blandly, one can say that nirvana is not the kind of thing towards which affective states of Desire (=Craving), in the Buddhist pejorative sense, can be directed."[53] Collins tries very carefully to distinguish between positive "aspiration" and negative "desire" because to a large extent "desire" is seen as overwhelmingly negative in Buddhism. Rhetorically this is always the case; one will never read a Buddhist text that counsels one to "desire." And yet this does nothing to diminish the actual paradox, and as we have seen, the *Majjhima-Nikaya* does portray the two desires as two types of "craving." Further, the very first moments of the path are based on *shradda,* "faith" in the four noble truths, and such "*shradda*" has a strong affective quality. Gethin describes it as "a state of trust, confidence, affection, and devotion inspired by the person of the Buddha and his teachings."[54] Further, as Collins himself notes, the individual's feeling is engaged even in the higher reaches of the contemplative path up until the third *jhana* or meditative trance; one feels a higher "happiness" or "*sukha.*"[55] And as we saw earlier with our discussion of volition, *chetana* or intention is a broad term referring to the individual's moral agency in both intellectual and affective ways. In order to transform the individual, the Buddhist path engages the monk at all levels of human existence. Such a balanced view of desire and affectivity is not surprising, since another aspect of the "middle way" is that it steers a way between sensual indulgence on one hand and violent asceticism on the other. The Buddhist path, rather than eradicating initially all desire and all affectivity, begins by refining and transforming these things to its own ends.

Perhaps the most famous story illustrating this is the story of Nanda in the Jatakas.[56] According to the story, Nanda was the Buddha's younger brother, who joined the order after being initially converted by the Buddha. However, Nanda was married to a woman named, in Warren's translation, "Belle-of-the-Country." When Nanda left, she cried for him to return; the text states that "her speech remained in the venerable Nanda's mind, so that he became love-sick, and discontented, and pined away until the net-work of his veins showed on the surface of his body." The speech of his wife lives in his mind and creates a visceral, physical sickness. Nanda's attachment is both mental and affective, and his suffering takes place on both planes. The Buddha witnesses the situation and decides to save Nanda. He brings him to one of the higher heavens and shows him "five hundred celestial nymphs," who, he says, will be Nanda's if he undertakes "the duties of a monk."[57] Driven by his desire for the nymphs, Nanda throws himself into the monastic life. After he has done this, however, the Buddha tells the other monks that he has promised Nanda the nymphs. Members of the Sangha go to Nanda and shame him into a higher recognition:

> "Is it true, as they say, brother Nanda, that in the presence of the gods assembled in the Heaven of the Suite of the Thirty-three you took The One Possessing the Ten Forces as guarantee for some celestial nymphs, if you performed the duties of a monk? If that be so, is not your chaste religious life all for the sake of women? All for the sake of your passions? What is the difference between your thus doing the duties of a monk for the sake of women, and a laborer who performs his work for hire?"
>
> This speech put the elder to shame, and made him quite dispirited. And in the same way all the eighty great disciples, and the remaining priests also, shamed the venerable Nanda. And realizing that he had behaved in an unworthy manner, in shame and remorse he summoned up his heroism, and attained to insight and to saintship.[58]

In practicing the initial stages of the path, even with an improper desire for sexual gratification, Nanda comes to a certain kind of knowledge and realization that allows him to be shamed later by the members of the Sangha. It is because of the knowledge derived from praxis that Nanda is finally able to realize his past errors. But Nanda can only do this by working in and through his initial desires, and the Buddha realizes this. Incidentally, the communal force of this story also should not be taken for granted; it is not the Buddha who shames Nanda, since it was the Buddha who promised the nymphs. Rather, the other monks hold Nanda to account.

Skillful Means: Language and the Cultivation of Desire

Richard Gombrich has suggested that the Fire Sermon, when considered in the context of the *Mahavagga,* is actually the enlightening conclusion of a narrative whose main thrust is not only preaching ultimate truths in the Buddhist tradition but also showing the Buddha's ability to preach differently to different individuals, his use of what would later be called *upaya,* or skillful means.[59] The concept of *upaya,* to be sure, exists as a concept only in the Mahayana. Nevertheless, the idea can be found in the Pali canon,[60] and, in fact, throughout the Warren volume. Briefly put, the idea of "skillful means" refers to the Buddha's ability to communicate to every listener in the manner most appropriate to that person's ideological, intellectual, and affective situation. Indeed, *upaya* often entails not directly confronting the listener with Buddhist truths, but rather bringing them a certain way toward the ultimate truths through various strategies, ruses, and fictions. Gombrich cites an excellent passage from T. W. Rhys Davids, describing Buddhist *upaya:*

> Gotama puts himself as far as possible in the mental position of the questioner. He attacks none of his cherished convictions. He accepts as the starting-point of his own exposition the desirability of the act or condition prized by his opponent. . . . He even adopts the phraseology of his questioner. And then, partly by putting a new and (from the Buddhist point of view) a higher meaning into the words; partly by an appeal to such ethical conceptions as are common ground between them; he gradually leads his opponent up to his conclusion. This is, of course, always Arahatship.[61]

Rhys Davids is referring here to the tendency of the Buddha to take on the beliefs and perspectives of those he is engaging, as well as his ability to use the various modes of representation used by those people. For example, as we will see with the *Mahavagga,* the Buddha, when preaching to the worshippers of Agni, actually assists them in the fire sacrifice, setting the fuel for the sacrifice aflame and quenching the flames later. On one level, he partakes in the sacrifice in order to befriend the priests. On the other hand, this act provides a sign of the Buddha's superior power and his ability to "quench" the fires of desire and attain *nibbana.* Such an ability to invade subtly the discourse of his opponents has prompted Michael Pye to term the Buddha's method a "correlational technique."[62]

The Buddha's ability to speak differently to different peoples manifests itself in a special linguistic prowess: the Buddha is able to communicate to them not only in and through their own ideological predispositions but also through a great variety of linguistic forms and genres. Michael Pye, in his important book *Skilful Means,* has noted that the Buddha's teaching takes form in many different discursive genres:

This fundamental conception of the manner of the Buddha's beginning to teach has far-reaching implications. A teaching which relates to diverse needs in a differentiated world clearly requires a great flexibility and this was legitimated by the way in which the Buddha's own activity is understood. The flexibility of Buddhist teaching has many aspects. For one thing it is expressly permitted to be translated into many languages, and the use of any one language, whether it be Pali or Chinese, as a kind of special holy language is secondary. A great variety of literary forms is accepted as appropriate in all schools of Buddhism, and it has been seen that in The Lotus Sutra the various genres of Buddhist teaching are all conceived in terms of the Buddha's skillful means. Even the rules of religious practice submit to many re-adjustments. The laxity of the Mahasanghikas and the Mahayanists has found its way into the histories of Buddhism, but the analogous flexibility of Theravada discipline is often overlooked. In general it is fair to say that the idea of a differentiated yet consistent teaching was the basic style of pre-Mahayana Buddhism anyway, presumed to stem from the Buddha himself. Skillful means is the Mahayana name for this style.[63]

The truth of the Buddhist path is, in one sense, absolute. In another sense, however, it can be differentiated for practical purposes. Most of all, it can be translated. Pye is right to observe that the idea of a "sacred language" here is secondary. The Vedic ritual could only be performed in the sacred language of Sanskrit; the power of the entire cosmic order was embodied in this one language. The Buddha's teaching, however, can be effectively translated into other languages. The fact that the original Buddhist teachings were written in Pali, not in Sanskrit, brings this relative linguistic freedom starkly to the forefront. The Buddha's teaching does not rely on a single language, nor does it rely on a single genre. In fact, it does not depend on any single formulation of the doctrine. The Buddhist doctrine is based on strategy, on how to bring any particular individual to the highest goal, though this goal may be many rebirths away. The Buddhist path may lead to a single truth, that of *nibbana*, but this path and this goal can be represented in a myriad of ways, in a myriad of genres.[64]

Early Buddhist theories of interpretation and signification also insist on the fact that truth can be represented in many different ways, depending on the soteriological needs of the moment. *Nibbana* was the ultimate referent of the texts and practices of the Path, but it could be represented through a variety of textual representations. Buddhist hermeneutics operated with a similar assumption; some may be surprised to learn that Buddhism insisted, as did Christianity, on distinguishing between the "spirit" and the "letter" of a text, or rather, the intention and meaning of the text and its manner of expression. Etienne Lamotte has noted that for Buddhist interpreters, "The meaning is single and invariable, while the letter is multiple and infinitely variable. Buddhist exegetes often wondered anxiously whether one and the same entity or one and the same truth was not concealed under different terms."[65] Such a theory implies a unitary truth hiding beyond a multiplicity of particulars, mirroring the basic soteriological division between the realm of time and multiplicity and the atemporal, unified *nibbana*. But this, in turn, is an ancient trope that harkens all the way back to the *Purusha-sukta* of the *Rig Veda*, in which the whole, primal "person" was divided in making the universe. Franklin Edgerton has argued that such motifs led, in the later Vedic texts, to reflection on how the whole of a person strangely exceeded the sum of its parts.[66] The difference here is that the meaning does not seem to be imminent in the words themselves; the words bear witness to a truth that lies outside them, but they are not infused with that very truth. Again, language is only sacred by virtue of that to which it points. To take the language as an end in itself is to perform a kind of Buddhist idolatry. The lowest form of learner in early Buddhism is the one who grasps on to the letter of the teaching but does not discern the inner meaning.[67]

The problem with such a hermeneutics, of course, is that the emphasis must be placed on discovering this "spirit" behind the letter. Hence, the exegetes in Lamotte's explanation could become "anxious" in considering the multiplicity of forms. The problem of discovering such intention was real. But the Buddhist doctrine of *upaya* became a way of dealing with this hermeneutical complexity. The Buddhist schools held that

> the antinomic character of his [i.e., the Buddha's] teaching was only apparent and that his final view could be ascertained. Seeking to determine this final view became an overriding concern in Buddhist hermeneutics, and it is not surprising that the doctrine of upāya, of the Buddha's skillful methods of teaching the doctrine, which caused such problems in the interpretation of scripture should itself become a principle by which that interpretation was undertaken.[68]

In other words, the idea that the Buddha would teach different things to different people depending on their capacity for understanding became a difficult reality to negotiate when Buddhists analyzed their texts for the Buddha's core teachings. In a way, the entire corpus became the text behind which the exegetes attempted to ascertain an intention. But the idea of *upaya* eventually became a hermeneutical principle rather than something simply analyzed in the texts themselves. Thus exegetes could explain contradictions in doctrine by ascribing them different levels of maturity, understanding, and figurative expression. The ultimate verification that one has ascertained the meaning of the Buddhist path is the actual moment itself of *nibbana*.[69] Thus the meaning of Buddhist texts is never fully given, until the final moments of awakening at the end of the path. And such a meaning is one that no words themselves could ever embody.

In a very real way, because the ultimate meaning of the path is always deferred, every stage along the path becomes an instance of skillful means. The Buddhist tradition holds that a monk cannot be tossed into *nibbana* but must move through many different levels of intention, understanding, and insight. At each moment, the discourse used is provisional, meant to move the monk to a different level of understanding. After the teaching has been used, it is seen as provisional and laid aside for a higher teaching. The canonical image for this is the raft that takes the monk across the river to the farther shore, and then is discarded as he moves onto land.[70] The path is, in a way, self-destructing or, as the Fire Sermon would have it, "on fire"; each teaching or doctrine is measured by its ability to take one to a certain stage along the way. After that stage has been reached, the teaching is discarded.[71]

Richard Gombrich on the Fire Sermon in the *Mahavagga*

This excursus into Buddhist theories of language and hermeneutics is vital in our evaluation of the Fire Sermon because it helps us understand the sermon's place in the *Mahavagga*. The Fire Sermon as it appears in Warren represents the Buddha's ultimate teaching on desire and grasping. However, I believe that Eliot knew more of the significance of this sermon, based on his work with early Buddhist texts. Indeed, a full translation of the *Mahavagga* appeared in Max Müller's *Sacred Books of the East* series, published in 1881. Richard Gombrich has convincingly shown that the Fire Sermon only takes on its true significance at the end of a long narrative at the beginning of the *Mahavagga* that not only shows the conversion of the priests of Agni but also provides a model for what would later be known as skillful means.[72] I would take this reading one step further and argue that the linguistic basis for skillful means is also presented here. The priests of the Vedic sacrifice were also the poets of the Vedic hymns, and Agni, the god of the sacrifice, was associated in some hymns with Vac, the goddess of sacred speech. The conventional nature of language enables the Buddha to adapt his message to his audience. The belief that language is conventional removes the divine authority from sacred speech and paves the way, in the Buddhist context, to locating authority in the truth of enlightenment itself.

I have already presented the basic ideological doctrines that "fire" was meant to represent in the Fire Sermon. I noted that the flames are the three flames of "passion," "hatred," and "infatuation," and that they are meant to express the passionate attachment of human beings not only to objects in the world but to themselves as selves. Further, following Gombrich and Collins, I suggested that this imagery was intended to reappropriate the symbolism of the three fires of the Vedic sacrifice, as well as the fires of the Vedic householder. In his elucidative reading of this episode from the *Mahavagga*, Gombrich also shows how this very reappropriation is in fact a paradigmatic instance of what would later be called skillful means: the Buddha adopts the imagery of the interlocutors and revalues it.[73] Discussing the Fire Sermon's Pali title, *Aditta-pariyaya* ("the way of putting things as being on fire"), Gombrich notes, "When he [i.e., the Buddha] resorted to figurative or other indirect modes of expression, this is called *pariyāya*, literally 'a way round'; it is 'a way of putting things.'"[74] Thus, even the traditional title of the text highlights the Buddha's ability to manipulate figurative language and various genres of discourse to his own ends. We should not abandon the idea that this passage provides a "sermon," however. This text presents the genre of the sermon as not only a vehicle to convey information to the listeners, but as a deployment of figurative language to inspire a change of heart; the Buddha wants to change the way the world is seen and to move his listeners to different types of action in the world. The text implies that such genres are necessary in the Buddhist path.

The beginning of the *Mahavagga* contains one of the most important passages of all for later developments of the concept of skillful means, the famous story of Brahma's pleading.[75] The beginning of the story depicts the Buddha after his enlightenment, meditating upon the chain of dependent origination.[76] Shortly thereafter, the text depicts the Buddha in debate with himself over whether he will actually preach the *Dhamma*. He is initially inclined not to do it, as the teaching is very difficult to comprehend, and most people are too mired in desire to do so. If he were to preach to such people, thought the Buddha, "there would result but weariness and annoyance to me."[77] At the prospect of the Buddha remaining silent, the god Brahma three times pleads desperately with the Buddha to preach the *Dhamma*.

The Buddha accedes to Brahma's request and does so in a manner that implies that he will indeed need to preach to a whole range of aptitudes in his ministry. The *Mahavagga* describes the scene:

> Then the Blessed One, when he had heard Brahma's solicitation, looked, full of compassion towards sentient beings, over the world, with his (all-perceiving) eye of a Buddha. And the Blessed One, looking over the world with his eye of a Buddha, saw beings whose mental eyes were darkened by scarcely any dust, and beings whose eyes were covered by much dust, beings sharp of sense and blunt of sense, of good disposition and of bad disposition, easy to instruct and difficult to instruct, some of them seeing the dangers of future life and sin . . .
>
> . . . and when he had seen them, he addressed Brahmā Sahampati in the following stanza: "Wide opened is the door of the Immortal to all who have ears to hear; let them send forth faith to meet it. The Dhamma sweet and good I spake not, Brahma, despairing of the weary task, to men."[78]

138   DESIRE AND THE ASCETIC IDEAL

The Buddha makes his decision out of his compassion, awakened by Brahma's pleading. The text compares the Buddha's own "all-perceiving" eye with the defiled "mental eyes" of those in the world. Their different aptitudes are here represented by different levels of "dust" miring their sight. The implication, however, is that when the *Dhamma* is preached to them, their sight can also become pure (eventually), much as the Buddha's eye is pure. The Buddha does not place his own understanding at a divine distance from those to whom he will preach. Their sight is mired by dust, but that dust can and will be removed, to enable them to see reality as it is. The "door of the Immortal is open to all who have ears to hear": if they send forth faith, the *Dhamma* will meet them halfway.

In his analysis of this passage, Gombrich notes the irony that it is Brahma who grovels in this way toward the Buddha, especially given the importance of the term *brahman* in early Indian religion.[79] In the Upanishads, the highest form of knowledge was the realization of the oneness of one's own *atman*/self with *brahman*, the sacred power of the universe. The term *brahman*, however, had a wide set of significations and associations at the time of the Buddha. *Brahman* could mean any true statement, or it could refer to the Vedas themselves.[80] It could also refer to the Brahman priest of the Vedic sacrifice, whose duty it was to follow the entire sacrifice in his mind, identifying and remedying the mistakes committed in the proceedings.[81] Finally, the related term "Brahmin" refers to the *varna* of the priesthood in general, those qualified by lineage and education to wield the power of the sacrifice. Given this web of signification, Gombrich notes how outrageous the passage from the *Mahavagga* actually is: "So here the epitome of all that brahmins hold sacred is presented, in personified form, as humbling himself before the Buddha, declaring that the Buddha has opened the door to immortality (which brahmins had claimed to lie in or through Brahman), and begging him to reveal the truth to the world."[82] Further, I would add, the more egalitarian sense of the Buddha's teaching is also apparent. The truth the Buddha possesses may be possessed by all sentient creatures. It will not be wielded only within the confines of the ritual field but will be pronounced in the debate halls and the civic parks.

This passage at the outset of the *Mahavagga* merely sets up the rest of the narrative, which is, as Gombrich persuasively argues, an allegory ultimately regarding the Buddha's power to teach and to teach differently at different stages of the way.[83] The text describes the Buddha's first converts to the Sangha. After converting them, he sends them forth to preach the *Dhamma,* "which is glorious in the beginning, glorious in the middle, glorious at the end, in the spirit and in the letter; [they are to] proclaim a consummate, perfect, and pure life of holiness."[84] Note the hermeneutical distinctions the Buddha presents as he sends his monks out: the *Dhamma's* "beginning . . . middle . . . end" could refer to the discourses the monks will use, or they could refer to different teachings at different stages of the path. We have already discussed the distinction between the "letter" and the "spirit" of the text, and here the Buddha asserts that both levels are "glorious."

Shortly thereafter, the text dives into the narration of the Buddha's conversion of the Vedic ascetics, or Gatilas, worshippers of Agni, the fire god of the sacrifice. The Buddha visits the land of three of their leaders, Uruvela Kassapa, Nadi Kassapa, and Gaya Kassapa. As he visits Uruvela Kassapa, he asks to sleep "where your (sacred) fire is kept."[85] While sleeping in the fire house, the Buddha twice does battle with a "Naga (or Serpent) king of great magical power, a dreadfully venomous serpent,"[86] who battles him with fire. The battles are, apparently, quite a spectacle:

> When he saw that Kassapa had given his permission, fearlessly He, who had overcome all fear, entered. When the chief of Serpents saw that the Sage had entered, he became irritated, and sent forth a cloud of smoke. Then the chief of men, joyful and unperplexed, also sent forth a cloud of smoke. Unable to master his rage, the chief of Serpents sent forth flames like a burning fire. Then the chief of men, the perfect master of the element of fire, also sent forth flames. When they shone forth both with their flames, the Gatilas looked at the fire room (saying), "Truly the countenance of the great Samana is beautiful, but the Nāga will do harm to him."
>
> And when the night had elapsed, the flames of the Nāga were extinguished, but the various-coloured flames of Him who is possessed of magical powers remained. Dark blue and red, light red, yellow, and crystal-coloured flames of various colours appeared on the Angirasa's body. Having put the chief of Serpents into his alms-bowl, he showed him to the Brāhmana (saying), "Here you see the Nāga, Kassapa; his fire has been conquered by my fire."
>
> And the Gatila Uruvelā Kassapa, having conceived an affection for the Blessed One in consequence of this wonder, said to the

140   DESIRE AND THE ASCETIC IDEAL

Blessed One: "Stay with me, great Samana, I will daily provide you with food."[87]

The first thing to note is the aesthetic quality of the battles: the Naga and the Buddha both fight with flames, but the Buddha's flames are "various coloured."[88] Indeed, the Gatilas (those who will later be thoroughly converted) are struck by the beauty of the Buddha's display: "Truly the countenance of the great Samana is beautiful." The end result of the battle is not the conversion of the Gatilas; rather, it is the fact that Uruvela "conceived an affection for the Blessed One" and offers to supply him with food. The Buddha's display of wondrous power not only impresses the Gatilas aesthetically but induces one of their leaders to feel affectively connected with the Buddha. This affective connection will clearly be surpassed at the moment of the Fire Sermon, but for now it seems a necessary prerequisite to full conversion.

Part of what inspires this affection is the fact that the Buddha rids the Kassapas of a serpent who has been living in the sacred fire house. This would seem to be a benefit to the fire sacrifice practiced by the priests. Indeed, later in the narrative the Buddha performs activities that help the priests with the sacrifice: he chops wood for them, lights the fires, and extinguishes the fires. The Buddha begins by assisting the priests in their own activities. But the Buddha's display against the Nagas also subtly places him in a superior position to Agni, who, apparently, cannot rid his own house of the Nagas. In fact, he is not even personified as Brahma is. Further, as Gombrich notes, the Buddha is called an "Angirasa," a title that places him in direct conflict with the god of the sacrifice:

Āṅgirasa is a Vedic *gotra*, and it is by virtue of being a Gautama, says Brough, that he is so addressed. . . . In the *Ṛg Veda*, however, Aṅgiras is a class of supermen, standing between men and gods, and Agni, the personification of fire, is the first and foremost Aṅgīras. In other texts too the Buddha is called Aṅgīrasa when he is said to shine very brilliantly. . . . So in this passage he is virtually impersonating Agni, the brahmins' fire god. This looks less like a debate than a takeover bid.[89]

Agni is the foremost Angiras because he is the mediator between human beings and the gods who benefit from the offerings of the sacrifice. By burning the offerings, Agni takes them to the gods. The Buddha places himself in the position of mediator, but in his case he is a mediator between human beings and the ultimate truth, the tranquility of *nibbana*. In this sense, just as Agni sets flame to the offerings of the sacrifice, the Buddha makes an "offering" of the entire world, showing all things to be "on fire." Further, his mediation proceeds first through miracles, aesthetic displays of power, and compassionate works that build affection; only later does it culminate in an unvarnished discourse of truth. Indeed, the text itself attempts to elicit an aesthetic reaction, since it switches to verse, to *arya* meter, to describe the Buddha as Angirasa.[90] Gombrich is surely correct to insist that the text's long preface to the final act of preaching the Fire Sermon is meant to draw attention to the Buddha's "skillful means," his ability to appropriate the opponent's imagery, enter into his thought-world, and prepare them through various stages for the final, ultimate teaching.[91] The text in fact shows us the various stages of conversion, from the initial affection to a realization of error, to the final decisive awakening.

Asceticisms Compared

Eliot's own "Fire Sermon" concludes with the "Song of the (three) Thames-daughters."[92] This song culminates in a complex sonnet.[93] The traditional form of romantic love has become an expression of Schopenhauer's pessimism in which the characters have been robbed of meaningful existence. The first invokes Dante's La Pia from *Purgatorio* and sings of sexual violation, "'Supine on the floor of a narrow canoe.'"[94] The second sings of a song of repentance after a violation; she cannot bring herself to moral outrage: "'I made no comment. What should I resent?'"[95] Existence could not promise her anything, nor could her lover.[96] There is nothing to resent, because there has been nothing promised. And the third, singing the sestet, echoes the obsession with nothingness we have seen earlier in the poem, especially in the dialogue scene: "'I can connect / Nothing with nothing . . . My people humble people who expect / Nothing.'"[97] Like the previous daughter, this daughter's "people" expect "nothing" from existence. There is no reason to engage with life, for life makes no promises.

And yet, A. D. Moody, Nancy Gish, and Cleo Kearns have argued that there is a hint of promise here. Moody asserts that part of the promise lies in the utter clarity and honesty of the Thames daughters. They have

142   DESIRE AND THE ASCETIC IDEAL

achieved a vital self-knowledge: "The speakers express their state fully and lucidly in the bare essentials. And this honesty, this articulate integrity, is the rarely heard voice of self-knowledge, giving a direct vision of the life that is being lived."[98] This would seem to imply that out of their suffering, they have achieved a level of transcendence to be able to reflect upon and compose it. Likewise Donald Childs sees them as presenting a "judgment" on that which they represent, singing to express "a desire to escape desire."[99] And Nancy Gish sees promise in the ability of the Thames daughters to "tell their own stories and set them in the ironic context of the changing river and changing behavior."[100]

On the other hand, Kearns persuasively argues for a positive valence to the song based on the Buddhist perspective (and the section's title clearly invites this perspective), though I believe even she does not fully grasp the ascetic potential of these lines. In her reading, the recognition of the "nothingness" of all things is crucial in regarding other beings ethically and in ultimately achieving the Buddhist soteriological goals, though she believes that the end of the song ultimately comes to rest in nihilism.[101] However, the idea of "connecting" nothing with nothing is a relatively good description not only of the crucial soteriological recognition but of the Buddhist path itself, which connects objects in the world that may be seen as conventionally real but are ultimately empty of any essence, really nothing. The prospect of connecting nothing with nothing in that instance may imply a telos for the sake of which those things are connected, a signified that lies in the distant future, at the end of a process of development and cultivation. The Buddha can use "nothingness," can use empty phenomena and empty texts to bring his listeners to higher realizations.

It is perhaps no coincidence then that this meditation comes in the sestet, which can be seen either as an intensification of the pessimism of the octave or a turn from it. Here it is both. The dual vision the poem provides on pessimism mirrors the dual vision it has provided throughout on death. And yet, the sonnet form hints again at musical seduction. It is, after all, an erotic form, though often one expressing alienation from the beloved. In this context, it is a song form, an ordered organization of thought and emotion, that points to nothingness. The sonnet itself connects nothing with nothing. It is a bid for compassion—as is La Pia's prayer—and a transformation of suffering. And it leads into allusions to two ascetic texts that stress the ascetic potential of the metaphysical marginalization of objects in the world.

The poem concludes with what Eliot refers to, in his bizarre endnotes, as a "collocation" of ascetic fragments. He writes, "The collocation of these two representatives of eastern and western asceticism, as the culmination of this part of the poem, is not an accident."[102] The poem reads:

> To Carthage then I came
>
> Burning burning burning burning
> O Lord Thou pluckest me out
> O Lord Thou pluckest
>
> burning[103]

The references to burning most obviously evoke the Buddha's Fire Sermon in its diagnosis of the errors of human desire. Likewise, the first Augustine reference ("To Carthage then I came") explores the ethical consequences of the diseased will:

> To Carthage I came, where there sang all around me in my ears a cauldron of unholy loves. I loved not yet, yet I loved to love, and out of a deep-seated want, I hated myself for wanting not. I sought what I might love, in love with loving, and safety I hated, and a way without snares. For within me was a famine of that inward food, Thyself, my God; yet, through that famine I was not hungered; but was without all longing for incorruptible sustenance, not because filled therewith, but the more empty, the more I loathed it. For this cause my soul was sickly and full of sores, it miserably cast forth, desiring to be scraped by the touch of objects of sense. Yet if these had not a soul, they would not be objects of love. To love then, and to be loved, was sweet to me; but more, when I obtained to enjoy the person I loved.[104]

The passage picks up on the wandering theme from the end of book 2. Because Augustine does not rest in the peaceful stasis of divine love, he wanders abroad in search of objects upon which to exercise his lust. This is rhetorically reinforced by the movement in the first line: "To Carthage I came." Given the division of the self presented at the end of book 2, it is significant that Augustine has not yet turned within, to come to *himself,* as it were. Rather, he comes to the city of Carthage, "where there sang all around me in my ears a cauldron of unholy loves." Pusey takes some poetic liberties here: Augustine actually imagines himself within a "frying pan" (*sartago*),[105] heated by flames from below. His frying pan sizzles; it makes noise all around him (*circumstrepebat*) as its contents burn.[106] Heated desire gives rise to noise, or perhaps even to anguished human shouts. It is an image of captivity, the soul trapped in the heated pan, incapable of resisting the compelling power of desire's intense heat. In fact, the soul is even incapable of desiring such freedom: "and safety I hated, and a way without snares."

What exactly does Augustine think love is at this moment in the text? He uses the imagery of hunger to describe the love to which he drove himself, though he describes this in a negative way: "For within me was a famine of that inward food, Thyself, my God; yet, through that famine I was not hungered; but was without all longing for incorruptible sustenance, not because filled therewith, but the more empty, the more I loathed it." Augustine does not hunger for the divine food, and the emptier he is of such fare, the less he desires it. The implication is that Augustine does hunger for other fare, for that which can be physically consumed. As he fills himself with the satisfaction of his lusts, he becomes more empty in his soul. Love, therefore, for the young Augustine, is the search for physical objects of love that can be consumed into the body. It is a subsuming of the other into the self.

And yet Augustine's rhetorical brilliance shines through here. Just as he suggests that the beloved is like food to be taken within the self, he asserts that at the time his senses desired to be stimulated from without. He writes that his soul "miserably casts itself forth, desiring to be scraped by the touch of objects of sense. Yet if these had not a soul, they would not be objects of love." The soul, in its movement into the outside world, casts itself on its own agency toward objects. But the soul desires to have these objects "scrape" it. The soul looks for the influence of the object on the self. But this kind of contact only comes through the love of another soul, another vital principle, influencing the self in a reciprocal way. The young Augustine does not view his relationships in this way; he "defiled, therefore, the spring of friendship with the filth of concupiscence, and [. . .] beclouded its brightness with the hell of lustfulness." To see another human being as just another object in the world is to make a mockery of love's true friendship, to reduce the soul's mutual relation with another human being to a relation of the self with an object. Thus Augustine looks to "enjoy the person I loved."

It is here that we have our first provocative analogy with the earlier Buddhist texts. The suffering human being, in Theravada Buddhism, grasped or consumed objects in the world, drawing them into consciousness through its intentionality, *chetana*. Language marked and enabled this desire by giving nominal reality to impermanent entities. The individual mired in this grasping was fated to continue by projecting this grasping into future states of consciousness. Augustine's text more strongly emphasizes the social nature of language and the immediate ethical consequences of reification yet agrees that linguistic categories perpetuate sinful human desires, instantiate attachment, and pervert the will. Whether the concept of *chetana* is similar or analogous to Augustine's idea of the will is a matter of some scholarly debate, and I cannot enter fully into that discussion here.[107] What I would simply like to observe (and what I think Eliot's poem is prompting us to observe) is that both Buddhist intention and Augustinian will seem to refer to the overwhelming existential orientations that encompass intellectual understanding, human motivation, and affectivity.

Given this stringent critique of desire, it may seem strange, then, that the second passage cited by Eliot ("O Lord Thou pluckest me out / O Lord Thou pluckest") is one that validates beautiful human artifacts, albeit with qualification. Augustine's passage decrying sinful human desire is placed side by side with a later passage insisting on the presence of divine paradigms of beauty inherent in human artistic works. The passage comes as Augustine meditates on the temptations of the eyes, yet the resonances go much further. The passage is worth quoting in full:

> What innumerable toys, made by divers arts and manufactures, in our apparel, shoes, utensils and all sort of works, in pictures also and divers images, and these far exceeding all necessary and moderate use and all pious meaning, have men added to tempt their own eyes withal; outwardly following what themselves make, inwardly forsaking Him by whom themselves were made, and destroying that which themselves have been made! But I, my God and my Glory, do hence also sing a hymn to Thee and do consecrate praise to

Him who consecrateth me, because those beautiful patterns which through men's souls are conveyed into their cunning hands, come from that Beauty, Which is above our souls, Which my soul day and night sigheth after. But the framers and followers of the outward beauties derive thence the rule of judging of them, but not of using them. And He is there, though they perceive Him not, that so they might not wander, but *keep their strength for Thee,* and not scatter it abroad upon pleasurable wearinesses. And I, though I speak and see this, entangle my steps with these outward beauties; but Thou pluckest me out, O Lord, Thou pluckest me out; *because Thy loving-kindness is before my eyes.* For I am taken miserably, and Thou pluckest me out mercifully; sometimes not perceiving it, when I had but lightly lighted upon them; otherwhiles with pain, because I had stuck fast in them.[108]

Augustine once again brings up the specter of solipsism, describing how human beings become trapped in a round of sinful desiring. He denigrates created human artifacts as "toys," though he also realizes that such artifacts surround human beings on the most basic levels of lived existence. These are our "apparel, shoes, utensils and all sort of works, in pictures also and divers images." These are artifacts we literally cannot do without. At the same time, these are images that are made specifically to "tempt" human beings, to provoke more diseased desire. Humans are guilty of "outwardly following what themselves make, inwardly forsaking Him by whom themselves were made, and destroying that which themselves have been made!" Augustine's analysis is reminiscent of Buddhist theories of attachment; human beings trap themselves in the external artifacts of their own making, and this attachment is self-perpetuating. However, Augustine's problem, in distinction to that of the Buddha, is that these artifacts alienate the self from its inner reality, the place within where God speaks to the soul. The Buddhist analysis of consciousness seeks to end human consciousness so that the practitioner may experience the serenity of *nibbana.* Augustine thinks that the knowledge of God will be a nondiscursive mode of knowing, but his emphasis lies in the issue of the alienation from the God within and beyond. This alienation reproduces itself, involving the sinner in a cycle of alienation and repetition in which desire moves from external object to external object without rest. As the self moves further and further away from the divine speech within, it reiterates its sinful ways and slowly destroys the self.

The crucial turning point in the passage comes as Augustine produces a "conversion" of sorts within his own prose. At the midpoint of the passage Augustine's prose turns from a lament into a psalm of praise and sacrifice, in which the author praises the source of his own existence and regeneration. Pusey translates the verb *sacrifico* as "consecrate," though he gives the initial Latin in a footnote: "Sacrifico laudem Sacrificatori meo."[109] Praise is offered as a sacrifice to the God who sacrificed himself for the author's regeneration. Augustine's conversion is therefore placed at the turning point of this passage. This conversion occurs as God validates beauty, and serves as a guard against becoming ensnared in it.

The defense of beauty emerges from an assertion of the natural goodness of God's creation, a goodness that shines forth even in the sinful artifacts of human beings: "those beautiful patterns which through men's souls are conveyed into their cunning hands, come from that Beauty, Which is above our souls, Which my soul day and night sigheth after. But the framers and followers of the outward beauties, derive thence the rule of judging them, but not of using them." Human souls still operate with the divine criterion of beauty, but the beauty that is delivered over to their "cunning hands" (*in manus artificiosas*)[110] becomes distorted. Likewise, the "framers and followers of the outward beauties" possess a faculty of judging beauty that is also divine. However, though these human creators operate with the divine standards of judgment, they do not know how to "use" their talents to praise God and move closer to God. In many ways, Augustine's text is meant to give an example of how the rule of beauty can be followed in praising God and moving more and more toward an encounter with the inner beauty, God's presence to the soul. In this, Augustine mirrors the rhetoric of Ambrose in book 5, which works its way into Augustine's mind, seducing him onward toward conversion:

> I hung on his words attentively; but of the matter I was as a careless and scornful looker-on; and I was delighted with the sweetness of his discourse. . . . For though I took no pains to learn what he spake, but only to hear how he spake . . . yet together with the words which I would choose, came also into my mind the things which I would

148 DESIRE AND THE ASCETIC IDEAL

> refuse; for I could not separate them. And while I opened my heart
> to admit "how eloquently he spake," there also entered "how truly
> he spake;" but this by degrees.[111]

Augustine first experiences the "sweetness" and the pleasure associated
with Ambrose's rhetoric, but this pleasure enables the truth of the discourse to burrow its way into Augustine's mind slowly, "by degrees." The
aesthetic moment provides the gate to a higher level of truth. Augustine's
heart opens with beauty, and he inadvertently allows the truth in.

Augustine, however, knows that he has not arrived at the culmination
of the ascent. He is a work in progress, and he still stumbles on external beauty: "And I, though I speak and see this, entangle my steps with
these outward beauties; but Thou pluckest me out, O Lord, Thou pluckest me out." Despite Augustine's conversion, he still becomes entangled
in improper desire and imperfect beauty. God's intervention is needed
to "pluck out" Augustine's soul from the traps in which it becomes entangled, and at times this is a painful moment: "Thou pluckest me out
mercifully; sometimes not perceiving it, when I had but lightly lighted
upon them; otherwhiles with pain, because I had stuck fast in them."
The judgment of beauty develops, and God's grace must extract the soul
from its entanglement in beautiful images, pictures, and texts when such
attachment is detrimental to the soul. However, in a way, such attachments will always at some point be detrimental to the soul, since they are
not God. God alone is to be loved for His own sake, and all other things
for the sake of God. So even the beautiful artifacts made in the spirit of
praising God must ultimately give way to a more profound communion
and a deeper insight.

We begin to see yet another broad analogy with the Buddhist texts,
this time with the concept of *upaya*, or skillful means. The Buddha relied, in the *Mahavagga*, on displays of great beauty to establish bonds
of affection with the priests of Agni. Only later did he "pluck them out" of
aesthetic desire to bring them to the ultimate Buddhist truth. In fact,
though the Buddha was enlightened, he entered into the Vedic ideologies,
subtly modifying them for his own purposes, bringing the priests to a
place where they could perceive a greater truth. The early Buddhist texts
walk a fine line on the idea of beauty. It appears to be necessary at the
outset of the path, but the beauty of these texts must also be overcome.
The Buddha is "skillful" precisely because he knows how to "play with

fire," wielding dangerous linguistic, figurative fireworks for his own purposes. Likewise, for Augustine, the beauty of the world attests to God, who is Beauty itself. God's agency is needed to move the believer beyond earthly beauty to its Source. Still, as we saw with the Buddha, God must use the existing texts and ideologies to bring the self to a larger truth; in order to reach this situated self, God puts affectivity to use, engaging the individual through feeling and thought. Just as the *Mahavagga* will revalue and reappropriate Vedic images and narratives in an effort to reach its listeners through familiar tropes, so too will *Confessions* wrest classical myths and tropes from their sources, correlating them with biblical imagery in an effort to dislocate and relocate the reader's understanding.

As with the Indian texts, the progress toward the soteriological goal for Augustine is the cultivation of memory and desire, to the point where the self is effaced at the culmination of the path. Indeed, Eliot's poetry loses the "me" in its lines: "O Lord Thou pluckest me out / O Lord Thou pluckest."[112] Kearns, in fact, notes that not only is the "me" gone, but the progress of the verse eliminates the "Lord" here too, "leaving only the process of burning."[113] Paradoxically it is in and through the cultivation of the self and the exploration of memory that the self transcends its own solipsism, that it escapes its own self-destructive understanding and habitus and becomes united with the divine. God's intervention in Augustine's life plants its "seeds" in his memory, and these seeds insinuate themselves over time to take control of his existence. Augustine's own act of writing the *Confessions* is an attempt to exercise the memory, seeking these seeds of God's intervention in the hopes of moving closer and closer again to that light of Being, that voice in the heart of the self that declares itself to be the Creator.

I would therefore argue that Eliot presents *Confessions* and the early Buddhist texts side by side to draw a comparison between the processes by which desire is fueled and those by which the ultimate goal of a soteriological path is reached. In the Fire Sermon, fire depicts the desire that fuels the round of *samsara,* the desire that works through all of the senses. It also depicts the ultimately unreal, nonessential nature of things in the world and the process by which this nonessential nature is realized; that is, through the causal analysis of the Buddha and the practices of the path. The Fire Sermon realizes that *nibbana* means the extinguishing of desire along with all its instruments, including language. Yet it also knows that, like Augustine's text, language can have a positive role to play in the

150   DESIRE AND THE ASCETIC IDEAL

pursuit of the soteriological goal, pointing beyond itself to its ineffable consummation.

Language is enabled, for both Augustine and the early Buddhists, when the influence of the "other" beyond language (either the enlightened Buddha or God) enters into the linguistic categories, metaphors, and narratives of the time, and transforms them for soteriological purposes. Both God and the Buddha utilize "skillful means" to draw human beings toward the truth. In entering into these categories, they interrupt them and modify them, shifting the ideological emphases and beginning the subtle technologies of salvation. Such a model of being drawn through language by an influence beyond language may seem strange outside a religious context, but Eliot, in the final section of *The Waste Land,* places this concept in both a theological *and* ethical context.

The jarring dissonance is the strongly theological slant of Augustine's path and the intentionally, polemically nontheological teaching of the Buddha. Augustine's God is the fullness of Being that *itself* has agency; there is no such fullness for the Buddha, and *nibbana* has no such agency. Further, influenced by Neoplatonism, Augustine's God is the God of beauty; the experience of the beauty of the world plays a much larger role in Augustine than it does in the Buddhist texts, mainly because Augustine is concerned with maintaining the goodness of all creation in light of the challenges of theodicy. This tension is partly resolved and partly exacerbated in the final section of *The Waste Land.* Eliot in his conclusion prefers the comparison with the more theologically inclined Upanishads. However, in the final section, the poem depicts a situation in which the divine voice within the heart can only be heard when the self is made so empty that the voice can resound. And this, ultimately, may be one reason the end of section III feels so severe. If one is too attached to selfhood, losing it will seem the worst form of torment. The prospect of transcending it will be horrifying. If one sees the self as alienating, as many Western mystics did, its loss is ultimate gain.

In light of Buddhist-Christian polemics in the nineteenth century, Eliot's juxtaposition would initially seem to be one of two jarring worlds. Augustine's contemplative path, with its Neoplatonic emphases on the pursuit of Beauty and the striving after the One of absolute Being, would seem to be at odds with the relentless critique of essence found in the early Buddhist texts. There is no doubt that Eliot wishes the reader to experience the dissonance of these two different soteriological imperatives. But Eliot also wants to provoke the two traditions into a situation of mutual illumination in which the tensions between the two do not impede the curious consonances from emerging. Ultimately, Eliot seems interested not in comparing the final referents of these texts, but rather in perceiving *how* they conceive religious language and its implication in the contemplative path.

5

TRANSCENDENCE REVISITED

Hallucination and Literary Asceticism

In reading the conclusion of *The Waste Land*, I intend to make use of Calvin Bedient's hermeneutical lens. Recall from chapter 3 that Bedient emphasized the performative nature of *The Waste Land*, suggesting that the poem be viewed as a series of poetic performances with the goal of approaching an Absolute beyond history and language.[1] Bedient argues that the concluding section of Eliot's poem represents the performance of an "allegory" of ascent that leads to "a more austere and syncretic metaphysics of the unnameable."[2] This allegory takes the form of a "metaphysical vision" that Bedient asserts begins with the mysterious "third" that appears in the poem.[3] With this interpretation I am in substantial agreement. Indeed, I want to highlight the role the Indian texts play in representing the culmination of this allegory and in theorizing such an ascent that proceeds in and through fragments combining thought and feeling. I suggest that the protreptic pedagogy of the Upanishads and the Buddhist *upaya* provide a model for thinking about this gradual ascetic performance. In other words, the Indian texts provide not only the imagery for the allegory but also resources for conceptualizing such an ascent in the first place.

In the previous chapters, we saw that section III of *The Waste Land* ended with a complex comparison between Augustine's *Confessions* and the Buddha's Fire Sermon, one that evoked the Buddha's concept of skillful means, or *upaya*. The poem momentarily reaches the possibility that desire can be engaged in a path of cultivation leading to liberation from the cycle of memory and desire. In this chapter, I examine the poem's presentation of Indian materials at its conclusion. I argue that *The Waste Land* utilizes passages from the *Brhadaranyaka Upanishad* in presenting itself potentially as a constituent part of a similar path of contemplative and ethical praxis. Such a praxis attempted to provide "seeds" of memory to challenge the presumptions of the self and lead the self to release from its own solipsism. In *The Waste Land,* this release could only come in a realization of the emptiness in the heart of the self and a surrendering of the self's pretensions to sufficiency.

It may seem strange that, after the Buddhist fragments earlier, the poem invokes the Upanishads at its conclusion. However, I suggest that this reinforces the poem's focus on *upaya* and ascetic cultivation. Recall Jonardon Ganeri's observation that the kind of teaching represented in the *upaya* doctrine, a protreptic pedagogy, had its forebears in the Upanishads:

> The startling idea of the Hindu Vedantins, again, is that the way out of colossal error is to embed within the illusion the catalyst of its own destruction. The Upanishad is a "Trojan text," a false gift that will blow up in the mind of its recipient, destroying the error of which it too is a part. It is a false vehicle with a true content. Here I will introduce the idea of a "procedural use of reason," that application of reason and argument that levers one out of error, itself a practice of truth. It will seem that what one needs is to be able to appreciate a text, as one does a painting; if the text or the painting then turns out to be a fake, and can be seen to be so as a result of one's appreciation of it having done its inner work, does that really matter so much?[4]

Ganeri characterizes the Upanishads as self-destructive texts; once they have done their work in situating the self in a certain way, they undo themselves, reducing themselves to silence. Such texts are "performative" and "transformative,"[5] challenging the reader to perform the interpretation to bring them to a higher level of understanding. Once this happens, the performance is marginalized; it was necessary at the time, but it has been transcended. As an example, Ganeri gives the tale of Indra and Virocana in the *Chandogya Upanishad,* 8.7.1–8.12.6. In this story, the two gods ask Prajapati several times about the truth of the self. Indra, pondering each answer, comes to know its inadequacy, returning to Prajapati for instruction. Each time Prajapati gives a more detailed account until he reaches his ultimate teaching. Ganeri characterizes each inferior teaching as a "preparatory condition" for the higher ones.[6] Ganeri finds this graduated process of teaching to be operative throughout the Upanishads. Further, since the self cannot be an object among objects for the Upanishadic authors, the student must operate by considering the metaphors, similes, and differing conceptions of the truth of the self at different times, in the hopes of obliquely grasping the truth of the self in the gradual process of coming to an understanding.[7] For Ganeri, the Upanishadic tradition and the Buddhist tradition are united in emphasizing the necessity for engaging in such "practices of truth."[8]

In *The Waste Land*, Eliot chooses an Upanishadic passage—the myth of the thunder—that highlights the ability of language to conceal and reveal, to signify and be marginalized, in a path of ascetic development. It is also a passage in which Prajapati, much like the Buddha, acknowledges the legitimacy of different representations of truth and understanding. Prajapati speaks the same truth to gods, demons, and humans, and these classes receive the truth differently according to their capacities. Prajapati acknowledges that each interpretation has legitimacy, that the teaching can take different forms depending on the listener's situation. And his injunctions issue forth in praxis, not simply in intellectual truth. The understanding of truth goes hand in hand with activity.

The dream passages from the *Upanishad* cited in the poem, on the other hand, depict the dream state as a path of image and memory through which the self passes on the way to the oblivion of deep sleep. *The Waste Land* places itself potentially within such a path, mobilizing the fragments of memory and asking whether they can draw the self onward toward a loss of self. Eliot uses the thunder passage from the *Upanishad* to signify the divine speech in the heart of the self, a speech that transforms desire and enables selfless activity in the world. Most importantly, the presence of the *Brhadaranyaka Upanishad* at the conclusion of the poem, at the very culmination of ascesis, provides a crucial conclusion to Eliot's meditation on solipsism. The Indian texts in the poem both represent the reality of divine address and show themselves to be fragmentary constituents of the path toward the silent end point of ascesis. In *The Waste Land*, the textual productions of the cultural, geographical other have a potential to challenge the understandings of the self, while at the same time enabling the self to continue the process of re-signification. In other words, they both challenge and enable poesis.

All this might seem to some to drastically overread the end of the poem as an unambiguously positive, religious conclusion. To some extent this is correct. In reality, the positive fragments here appear as a dubious hallucination. They emerge as dreams from within a pessimistic framework. In terms of Eliot's early philosophy, it is one point of view or perspective taking another into consideration as a possibility. In *Knowledge and Experience,* Eliot writes, "For we vary by passing from one point of view to another or . . . by occupying more than one point of view at the same time, an attitude which gives us our assumptions, our half-objects, our figments of imagination; we vary by self-transcendence."[9] When one attempts to occupy two points of view, the possibility exists that one will consider first one and then the other as hallucinations or dreams. From one perspective, the other perspective may first make a claim on oneself as a kind of dream, something unreal. I am suggesting that a premodern, ascetic ideal emerges in *The Waste Land* as just such a hallucination, daring the speaker to make a leap, and making the ending of the poem ultimately ambiguous. For this is an element of the poem that has not been sufficiently recognized: the ending of the poem is not ambiguous because its religiosity is being challenged by pessimism. The poem is ambiguous because its pessimism is being challenged by premodern, ascetic religion. My task here is to attempt to articulate how that other point of view appears in the poem. Ultimately, Eliot's poem puts the reader on trial, inciting him or her to decide whether a positive reading is even possible. Significantly, this very possibility is opened up by the presence of Indian texts in the poem.

The Beginning of the Vision and the Mysterious Third

Ultimately what is at stake in this conclusion is the status of human desire. In chapter 4, we examined Eliot's depiction of Baudelaire's engagement with the modern city. Eliot claimed that Baudelaire attempted to inhabit contemporary images of the city and to create new ones in order to liberate his readers. In examining Paris, Baudelaire is "presenting it as it is, and yet making it represent something much more than itself."[10] This excess in the depiction of the city mirrors the excess in human desire, a desire that aims beyond its relationships to something more. Eliot writes: "the reaching out towards something which cannot be had in, but which

156   DESIRE AND THE ASCETIC IDEAL

may be had partly *through*, personal relations. Indeed, in much romantic poetry the sadness is due to the exploitation of the fact that no human relations are adequate to human desires, but also to the disbelief in any further object for human desires than that which fails to satisfy them."[11] As Eliot states earlier, however, the recognition of suffering and the insufficiency of the "purely natural" and the "purely human" itself implies already the presence of the supernatural.[12]

The opening to section V begins with desire, or rather, thirst. This is a thirst both physical and spiritual. The speaker expresses not only the need for water but also the death and absence of a Christ-like figure: "He who was living in now dead / We who are living are now dying."[13] The anxiety here is of death, the death of this figure and the seeming impossibility of resurrection, and perhaps the anxiety that the "he" who is dead was ever only purely natural. The opening also, however, alludes to the beginning of the poem. The possibility for spring rain hovers on the horizon, with the "thunder of spring over the distant mountains."[14]

Recall that at the very beginning of the poem, rain was used in a complex metaphor to describe the purely immanent, solipsistic round of memory and desire, resonating with Schopenhauer's negative view of desire. The speaker in section V does not seem to await rain from the spring thunder. It is and is not expected, it is and is not desired. The question the poem raises is whether this rain—if it comes—will represent repetition or something more. In other words, will the awakening of desire again be purely natural and solipsistic, or will it be transformative? Another way of thinking about this is in thinking about the memory of the "he" who is now dead. Will this memory lead to a different kind of desire, or merely more of the same? And simultaneously, is the thirst of the speaker natural, or is there a presence of the supernatural within that thirst?

Just as Eliot's Baudelaire envisioned beatitude through suffering, this speaker has a visionary moment, though its ultimate significance, whether divine vision or hallucination from exhaustion, will remain ambiguous. On the verge of a literal and figurative death, a bizarre vision suddenly begins and continues right up until the very end of the poem, a vision that hovers on the edge of prophecy and hallucination.[15] It is an imagining of renewal, but one that emerges from an engagement with other human beings and a realization of the mortality of the self. Crucially, it begins by imagining not only an absent divine third but also the human dialogue partner:

> Who is the third who walks always beside you?
> When I count, there are only you and I together
> But when I look ahead up the white road
> There is always another one walking beside you
> Gliding wrapt in a brown mantle, hooded
> I do not know whether a man or a woman
> —But who is that on the other side of you?[16]

The temporal markers in this passage are significant. Whereas the opening of the section situated itself as "after," here the focus is on the present. The trochaic substitution on "always" places a dual emphasis on "walks always"; the temporal marker leaps out of the rhythmic texture. The mysterious "third" is always present next to the speaker's companion as they walk, now into the future. The fact that they are walking not only emphasizes the "now" of the interaction, but also gives the hint of a teleological dimension. Such a dimension had been crucially lacking earlier in the poem: Eliot's Londoners walked wearily without a telos, looking down at their feet. In contrast, in this passage Eliot's speaker constantly looks forward and over at his companion, whose presence has suddenly seemed to direct the self's attention both toward the future and toward the mysterious third. Ironically, when the self *gives* that attention to the third, it disappears.

Eliot tells us in his notes that this passage alludes to the Antarctic expedition of Ernest Shackleton: "it was recorded that the party of explorers, at the extremity of their strength, had the constant delusion that there was *one more member* than could actually be counted."[17] Rainey provides further details, giving Shackleton's own account of the vision, in which the explorer asserts that there always seemed a fourth person walking with him and his three companions. Shackleton could not explain the feeling: "When I look back at those days I have no doubt that Providence guided us, not only across those snow-fields, but across the storm-white sea.... One feels 'the dearth of human words, the roughness of mortal speech' in trying to describe things intangible, but a record of our journeys would be incomplete without a reference to a subject very near to our hearts."[18] Shackleton's description does not claim to be able to describe exactly what was felt with his companions, but it exists as testimony to a shared, felt experience at the limits of physical endurance. Further, for Shackleton it is an experience of Providence, of a guiding force to their travails. Shackleton and his men follow Providence into the Antarctic whiteness, as if they wander into the ineffable whiteness of a page, its letters left behind.

The more obvious allusion here is the appearance of Jesus to two disciples on the road to Emmaus after his resurrection. The travail of the speaker after the crucifixion is mirrored in these disciples who despair of ever seeing the Christ again. The disciples do not recognize Jesus, for "their eyes were holden that they should not know him."[19] But as they walk and discuss the death of Christ, Jesus begins to expound the tradition of prophecy concerning the Christ: "Ought not Christ to have suffered these things, and to enter into his glory? / And beginning at Moses and all the prophets, he expounded unto them in all the scriptures the things concerning himself."[20] Christ prepares the disciples for an ultimate recognition by placing himself within a prophetic tradition. Finally, it is only with the breaking of the bread, symbolic of Christ's crucifixion and the communal meals of the early church, that the eyes of the disciples are opened, and they recognize him. It is when they come to this realization that Jesus disappears: "And their eyes were opened, and they knew him; and he vanished out of their sight."[21] The disciples are left with the physical reaction they had when he spoke to them, and when they heard the Scriptures explained: "And they said one to another, Did not our heart burn within us, while he talked with us by the way, and while he opened to us the Scriptures?"[22]

Both passages deal with visions that are on the borderline between reality and hallucination and that describe a play of presence and absence. For example, on initial consideration, the vision Shackleton describes seems likely to have been a pure hallucination, and yet the feeling of the fourth is shared by the companions. If it was a hallucination, only a dream, it was a shared one. The disciples on the road to Emmaus suffer as well, though they, like the mountain figure, suffer from the absence of the teacher Jesus. They travel with the resurrected Lord, and yet when they can finally put a name to him, identify him positively through the reenactment of the Last Supper, when they realize his presence, Christ disappears from their sight. Christ's epiphany to them is only momentary.

Eliot's speaker, like the disciples, places himself after the death of an important figure, in the moment of remembered absence. And like Shackleton, he has his hallucination on the limits of physical and mental endurance. But even more unusually, the speaker of Eliot's poem hallucinates not only the "third," but a "second" as well. He addresses a "you," but there has not been a companion up until this very moment. Further, in the context of the image, the "third" is seen only out of the corner of the pilgrim's eye, across the body of the walking companion, never when the speaker looks directly at both. The "third" disappears under the scrutiny of direct vision and can only be seen obliquely. And even when seen, it is seen "hooded," in a "brown mantle," seemingly without gender ("I do not know whether a man or a woman"). The ambiguous gender of the figure echoes Tiresias from section III. The shape is discernibly human, but hidden under a veil.

Taken in the context of the problematics given at the beginning of the poem, however, we begin to see the possible beginnings of a solution to the solipsism of the self. The "third," perhaps a divinity that lies beyond humanity, appears in human suffering and in human discourse and makes itself known through visions whose reality can only be provisional. So provisional are they that their veracity can always be challenged within the vortex of cultural memory. The third also represents a mediating image, an image the speaker wishes to share with the imaginary companion.[23] The speaker continues to make appeals to the companion, asking him or her whether they share the vision: "Who is the third who walks always beside you? . . . But who is that on the other side of you?" Thus the speaker imagines an other and imagines an attempt to prompt the other to recognize the vision the self holds of the divine third.[24] The mutual recognition of the third would establish a new point of view and indicate a self-transcendence enabled by the other's recognition. Hence we have in a few brief lines the problem and potential of a poet writing for an audience, offering the "image" that occurs to him or her, imagining the other to whom he offers his vision. The appearance of the "third" has vast consequences for the self's journey through the self. Suddenly a startling vision emerges, culminating in the description of music welling up through "empty cisterns and exhausted wells"[25] and the arrival at the "empty chapel"[26] filled only with the bones of the dead: "dry bones can harm no one."[27]

Figuring Divine Speech through the *Upanishads*

After the chapel is reached, it would seem that the vision is completed. But Eliot reserves the final ironic surprise for the end, a description, not

160 DESIRE AND THE ASCETIC IDEAL

of a grail or the body of Christ, but of rain both given and withheld, and an extended, self-conscious interpretation of the *Brhadaranyaka Upanishad*.[28] Where one expects rain, one finds instead the injunctions of this Indian text and a novel set of interpretations of it. I suggest that it is to some extent the India of the BU that Eliot imagines as the "second" with whom to envision his divine "third" (though the issue of translation will raise an important qualification, as we will see later). Eliot's engagement with the *Upanishad* is complex and will reward close scrutiny, for it is only by engaging with the fullness of the references here that we can gain a more complete sense of *The Waste Land*'s exploration of poetry's representation of otherness. Eliot writes:

> Then a damp gust
> Bringing rain
>
> Ganga was sunken, and the limp leaves
> Waited for rain, while the black clouds
> Gathered far distant, over Himavant.
> The jungle crouched, humped in silence.
> Then spoke the thunder
> DA
> *Datta:* what have we given?
> My friend, blood shaking my heart
> The awful daring of a moment's surrender
> Which an age of prudence can never retract
> By this, and this only, we have existed
> Which is not to be found in our obituaries
> Or in memories draped by the beneficent spider
> Or under seals broken by the lean solicitor
> In our empty rooms[29]

Ganga, the Ganges river, is "sunken"; it suffers from a lack of rain, just as the empty cisterns and wells do, just as the pilgrim does wandering in the mountains. The vegetation imagery echoes the very first lines of the poem, in which the dead land was "breeding" lilacs, and "mixing" memory and desire. There, the allusion was to the round of rebirth, of *samsara,* with the rain imagery designating the solipsistic round of desire. Here, water does not have the pejorative reference; it is beneficial and expected, and the plants need it for sustenance. Neither is the vegetation imagery negative: in fact, we have not only isolated flowers, we have a whole jungle, composed of "limp leaves" that "waited for rain." The speaker also refers to the jungle in animal terms: it "crouched, humped in silence" like a beast ready to spring. Unlike the animal imagery depicted elsewhere in the poem, the springing of this beast provides a sense of expectation. The beast awaits the desire the thunder will enable.

The rain expected now is not the water of harmful desire; rather, it is rain that emerges from the speech of the thunder, the voice of the creator god Prajapati from the BU. On another level, the transformation in the imagery of nature bears witness to the potential transformation within the self. The poem thus now mobilizes representations of nature to depict not the chaos of existence but the divine influence operating through it. The poem also represents the divine influence using motifs from a foreign text. Eliot explicitly references the translation of the BU from Paul Deussen's *Sixty Upaniṣads of the Veda*:

1. Three kinds of son of Prajāpati lived with their father Prajāpati as pupils (*brahmacaryam ūṣuḥ*), the gods, men and the demons. After they had lived as pupils with him, the gods said: "Instruct us, O Lord!" Then he uttered to them the syllable "*da*."–"Have you understood it?" he asked.–"We have understood it" they replied, "you have told us that we should control ourselves (dāmyata) [*sic*]."–"Well" he said, "you have understood it."

2. Then men said to him: "Instruct us, O Lord! [*sic*]" Then he uttered to them also this one syllable "*da*." "Have you understood it?" he asked.–"We have understood it" they replied, "you have told us that we should give (alms or gifts) (*datta*)."–"Well," he said, "you have understood it."

3. Then the demons said to him: "Instruct us, O Lord!" Then he uttered to them also this one syllable "da" [*sic*].—"Have you understood it?" he asked.—"We have understood it" they replied, "You have told us that we should have compassion (*dayadhvam*)."—"Well" he said, "you have understood it."

    That divine voice, the thunder, even repeats this when it thunders uttering 'da,' 'da,' 'da,' which means "control yourself, give alms, have compassion."—Therefore, one should practice these three utterances: self-control, giving of alms and compassion.[30]

162   DESIRE AND THE ASCETIC IDEAL

The three classes of beings ask their questions after having lived with Prajapati and studied the Vedas at his feet. From the outset the passage stresses the father/son, teacher/student dialectic. The passage unfolds in request and response: the classes demand more instruction than simply the Vedic injunctions, and each time they demand that Prajapati responds. He responds, however, in syllables of pure sound, a sound the myth later associates with that of thunder. Hence, the syllable "da" (lowercase for Deussen) as spoken by Prajapati has yet to take on any semantic, linguistic significance. Only in the reception of the sound and in the response by the pupils does the natural sound become signification, the root and support of each of the Sanskrit terms: *damyata, datta, dayadhvam.*[31]

Further, although Prajapati speaks in pure sound, the sound of one syllable, he demands comprehension of his pupils. To each class of being he asks, "Have you understood it?" The sound may be pure sound and in a very real sense ineffable, but the creator god demands that it be understood, given linguistic form for comprehension. And the divine speech is understood properly by the three classes, though understood differently. The beings receive the divine voice and use it as a basis of their comprehension. Thus their language bears the mark of the instruction already within it; it takes the instruction, the divine injunction, and mirrors it back to the creator in semantic form. The significance of each term, moreover, is an injunction related to ethics or praxis: the control of the self, the giving of alms, and the practice of compassion. Likewise, Eliot takes the Sanskrit of the original, filtered through the German translation of Deussen, and uses it as a basis for his own attempt at comprehension. In assessing this passage, therefore, Kearns is correct to see the focus on both the projections of the interpreters and the "datum" of the voice itself.[32] She also importantly observes that Eliot changes the order of responses from the original text.[33] What is also true, though, is that the voice of the thunder is a demand for interpretation; it is a voice coming from outside of the self, directing the self beyond itself to venture an interpretation. The speaker feels an imperative for comprehension in the text of the cultural "other"; the words of the BU have a sacred force for the poetic speaker. And, as we will see, as in the myth, the speech of the divine other results in an understanding of ethical praxis.

Most scholars of Eliot acknowledge the influence of this passage on the poem, since Eliot himself references it in his endnotes. However, scholars very rarely look at the next passage of the Upanishad that is directly related, in which the sound of Prajapati is located within the heart, *hrdayam*. Kearns herself does not look so far. Once again, the syllable "da" appears as the very heart of the word meaning "heart":

> The heart (hrdayam), it is the Prajāpati, it is the Brahman, it is all (everything). The same consists of three syllables *hr-da-yam*. The first syllable is hr; to him who knows it, his own people and others (strangers) offer tributes (gifts) (abhiharanti). The second syllable is da; to him who knows it his own people and others give gifts or donations (dadati). The third syllable is yam; he who knows it, enters (eti) heaven.[34]

It is as if the author of the Upanishad were himself part of the previous story, incorporating the divine speech of Prajapati into his explanation of the heart. This passage, however, complicates Prajapati's location. In the previous myth, Prajapati was distinct from the classes of beings, speaking to them from a distance and granting instruction. Here, Prajapati, equated with the *brahman,* the "all," resides deep within the heart. Taken together, the myth and the gloss on *hrdayam* re-create a common Vedic and Upanishadic trope, that of the divine being both transcendent to the self and imminent to the self. Likewise, in the earliest Vedic hymns, Purusha was both the primal sacrifice imminent to every part of creation and yet strangely beyond the sum of his parts.

Eliot's poem does not mention the name of Prajapati, whose voice it is that speaks in the BU. And yet it is the thunder, transcending the "limp leaves" of the jungle, that speaks divine syllables from the sky. We have moved from the anguished cries of the opening of the section, to the music emerging out of and leading one toward the empty cisterns and wells, to a pronouncement of pure sound. The divine voice, non-semantic and ultimately ineffable, resounds like the music in empty wells. Eliot, unlike Deussen, gives the syllable in capital letters, emphasizing the pure sound quality of the thunder. The self also responds to the thunder, just as the different classes of beings do in the BU myth. However, Eliot also immediately invokes the *hrdayam* passage: "DA / *Datta:* what have we given? / My friend, blood shaking my heart."[35] The "DA" sound of the thunder now becomes the beating of the heart. It has an aural, visceral impact on the speaker. Divinity now potentially lies both transcendent to and within the self.

164 DESIRE AND THE ASCETIC IDEAL

Bedient is correct to note that there is nothing "romantic" informing the three injunctions or responses that follow.[36] The speech of the god has ultimate agency here. Nevertheless it leads to a physical response in which both divine and human come to interact with each other. Gish has noted that not only does the thunder have the most authoritative voice in the poem, but also that this episode marks the first time that "the divine voice has elicited a positive response."[37] Agency is ambiguous in this passage, as the speaker describes the ultimate moment of self-surrender: "My friend, blood shaking my heart / The awful daring of a moment's surrender / Which an age of prudence can never retract."[38] On one hand, it is the heart, the metaphorical expression of the Absolute, that pumps blood throughout the body, causing the visceral, physical reaction. On the other hand, the speaker specifically says that it is the "blood shaking my heart," as if the influence were the other way around. Further, the act of surrender is itself paradoxical: it is a giving up of control, through an act that is itself a moment of control. It is a seemingly impossible moment, in which desire leads to its own marginalization, in which one seeks to lose agency through an act of agency, and desires not to desire. And yet, only divine speech can call forth the paradoxical response of the self.[39]

The speaker ratchets up the paradox further, claiming that it is only through such moments that human beings have "existed" at all:

> By this, and this only, we have existed
> Which is not to be found in our obituaries
> Or in memories draped by the beneficent spider
> Or under seals broken by the lean solicitor
> In our empty rooms[40]

"This" here refers to the "awful daring of a moment's surrender," the daring in which the self, in response to the divine, releases control of itself. This daring is that by which human beings have existed, and yet it is not a part of temporal, linguistic existence: it is not found in the language of "obituaries," or in the discursive memory, or under the solicitor's "seals," in the will left by the deceased. The self's "obituary," the summary of a life upon death, casts a glance into the past, representing the accomplishments of a recently deceased person. It is a text from which the referent has definitively withdrawn. The will that is "sealed" is a document that looks to the future, that continues the self's influence even after death, though it is also subject to contestation and interpretation. Language is once again implicated in the round of memory and desire. Language itself cannot represent directly those moments of response and surrender, and yet we are led to believe that those moments truly call us into existence.

Mobilizing Memory: The *Brhadaranyaka Upanishad* on Dreaming

What makes this passage even more difficult to parse is Eliot's use of the spider imagery, once again a reference to the Vedic imaginary. The spider does, in fact, also appear in the BU, in a crucial passage dealing with dreaming:

16. Then Ajātaśatru asked: "When this man was asleep here, where was that spirit consisting of knowledge (vijnanamayaḥ puruṣaḥ) and from where has it now come here?"—Gārgya did not know (the answer to) it.

17. Ajātaśatru said: "When one is thus asleep, then that spirit, consisting of knowledge, has taken (withdrawn) in itself through its knowledge, the knowledge of those vital organs and lies in that space (ākāśa) which is inside the heart; when that spirit seizes those (senses) withdrawn in itself, then people say that the man goes to sleep (*svapiti*) then the (sense of) smell is seized and withdrawn, the speech is seized (and withdrawn), the sense of sight (eyes) is seized and withdrawn, the sense of hearing (ears) is seized and withdrawn, the power of thinking (*Manas*) is seized and withdrawn.

18. "Then where he wanders or moves about in the dreams, they are his worlds; then he is, as it were, a great king or as it were a great Brahmana or he, as it were, moves above on high and down below. And just as a great king takes his subordinates with him and wanders about in his realm according to his pleasure so also he takes around with himself those vital spirits and carries them around in his body, according to his pleasure.

19. "When, however, he is in deep sleep, and is not conscious of anything, then the twenty-seven thousand arteries named as *hitaḥ* ('the benevolent ones') circulate from the heart in the

166 DESIRE AND THE ASCETIC IDEAL

> pericardium and just as a young lad or a great king or a great Brāhmaṇa, having enjoyed abundant bliss, reposes, so also he then reposes or rests.
>
> 20. "Just as the spider goes out through its threads, just as the tiny sparks spring forth out of the fire, so also all the living spirits, all the worlds, all beings originate, out of the Ātman;—His secret name (upaniṣad) is 'the reality of reality'; the living spirits are the reality and he is their reality."[41]

Once again, as with the previous passage selected by Eliot, the heart is presented as the important point in the human being for encountering the "reality of reality." The passage depicts the different stages of sleep (dreaming and deep sleep) as a slow retraction of the self into itself, with all its sense faculties. The self that journeys into the heart is the "spirit consisting of knowledge" (*vijñanamayaḥ puruṣaḥ*). I take this to mean the self that possesses the higher knowledge, the *vijñana* of the reality of the "Ātman." It is this self that gradually takes with it all of the faculties of sensation, including speech and the "power of thinking," the *manas,* or mind. It is because the self brings these sense faculties with it into the heart that it is able to create worlds for itself in its dreaming: "Then where he wanders or moves about in the dreams, they [i.e., the faculties of sense and thought] are his worlds."[42] In other words, it is the memory of the world belonging to the various sense faculties that allows the self to create its dream worlds. The self draws these faculties along with it as a king leads his retinue or "subordinates," and they serve to satisfy its/his "pleasure."

However, the self passes from images to repose, and from pleasures and traveling to their cessation in "deep sleep." The self rests in the heart without any dreams. It is this stage in the self's journey inward that the author uses the spider imagery to explain. The spider spreads itself out into the world through its web just as the Atman spins itself out into the universe, giving rise to "all the living spirits, all the worlds, all beings." Likewise, the self's slow withdrawal into itself resembles the spider's retraction of its webs into itself. This image of slow withdrawal into the self mirrors the journey of Eliot's pilgrimage, from the suffering of the world, through poetic/dream vision, into the deep recesses of the self, where the pure sound of thunder resonates. Here, we must also surely remember the Buddhist notion of *upaya* and the aesthetic valence of Augustine's ascesis sketched in the last chapter. In both of these models of ascesis, the subject's feeling is engaged through the texts of the tradition, as he or she moves toward a deeper rest beyond these things. But the withdrawal within presupposes the engagement with the world enshrined in memory. Therefore the process is paradoxical—to withdraw one must engage.

Of equal interest, however, is the related account of dreaming in BU, an account that seems to be a gloss on and expansion of the previous account. In the longer version of the dream theory, the author/redactor reinforces the portrayal of the dream state as a middle realm between the extremes of the sense world and the world of deep sleep. There again the self creates worlds for itself. The author, however, expands on the description of the state of deep sleep, in which the self loses the distinction between self and object and comes to find itself with its desire fulfilled and even beyond any desires at all:

> Because, just as one, embraced by a beloved woman, has no consciousness of that which is outside or inside, so also the spirit, embraced by the self of the nature of knowledge (*prajñena ātmana*, i.e., the Brahman) has no consciousness of what is outside or inside. That is the essential form of the same (self) in which it is one with all its desires appeased or fulfilled, one desiring its own self, one without desires and separated (free) from desire.[43]

The text likens the moment of absorption to a moment of sexual bliss in which there is no sense of distinction between self and other. Yet crucially, there is an otherness within the self with which the phenomenal self communes. Likewise, the final moment of union of the self with the "self of the nature of knowledge" is one in which desire is both satisfied and transcended in the other's embrace. Crucially for our purposes, this state of fulfillment and indistinction is represented later in the passage as a body of water: "Just like water (pure—Kath. 4.15), it [i.e., the true self] stands alone as the onlooker without a second one, it is, O great king, the Brahman of this world."[44] The BU depicts the self within the self as constant and without self-object distinction, like a body of water without divisions, in which all desires are gathered up and calmed, like a calm ocean. One is reminded of Patanjali's description of the end state of meditation as the "Rain cloud of [knowable] things."[45]

In Eliot's poem, the spider becomes a symbol of an otherness lying within the very heart of the self. The web the spider spins here is the

168   DESIRE AND THE ASCETIC IDEAL

web of memory, and we have seen a sense of self in *The Waste Land* that is trapped within the round of memory and desire. The spider itself lies beyond that and yet is not divorced from it. The BU associates the web the spider weaves not only with the sense faculties the self is able to withdraw from the world but also with the dream world itself that takes its imagery from the memories of the sense world. Yet the spider is "beneficent": though it drapes the memories that lead to the round of suffering, it also enables the memories that can potentially begin the escape from that round. In the BU dream sequences, one must pass through the realm of dreams before attaining union with *brahman* in deep sleep. As Kearns notes, the dreaming self in the BU is in an "in-between" state that contains the "potential for liberation or rebirth."[46] Though the moments of surrender may not be able to be directly represented in the texts of the past or the predictions of the future, memory is able to grasp the allusions to those moments of "embrace" and surrender that are just glimpsed obliquely in those texts. Eliot presents poetry as perhaps providing the positive seeds that orient the self toward those moments of surrender. As we shall see, poetry also has the capacity, in its musical qualities, to awaken an awareness of what is beyond the self, thereby challenging self-involvement and training the self in compassion.

The Second Heartbeat: Compassion and the Imagination of Otherness

Eliot's second "heartbeat" translates the BU's injunction to "have compassion" (or as Eliot writes in his notes, "sympathise")[47] in a commentary on the imagination of otherness. The otherness in this extended poetic translation extends to both the otherness of the divine and the otherness of human beings. Whereas the first commentary on the thunder's utterance focused on the journey into the self, the second explores the imagination of otherness:

> Da
> *Dayadhvam:* I have heard the key
> Turn in the door once and turn once only
> We think of the key, each in his prison
> Thinking of the key, each confirms a prison

Only at nightfall, aethereal rumours
Revive for a moment a broken Coriolanus[48]

Eliot, in his endnotes, directs the reader to a passage from Dante's *Inferno* (XXXIII.46–47) and to F. H. Bradley's *Appearance and Reality,* on which Eliot wrote his dissertation. The passage from the *Inferno* describes the sins of Ugolino della Gherardesca, who was imprisoned by Archbishop Ruggieri of Pisa along with his four children. The archbishop left the five to starve to death, and Ugolino, in order to survive, ate his four children upon their deaths.[49] According to Eliot, Ugolino heard the key "turn in the door once and once only," as the guards locked the door to his cell, never to be opened for him again.[50]

At the same time, Eliot psychologizes the image, through a reference to Bradley. In his endnotes, he quotes from Bradley's text:

> My external sensations are no less private to myself than are my thoughts or my feelings. In either case my experience falls within my own circle, a circle closed on the outside; and, with all its elements alike, every sphere is opaque to the others which surround it. . . . In brief, regarded as an existence which appears in the soul, the whole world for each is peculiar and private to that soul.[51]

The passage from Bradley provides a statement of unmitigated idealism, in which the consciousness of each individual closes in upon itself. Bradley uses the metaphor of a circle to describe experience: the "soul" lies in the middle of a bounded "closed" circle. Other human beings cannot be interpreted by the "soul," since "every sphere is opaque to the others which surround it." Combined with the story of Ugolino, this passage becomes a barbaric one, operating on two levels. First, the self becomes like a prison, locked by a mysterious jailor. The soul, devoid of any access to the outside world, devours its own contents in its slow descent into death. On another level, and perhaps more to the point, the soul that is closed off from other human beings, without any awareness or acknowledgment of their existence, devours them to satisfy its own hunger, imprisoned within the self and devoid of the compassion that is the BU's injunction.

Eliot seems to suggest that it is precisely the experience of sympathy or compassion that challenges such an idealism. Sympathy is a response to the other who makes a moral claim on the self. It bears witness to the "key" beyond the self that makes the self aware of a world beyond itself not subject to its control and "consumption." It is the experience of sympathy, of an emotional and imaginative reaction to the other, that provides the "key" to unlocking the door to consciousness. The *Oxford English Dictionary* defines "sympathy" in two ways that are pertinent here. First, it is a response to suffering: "The quality or state of being thus affected by the suffering or sorrow of another; a feeling of compassion or commiseration." The second definition expands the notion of feeling and sympathy, stressing the responsive nature of sympathy: "The quality or state of being affected by the condition of another with a feeling similar and corresponding to that of the other; the fact or capacity of entering into or sharing the feelings of another or others; fellow-feeling. Also, a feeling or frame of mind evoked by and responsive to some external influence."[52] The influence of other human beings on the self makes itself known through the "feeling" and "emotion" that "moves" the self from its position of self-contained stasis to a more active engagement of solidarity. Such an influence challenges the supposed inviolability of the self. The common trait between the two definitions is that sympathy is, even in the first instance, not a function of reasoning, but an imagination of the other's suffering and a response in feeling or emotion. For Eliot, the medium best suited to engaging with matters of feeling and emotion, and to connecting these matters with thought, is poetry.

The "key" the speaker mentions in this passage is a remembered one: the key was "heard" once in the past. Eliot once again highlights the *sound* of that which lies beyond the limits of the self, drawing the self beyond itself. The memory of this sound drives the self to "think of the key" again. The invocation of sound draws attention back to the aesthetic moments of the vision. Sound drew the speaker on toward the empty chapel and the culminating moment of divine speech. It is poetry's capacity to merge vision and sound that is evoked as an integral part of the path. In its affective dimension, poetry has the capacity to generate sympathy and challenge the pretensions of the self, all the while drawing memory back to previous significant moments of sympathy. And yet, those isolated moments of sympathy also highlight the self's ordinary self-involvement. In thinking the moment of sympathy, "each confirms a prison." The moments of "self-surrender" in sympathy are few and far between, and yet the self realizes their liberating potential.

Eliot's passage also comments on poetry itself, challenging the severity of Bradley's idealism. Poetry, in its physical, affective dimension, makes the reader aware of human otherness in a more visceral way. Poetry's form makes the reader aware of the motions of otherness by stirring an affective response in the self, though it also conceals the personal depths of that otherness. Eliot holds open the possibility that poetry can awaken a sense of sympathy and, in doing so, begin to bridge the distance between the fragments of human existence. Once again, it is sound that signals the hidden wholeness never to be fully attained: "Only at nightfall, aethereal rumours / Revive for a moment a broken Coriolanus."

In Shakespeare's play, Coriolanus, an absolutist Roman consul loathe to patronize the fickle crowd, is torn apart by the Volscians (with whom he has sided against Rome) for sparing the city of Rome. Coriolanus's pity results from the impassioned appeal of his mother, Volumnia, whom the Romans send as an emissary on their behalf. Volumnia gives a long speech in which she urges reconciliation between Rome and the Volscians. Ultimately, however, she eschews argument and appeals to Coriolanus's compassion or sympathy, directing his attention to his son: "Nay, behold's, / This boy that cannot tell what he would have, / But kneels, and holds up hands for fellowship, / Does reason out petition with more strength / Than thou hast to deny't."[53] Coriolanus's change of heart, appropriately, occurs in silence, as he takes his mother by the hand: "(Holds her by the hand silent)."[54] Just as Volumnia eschews argument, Coriolanus will not reason to a conclusion of the crisis but will react with feeling. His moment of sympathy marks the moment in the play when Coriolanus sets aside his rigid ideals in ethical regard for another.

The theme of "revival" in this passage mirrors the resurrection theme from earlier in the poem and carries with it a hermeneutical valence. Coriolanus can be interpreted through the hermeneutical "key" of sympathy. He is revived in memory through a hermeneutic in which the reader's compassion enables him or her to understand other instances of it. The reader's experience of sympathy allows him or her to come to terms with a surrender of the self that occurs silently, beyond language. Only "at nightfall," in the dark, can one hear the "aethereal rumours" that signal the wholeness beyond this fragmentation. But again, we get a hint of that unity from the influence of something beyond the self, here given as "aethereal rumours" one can just barely hear.

172 DESIRE AND THE ASCETIC IDEAL

The Third Heartbeat: The Joyful Cultivation of the Self

In the final gloss on the BU, the focus turns to a representation of both self and other in an image that reconciles the water imagery of the poem with the central images and ideas from the Upanishad. It is also here that we find a recollection of the poem's previous evocation of asceticism. The poem presents the union of the heart, the image of the most intimate self, with the other who is a nameless "hand":

> DA
> *Damyata:* The boat responded
> Gaily, to the hand expert with sail and oar
> The sea was calm, your heart would have responded
> Gaily, when invited, beating obedient
> To controlling hands[55]

The water imagery in this passage brings with it the whole range of allusions built up around it throughout the entire poem. With the opening passage of the poem, water represented the desire that propelled one through the round of *samsara,* of memory and desire. In this section of the poem, water (or the lack thereof) represented a necessary physical and spiritual nourishment after which the mountain figure thirsted. The speaker's vision included a potentially rejuvenating rain, a potentially transcendent desire, a desire as gift of the divinity beating in the heart of the individual. The peace in the heart of the individual was depicted as a body of water in the dream passages of the BU.

Now the "hand" of an other guides the self. Or, rather, the speaker now envisions the possibility of a desire not at odds with divine dictate, a desire put at the service of divine and human "others." Eliot envisages an obedience that responds to instruction "gaily."[56] As with the BU passage, the divine influence calls forth a response from humanity. Hugh Kenner notes that the poem at this point also extends this possibility of control to another, in a potential crafting of intersubjectivity, an "imagined instrument of a comparably sensitive human relationship."[57] As the result of the divine dictate of the BU, I believe we are at least allowed to conjecture a reference here to the divine as well. The word "gaily" occurs twice in the passage to describe responses, either actual or possible, to the control of the other. The obedience of the heart, "beating obedient / To controlling hands," is a visceral experience that enhances and enables the self, bringing joy rather than anguish. The influence of the divine is an "invitation," not a command, though an invitation that requires the "awful daring of a moment's surrender." The continuing path of ascesis can now be undertaken, not as a masochistic self-torture, but as an enabling process of self-cultivation.

Eliot's depiction of this experience also takes into consideration the beginning of the vision, in which both the human other and the divine other were co-imagined. In all three sections of the thunder passage the speaker refers to others, to "we" and "you." Here, according to the speaker, the boat "responded" once already to the "expert hand." He then states, "your heart would have responded / Gaily, when invited." The verb tenses are important here: the boat responded once to the "expert hand," but this passage is directed to another who has not had this experience, "Your heart *would* have responded" (emphasis mine). The event happened, but not to the other. If certain conditions had been met, then the other would have responded. As with the vision earlier, Eliot's poetry attempts to imagine both human and divine "other" simultaneously, in an experience that would fulfill both and envelop both "gaily" (a repeated word in this passage). And the appeal through poetry, like the divine appeal, is an "invitation" to sail, rather than a conquest of the will.

Conclusion: Performing the Fragments

If we take a step back then from our own traversal of Eliot's finale, we see an interesting trajectory develop, one that mirrors to a certain extent the dream myths of the BU as well as the Buddhist *upaya* theory described in chapters 2 and 4. In the BU, the self journeys from the waking state, through dreaming, to the repose of deep sleep, united with the "reality of reality,"[58] the spider whose webs create the fabric of reality for the self. The journey through dreams is a journey through memory; memory provides the images and tropes through which the self composes its dreams. The merging with ultimate reality occurs at a moment in which the deeper self, the "self of the nature of knowledge," embraces the temporal self. This embrace, likened to a sexual embrace, leads the self into perfect union with *brahman,* beyond any subject/object duality. The knowledge attained in deep sleep is a higher knowledge, not one predicated on a knowing subject comprehending detached, separate objects.

174   DESIRE AND THE ASCETIC IDEAL

I suggest that the trajectory of Eliot's final passage mirrors this passage from wakefulness to deep sleep, through the dream state, except that in *The Waste Land* the dream state represents the vision of the intensely suffering mountain figure and the potential sound of the divine calling him through his vision to emptiness. The speaker's suffering, the suffering in the absence of the divine, leads to an extended "vision," a string of fragmentary images giving imaginary shape to that which is desperately needed, a desire enabled by divine call. Like BU's dream state, the speaker's vision is a reconfiguration of memory: images, metaphors, and allusions from the previous sections of the poem implicate themselves, but this time joined to the task of searching for the Absolute. The vision attempts, by mobilizing these memories and listening for the divine sound, to give imaginative expression to the emptiness of the self, to merge with an emptiness that is simultaneously the source of renewing rain. It is in and through memory, therefore, that the Absolute is reached. This vision becomes also a potential mode of envisioning the entire poem as a dream vision whose fragments may be efficient in approaching its ineffable ending.

However, as we recall from the beginning of the poem, memory is a vexed topic for *The Waste Land*. It is a pole in the samsaric cycle of memory, desire, and rebirth. Desire and memory, unpurified, lead to the perpetuation of evil acts and their consequences, driving the self to repetition, trapping it in solipsism, and robbing the self of agency. The water imagery early in the poem depicts the self tossed about by desire and attachment. The prospect of an action driven by an unselfish desire, a desire not determined by selfish motives, is not even entertained. At the end of the poem, however, a positive view of memory and desire emerges, though not unambiguously, and the possibility of desire purified by the embrace of the Absolute becomes the focal point of the vision.

The three commentaries on *Datta, Dayadhvam,* and *Damyata* show that the pulsing of the thunder within leads to the surrender of the self, the possibility of compassion, and the joy of a praxis guided by the "controlling hands"[59] of the divine. The heart becomes the water depicted as the deep sleep of the BU, the ocean of repose, but now figured as the rains dispensed in the divine thunder. The price of repose, however, is the death of the temporal self, the realization of its emptiness. The culmination of the path of the speaker is a path in which the self must be "surrendered." It must recognize itself in the frailty of decay and the emptiness of the grail chapel.

The culminating ascetic moment of *The Waste Land* comes at its very conclusion. Eliot ends the poem with his famous "Shantih shantih shantih," translated by him in his endnotes: "Repeated as here, a formal ending to an Upanishad. 'The Peace which passeth understanding' is our equivalent to this word."[60] The blank page after "shantih" signals the ineffable moment that escapes and yet gives rise to language. I agree with Kearns in seeing one of the possible interpretations of the ending moments of the poem as the work of a mind attempting to focus itself in the final moments of meditation, as thoughts well up once more in spasm.[61] She notes that the final lines represent in this sense the "goal of meditation."[62] Yet I also agree with her that the ending has again a dual valence; one can see it as a pessimistic death or a transcendent one.[63]

Likewise, depending on which side one adopts, one would view the endnotes differently. They could represent the fragments of consciousness shattered apart by divinity or the pedantic notes of a poet-scholar. The former interpretation requires some explanation.[64] After we read the poem, we are given a list of fragments, some just references, some quotes, in Italian, Latin, English, German, and Sanskrit. *The Waste Land* is the only poem for which Eliot provided such "notes," though the reader might have wished for them in some of his other works. *Four Quartets,* for example, is just as complex in allusions as *The Waste Land* but contains no such apparatus. Further, as explanatory, they are not comprehensive; many crucial allusions are not mentioned.

There is in one sense, therefore, a circular structure to the poem: its beginning presupposes its end, and the notes document the coalescence of fragments that made the poem possible in the first place. In another sense, however, the poem is not cyclical. What is shown in the compilation of fragments, in the collage of memories, is an *ascesis,* and then a shattering of the subjectivity into fragments by that which lies beyond it. The endnotes reveal the fragments that have been used in the ascent. At the same time, they bear witness to a force from beyond the self that has both enabled and ultimately dismantled this approach. In this, it points beyond solipsism. In this sense, *The Waste Land* as a poem could be regarded as one single attempt at *ascesis,* one single approach to the other. Presumably, the speaker of the poem will now have to rearrange

176   DESIRE AND THE ASCETIC IDEAL

the fragments and at the same time rearrange the self, based on the shattering and surrender that has occurred. Just as a poet withdraws from his or her work in the very process of writing it, so too does the divine withdraw from the self here, enabling new striving even in its passing.

Is Eliot saying that true poets must be contemplatives? The answer lies in Eliot's representation of the dream state, a stand-in for the work of literature. The speaker there is drawn on by oblique visions of the divine and the sounds of music: the "fiddled whisper music," the whistling of the bats, the "tolling reminiscent bells," and the "voices singing out of empty cisterns and exhausted wells." Sound seems "ethereal" but is a physical phenomenon that resonates physically with the listener. Thus also the experience of the divine is a visceral and aural experience; the thunder is pure sound, and it shakes the heart in its speech. Later it will be the sound of the key in the prison door that the speaker remembers ("I have heard the key") in the hope of finding release from the cannibalistic prison of the self.

The presence of the divine Other emerges through affective experience. Eliot seems to be suggesting that aesthetic, affective experience has the potential, because it clearly calls forth a reaction of the subject to something from outside of it, to approximate the more complete, visceral encounter with the divine Other. Affective experience, whether of another person or a textual expression of such a person, possesses the potential to challenge the pretensions of the self through feeling, generate compassion, and prepare the self for a more complete surrender to the Absolute. Eliot makes precisely this point in his 1929 essay on Dante, where the textual, human, and Divine "others" are elided:

> The experience of a poem is the experience both of a moment and of a lifetime. It is very much like our intenser experiences of other human beings. There is a first, or an early moment which is unique, of shock and surprise, even of terror (*Ego dominus tuus*); a moment which can never be forgotten, but which is never repeated integrally; and yet which would become destitute of significance if it did not survive in a larger whole of experience; [and] which survives inside a deeper and a calmer feeling.[65]

It is poetry specifically and literature more broadly, in its formal properties, its rhythms, rhymes, and music, that can call forth a more complete response of the individual, here an experience of "shock" or "terror." And since the self moves toward the divine in part through affectivity, poetry becomes the most appropriate form for pursuing it. Poetry unites the fragments of knowledge represented in the endnotes into a new whole of feeling and a new possibility for compassionate self-surrender. It attempts the reconciliation of disparate fragments of knowledge but also aims at the ethical transformation of both poet and reader. Scholarship, with its endnotes and its attempts at a purely intellectual synthesis, only meets part of the requirement.

If it is indeed in and through reading that compassion can be generated by attentiveness to the movement of the textual production of the other, it is significant that one of the "others" by which Eliot has been influenced is the *Brhadaranyaka Upanishad*. This is the case to such an extent that Eliot even compares his own poem to an Upanishad. The ending of the poem ("Shantih shantih shantih") is, according to Eliot, the formal ending to an *Upanishad*. We do not need a set of notes to tell us that the formula also represents the formal ending to his own work.[66] Eliot's own path of following the music of the divine has decisively been a path through the Indian sources.[67] Gish has noted that the passage from the BU represents "the nearest thing to a last word" in the poem.[68] Yet, as Eliot realizes, the issues of translation are complex. It is to a *translation* of the *Upanishads* by Deussen that Eliot points in his endnotes, not to a critical source in Sanskrit. Translations of Indian sources formed a part of the store of memory from which the poet strives to cross-signify the world. Engaging with them was not optional. The attempt to engage with Indian sources bears witness to their profound influence on Eliot; his poetry is a response to the "surprise," "shock," or even "terror" provoked by an encounter with them. And just as the thunder of Prajapati demanded a response of comprehension from his children, so too did the Indian texts, in the feeling they evoked and the demands they made, call forth a response from Eliot the reader.

But Eliot also realizes that the cultural other, like the divine other, can only be viewed obliquely. In the vision of part V of the poem, the speaker must imagine both the mysterious third *and* the dialogue partner. The understanding of both is provisional, liable to error, further fragmentation, and reform. And yet, if engagement with texts is part of the ethical path, then the imagination of otherness is inescapable; it is part of any hermeneutics. In any engagement with a text that makes a claim on the reader, there is an attempted imagining of the other perspective embodied in the text and an attempt to listen to the text's address. Further, if reading as a practice is critical in preparing the self for transcendent experiences, then, for Eliot, the Indian sources are part of that process of cultivation. They already, through translation, cross-signify reality, and the familiar language already bears the influence of the foreign texts. The understanding of the self through language necessarily entails an engagement with texts of the cultural other that have surreptitiously influenced the significations of that language. Therefore, the understanding of all texts changes with the introduction of new texts. This is a point Eliot makes strongly in "Tradition and the Individual Talent," though admittedly without the cross-cultural valence.[69] In influencing the home language, these texts change, if ever so slightly, the interpretation of the classic texts of a cultural textual tradition. In other words, the culture becomes more hybrid.

For Eliot, the "third" he imagined may have been the divine, or God, or the Absolute, but one of the dialogue partners across whom he had to look, for *The Waste Land,* seems to have been India. Eliot's "imagining" of India relies on using the textual expressions of India's past alongside the textual expressions of Europe's past in an attempt to raise memories that would disrupt and reform the present. However, the provisional nature of poetry makes this comparison an invitation. Given the poem's explicit positing of various "others," this is inevitable. As I argued earlier, for all its shifting tones, characters, and languages, *The Waste Land* focuses on moments of domination of various others: the sexual other, the geographical other, the theological other, the aesthetic other; hence the images of rape and violation throughout the poem. Eliot's poem is an attempt to imagine these "others," while at the same time realizing that it could be another instance of such violation. The very diagnosis of desire presented in the poem implies as much.

Eliot was surely attracted to the fragmentary, redacted nature of the Upanishads; they mirrored his perception of fragmentation, difference, and disjunction in modern Europe. He realized that the question of diversity and perspective had already been decisively raised, regardless of what the poet thinks or does not think. But Eliot would insist that along with the reality of perspective is the awareness of that which lies beyond. For Eliot thinks that the pursuit of reality, of truth, of perhaps God emerges from the encounter of more than one perspective. It takes the influence of an other to raise the issue of something lying beyond the self; otherwise the self would have no awareness of that which exceeds it. The disruption that takes its source from the other opens up the experience of perspective by calling the self forth from its solipsism. Such disruption enables the self to perceive the world differently. Far from putting an end to the pursuit of truth, the presence of the other inaugurates it. The tragedy, therefore, is not that dialogue and comparison take place; the tragedy is that, by refusing comparison, the influence of the other on the self is not acknowledged. The self is envisioned as solitary and allowed to remain locked in its prison, feeding on its own, refusing to share signification, desperately blind to that which lies beyond.

6

LANGUAGE IN THE MIDDLE WAY

T. S. Eliot's Engagement with Madhyamaka Buddhism in *Four Quartets*

In this chapter, I demonstrate how certain foundational Buddhist conceptions of language and causality, embodied in the tradition by the concept of the "middle way," played a central role in T. S. Eliot's philosophical and poetic orientation, especially as evidenced in *Four Quartets*. It was Eliot's affinity for these ideas, ideas appearing in both earlier Theravada and later Mahayana texts to which he had access, that appeared in key moments of his poetic corpus. More specifically, I develop the suggestion offered by Jeffrey Perl and Andrew Tuck that the work of Nagarjuna, the second-century founder of the Madhyamaka school of Buddhism (the "Middle Way" school) played an important role in T. S. Eliot's intellectual development. To be sure, there has been in Eliot scholarship an engaging debate on how deeply Eliot knew the work of Nagarjuna, though we know he was introduced to Nagarjuna's thought in classes with Masaharu Anesaki at Harvard. Regardless of how one comes down on this issue, it is nevertheless true that Nagarjuna codifies and systematizes some of the major trends in the Buddhist texts to which Eliot had access more broadly. I therefore use Nagarjuna's major text, the *Mulamadhyamakakarika*, as a lens through which to gauge Eliot's indebtedness to Buddhist texts in *Four Quartets*. My success, I hope, will be gauged from the interpretive possibilities that open up once one puts Eliot's text in hermeneutical conversation with the Buddhist texts, Nagarjuna's in particular.

I suggest that Eliot's allusions to the "middle way" in *Four Quartets* reflect Nagarjuna's causal analysis and linguistic theories. I argue that Eliot, following Nagarjuna's "middle way," presents a view of time and causality that insists that things in the world cannot be considered either as impermanent or as lacking a causal continuity. Because of this, language, though it has the potential to deceive by reifying things in the world that are ultimately impermanent, also has a chastened sense of reference, able to signal elements of life that have some abiding, dependent regularity. In Kearns's terms, Nagarjuna avoids the extremes of "logocentric formulation" and "the silence of despair" for a "middle state" of linguistic dependence.[1] Thus, for Eliot and Nagarjuna, language has the potential to index both life's sufferings and its saving moments of illumination, two elements of human existence to which religious paths of cultivation consistently bear witness. Both see language as holding open the possibility of a soteriological path of writing and praxis that eventually, in its culminating moments, leads to a paradoxical loss of subjectivity.

Cleo McNelly Kearns reports that Eliot was introduced to the Mahayana during his graduate studies at Harvard through a lecture series taught by Masaharu Anesaki in 1913–14. Anesaki devoted significant time to a presentation of the Madhyamaka, primarily in reference to the work of its founder, Nagarjuna.[2] Kearns warns us, however, that there "is no evidence that Eliot read any of the works of Nagarjuna or studied his thought outside the context of Anesaki's general introduction. (In fact, his notes tell us that he missed three lectures, including one specifically devoted to Nagarjuna)."[3] Despite this, as Kearns notes, Anesaki did talk quite a bit about Nagarjuna in the other lectures, so Eliot was probably aware of the basic philosophical teachings. Further, it is not out of the question that Eliot could have acquired a translation of Madhyamaka texts if he desired; as Andrew Tuck has pointed out, one of Candrakirti's commentaries on Nagarjuna's *Mulamadhyamakakarika* was partly available in translation by Eugene Burnouf.[4] Other than this speculative possibility, however, we simply do not know definitively what kind of engagement Eliot may have made with Madhyamaka texts outside of classroom study. Nevertheless, Jeffrey Perl and Andrew Tuck have argued that evidence in the philosophical notebooks points to a deeper awareness of Madhyamaka than Kearns initially allows. They argue that Eliot latched on to Nagarjuna's formulation of the "middle way," an analysis of the world poised between philosophical nihilism and essentialism, that resulted in the recovery of the utility of social convention cleansed of essentialist tendencies.[5] They cite Eliot as writing, in some unpublished lecture notes from 1913–14: "A view is false in one sense, true in another. This kind of synthesis is characteristic of Buddhism from its very beginnings under the name of middle path. . . . Life is neither pain nor pleasure. The views that the world exists or not, both are false, the truth lies in the middle, transcending both views."[6] As we shall see, this does indeed closely resemble the kind of philosophical argument made by Nagarjuna in the seminal text for the Madhyamaka, *Mulamadhyamakakarika* Nagarjuna does attempt to maintain some sense of conventional reality of existents, even while denying that they possess an eternal, independent essence. Entities exist conventionally but do not ultimately exist. It is also true that Anesaki claims that this sort of analysis is shared broadly by the tradition.

Perl and Tuck also claim that Eliot uses Nagarjuna's famous declaration of the identity of *nirvana* and *samsara* to describe the process of a soteriological path that returns one to the world (previously experienced as the round of suffering, *samsara*) now seen anew in a soteriologically efficacious way, as empty (*nirvana*).[7] Further, they see Nagarjuna's supposed eschewal of all philosophical "views" as a possible source of Eliot's contextualized embedding of truth claims within discrete discursive contexts: "he [i.e., Eliot] was concerned to affirm the contextual validity of all theoretical statements: any theory will possess a significance and function within a limited system of beliefs and practices. . . . Eliot rejected the philosophically standard presupposition that belief in an ideology necessitates belief in its exclusive access to truth."[8] Consequently, they argue, such a view of discourse allows Eliot to reconceive philosophical practice, not as allied with the free exercise of sovereign reason, but as a soteriological practice.[9]

As may be apparent from this short summary, Perl and Tuck have glimpsed tantalizing allusions to Nagarjuna, but the evidence they present suggests rather than proves the influence of Madhyamaka on Eliot's work. To be sure, they have identified important themes shared by both Nagarjuna and Eliot; the parallels are striking. Kearns makes precisely this point, while simultaneously lamenting the lack of clear textual evidence of influence: "For Eliot, too, this notion of an 'in-between' or middle state that will not rest either in a logocentric formulation or in the silence of despair imposed by interdicting it completely is crucial."[10]

I presently suggest that the evidence from Eliot's notes is a bit stronger than Kearns allows, though the uncertainty still remains. I also show that some of Nagarjuna's arguments appear in nuce in translations of Theravada texts upon which Nagarajuna built and that Eliot certainly knew. Finally, I suggest that ultimately an understanding of Nagarjuna's method of argumentation sheds light on Eliot's poetry itself, and this is ultimately what matters. If Perl and Tuck want to argue the strength of Nagarjuna's influence on Eliot's philosophical formation, it would make sense to show how these ideas shape the texture of the poetry itself. Such an analysis, though not proving influence, would at least make the argument more persuasive. Kearns herself sees such an avenue as potentially enlightening, so to speak. She writes that "the parallel between Nagarjuna and Eliot . . . is so rich in potential that problems of tracing direct influence ought not to prevent its further pursuit."[11] It is just such a pursuit I undertake here, but only through a close attention to the details of Eliot's poetry (in this case, *Four Quartets*). Hopefully such an analysis will lend credence to the important work done by Perl and Tuck, while highlighting the provocative parallels noted by all of the commentators.

Language and the Finitude of the Self in *Four Quartets*

I begin the discussion by exploring how the invocation of the "middle way" emerges for Eliot in *Four Quartets*. I hope to show that this happens after Eliot lays out a very Nietzschean view of language in "East Coker." Then, after raising a hermeneutical dilemma about that view at the end of "East Coker," I turn to Nagarjuna's theories of language as a way of helping us solve this dilemma and understand the transition from "East Coker" to "The Dry Salvages." Finally, I return to *Four Quartets*, now with an understanding of Nagarjuna's thought, to see how the Buddhist's text helps us see a distinctive movement of Eliot's poetry.

Eliot alludes to the "middle way" explicitly twice in *Four Quartets*, both instances in "East Coker." Significantly, both references occur as the four-poem sequence approaches its own "middle," the transition from "East Coker" to "The Dry Salvages." Though realizing that the poems were not initially published together, I believe there is a highly sophisticated plan reaching across the *Quartets*, one that is very much influenced by the Buddhist analyses of causation and signification. Consequently, I argue that the placement of these allusions toward the middle of the sequence is intentional, signaling to the reader a crucial change of vision in the course of the poems, from a realization of transience to an

184   DESIRE AND THE ASCETIC IDEAL

appreciation of that which abides, and from a meditation on that which language falsifies to an insistence on that which it signifies. In order to demonstrate this, I first explore the context in which these allusions are made and then show how an understanding of Nagarjuna's Madhyamaka answers some crucial questions that will emerge in the course of the analysis.

The first reference to the middle way appears, in part II, in the midst of a discussion of language's inability to represent a world that is in perpetual flux. Indeed, the problem of transience emerged fully in part I of the poem, through a discussion of the cycle of human desire and generation. There the poet depicts the dance of men and women around a bonfire as emblematic of the desire that characterizes embodied, sexual existence. The dancers move "Round and round the fire / Leaping through the flames, or joined in circles,"[12] as generations come and go in a seemingly incessant "round" of birth, decay, and death.[13] Eliot describes this cycle as "The time of the coupling of man and woman / And that of beasts. Feet rising and falling. / Eating and drinking. Dung and death."[14] Existence as depicted here is a material, beast-like one of coupling, eating, defecating, and dying. Bodily rhythms, the rhythms of life, enchain the human being in a temporal existence in which one is moved in the cycle that itself will continue long after the individual has spent his or her desire.

Part II takes the depiction of transience and desire from the first section and develops it in terms of language, epistemology, and poetry. In fact, it is in this passage that Eliot presents a view of language that sounds remarkably like that of Nietzsche. Eliot begins his discussion of language by meditating on human finitude and the potential for epistemic error. In the middle of this section, Eliot writes:

> There is, it seems to us
> At best, only a limited value
> In the knowledge derived from experience.
> The knowledge imposes a pattern, and falsifies,
> For the pattern is new in every moment
> And every moment is a new and shocking
> Valuation of all we have been. We are only undeceived
> Of that which, deceiving, could no longer harm.
> In the middle, not only in the middle of the way

LANGUAGE IN THE MIDDLE WAY 185

> But all the way, in a dark wood, in a bramble,
> On the edge of a grimpen, where is no secure foothold,
> And menaced by monsters, fancy lights,
> Risking enchantment.[15]

First, of course, any allusion to the "middle of the way" has to evoke the beginning of Dante's *Inferno:* "In the middle of the journey of our life, I came to myself in a dark wood, for the straight way was lost."[16] The beginning of Dante's monumental journey begins in a "dark wood," made more confusing by the sleep that still hangs about his head: "I cannot really say how I entered there, so full of sleep was I at the point when I abandoned the true way."[17] Dante's journey will be one from darkness to light, from obscurity to clarity, and from sleep to an uninterrupted attentiveness to the Divine. Thus, the opening of the poem stresses the temporal finitude of the individual and the epistemological obscurity of the mind just awakening, not yet graced with insight. Eliot makes clear that Dante is behind this passage, redescribing Dante's "dark wood" as a "bramble" or "the edge of a grimpen, where is no secure foothold." (In fact, Dante himself relates how he had to proceed up the mountain "so that my halted foot was always the lower").[18]

In addition, Dante encounters three beasts, a leopard, a lion, and a she-wolf. In *Inferno,* these animals' significances are unclear, but they certainly represent sins prohibiting Dante from ascending the mountain.[19] Hence, like Eliot, Dante is "menaced by monsters." The animals in Eliot's poem hearken back to the same kind of bestiality and carnality represented in the first part of "East Coker." In part II, that carnality is placed firmly within the meditation on epistemology. The poet is "menaced by monsters, fancy lights, / Risking enchantment."[20] The pilgrim in the "dark wood" can only see the "monsters" and "fancy lights" that appear to him. To trust them, to take them as true, is certainly to "risk enchantment." And given the allusion to Dante, one can assume that these "monsters" and "fancy lights" are not at all benevolent.

This bleak view of the "middle of the way" is prepared by the lines on signification that immediately precede it, lines that very much resemble Nietzsche's theories of discourse. Eliot began this passage with a poet's frustration in "the intolerable wrestle / With words and meanings."[21] Later in the passage he dilates on this struggle: the individual mired in temporality cannot resort easily to the "knowledge derived from experience," because "[t]he knowledge imposes a pattern, and falsifies, / For the pattern is new in every moment."[22] In this view, the world is in complete flux, and the attempt to gather knowledge is really an imposition of a pattern upon that world. The individual must impose human patterns of knowledge upon the world, creating distinctions within a reality that is inherently indistinct. The pattern falsifies because, in reality, "the pattern is new in every moment." Eliot attempts to illustrate his meaning by changing the meter in the middle of the latter line, from the preliminary anapests to the concluding iambs after the word "new," rhythmically depicting a change of "pattern." As soon as a pattern is established, the transience of reality has ensured that that which was signified is now no more. While scripted metrics may be preserved on the page, the world has changed into a new pattern, making the knowledge once gained immediately obsolete and illusory. Thus "We are only undeceived / Of that which, deceiving, could no longer harm."[23] Only in retrospect, once we have been undeceived, can we actually know that which deceived and has harmed us. And the mode for this sudden realization is nowhere mentioned. However, it should also be noted that, in Dante, the opening lines, with all their foreboding, mark the moment of supreme optimism, for it is only with the graced awareness of obscurity and error that one can hope to overcome it. This depiction of the beginning of the soteriological path will become important later in the analysis.

Further, each attempt at knowledge represents a "valuation," not an instance of rational objectivity. As with Nietzsche, thinkers are immersed in the process of valuing and asserting the will to power, of forging an order where none exists. Our language manifests not an unchanging truth about the world, but the residue of former valuations that were made, not because of their truth value, but as part of the complex of exertions of the will to power. The meter nicely captures the rupturing effect of Nietzschean valuations: the term "Valuation" captures one's attention immediately, coming as it does at the beginning of the line. It also changes the metrical pattern from the iambs of the previous line to the "shocking" trochaic meter of "valuation." Remember Nietzsche's famous assertion that truth was a series of metaphors that "after long usage seems to a nation fixed, canonic, binding; truths are illusions of which one has forgotten that they are illusions."[24] In this sense, the animal references from part I and from Dante become particularly poignant:

language usage here has nothing to do with reasoning, but with a more primal self-assertion of existence.

For the poet in this part of the poem, the meditation on the obscurity of knowledge emerges from an initial dissatisfaction with poetic utterance itself, "the intolerable wrestle / With words and meanings."[25] In fact, the portion of free verse in the second half of part II follows immediately after the formal sequence of more or less strict iambic tetrameter lines describing nature as engaged in "constellated wars / Scorpion fights against the Sun / Until the Sun and Moon go down / Comets weep and Leonids fly / Hunt the heavens and the plains / Whirled in a vortex."[26] With the line "That was a way of putting it—not very satisfactory,"[27] the poet recognizes the paradox of describing the disordered world in fixed linguistic form.[28] To tread this "middle way" is therefore truly to "risk enchantment," the enchantments provided by the tendency of language to falsify and of words to slip away from their meanings or fail to carry the burden of communication and reference. In fact, we find that the whole meditation on falsifying and imposing patterns is really a meditation on the ability of language, once fixed on the page, to accurately represent a reality that always temporally outstrips it. The epistemological uncertainty expressed in the echoes of Dante therefore are intertwined with issues of language and signification. To be a pilgrim on the *via viatoris* of human time is to be susceptible to the "enchantments" of human language and knowing.

The second reference to the "middle way" emerges only after the poem prepares for it with a series of passages challenging the pretensions of the self. These passages explore dispossession and the insubstantiality of the self as soteriological goods. Part III moves the meditation on transience to a profound negation and detachment in which all human representation and all human desire is depicted as in some way suspect and soteriologically inefficient:

> In order to arrive at what you do not know
>> You must go by a way which is the way of ignorance.
> In order to possess what you do not possess
>> You must go by the way of dispossession.
> In order to arrive at what you are not
>> You must go through the way in which you are not.[29]

The reader here is left only with paradox: to know, one must be ignorant; to possess, one must dispossess; to arrive at a new identity, one must abandon the self and "go through the way in which you are not." The more the self asserts itself, the further from any soteriological goal it moves. The exposition on transience and desire and the critique of language have led in part III to a thorough-going skepticism regarding all human knowing and intention. Paradoxically, humans must intend not to intend, and relinquish when they hope to possess, and desire to end desiring.

Part IV then focuses the negating analysis of part III onto the human subject itself, pointing to the problem of desire as requiring drastic remedy from outside the individual. The verses figure Christ as the "wounded surgeon" who "plies the steel / That questions the distempered part."[30] Christ is a doctor who heals by cutting away and shaping; his care is "[t]he sharp compassion of the healer's art."[31] Eliot's depiction suggests that human beings are made up of "parts" that can be cut away, a set of physical constituents that are in turn also susceptible to the surgeon's knife. The "steel" of the surgeon's instrument, tempered in fire and purified, itself must heal the "distempered part" of the human body that has not yet been purified. The affliction of the patient here is fever, the inflammation of the body, the increase in body temperature. The body is consumed by the flames of desire; it needs to be consumed by the flames of purification that can "temper" it. Christ the healer wields an instrument, the instrument of his "art," that has itself been tempered in flame. Christ simultaneously cuts away and shapes the patient into his work of art, ironically a fragmented work. The art of this physician, then, is to pry the self away from its bodily attachments, desires, and pretensions by showing the depths of its temporal finitude and error. Thus, the poet ironically notes that "to be restored, our sickness must grow worse."[32]

Only the abandoning of the quest for the sovereign self, enabled by Christ, will lead to the ultimate healing of the individual. Christ's passion, alluded to in the last lines of the section, becomes a reminder of human error and mortality, as well as the prime example of perfect self-sacrifice and divine self-emptying:

> The dripping blood our only drink,
> The bloody flesh our only food:

In spite of which we like to think
That we are sound, substantial flesh and blood—
Again, in spite of that, we call this Friday good.[33]

The gruesome reminder of Christ's Passion serves as a reminder of human physical mortality as well as the sin that would lead Christ from the last supper to the passion on Calvary. The Eucharistic meal here is bread and wine, but even more so a prefiguration of the following day's butchery. This is a vicious, bloody, cannibalistic meal, shot through with sin. Christ's passion shows the hungry, desiring self, the self that consumes food, information, and Others, as sinful. And it is "in spite of" Christ's human suffering that we posit ourselves as "sound, substantial flesh and blood." According to the *OED*, "sound" can mean "not affected by disease, decay, or injury," as well as "of things or substances: solid, massive, compact," and "of a solid, substantial, ample, or thorough nature or character."[34] In this passage, humans are not healthy physically, epistemically, or morally, and neither are they "solid" or "substantial." Flesh and blood can be chewed and changed by bodily processes. This resonates in turn with the surgery metaphor. Once Christ cuts away the body, part by part, no substance emerges. It is not coincidental, I think, that such an analysis echoes Buddhist assertions that a self "is not found" in philosophical analyses, as we shall see shortly.

The Eucharistic reference also implies Christ's triumph in spite of humanity's sinful desire. This triumph is accomplished not only in his suffering but also in the shaping capacity of the ritual path. Good Friday is but prelude to the Resurrection, and the Eucharistic meal, as means of grace, leads to the resurrection of Christ in the lives of believers. The Eucharist, the ritual path, becomes the razor through which Christ begins to temper the passions of the faithful, transforming their consuming desire from within and fulfilling those desires beyond expectation. The Eucharistic reference here, after a rather Buddhistic analysis, points to an Anglo-Catholic formulation of the Impossible, the eradication of desire in and through desire. But it is precisely because the human being is mutable, not "substantial," that Christ can cut and shape human life into art.

Finally, after exploring finitude, mortality, and epistemic uncertainty, in part V of the poem, we get a recapitulation of the theme of the "middle way," this time beginning with an echo of the critique of language from

190   DESIRE AND THE ASCETIC IDEAL

the earlier passage, but moving to a different resolution than negation. This passage will reward a very close scrutiny. Eliot's evocation of the "middle way" returns to the meditation on poetic making from part II:

> So here I am, in the middle way, having had twenty years—
> Twenty years largely wasted, the years of *l'entre deux guerres*—
> Trying to learn to use words, and every attempt
> Is a wholly new start, and a different kind of failure
> Because one has only learnt to get the better of words
> For the thing one no longer has to say, or the way in which
> One is no longer disposed to say it. And so each venture
> Is a new beginning, a raid on the inarticulate
> With shabby equipment always deteriorating
> In the general mess of imprecision of feeling,
> Undisciplined squads of emotion.[35]

Interestingly, the dismantling of the pretensions of the self from the previous section is followed by the speaker's renewed self-assertion, "here I am, in the middle way, having had twenty years." The critique of "substantial flesh and blood" has done nothing to remove the temporal existence of the poet or the reality of a world plagued by the violence of "*deux guerres.*" The self may not exist in an ultimate sense, but that realization has not eradicated the struggle of the temporal self for linguistic expression and discovery, a struggle that Eliot describes slightly differently now. Rather than stressing the hopeless falsification that human knowledge and language impose upon the world, he depicts verbal description as something that can and must be undertaken again and again: "every attempt / Is a wholly new start, and a different kind of failure." Note the strange position of the word "Is" at the beginning of the line, receiving the visual and perhaps even auditory stress here. The same occurs later at the beginning of the line "Is a new beginning." Regardless of what it may mean to exist, the attempt itself, the renewal of struggle, is something that exists most strongly here. The poet does not indulge in despair but rather expresses a renewed sense of striving, albeit in a tone suffused with stoic resignation; the poet does, after all, write from the experience of two world wars, the poet's "deux guerres." An awareness of language's shortcomings has not eradicated the need to use it. Ventures and attempts, beginnings and new starts: these things possess a vivid reality for the poet. Further, human knowing is not so deprived as to prohibit the poet from knowing that each attempt itself is a "new start, and a different kind of failure." For the poet to say that "one had only learnt to get the better of words / For the thing one no longer has to say, or the way in which / One is no longer disposed to say it" implies that the poet had a "thing" to say, or something for which a particular expression is no longer adequate. Though "each venture" is a "raid on the inarticulate," the poet implies that there is still something to be gained from articulating and rearticulating.

The kind of articulating here, whose raw materials are an "imprecision of feeling" and "Undisciplined squads of emotion," is precisely the poetic articulation Eliot describes in "Tradition and the Individual Talent." The terms "feeling" and "emotion" are thus charged terms for Eliot, used frequently in his critical writing. In "Tradition," these are the two "elements" that the poet converts into poetry. In this essay Eliot characterizes the poet as a type of "catalyst" that joins emotion and feelings into different poetic configurations; he or she is a "medium in which special, or very varied, feelings are at liberty to enter into new combinations."[36] These two terms, "emotion" and "feeling," admittedly have very vague significance for Eliot in this essay, but they do seem to have different valences. The confusion is heightened by the fact that Eliot does not, I think, use them in their more colloquial senses. He writes, "The effect of a work of art upon the person who enjoys it is an experience different in kind from any experience not of art. It may be formed out of one emotion, or may be a combination of several; and various feelings, inhering for the writer in particular words or phrases or images, may be added to compose the final result."[37] "Emotion" in this passage seems to be an internal, subjective reaction, the "effect of a work of art upon the person who enjoys it." "Feeling," on the other hand, seems to refer to something that inheres in particular words or images for the author. It seems to invoke the poetic effect connected with either the mimetic quality or the sensuous texture of words. Hence, feelings are "words or phrases or images," all of which have a sensuous reality for either poet or reader. At any rate, both feeling and emotion seem to be "passions" in the sense that they represent something that happens to the poet or reader, an experience of the influence of an external force on the creating mind.

The poet's craft depends on "a continual self-sacrifice, a continual extinction of personality"[38] in order to allow these external influences to accumulate and form different combinations within the mind. The mind of the poet is "a receptacle for seizing and storing up number-less feelings, phrases, images, which remain there until all the particles which can unite to form a new compound are present together."[39] The poet/bricoleur must continually extinguish the personality in order to "store up" all of these feelings and to allow them to suggest to the mind new combinations, new poetic feelings on their own. Thus Eliot takes great pains to delineate both the active and the passive aspects of poetic creation, stressing the "givenness" of the materials with which the poet actively creates: "the more perfect the artist, the more completely sepa-rate in him will be the man who suffers and the mind which creates; the more perfectly will the mind digest and transmute the passions which are its material."[40]

This process of self-sacrifice and recombination, for Eliot, is that by which the poet, in a new situation, encounters tradition as well. Old and new consort to form a new utterance that speaks to a contemporary au-dience. The poet must be aware of the meaning that is shared across the years as well as the contours of the modern situation. This awareness, the poet's "historical sense . . . is a sense of the timeless as well as of the temporal and of the timeless and of the temporal together."[41] As Eliot makes clear in the essay, this historical sense is not a blind obedience to historical authority, but a process of recovery in the present that must be worked for by the poet: "Tradition . . . cannot be inherited, and if you want it you must obtain it by great labor."[42] Thus, the timeless within the temporal must be continually sought out, worked out, recovered through great poetic effort, and "transmuted" into new feeling, new text(ure).

It is precisely this theory that seems to be evoked in our passage from "East Coker." The middle way now represents, not epistemolog-ical uncertainty, but a view of poetic making that stresses the continual recommencing of textual signifying, the constant recovery of meaning, "the fight to recover what has been lost / And found and lost again and again."[43] And this process, as in "Tradition," is one that takes into con-sideration not only the individual's imposition of order onto the world but also the self-sacrifice of the poet and the reception of data from out-side the individual. Poetic creation takes place through both "strength and submission,"[44] and that which is to be "conquered"[45] must also be "recovered."

Buddhism and the "Middle Way"

Why this move from language's utter inability to signify to a historically informed view of poetic creation's ability to recover and reiterate? I believe the answer becomes clearer if we view the allusions to the "middle way" in "East Coker" through the lens of Madhyamaka Buddhism, the self-proclaimed "middle way" school. The founder of this school, Nagarjuna, presents, in his seminal text *Mulamadhyamakakarika* (henceforth "MK"), an analysis of causality that results in the declaration that all phenomena are both empty and conventionally existent. I believe Eliot has in mind here such a causal analysis, in which words themselves are shown to be both empty and yet pragmatically efficient. This is not to say that this is the only way to read the *Quartets,* or that Eliot's work is a hidden Buddhist polemical tract (though I do think Eliot's Christianity has a strong Buddhistic character). Rather, what I suggest is that a tarrying among the verses of Nagarjuna's thought will unlock yet another dimension of Eliot's complex poetry, clarifying one of its central structural elements. Therefore, it will benefit us to take a closer look at Nagarjuna's text and the view of causality and language presented there.

I rely in this presentation primarily on Jay Garfield's translation of the text, as well as his excellent commentary on it, which I find particularly illuminative of the poetry at hand.[46] The magnitude of my debt to his interpretation is significant and should become clear over the following pages; it is his interpretation of Madhyamaka I hope to present as clearly as possible. At the same time, I believe that Garfield's analysis describes the dialectic that is already identified as proper to Nagarjuna by Masaharu Anesaki in Eliot's notes for his philosophy class. Anesaki's discussion of Nagarjuna takes place against an implied accusation of nihilism, an accusation we saw in chapter 1 as influenced in part by Schopenhauer's embrace of the tradition. Anesaki's answer is to insist that Nagarjuna saw his thoughts as pointing to the reality of a Buddha nature. In this his understanding is unlike that of Garfield, though it is consistent with Tiantai: "Buddhism minus Buddha might have become a thorough nihilism. Nagarjuna *as a philosopher alone* might be taken as a pure nihilist, but he emphasizes on the other hand the Buddha nature."[47] Anesaki does not articulate how the concept of a Buddha nature figures into Nagarjuna's philosophy, and he clearly distinguishes Nagarjuan's philosophy from his own Tiantai Buddhism. To be sure, Anesaki's interpretation is highly controversial, and he interprets Nagarjuna as having the same teaching on the reality of the Buddha nature as the *Lotus Sutra*. We explore this part of Anesaki's teaching later in the next chapter.

Such a quasi-theological interpretation of this text is not shared by contemporary interpeters such as Garfield. Nevertheless, Anesaki does go on to identify Nagarjuna's dialectic in a very similar way. In fact Anesaki goes out of his way to distinguish this dialectic from the more theologically inflected Tiantai interpretation. In Eliot's notes, we find:

1. Being   dialectic of Nagarjuna
2. non-being
3. madyama[48]
4.

According to Anesaki, Nagarjuna's initial reference point is a mistaken interpretation of the world as consisting of things as having being. This view is then treated through rigorous philosophical analysis to be mistaken; things in the world lack being or are empty. Nagarjuna's linguistic analysis, though, prohibits our positing reality to the term "empty." Therefore, the resolution to the dialectic is to see things as being neither real nor unreal, as being conventionally real and ultimately unreal. Anesaki then goes on to give his understanding of Tiantai that distinguishes it from Nagarjuna's dialectic. He insists that there is an "ultimate"[49] that lies beyond dualisms. He asserts, "The ultimate which conditions being and non-being lies beyond both, but manifests itself in neither."[50] In other words, to refuse dualisms is to see all conceptualizations as conditioned by a more profound reality—for Anesaki, the Buddha nature.

Now as it stands, I believe that Eliot's interpretation of Buddhism in *Four Quartets* to be in sympathy with Anesaki's quasi-theological tendences. I explore this in the next chapter. However, I also suggest that Eliot plays with something like Nagarjuna's dialectic in regard to language use in the poetry. For Eliot, this means considering language and causality in a manner that reflects Nagarjuna's dialectic as it appears in his lecture notes. For Eliot in *Four Quartets*, this dialectic becomes a reflection of philosophical skepticism that opens up a soteriological dimension to human existence. In exploring this dialectic, Garfield's commentary is illuminating of a crucial trajectory of the poetry. As Garfield insists, in order to understand the Madhyamaka, it is absolutely crucial to understand what they are arguing against. Otherwise, it is very easy to interpret their texts simplistically as nihilistically denying *any* existence to objects and the self. As we will see, to interpret Nagarjuna this way would be to miss his unique philosophical contribution. The Madhyamaka argues against a specific notion of essence, or *svabhava*. Jay Garfield defines this notion as follows: "essences are by definition eternal and fixed. They are independent. And for a phenomenon to have an essence is for it to have some permanent independent core."[51] Such an essence would be self-caused, impervious to change, and without reliance on any temporal conditions whatsoever for its existence. For something to have essence, *svabhava,* would be for that thing to be in some sense free from temporal dependence.

To such a notion of essence, Nagarjuna applies a very particular version of the Buddhist concept of *pratityasamutpada*, the chain of dependent origination that explains how all things exist and retain the consequences of their actions within *samsara,* the round of desire, suffering, and rebirth. This analysis of dependence becomes the basis for the conception of the "middle way." Steven Collins has described how, from the very earliest textual strata of the Buddhist tradition, such a description of the conditioned nature of all things was seen as a "middle way" of sorts:

> Just as in the Buddha's first sermon the Eight-fold Path was the Middle Way between the extremes of sensual indulgence and ascetic self-torture, so here in the conceptual sphere, the teaching of Dependent Origination is a middle way between the two extremes of eternalism and annihilationism. "The same man acts and experiences the result—this is eternalism. One man acts, another experiences the result—that is annihilationism. Avoiding these two extremes, the Enlightened One gives a teaching of the Middle Way"—that is to say, Dependent Origination. In another place, the two extremes are said to be "existence" and "non-existence."[52]

Collins notes that the idea of the middle way, first described as a soteriological path of detachment between self-punishing asceticism and sensualism, in philosophical discourse becomes a conceptualization of the self between eternalism and annihilationism, allowing the Buddhist to argue the conditionality of the self while maintaining a sense of ethical responsibility. Only by maintaining some belief that the self suffers the ill consequences of its attachments, regardless of how devoid of essential unity it is, can the Buddhist defend the system of karma upon which the

196   DESIRE AND THE ASCETIC IDEAL

Buddha's soteriology depends. The Buddhist therefore argues against the belief that "there is an entity which is denoted by the grammatical subject of verbs . . . the Buddha's reply asserts the existence of an event described by the verbal notion, but denies that it is legitimate to infer the existence of the real subject from the verbal form."[53] The philosophical trick for the Buddhist becomes criticizing the "I," while still granting it some agency vis-à-vis the "verbal," the practical sphere of ethical action.

It is not only the "I" that has no abiding essence, but anything that falls under this understanding of causation, that is, everything. Our language then as a whole deceives us into thinking of things in the world as permanent rather than dependent conglomerations. In Henry Clark Warren's collection (that we know Eliot used), we find this passage from Buddhaghosa:

> Just as the word "chariot" is but a mode of expression for axle, wheels, chariot-body, pole, and other constituent members, place in a certain relation to each other, but when we come to examine the members one by one we discover that in the absolute sense there is no chariot . . . in exactly the same way the words "living entity" and "Ego" are but a mode of expression for the presence of the five attachment groups, but when we come to examine the elements of being one by one, we discover that in the absolute sense there is no living entity there to form a basis for such figments as "I am" or "I"; in other words, that in the absolute sense there is only name and form. The insight of him who perceives this is called knowledge of the truth.[54]

Buddhaghosa claims that words simply draw together elements that we take to be a really existing thing. We cannot initially do without these "modes of expression"; they provide us with our initial understanding of the world. Nevertheless, the things they signify do not exist in an "absolute sense." We have here then the beginning of the distinction between conventional and ultimate truth that would become so important in the Mahayana, of which Nagarjuna is a part. Collins notes that the early Buddhist notion of "two truths" usually refers to a distinction between higher and lower teachings, or the very distinction between language and the lack of essence of a thing.[55]

Codifying and expanding some of these earlier trends, Nagarjuna embraces the notion of the "middle way" as that which orders the whole of the Buddhist tradition, and consequently his text begins first and foremost with a thorough analysis of the impossibility of essence in a world of temporal conditionality. Dependent Origination is thus the chief ontological commitment of the text, asserted in the very first verses:

1. Neither from itself, nor from another,
   Nor from both,
   Nor without a cause,
   Does anything whatever, anywhere arise.

   . . . .

6. For neither an existent nor a non-existent thing
   Is a condition appropriate.
   If a thing is non-existent, how could it have a condition?
   If a thing is already existent, what would a condition do?[56]

The first verse presents a version of the Madhyamaka "tetralemma," a four-part analysis that supposedly takes into consideration all possible philosophical accounts of causation. From Nagarjuna's view, no existing thing can be the cause of itself, nor can an existing thing contain within itself the inherent potential to become a particular kind of essential thing.[57] Essences do not change or develop and do not depend on temporal conditions for their existence. Likewise, no essence can emerge from another unchanging essence: the very idea undercuts the autonomy of essence. If an entity is caused by another, brought about by another, it cannot be independent.[58]

If we cannot argue either of the first two options of the tetralemma, then we cannot argue the third, which combines the first two options by claiming that an essence emerges from both self and other. Finally, we cannot make the ridiculous claim that entities arise in the absence of conditions. This echoes the epistemological point raised above; if there were an entity separate from conditions, it would be impossible for us to know about it in the first place. Thus verse 6 summarizes the causal analysis. An independent existing thing that is truly an essence could not be contingent; it would have no conditions: "If a thing is already existent, what would a condition do?" A nonexistent thing also could not possibly be conditioned: "If a thing is nonexistent, how could it have a condition?" Thus we are left with the apparent paradox that things in this world, including selves, neither exist nor do not exist. Conditioned things cannot be essences, yet we also cannot say that they don't exist in some way. For Nagarjuna, such entities are empty, *shunya*.

Nagarjuna begins by dismantling a particular view of entities and causality, showing it to be incoherent. When we attempt to consider entities as conditioned, it becomes impossible to grasp on to something we can hold to be essential. Later in the text, Nagarjuna shifts his causal analysis to a more detailed analysis of the subject, epistemology, and language. This analysis begins to emerge in chapter 9 of the text, in which Nagarjuna takes the "dependence" on which he so rigorously insisted in the first chapter to assert the dependence of the self on objects exterior to it. The analysis of objects in the world is now turned back on the subject: "Someone is disclosed by something. / Something is disclosed by someone. / Without something how can someone exist? / Without someone how can something exist?"[59] Garfield notes in his commentary on the verse that Nagarjuna is asserting "the corelativity and interdependence of subject and object. Subjectivity only emerges when there is an object of awareness . . . the idea of an object with no subject is contradictory."[60] The concept of dependence therefore holds for the very relationship of knowing. Human subjectivity exists in a relationship of dependency from moment to moment on objects external to the subject. Subjects and objects are "disclosed" by one another in a temporal relationship, with neither receiving epistemic primacy in Nagarjuna's analysis.

Subjectivity depends on a relationship with externality, on the disjunction of self and otherness that, in a Buddhist context, will lead to an unfortunate grasping of self, the "I," as "mine." It is precisely this point that Nagarjuna makes in chapter 18 of MK, an important chapter that elucidates the relation between grasping, consciousness, and language:

4. When views of "I" and "mine" are extinguished,
   Whether with respect to the internal or external,
   The appropriator ceases.
   This having ceased, birth ceases.

5. Action and misery having ceased, there is nirvana.
   Action and misery come from conceptual thought.
   This comes from mental fabrication.
   Fabrication ceases through emptiness.[61]

LANGUAGE IN THE MIDDLE WAY   199

Here views of "I" and "mine," "internal" and "external," must be released in order for liberation from rebirth to occur. But given the previous analysis of subjectivity, these views imply far more than simple greed or possessiveness. They refer, rather, to the very operations of consciousness itself, which "appropriates" externality as part of itself. Garfield explains: "By 'appropriation,' Nāgārjuna indicates any cognitive act by means of which one takes an attribute or entity as one's own, or as part of one's self."[62] Even though one cannot think the subject without the object, the manner in which these objects are identified *as such* and are likewise appropriated by consciousness will depend upon some sort of subjective act of grasping. This is precisely what Nagarjuna goes on to explain in verse 5, where mental fabrication leads to conceptual thought, which leads constantly to the wrong kind of action and appropriation, and therefore to continued suffering. Mental fabrication claims aspects of externality for the self by making them into objects for appropriation. It is precisely this aspect of consciousness that reifies external existents into essences, creating the ontology within which the subject lives.[63] So the self is not "other" to its objects—it in part constitutes them. It is also not the same as those objects—it has a distinct existence.

Verse 7 then goes on to present the paradox of selfhood, while bringing the problematic of language firmly into the purview of the previous statements on mental fabrication. Language, it turns out, has nothing substantial to which to refer, nor does it possess in itself any essential reality. Nagarjuna writes:

> 7. What language expresses is non-existent.
> The sphere of thought is nonexistent.
> Unarisen and unceased, like nirvana
> Is the nature of things.[64]

Verse 7 brings the crisis to a head: not only is what language expresses empty, but the sphere of thought is also empty. Language and thought fabricate the distinctions of the world. The external world exists without such distinctions, and it is only through human mental fabrications that a world of objects exists to begin with. The world exists for human beings as part of human consciousness. This does not, however, mean that there is no external world.[65] Note that Nagarjuna claims that "what language *expresses* is non-existent" (emphasis mine). Language and thought both fabricate and express, and express through fabricating.

200   DESIRE AND THE ASCETIC IDEAL

Those things that language expresses, the phenomena of the world, are empty. But language can still express phenomena. Garfield explains this tension as follows: "To say of a thing that it is dependently arisen is to say that its identity as a single entity is nothing more than its being the referent of a word. The thing itself, apart from the conventions of individuation, has no identity. To say of a thing that its identity is merely a verbal fact about it is to say that it is empty."[66]

The seeming equivocation in Garfield's commentary here actually reflects the deliberate ambiguity in Nagarjuna's text: there are referents to words, and yet words serve as establishing conventional reality through individuation. All things are "conventionally existent but ultimately empty."[67] Hence, we get the conclusion to the sequence from chapter 18:

> 8. Everything is real and not real,
>   Both real and not real,
>   Neither real nor not real.
>   This is Lord Buddha's teaching.

. . . .

> 10. Whatever comes into being dependent on another
>   Is not identical to that thing.
>   Nor is it different from it.
>   Therefore it is neither nonexistent in time nor permanent.[68]

The conclusion to this important chapter combines Nagarjuna's view on language and the self with the analysis of temporal dependence that he had developed in earlier chapters. He compounds the epistemic ambiguity with his previous causal skepticism. Any thing that comes to be, dependent on conditions, cannot be the same as those conditions, for we speak of a different, transient entity. Nor can it be said to be free of those conditions, precisely because it is dependent. Thus it is neither "nonexistent in time nor permanent." It is "both real and not real." Further, note the temporal tension expressed here. Even though entities change, we cannot say that the later version of the entity is the same as the earlier, nor can we say that it is completely different from it. We cannot say it is the same, since obviously it has changed, and we cannot say it is completely different, for that would be to reify a later stage of the entity, granting it some form of independence from its conditions. Rather, the entity exists in temporal tension.

Take the self: if the self comes into existence in juxtaposition to the objects of the world, its subjectivity is dependent on those conditions. The self is not identical to those conditions, nor can it be said to be completely other from them. It requires that externality as its co-constituting other. Further, as above, we cannot say that each temporal moment of the self is the same as, or different from, the moments that preceded it. The self exists in temporal tension. Or, consider language: it emerges dependent on the exterior world, yet it shapes that world for human consciousness. It cannot be said to be identical with the world, nor can it be said to be completely different from it. Language itself is dependent. Daniel Arnold has made precisely this point in describing Nagarjuna's views on language:

> Nāgārjuna... insists that precisely because all things are dependently originated, *our accounts of them, too, are dependent*—dependent, that is, on the fact that phenomena exist and we are able to describe them. Because our descriptions so depend they must not be understood as providing metaphysical explanations that operate as though they referred beyond phenomena to "the reasons *for* phenomena"; and, also because our descriptions so depend, phenomena are not allowed to be replaced by our descriptions of them. That is, they exist.[69]

I would also stretch the point and assert that each instance of linguistic utterance depends on the entire context of language that precedes it. Language usage is itself dependent on a linguistic history of effects that makes that usage neither completely the same nor different from prior usage. Regardless of this, however, the import of the prior analyses is that if we give independent, inherent existence to any of the entities above, we remove them from the world of dependence. Yet this is absurd, for as Garfield notes, "Emptiness is important because it is the only way that things can exist."[70] Emptiness, dependent origination, the tension of a temporally bound being, is the only way that this being can exist in any way we could know. Otherwise an entity would be completely beyond our realm of experience, completely beyond thought and language.

Nagarjuna shows the depth of language's dependence when he asserts paradoxically that his *own* designations of things as "empty" are also empty. It is in this move that Nagarjuna reveals the full significance of the linguistic "middle way," demonstrating the dependence of Buddhist

202   DESIRE AND THE ASCETIC IDEAL

discourse itself on previous instances of reification. In chapter 24, verse 8, Nagarjuna argues: "Whatever is dependently co-arisen / That is explained to be emptiness. / That, being a dependent designation, / Is itself the middle way." Garfield's commentary on the text explains that Nagarjuna is asserting the "emptiness of all phenomena."[71] In other words, you must first perceive phenomena before claiming they are empty; the designation "empty" depends on the previously reifying nature of language. If nothing were ever reified, seen as a substantial unity, there would never have been a need for the teaching of emptiness, for neither would there have been suffering itself. The teaching responds to a set of conditions and is dependent on those conditions, as in analyzing a table, for example:

> No conventional table, no emptiness of the table. The emptiness is dependent upon the table and is, therefore, itself empty of inherent existence, as is the emptiness of *that* emptiness, and so on, ad infinitum. To see the table as empty, for Nāgārjuna, is not to somehow see "beyond" the illusion of the table to some other, more real entity. It is to see the table *as conventional; as dependent.* But the table that we see when we see its emptiness is the very same table, seen not as the substantial thing we instinctively posit, but rather as it is. Emptiness is hence not different from conventional reality—it is the fact that conventional reality is conventional. Hence it must be dependently arisen since it depends upon the existence of empty phenomena.[72]

Thus, "emptiness" does not refer to an essence lurking beyond the shadowy phenomena of this world. Being a dependent designation, it describes the state of phenomena themselves.[73] This also opens the way for the second important point that Nagarjuna makes at the end of the text, the identity of *samsara* and *nirvana.* Because the designation of emptiness is dependent on phenomena, the realization of this emptiness, the soteriological telos of *nirvana,* depends upon the prior positing of conventional phenomena. *Nirvana* becomes a way of seeing the world accurately (as empty); it is a shift in how the conventional world is perceived, not the positing of a separate realm of emptiness separate from the world of phenomena.[74]

Most importantly, it is precisely because the world is empty that *nirvana* can be attained in the first place. The fact that all things are dependently originated means that suffering also arises in dependence, and that to eliminate those things upon which suffering depends means eliminating suffering itself. Thus, as Garfield rightly points out, emptiness is the basis of the whole practice of Buddhist life: "the path only makes sense, and cultivation of the path is only possible, if suffering is impermanent and alleviable and if the nature of mind is empty and hence malleable."[75] The fact that all phenomena are empty makes the idea of self-cultivation, of striving for improvement, cogent. As in Eliot's "hospital," the self can only be cultivated if it is not essential, and its suffering not permanent.[76] Kearns explains that a "purpose of this apparently paradoxical assertion that nirvana and samsara are 'not different' is . . . so that the Madhyamika . . . does not evade temporality but works through it."[77]

Near the conclusion of the chapter 24, Nagarjuna shows that the soteriological potential of the Buddhist path is precisely what is at stake. At issue is the reality of suffering: suffering must be real enough to be a problem for human beings but must not be seen as essential and incapable of changing:

> 23. If suffering had an essence,
> Its cessation would not exist.
> So if an essence is posited,
> One denies cessation.
>
> . . . .
>
> 25. If suffering, arising, and
> Ceasing are nonexistent
> By what path could one seek
> To obtain the cessation of suffering?[78]

Nagarjuna ends with a soteriological concern, now filtered through his sophisticated linguistic and causal analysis. In order for the cultivation of the Buddhist path to be both possible and necessary, suffering must be seen to have reality, though not essential existence. If essence is posited of suffering, suffering cannot end. But if suffering has no abiding existence whatsoever, if it has no consequences, there is no need for the disciplines of the path. Likewise, the self must be seen as abiding enough to bear the consequences of its previous actions and mutable enough to be reformed.[79] So Nagarjuna's thought seeks to index and hold open the possibility of the ultimate, unresolved Buddhist paradox, the overcoming of desire and attachment in and through the discipline of desire and the proper attachments. One must desire not to desire.

204   DESIRE AND THE ASCETIC IDEAL

Language and Causality in *Four Quartets*

Finally turning back to Eliot, we find a new way of thinking about how causality and representation are presented in the *Quartets*. To begin, recall that the first meditation on the "middle way" represented the bleakness of epistemological uncertainty. As with Nietzsche, language and thought impose false patterns on the world: "The knowledge imposes a pattern, and falsifies, / For the pattern is new in every moment."[80] Further, the poet portrayed knowledge as an ever-developing series of human (all too human) valuations that are made only to be overcome later by more potent valuations: "And every moment is a new and shocking / Valuation of all we have been."[81] The "middle way" is therefore pictured as Dante's dark mountainside at the outset of *Inferno*, where the pilgrim is threatened with carnality, bestiality, and illusion. Eliot's speaker decides that "The only wisdom we can hope to acquire/ Is the wisdom of humility: humility is endless."[82] Suddenly, in parts III and IV, "East Coker" plummets into a relentless negation, into (literally) a cutting away of illusion and desire. We are finally brought face to face with a very Buddhist-like analysis, in which human parts are cut away by Christ the surgeon; the notion that we are "sound, substantial flesh and blood" is given up, and the reader wonders where the poet could possibly go next. Both language and the self are, in Nagarjuna's terms, "empty." Yet at the same time, the inessential nature of the self, the self's vulnerability to suffering, change, and decay, allows Christ to sculpt the self into a work of art with his tempered scalpel. The instrument by which Christ accomplishes his "art" is the ritual sphere, the path of devotion in which human consumption is defeated from within by the Eucharist, in moments of impossible transformation. As with Buddhism, desire is defeated initially from within desire.

In part V, we find a reassertion of the poet's subjectivity: "So here I am in the middle way."[83] The "I" that was just dismantled appears again in temporal, spatial existence: "I," "here." Some sense of subjectivity remains, even after the dismembering analysis of part IV. The "I" has been seen to be ultimately empty, yet its reality as one engaging with language and practice persists. In Nagarjuna's language, the ultimate reality of the self and the world has been glimpsed, but the conventional self persists in the activity and passivity of the salvific path. Further, we have the emergence of a rhetoric of recovery, linked with Eliot's own notions of poetic making, notions not only of the merging of feeling, thought, and emotion, but also of making the past present through a poetic process inescapably informed by an awareness of the past. The poetic process becomes "the fight to recover what has been lost / And found and lost again and again."[84] Eliot's poetic process is that whereby emotion is reconciled with feeling, the interior with the exterior, and action with passion.

Most importantly, this change in rhetoric marks a change in the overall intellectual trajectory of *Four Quartets*, for, following the evocation of the "middle way," "The Dry Salvages" obsesses about the presence of the past; it speaks of that which abides, of the repeating patterns of time, of the temporal and human regularities upon which language and knowledge depend. Consider the image of the edge of the ocean, "the beaches where it tosses / Its hints of early and other creation."[85] The beach shows forth the wreckage of former times, the detritus that remains after these artifacts have been used and abandoned. Their creators have disappeared, but they remain as hieroglyphics to be read and pondered. Or consider this passage from part II:

> It seems, as one becomes older,
> That the past has another pattern, and ceases to be a mere sequence—
> Or even development: the latter a partial fallacy
> Encouraged by superficial notions of evolution,
> Which becomes, in the popular mind, a means of disowning the past.
> The moments of happiness—not the sense of well-being,
> Fruition, fulfillment, security or affection,
> Or even a very good dinner, but the sudden illumination—
> We had the experience but missed the meaning,
> And approach to the meaning restores the experience
> In a different form, beyond any meaning
> We can assign to happiness.[86]

We hear that this illumination "Is not the experience of one life only / But of many generations."[87] Suddenly, the past has a pattern and is no longer merely a sequence of separate moments (nor a teleological, evolutionary progression). Certain experiences belong not to one generation, but to many. This experience cannot be "disowned," but remains a part of human temporal experience. And we find that one such experience to which the past attests through a series of attempted figurations is that of humanity's "sudden illuminations," which cannot be fully expressed, but can be approached by successive generations of writers through different "forms" that linguistically transform the experience.

Not only do the traces of illumination abide, but so do the other "ineffable" experiences of "agony":

> Now, we come to discover that the moments of agony
> (Whether, or not, due to misunderstanding,
> Having hoped for the wrong things or dreaded the wrong things,
> Is not in question) are likewise permanent
> With such permanence as time has.
>
> . . . .
>
> Time the destroyer is time the preserver.[88]

Suffering here is not only physical, but mental and emotional as well: it is caused by "misunderstanding," or improper hoping, or improper fearing. Moments of pain and the consequences of error remain within human selves, once again placing the persistence of suffering at the heart of "The Dry Salvages." The experience of suffering seems, for Eliot, to be a vivid reminder that we are the inheritors of any type of pain we have previously experienced. These marks of pain abide, but only with "such permanence as time has." The self retains the memory of agony, but the poet implies that the pain is not eternal or essential; there is a possibility of its ceasing. For we are also inheritors of the sudden illuminations as well, both those of our own lives and those within a broader historical context, that we can strive to recover. To invoke the presentness of the past in suffering is also to open the possibility of the recovery of the past.

What we see, therefore, in the references to the middle way in "East Coker," is a change in emphasis from that which changes to that which abides, from that which is imposed upon reality to that which influences the individual from without, from that which language falsifies to that which it signifies. I therefore suggest that Eliot's allusions to the "middle way" signal the moment in *Four Quartets* where Eliot's poetic persona moves to adopt something like Nagarjuna's dual perspective on causation and language. Just as Nagarjuna asserts that entities are dependent, that they cannot be said to be completely different from nor the same as the entities of previous moments, so too does Eliot take into consideration the constantly changing nature of temporality on one hand ("East Coker"), and the abidingness of entities on the other ("The Dry

Salvages"), and all the while preserving the salvific potential of language. True, this potential is hampered by the challenges of deception, illusion, and falsification, elucidated in the early sections of "East Coker." But the emptiness and transience described in "East Coker" is transformed at the end of it and is shown to be the precondition of the path of cultivation, of being shaped by Christ. For both Eliot and Nagarjuna, the realization of emptiness and suffering, based on the healing intervention of a teacher (Christ, the Buddha) enables the salvific process of cultivation toward an impossible telos. The emptiness or dependence of the subject exposes it to the suffering of the world, but also enables the *shaping* of the self through practice and words; the Christian believer consumes the Word but is in turn shaped by it through words and sacrament. Or, rather, the human being becomes the poem, the word of the Word through praxis and desire. Human suffering, that is, the existential condition of the self being acted upon, is transformed from within, into the therapeutic instrument of salvation.

Recall the soteriological import behind Nagarjuna's causal analysis. The purpose of the doctrine of dependent origination, from the earliest moments of the Buddhist canon, was to explain temporal becoming in terms of suffering. This meant that it not only had to attack notions of an eternal, essential self, but also to explain how a transient self could be said to suffer and need redemption at all. Nagarjuna's analysis attempts to accomplish both through an insistent assertion of dependence. The self is not an eternal essence; it is temporal and transient. But this does not mean that the self lacks the traces, both mental and physical, of its temporal experience of the world. The self acts and is acted upon. It is only because of this dialectic that the self's attachments to the world can be explained as soteriologically detrimental suffering. And it is only because of this dialectic that the self can begin its way upon the path through first developing the proper attachments. It must have a history of attachment as well as objects exterior to it to which it can be attached and from which it can consequently be liberated. The traces of bodily and mental suffering (in the broadest sense) must be considered to have at least as much reality as the continuing process of desiring and becoming. Therefore, in Nagarjuna's analysis, the self is dependent on previous versions of itself as well as upon the externality of that which it reifies.

On a linguistic level, what we find at the end of "East Coker" is a movement, after critiques of language, epistemology, and essence, to a reinstatement of the self, language, and external objects, but now as temporal and dependent. We find, as shown above, an insistence that there are aspects of human existence that can be figured and refigured, discovered and rediscovered. We find that language, inexact though it be, can express aspects of reality with some degree of success. And we find a reassertion of the self that strives toward a salvific goal, expressed at the end of "East Coker" in terms of the poetic search for meaning. Recall the soteriological valence of part IV of the poem that prepares the way for the culminating allusion to the "middle way." The realization of the emptiness of the self was figured as an operation of cutting away and shaping, undertaken by Christ the surgeon/artist upon the mortal, sinful subject. The world was portrayed as a soteriological hospital: "The whole earth is our hospital / Endowed by the ruined millionaire."[89] The healing that takes place within this hospital is not one we tend to enjoy, however, for it challenges selfishness and self-possession by dismantling the self. Yet the "I" that was reinstated in part V, the "I" of the middle way, is still a subject who suffers and stands in need of healing, and one who, like Dante, treads the path to salvation; there is still some sense of the subject who strives to "get the better of words" in order to express the "inarticulate" or to "recover what has been lost." The self acts and suffers "in the aspect of time / Caught in the form of limitation / Between un-being and being."[90]

For both Eliot and Nagarjuna, the reality of suffering opens up the possibility of signification, for suffering implies both the transience of the self and also the abidingness of the effects of action and suffering. Recall that, for Nietzsche, signification was impossible in a world of flux and becoming. Signification is impossible, as, in Eliot's words, "every moment is a new and shocking / Valuation of all we have been." This led Nietzsche to a revaluation of mythos, a radical reveling in the will to power and language's metaphorical potential. Neither Eliot nor Nagarjuna rests in such a view of temporality. Both suggest that such a view fails to take the realities of suffering and dependence seriously enough; the pain and effects of temporal existence persist and cannot be willed away. Because entities both change and abide, the possibility of reference remains. In "The Dry Salvages," Eliot gives us the ominous portrait of the "ragged rock in the restless waters"[91] upon which waves constantly crash: "In navigable weather it is always a seamark / To lay a course by: but in the sombre season / Or the sudden fury, is what it always was."[92] The rock is dependable enough to successfully navigate by and solid enough to wreck the storm-tossed ship. It is ignored at one's peril, and its reality is confirmed by the suffering it regularly causes. The rock becomes emblematic of the causes of human suffering in general, from epistemic and ethical error to physical pain.

This does not mean that both thinkers turn their backs on the fabrication involved in human knowing and representing, a fabrication upon which Nietzsche insisted. Both realize that any soteriological goal passes through an imperfect discourse that must describe the problem, suggest the solution, and point to the ultimate illumination, regardless of how ineffable it might be. The allusion in "East Coker" to "Tradition and the Individual Talent," in which the poet must deal with "feeling" and "emotion," in a dialectic of passivity and activity, deploys the kind of epistemic moderation Nagarjuna presents when he insists that words depend on externality on the one hand and subjective grasping on the other. In order to understand human knowing, one must take into consideration both human fabrication and that which happens to human knowers. Both are dependent on one another. Ultimately, for both Eliot and Nagarjuna, the middle way stretches discourse between past *and* future, interior *and* exterior, deception *and* expression.

As mentioned earlier, the "middle way" is also a reference to the beginning of Dante's pilgrimage from darkness to light, from obscurity to clarity, from desire to love. Eliot wrote of Dante in the Clark Lectures that, in his brand of mysticism, "the divine vision of God could only be attained by a process in which the analytic intellect took part; it was through and by and beyond discursive thought that man could arrive at beatitude."[93] The path to salvation for Eliot, as for Madhyamaka Buddhism, begins with discursive thought and cultivation, leading beyond it to a moment in which the individual's intentionality and desire are completely transformed and overcome. It is true that for Eliot, and *not* for Nagarjuna, this moment is the moment of Christian grace and love. Eliot will only go so far with the Buddhist. Nevertheless, both thinkers would realize the paradoxical nature of this moment. Both would assert that, prior to that moment, the striving to realize the transformation must pass through discourse relentlessly, rigorously, and with a profound humility in the face of ambiguity: "For us there is only the trying. The rest is not our business."[94]

7

PERFORMING THE DIVINE ILLUSION

Memory, Desire, and the Performance
of Form in "Burnt Norton"

In section II of "Burnt Norton," Eliot paradoxically describes the mystical "still point" that lies at the heart of all existence. In the process he uses a technical philosophical term to describe consciousness lifted beyond itself to see the will. The term is *erhebung*. In a brilliant reading of *Four Quartets*, Aakanksha Virkar-Yates has reminded us that this term refers to Arthur Schopenhauer's theory of the sublime.[1] In an analysis mainly focusing on Schopenhauer's theory of music, Virkar-Yates argues that what Eliot has done in *Four Quartets* is to substitute a metaphysics of love for Schopenhauer's metaphysics of the will.[2] The moment of *erhebung*, translated by Virkar-Yates as "exaltation,"[3] then becomes a moment when love becomes conscious of itself as well as the abiding presence of desire.

I suggest in this final chapter that Eliot once again alludes to the *upaya* concept, in imagery borrowed from the *Lotus Sutra*, to depict the moment of religious insight as itself part of a process of cultivation that involves thought and feeling. Schopenhauer's *erhebung* gets caught up in an ascetic path in a manner quite unlike Schopenhauer's own metaphysical assumption. As Virkar-Yates recognizes, this process of cultivation takes place in a context of increasing love and persistent desire. The metaphysics in "Burnt Norton" is the result of an initial bracketing of pure philosophical speculation. It results from a soteriological hermeneutics that seeks to remain true to both the reality of human suffering and the moments of soteriological insight, moments the poem describes in terms of selflessness and surrender.

The allusions to the *upaya* doctrine provide an intercultural point of comparison for the idea of a metaphysical absolute—either God or Anesaki's Mahayana Buddha—as leading human beings in their diversity to a soteriological endpoint. It becomes a way of conceiving the aesthetic and ritual cultivation of humanity in an inclusivist paradigm. It is therefore significant that Eliot's own model of Christian inclusivism is itself formulated in dialogical relation with the cultural other. Eliot's poetry is still Christian, but it is hybrid. Its hybridity, embodied in poetry, retains a provisional nature. In this, I believe it is an incipient comparative theology, incipient because it leaves systematic elaboration for a later time and context. Eliot's poetry is content to suggest potential starting points for such an endeavor. Those starting points have been thought and felt by validating the soteriological paths and insights of the religious other and thinking analogically.

Metaphysics and Vision

The opening of "Burnt Norton" is meant to bracket metaphysical claims through an analysis of temporal experience. This analysis opens up a soteriological dimension of human life by seeing moments of regret and moments of atemporal illumination as providing the patterns that make time meaningful. The poem brackets metaphysical claims by claiming that temporally immanent existence cannot possibly gain the kind of perspective on time that would make metaphysical speculation possible. On the other hand, the poetry does not close off another sort of escape from time, an experience of timelessness within time that is possible amid soteriological praxis. The poetry signals this through a poetic, experimental synthesis of two ideas, the Buddhist experience of the emptiness of the self and the Christian experience of selfless love. This synthesis is suggested by the juxtaposition of the lotus and the rose at the heart of the rose garden in "Burnt Norton." The poem—and the sequence—ultimately suggest that these two religious traditions make possible a meaningful existence in time by keeping alive and enhancing the memory of the transcendence of time. They mobilize time for its transcendence.

In its breathless set of opening lines, the outset of "Burnt Norton" patiently considers the possibility that time might have a formal teleology, only to immediately bracket it. It begins: "Time present and time past / Are both perhaps present in time future, / And time future contained in time past."[4] The key word at the outset is "perhaps." The present and the past may be "present" in the future: they may exist there already in some fulfilled form. The present and the future *may* be "contained" in the past, held there as a seed to develop. The poem evokes the potential for a teleology that may echo Aristotelian form. But the "perhaps" suggests that there is no way to obtain a bird's-eye view of time to know, philosophically speaking, whether time embodies a formal teleology. The opening of this poem situates us within time, and therefore also in a skeptical position about a metaphysics that may presume to be above it, at least in any sort of philosophical or scientific manner. This skeptical posture resembles Kierkegaard's criticism of Hegelian idealism in *Philosophical Fragments.*

From this moment of skepticism, however, the poem immediately moves to the soteriological. The priority of the poem changes from the potential of accounting for time in its entirety to the idea that temporal experience may give rise to the idea and necessity of redemption. The poem continues: "If all time is eternally present / All time is unredeemable."[5] Redemption only makes sense as a concept if we are within a temporal existence. If we live in a constant present, we are unchanging and static: if we are in a deficient state, we will remain in the deficient state; if we are in a positive state, we will remain in a positive state. Our existence is one of change, and change is typically perilous; it means we are always under the threat of losing what we have, of veering away from commitments, of being influenced by fortune or mortality. However, change is also the precondition of redemption. In a Christian context, if one is mired in sin, even that is not strictly speaking permanent. Our capacity for metamorphosis gives to our existence a salvific potential.

The evocation of redemption is crucial in understanding the contours of the next nine lines. The poem launches into a meditation on "what might have been"[6] and "the passage which we did not take . . . the door we never opened / Into the rose-garden."[7] In the context of the concept of redemption, I think that this can be understood in two different ways. In Eliot's poem, especially the broader sequence, the moment of love, of transcendence, strictly speaking "does not happen": it lifts one beyond temporal experience and the phenomenal self. It is, as Kevin Hart would term it, a "counter-experience,"[8] an experience beyond phenomenal experience, an experience of the "Outside"[9] to experience. And it is one that we "did not take" because it is an experience of gift, an experience that one cannot lay hold of.

On the other hand, the experience of time is also potentially the experience of regret. This potential experience comes from the trail of possibilities left behind after each temporal decision and act: "What might have been is an abstraction / Remaining a perpetual possibility / Only in a world of speculation. What might have been and what has been / Point to one end, which is always present."[10] The possibility that Eliot gives us is one of a gradually unfolding set of choices and circumstances, choices that cut off forever certain possibilities. If one chooses and actualizes one possibility, other possibilities are eliminated. We exist in the present, against a background of never actualized possibilities, and potentially a sea of regret and suffering.

The beginning of Eliot's sequence prompts the reader to consider the potential relation between these two experiences, of illumination and regret. This comes in and through the allusion to the garden of Eden. Eliot's garden at the beginning of "Burnt Norton" here is a "rose-garden" inhabited by voices of children. The image of the rose obviously raises the specter of love—both romantic love (alluding to the relationship with Emily Hale) and divine love, as the image of a rose represented the apex of heaven in Dante's *Paradiso,* beginning in canto 30.[11] It can also be associated with a lost innocence and an alienation from the divine, and therefore with a sense of primal spiritual loss. Regret can occur when the mind tears itself away from the present to become attached to the lost possibilities of the past. But regret can also suggest that there *was* a possibility that was more beneficial that was turned down, from which the self turned away. Regret is a backward glance to what might have been, but with the pain of realizing that the path that was chosen led to suffering. In personal terms, for Eliot this might have meant a response to the relationship with Emily Hale. In religious terms, the poem evokes imagery from the Garden of Eden, suggesting that humanity as a whole experiences a primal regret, that existence as a whole is beset by the regret that it turned (or turns) away from a unity with God.[12] Jewel Spears Brooker has insisted that such an experience of alienation was prepared for Eliot in Bradley's philosophy, where the fragmented consciousness is always already alienated from the wholeness of immediate experience, beyond subject-object dualism.[13]

I do not think the poetry refers to the Eden narrative in any kind of straightforward biblical way. Rather, I think the poetry means to invoke an experience of lack in or dissatisfaction with temporal experience emerging from within that experience itself. In analyzing St. Augustine's view of time in *Confessions,* Paul Ricoeur identifies a similar temporal tension as that of "Burnt Norton." Ricoeur describes Augustine's concept of the "*distentio animi,*" the stretching of the soul in temporal experience between the past, present, and future. After invoking Augustine's mystical experiences in *Confessions,* he writes: "But it is precisely this experience of eternity that has the function of a limiting idea, when the intelligence 'compares' time with eternity . . . the reverberation . . . of this negation that is thought on the living experience of temporality will not convince us that the absence of eternity is not simply a limit that is thought, but a lack that is felt at the heart of temporal experience."[14] Augustine both thinks of eternity as the eternal now against which human temporal experience unfolds, but also experiences it in moments of timeless illumination. These experiences of eternity give temporal experience a sense of loss or alienation. Eternity becomes the "lack that is felt at the heart of temporal existence." Eternity is not simply a speculative thought, but an experience that gives shape to the lived experience of the soul.

In Eliot's terms, temporal experience plays out against the background of an eternity too real for human beings to tarry in for very long. These moments therefore evoke both redemption and regret. The salvific moment casts into relief the present moment and prompts one to want to reapproach it. The memory of the past can therefore be a morass of regret, or it could contain the seeds of hope and emancipation. As Eliot writes in "Little Gidding," "History may be servitude / History may be freedom."[15] The sequence of poetry continues then to mine the past for traces of these timeless moments, in poetry, in other religious traditions, and in the Christian tradition. The oblique reference, in some cunning word play, to the "lotos rose"[16] brings both Buddhism and Christianity together as traditions oriented, in their own way, to time's other, both attempting to develop paths of cultivation that pursue the memory traces of timelessness to transcend temporal experience. As Eliot writes later in "Burnt Norton," "Only through time time is conquered."[17]

The poetry moves from a view of time in terms of possibilities and actualities now to a heightened vision rooted in memory. But this is a weird sort of memory: it is the memory of a door not opened or a passage not taken. The memory of something not done. Eliot writes:

Footfalls echo in the memory
Down the passage which we did not take
Towards the door we never opened
Into the rose garden. My words echo
Thus, in your mind.[18]

Again, there is a double speak here. This is the memory potentially tied to regret, the memory of something that didn't happen, that perhaps the speaker wanted to happen. But it is also the memory of "what didn't happen," a kind of counter-experience. Eliot's sequence centers on a double evocation: of regret and of counter-experience. The move into memory is what joins the two.

The "footfalls" in the memory refer in an immediate sense to words. The poetic speaker makes this association in the final lines above, but also in and through the parallel stresses at the ends of the lines: "did not take"; "never opened"; "My words echo." Though the reference to "we" here is ambiguous, it certainly encompasses the relation of poetic speaker to readers. The words of the poet are to echo in the mind of the readers like footsteps toward a "door we never opened." On one hand, this points to the specificity of the poetic text. This series of words, in this arrangement, in this circumstance, is particular to Eliot. To the reader, they are literally a path that they did not take. Eliot took it, and now no one else can take it as he has. The text stands forth against the white page in its utter specificity.

But what does that mean for the reader who will traverse the text? Are we simply left to read a dead experience? In other words, what is the point of the echo in the mind of the reader? The speaker seems to ask this question next: "But to what purpose / Disturbing the dust on a bowl of rose-leaves / I do not know."[19] On the other hand, the echoes in the mind represent a dynamic experience; the footfalls provoke the reader into a complex engagement between the footfalls of words—in this case, sensuous, music-laden words—and the reader's own memory. Yes, the words on the page represent a unique pattern that only one poet has created, but this pattern, when allowed to resonate in the mind of the reader, can potentially set the reader off on their own journey of memory.[20] The

216   DESIRE AND THE ASCETIC IDEAL

event of meaning represented here is one in which an event of thought and feeling on the page provokes the reader into a parallel experience of thought and feeling, in which they set off into their own memory, following a different set of echoes, in pursuit of that which did not happen, strictly speaking.

Finally, as mentioned above, the "we" is the human race: there is a mythological element to this journey through memory. The memory is potentially of a religious path not taken, a feeling of alienation or regret that accompanies our experience of time. It is the speculation of what time's "Other" would be like. As Paul Ricoeur says, the experience of time conjures also the idea of time's "Other." Here, the "Other" would be an existence that didn't fall into the distension of time, that didn't fall into a situation in which the self needed to be redeemed. The experience of time coincides with the experience of needing to be redeemed.

As the vision unfolds, however, it is clear that the journey through memory is also a journey through memory's deceptions. Memory is, after all, an impression of an experience, but one that can never be relied upon with certainty. The poetry describes memory as a trace of a profound experience, but one that strictly speaking is fictional. Eliot writes:

> Other echoes
> Inhabit the garden. . . .
> . . . .
> Through the first gate,
> Into our first world, shall we follow
> The deception of the thrush?[21]

The entrance into the rose garden is in some sense a return to the garden of Eden. Nevertheless, this also has obvious resonance with Dante's rose of paradise, the metaphorical representation of God's court in paradise. There, the rose is a metaphor for God's love written by God, and furthermore written not with words, but with redeemed human souls.[22] On the other hand, the poetry here repeats the word "first." This reinforces the mythological aspect of this memory-place. The memory here is of an alpha and omega, of a first world, and an eschatological telos, a communion in love, crafted through the artistry of God.

As a first world, Eliot may very well be drawing on the idea present in mystical texts that the path of desire is always initiated by the touch of divine love. This is, in fact, what John of the Cross asserts in his writings.[23] The search for God begins when God in Godself touches the soul with the fire of love. This is, in a sense, the beginning of another kind of "first world," a view of the world opened up by the touch of divine love. And that touch itself can only be retained in the memory, a memory that—however tenuous the details—points to the existentially liberating and significant nature of that touch. The memory preserves the trace and sets the soul off again in search of another such experience.

In another sense, though, the memory of a timeless moment must of necessity be deception. Here, the thrush is deceptive.[24] The thrush brings us into the garden through deception. The timeless can only be represented through deception. The door not opened *is* the door to the timeless. The atemporal cannot be represented in and through words. What we are looking at here is the approach to a timeless moment, represented as the primal garden, as the ultimate paradise, and as the timelessness of love. *These* are the things that lay behind the door we "did not take." The poetry gives us a journey into memory, exploring the door that was not opened. The door of the atemporal, of innocence, of love. And added to all of these, a journey of regret. The soul cannot retain a heightened moment; it falls away from it too easily, fostering an experience then of alienation and the reapproach of the soul. The moment of innocence provokes dialectically the recognition of the usual state of the soul, which always falls short of that innocence. The moment of illumination brings in its wake the harsh recognition of the soul's usual existence. It is just such a dialectic that Cleo McNelly Kearns has identified in the movement of surrender and recovery found throughout Eliot's corpus.[25] The self regained after the surrender is strictly speaking not the same.

It is at this point that Eliot provides us with an absolutely crucial reference to John of the Cross. In the *Spiritual Canticle,* John depicts one experience of God's presence in creation. The things of creation are given existence precisely because God looks at them. Eliot writes:

> And the unseen eyebeam crossed, for the roses
> Had the look of flowers that are looked at.
> There they were as our guests, accepted and accepting.
> So we moved, and they, in a formal pattern,
> Along the empty alley, into the box circle,
> To look down into the drained pool.[26]

218   DESIRE AND THE ASCETIC IDEAL

Eliot's own fascination with tradition opens up an intriguing interpretive possibility, especially given the journey into memory here. The "they" could be other voices/presences in the mind, that are making the trip with the poet, and that enter into the ultimate memory/vision here. They move "in a formal pattern," as the current poet and the previous ones enter into a formal relationship; they all become part of a pattern of representing the timeless. The poetry suggests a network of memory, a pattern of memories creating a memory-form within the mind, but again, a form of deceptions.

The poetry also alludes to John of the Cross's description of creation, given reality because of the gaze of God. John's presence can be felt strongly throughout "Burnt Norton," and Kevin Hart has observed that the presence of music in the garden alludes to the "silent music" of created things in the *Spiritual Canticle*.[27] Hart recognizes that the "eyebeam" image is a reference to a divine influence.[28] He is surely correct here, though he misses yet another reference to John in this image. John claims that all created things exist because God looks at them through the Son: "only with this figure, his Son, did God look at all things, that is, he communicated to them their natural being and many natural graces and gifts, and made them complete and perfect."[29] Creation is a vision that God has. There are therefore two things that are beyond the perception in this vision, and that suggest the presence of the supernatural: the "unheard music" and the "unseen eyebeam." The eyebeam makes the flowers visible, but it itself is not seen. It pervades and illuminates, and is hidden.

The poem suggests a vision from memory, a vision that is enabled by unheard music, and that is illuminated in the mind's eye by the unseen eyebeam. But if so, the vision is a *divine* illusion. It is an illusion to draw the poet to the ultimate image of the dry pool. This eruption of memory is a figuration of the timeless, and also in that figuration an experience of exile or alienation from it. The imagery here clothes the memory of the timeless and also marks that alienation. And the imagery, as *illusion*, brings the speaker of the poem to the center of the metaphorical garden, in which emptiness stands hidden by the illusion of illumination.

The things within the vision exist because they are seen by the eyebeam. The gaze of God is a creating gaze here. These things exist visually because they are looked at by God. We can see them only because God sees them first. God is creating an illusion for the speaker, is drawing the speaker further into the vision in and through illusion, toward the truth at the heart of the garden. And the truth is emptiness. Kearns notes that the moment represents an analogue to Buddhist *shunyata*.[30] God here is a poet, leading the earthly poet onward to the truth. And that truth is emptiness. But even *that* is an illusion. Even the emptiness in itself is an illusion. In Nagarjuna's terms, we see the emptiness of emptiness. It is "reality" within the context of the vision, but as part of the metaphorical mise-en-scène, it is still metaphorical. This is, incidentally, precisely a depiction of the "emptiness of emptiness" that I explore in the previous chapter. Indeed, Kearns has also cited this as a representation of something similar to Nagarjuna's insistence on the identity of *samsara* and *nirvana*.[31] The light and the music are the modes by which God signifies to the mind, but they too ultimately are metaphorical. They are also stand-ins for the sake of thought and feeling.

All of these tropes echo the earlier *Knowledge and Experience* in a fundamental way. The path that we did not take could be read as immediate experience: it is the innocence and the unity that lies beyond our conscious thought, that source of wholeness from which we have been alienated.[32] It is the "path that we did not take," but perhaps also that which can be revealed in extraordinary moments of ecstasy. Immediate experience must be empty, or represented as emptiness, since it is literally beyond time and representation and consciousness. This also, however, intimates that there is a level of the human person that is always already in contact with divinity, which is always already sensitive to the motions of music made upon the soul.

And this brings us to the heart of memory here, the center of this illusory scene, the pool itself, and its flower that brings together resonance from both Christian and Buddhist religious traditions. The text reads: "Dry the pool . . . and the pool was empty."[33] The pool here is one of sunlight, not water. It is "dry," and the verse repeats the term calmly. The pool is "brown edged," reinforcing the lack of water. The image is of a decaying pool, but suddenly irradiated: "And the pool was filled with water out of sunlight."[34] The light here is amassed. The pool is a container, but a container for light, which cannot really be contained in such a way. The phrase "water out of sunlight" is interesting: it seems the light takes on the form of water. But this is an illusion. As long as the

220   DESIRE AND THE ASCETIC IDEAL

light shines, one sees the water, and the lotos. When the sun is gone, one sees the empty pool.

At the heart of the scene lies the lotos, but a lotos that, through a verbal ambiguity, becomes juxtaposed with the rose. The text reads, "the lotos rose, quietly, quietly."[35] The immediate significance of the phrase signals the motion of the lotos resting above the amassed waters of light. The lotos is, of course, the representation of peace, contemplative calm, and selflessness in Buddhism, which I discuss further below. The term "rose" most obviously is a verb describing the motion of the lotos. However, the phrase also juxtaposes two flowers: the lotos and the rose. The rose in fact takes on a complex set of associations in *Four Quartets,* stemming from the rose garden in this section: purity, innocence, the past, paradise, unity. Eliot's chief referent here is Dante's rose of paradise, signifying the ultimate unity of the saints with God in love.[36] Eliot's poetry brings together the selflessness of Buddhism with the perfection of Christian love in the *Commedia.*[37]

This selflessness, this emptiness, even depicted in an illusion—an illusion of emptiness—is too much for the poetic speaker to handle. When the light is hidden, the speaker is virtually driven out of the garden:

> Then a cloud passed, and the pool was empty.
> Go, said the bird, for the leaves were full of children,
> Hidden excitedly, containing laughter.
> Go, go, go, said the bird: human kind
> Cannot bear very much reality.[38]

This passage repeats something we often see in Eliot: that emptiness can be seen either in a positive or a negative vein. It is frightening to those who live in the constant presumption that the self and the things to which it is attached are somehow substantially real. It is positive to those who have embraced the liberating possibility of selflessness. In this instance, that state of selflessness becomes a lost state of innocence, an innocence from which we as human beings have been alienated by temporal existence itself. The garden is inhabited by children, children who are seemingly laughing at the anxious human comedy before them, the comedy of human beings finding the truth for which we seek, and finding it to be very unlike what we thought it would be. The irregular meter from the trochaic "Cannot" and the spondaic "bear very" provide a harsh interruption of the otherwise iambic line, although one that also ends with the awkward clangor of the final "reality." The verse signals both the disruptive potential of a moment of reality and the harsh difficulty of the human attempt to come to terms with it.

What Eliot has done then in the first two sections of "Burnt Norton" is to sketch the possibility that conscious forms can give qualified existence to the illusory memories of the atemporal. Nevertheless, it is only in and through the pursuit of these memories that humans can attempt to be liberated from time. In fact, just such a possibility was obliquely signaled in section I by the reference to the lotos. A familiarity with the *Lotus Sutra*, with which Eliot was thoroughly familiar from his graduate studies, reinforces this overall reading of "Burnt Norton." For the *Lotus Sutra* is the classic text of Buddhist *upaya*, indeed, a sustained meditation on how an eternal Buddha nature can utilize fiction, ruse, and illusion to move the practitioner closer to a recognition of emptiness.

Anesaki and the *Lotus Sutra*

As noted above, Cleo McNelly Kearns identifies the lotus image as a traditional Buddhist one representing, in this instance, something like Nagarjuna's view of emptiness, a view with which I agree. However, I suggest that Eliot is also alluding strongly to the *Lotus Sutra* and its teachings on skillful means. In general, Kearns does not think that Eliot was as influenced by Mahayana Buddhism as he was by the Theravada.[39] In contrast, however, I suggest that the Mahayana is quite a bit stronger in *Four Quartets* by reading the text through the lens of the *Lotus Sutra*, especially as presented to Eliot by Anesaki.

The *Lotus Sutra* played a pivotal role in the early American and European encounter with Buddhism. Donald S. Lopez has admirably traced this encounter in *The Lotus Sutra: A Biography*. Lopez points out that the text was one of the first Buddhist texts translated in Europe, in 1839 (though not published until 1852), by Eugène Burnouf, the author of the massively influential *Introduction à l'histoire du Buddhisme indien* of 1844.[40] Indeed, according to Lopez, Burnouf initially conceived of the *Introduction* as a series of notes "intended to aid readers in understanding the *Lotus Sutra*."[41] Further, chapter 5 of Burnouf's translation appeared in *The Dial* in New England in 1844 (prior to its full publication in Europe).[42] Eliot would have read the text first in the English translation of Hendrik Kern, and indeed Anesaki refers to that translation in his Harvard course.[43]

Anesaki's chief concern in the part of the course dedicated to the Sutra was to explain the Tiantai understanding of it. We explored Anesaki's understanding of the Buddhist tradition more broadly in chapter 1. Kearns observes that Eliot's notes record that Anesaki drew attention to the *Lotus Sutra*'s tendency to find a place for different interpretations of Buddhism.[44] The passage from Eliot's notes states:

> Tientai has its sole basis in Saddharmapundarika [i.e., Lotus Sutra], but its philosophy is an attempt to consummate the distinctions of various schools as to the conception of reality. Tientai's ambition was a synthesis to embrace all views by elevating them (aufheben, Hegel) to his own standpoint. A view is false in one sense, true in another. This kind of synthesis is characteristic of Buddhism from its very beginnings, with the name of middle path.[45]

Anesaki is referring to the sutra's attempt to accord different schools of Buddhism different levels of truth. Anesaki envisions "lower" schools as being "taken up" or "elevated" in a quasi-Hegelian manner, their truths maintained in a higher synthesis that nevertheless transforms those truths. Lying behind this may be a conviction, articulated by Nichiren, that the Buddha realm is always already implicated in the complexity of reality, elevating that reality and working in and through it.[46] At any rate, I argue later that Anesaki's presentation of unity in diversity is also Eliot's strategy vis-à-vis other religious traditions in the totality of *Four Quartets*.

Indeed, the image of the lotus is described by Anesaki as providing a metaphor for this unity in diversity. He describes the lotus in terms of the central fruits and the diversity of flowers surrounding it: "The lotus alone is perfect, because it has many flowers and many fruits *at once*. The flowers + fruit are simultaneous. The real entity represented in the fruit, its manifestation in the flowers. Mutual relation of final reality and manifestation."[47] Eliot's notes are slightly ambiguous here, but I believe what Anesaki is doing is drawing attention to the distinction between the teaching of ultimate reality and different skillful manifestations of the teaching. By extension, the figure refers to the Buddha nature residing in emptiness and the diversity of skillful representations of that nature through *upaya*. Indeed Anesaki calls the fruit the "final reality," the reality that those manifestations are moving toward over time, their ultimate fulfillment. Anesaki goes on to make precisely this point afterward. He states, "Stages of progress in our attainment: diversity due to upayakausalya, educated method of B.; of wh. Sadd-pundarika is the consummation."[48] Thus the sutra itself is the culmination of the Buddha's teaching. All other teachings point to the *Lotus Sutra* as their final telos.

The truth of the sutra, however, is characterized by the text's ability to provoke its reader to become a Buddha. The notes state: "The truth manifests itself in 3 ways. 1. In all beings variously. 2. In Buddha. 3. In citta—the mind. The truth of existence is perfected in this book because this book incites us to Buddhahood. The book itself represents the truth of existence. (Chap. II.)."[49] The distinction between the conventional and ultimate truth that we have seen before, especially in our discussion of Nagarjuna, is implicit here as well. The ultimate truth is in emptiness, as Anesaki notes just after. The text points to this "entity" and enables its hearers to attain it. Its truth is in its ability to "incite" the hearer to this higher realization. The text itself is still conventional or language-bound, but its truth is measured in its ability to "incite." Here again the text's protreptic, performative nature is on display. At the same time this truth is already active in all beings through the skillful means of the Buddha. In this sense, the sutra makes manifest an always implicit Buddhahood.[50] The text both incites and manifests. For this reason, too, Tiantai Buddhists often discussed the potential for rapid enlightenment.[51] As we will shortly see, the sutra's conception of the Buddha is quasi-theological as all-knowing, eternal, and all-pervading. In contrast to Nagarjuna, emptiness for practitioners is ultimately becoming one with the Buddha-nature. The Buddha is always moving all beings to Buddhahood, and the text is the Buddha's highest skillful mean for doing so.

The utility of the text in achieving the Buddha's aims is thematized immediately in chapter 2. The Buddha describes part of his project for enlightenment:

> 61. If, O son of Sari, I spoke to the creatures, "Vivify in your minds the wish for enlightenment," they would in their ignorance all go astray and never catch the meaning of my words.

62. And considering them to be such, and that they have not accomplished their course of duty in previous existences, (I see how) they are attached and devoted to sensual pleasures, infatuated by desire and blind with delusion.

63. From lust they run into distress; they are tormented in the six states of existence and people the cemetery again and again; they are overwhelmed with misfortune, as they possess little virtue.

64. They are continually entangled in the thickets of (sectarian) theories, such as, "It is and it is not; it is thus and it is not thus." In trying to get a decided opinion on what is found in the sixty-two (heretical) theories they come to embrace falsehood and continue in it.

65. They are hard to correct, proud, hypocritical, crooked, malignant, ignorant, dull; hence they do not hear the good Buddha-call, not once in kotis of births.

66. To those, son of Sari, I show a device and say: Put an end to your trouble. When I perceive creatures vexed with mishap I make them see Nirvana.[52]

The *Lotus Sutra* assumes that the Buddha can see all creatures in their progress toward Buddhahood.[53] Brook A. Ziporyn observes that the text therefore attempts to show the reader the way that the Buddha sees all of us.[54] The Buddha describes the goal of his teaching, to have the idea of *nirvana* "vivify" the minds of creatures—to take a hold, animate, make the idea itself active in the mind. Though the Buddha preaches it and tries to bring the creature closer to understanding, it is the idea itself that animates. In other words, the text seeks to provoke a kind of ascetic desire, though the text would never rhetorically use this term. It is a strange type of desire though, the desire to be what we already are.

The problem is that creatures cannot even begin to understand this idea. Sentient existence is rooted in desire and powerful ignorance. Ignorance means they cannot immediately understand the fullness of the teaching. Nor, ultimately, can they understand the nature and ultimate telos of their own desire.[55] Creatures are "infatuated by desire and blind with delusion." How does one preach the absence of desire to those who exist in webs of desire? How does one educate one for whom desire and ignorance are intricately bound up? The Buddha describes this tortured web as having been built up over many existences. These creatures are stuck in the karmic realm, and they "people the cemetery again and again" in their rebirths.

Note that the Buddha claims they are "entangled in the thickets of (sectarian) theories, such as 'It is and it is not; it is thus and it is not thus.'" While the Buddha is concerned that these creatures are not able to allow the truth to vivify the mind, he also suggests that metaphysical entanglement is also a problem. The creatures are too caught up in debates over existence. To this, the *Lotus Sutra* is going to adopt the view of the "middle way," that things neither exist nor do not exist. They exist conventionally but are ultimately empty. Or, similar to Nagarajuna, the "'true' Nirvana is not the leaving of samsara, but samsara itself."[56] Metaphysical speculation drives creatures away from realizing their suffering and seeking its end.

As we saw with the Fire Sermon, the key to reaching creatures is to meet them where they are, in and through the categories and images constituting the webs of desire and ignorance that hold them. And so the Buddha says, "I show them a device and say: Put an end to your trouble . . . I make them see Nirvana." Somewhat surprisingly, the idea of the "three vehicles" is one such device that moves even highly developed monks to move beyond their complex ignorance to the higher understanding of the bodhisattva. Such devices apparently come in higher and lower forms. Lopez and Stone observe that the *Lotus Sutra* is significant in teaching that the three vehicles or paths (those of monks, "solitary Buddhas," and bodhisattvas) are really one vehicle, that of the bodhisattvas.[57] In other words, all are always in reality moving toward being bodhisattvas.[58]

The discourse goes on to say that the Buddha uses "jewel images," "images of Sugatas made of the seven precious substances of copper or brass," "beautiful statues," "images (of the Sugatas) on painted walls."[59] He goes on to mention "flowers and perfumes," "musical instruments . . . in order to celebrate the highest enlightenment."[60] As we saw highlighted in Anesaki's lectures in chapter 1, the text validates the aesthetic and ritual sphere as providing suitable means for engaging and redirecting the desire and intellectual faculties of the creature. As Eliot might put it, they redirect "thought and feeling" to a telos in which these find their completion, highest fulfillment, and annihilation.

226   DESIRE AND THE ASCETIC IDEAL

The Buddha can use these figures and "devices" because he has first gained crucial insight into the truth about the world. All creatures who are to become bodhisattvas have to attain this insight. The text states,

> Then the Tathāgata preaches to him: How can he who has not penetrated all laws have reached Nirvāna? The Lord rouses him to enlightenment, and the disciple, when the consciousness of enlightenment has been awakened in him, no longer stays in the mundane whirl, but at the same time has not yet reached Nirvāna. As he has arrived at true insight, he looks upon this triple world in every direction as void, resembling the produce of magic, similar to a dream, a mirage, an echo. He sees that all laws (and phenomena) are unborn and undestroyed, not bound and not loose, not dark and not bright. He who views the profound laws in such a light, sees, as if he were not seeing, the whole triple world full of beings of contrary and omnifarious fancies and dispositions.[61]

The awakened practitioner sees the world as empty or "void," lacking an abiding or stable essence. To see the world in this way is to see the world as a realm of "magic, similar to a dream, a mirage, an echo." This latter term, given the beginning of "Burnt Norton," is especially evocative. The world is made up of memories that are like echoes of utterances already spoken and over. If the bodhisattva is able to recognize this, though, it means he is beyond these illusions, he has transcended them. He "sees, as if he were not seeing" that "all laws (and phenomena) are unborn and undestroyed." They are unborn, meaning they are all merely products of the causal nexus. Phenomena do not exist as individuals apart from the causal chain. And as such, they cannot be destroyed per se, since they never properly existed in the first place. In a sense, the bodhisattva has one eye on the transcendent and one eye in the dream world. As a result he is able to manipulate that dream world in the most effective manner for whichever creature he is attempting to reach. He uses and enhances the "soteriological value of the world of phenomena."[62] Later in the text, it becomes clear that this is every creature. Indeed, the Buddha takes on cosmic, quasi-divine qualities as he approaches each creature over their series of lives to move them to *nirvana*.

The lotus itself becomes a "device" used to represent this detached bodhisattva. The text calls the bodhisattvas "these who are untainted as the lotus is by water: who to-day have flocked hither after rending the earth, and are standing all with joined hands, respectful and strong in memory, the sons of the Master of the world."[63] The bodhisattva is untainted by the world of phenomena, sitting calmly on top of it in peaceful repose, even as he has a root descending into the water. It is this detached mastery that enables the bodhisattva's immense powers to use any means to move creatures to *nirvana*. The lotus is a complicated image. On one hand, it represents detachment from the world and purity. On the other hand, it is self-consciously a figure and a stand-in for the text itself, which as a product of language is still a part of the world of echoes and illusion, though of illusions of greater or lesser efficacy. The lotus sits on top of the water, but its roots reach down into it. Likewise, the bodhisattva sits atop the world of phenomena and reaches down into it strategically. The text itself, though providing a configuration of verbal illusion, also points to the truth of the Buddha's enlightenment. It is a superior fiction. The lotus image is therefore, like the text, a self-deconstructing image, meant to signify and erase itself.[64] It is conventionally real and ultimately unreal. Like Eliot's dry pool, it signals emptiness but is itself still an illusion, though a higher one.

The reason the Buddha can wield textual devices in such a literarily crafty way is because of the immense power he has attained. This is described in the all-important chapter 16, after the Buddha has been asked what will happen to the truth of the dharma after Shakyamuni is finally extinct. The answer is that the Buddha attained "supreme, perfect enlightenment"[65] very long ago, "many hundred thousand myriads of kotis of Aeons ago."[66] It turns out that the Buddha has been around a long time and will continue to exist for the sake of all sentient beings. He in fact appears in every generation—and to every individual—in order to move them closer to *nirvana*.

> The Tathāgata considering the different degrees of faculty and strength of succeeding generations, reveals at each (generation) his own name, reveals a state in which Nirvāna has not yet been reached, and in different ways he satisfies the wants of (different) creatures through various Dharmaparyāyas. This being the case, young men of good family, the Tathagata declares to the creatures, whose dispositions are so various and who possess so few roots of

228   DESIRE AND THE ASCETIC IDEAL

> goodness, so many evil propensities . . . it is for the education
> of creatures, young men of good family, that the Tathāgata has re-
> vealed all Dharmaparyāyas.[67]

The Buddha appears to each generation in the manner best suited to their dispositions. The text even goes so far as to say that he "satisfies the wants of (different) creatures through various Dharmaparyāyas." He does this in spite of the fact that the "wants" are conditioned by ignorance and attachment. Not only is the Buddha not extinct, but he continues to appear over and over again to "educate" each generation. Indeed, Ziproyn thinks that the primary mark of Buddhahood in this text is the ability to educate with empathy.[68]

The Buddha can do this because he is detached from temporal experience itself. This enables the Tathagata to speak different truths at different times:

> Under his own appearance or under another's, either on his own
> authority or under the mask of another, all that the Tathāgata de-
> clares, all those Dharmaparyāyas spoken by the Tathāgata are true.
> There can be no question of untruth from the part of the Tathāgata
> in this respect. For the Tathāgata sees the triple world as it really
> is: it is not born, it dies not; it is not conceived, it springs not into
> existence; it moves not in a whirl, it becomes not extinct; it is not
> real, nor unreal; it is not existing, nor non-existing; it is not such,
> nor otherwise, nor false. The Tathāgata sees the triple world, not
> as the ignorant, common people, he seeing things always present
> to him; indeed, to the Tathāgata, in his position, no laws are con-
> cealed. In that respect any word that the Tathāgata speaks is true,
> not false. But in order to produce the roots of goodness in creatures,
> who follow different pursuits and behave according to different no-
> tions, he reveals various Dharmaparyāyas with various fundamen-
> tal principles.[69]

All things and all laws are present to the Buddha, meaning he sees them all from a detached perspective. The Buddha is therefore both transcendent to time and becoming, and also immanent within it. This allows him to speak truths that may not represent the fullness of Buddhist truth but will serve to educate creatures in a productive way, or to "produce the roots of goodness in the creatures."[70] It also means that the Buddha can be found in and among the complexity of phenomena.[71]

The Buddha begins to take on some properties that in Christianity are often attributed to divinity.[72] The Buddha for instance "is unlimited in the duration of his life, he is everlasting."[73] Later the text claims that the Buddha's "field" is "everlasting" and that he undertakes an "infinitude of my actions."[74] The picture of the Buddha is of a being always appearing, over generations, and always acting in appropriate ways for the sake of a diversity of predispositions. He explains that "knowing them to be perverted, infatuated, and ignorant I teach final rest, myself not being at rest."[75] Far from being a static reality, the Buddha's existence is active, always changing, diverse, and yet rooted in the peace of enlightenment.

In an important diversion from his usual way of discussing skillful means, the Buddha claims that part of his strategy is to prompt humans to think that he is absent, thus stoking desire for the absent Tathagata. When discussing the danger of creatures growing slack in their efforts, the Buddha claims that he will tell creatures that the appearing of a Buddha is rare, although it is not:

> Hence, young men of good family, the Tathāgata skilfully utters. [sic] these words: The apparition of the Tathāgatas, monks, is precious (and rare). By being more and more convinced of the apparition of the Tathāgatas being precious (or rare) they will feel surprised and sorry, and whilst not seeing the Tathāgatas they will get a longing to see him. The good roots developing from their earnest thought relating to the Tathāgata will lastingly tend to their weal, benefit, and happiness; in consideration of which the Tathāgata announces his final extinction, though he himself does not become finally extinct, on behalf of the creatures who have to be educated. Such, young men of good family, is the Tathāgata's manner of teaching; when the Tathāgata speaks in this way, there is from his part no falsehood.[76]

The Buddha leads people to believe that he is extinct in order to generate a "longing," a desire, to see the Buddha again. The desire of these creatures is therefore nourished by the Buddha's absence. The text is therefore depicting a process of education that not only engages with the thought and feeling of the practitioner, but that generates the proper kind of longing through the dialectic of presence and absence skillfully deployed by the infinite Buddha.[77] As a later verse puts it, "Let them first have an aspiration to see me: then I will reveal to them the true law."[78]

The dialectic of presence and absence, form and the unconditioned, is at the heart of Eliot's memory garden. At the heart of the temporal self is the eternal, the still point. In "Burnt Norton" this is represented by Dante's rose of paradise or by the Buddha's figure for poise and skillful detachment. Dante's own rose of paradise beautifully symbolizes the impossible reversal of desire. For both the Buddhist and Christian thinkers, the flower represents that which lies beyond language. It also represents the necessity of the image in order to move one beyond it. Both figures are poets of a sort who seek to place their texts within a process of ascent. Eliot's poetry moves from light and illumination to the image made possible by that light to the emptiness of the dry pool. And this image of the emptiness of the dry pool is still simply that: an image. It is an image conditioned by the exile of which it is a part. The way beyond the temporal forms, the way to the eternal, is in and through and beyond aesthetic forms, for "only through time time is conquered."[79] As we will see, though, the sensibility of unity-in-diversity embodied in the *Lotus Sutra* also pervades Eliot's sequence, informing at least in part his poetry's own Christian inclusivism.

Aesthetics and the Approach to the Absolute

What Eliot has given us in the first movement of "Burnt Norton" is a journey within the self, through memory, and through illusion, to the emptiness—and the liberation—at the heart of the self. That liberation is depicted as something that has happened in the past, an extraordinary moment, and one that can only be reapproached anew through illusion and figuration. The crucial figuration was the "lotos rose," bringing with it the allusion to Dante and the *Lotus Sutra*. The figuration keeps that memory alive and makes it an active possibility for the future as well. The memory of emptiness or transcendence keeps alive the possibility of it and indeed generates a different kind of desire for it.

Eliot says later in the sequence that memory can only be approached in a different form than the actual experience of the event. This is doubly the case when we're talking about the "counter-experience"[80] that Eliot describes here. It is, by definition, only approachable in and through figuration, which must inevitably falsify. In this passage, Eliot is describing the memory of that moment as itself clothed in illusion. Ironically, it is only in and through the illusion and the deception that the real is revealed and remembered. In the very next section, the poetry concludes:

Time past and time future
Allow but a little consciousness.
To be conscious is not to be in time
But only in time can the moment in the rose-garden,
The moment in the arbour where the rain beat,
The moment in the draughty church at smokefall
Be remembered; involved with past and future.
Only through time time is conquered.[81]

Here again, the motif of "time past" and "time future" emerges, but in a different key. "Consciousness" now is a more profound consciousness; time is ordinarily a mark of human consciousness, but here temporal experience alienates from the deeper awareness. Nevertheless, only in temporal experience can the memory of heightened consciousness persist and influence the direction of human life. If these moments are not represented in time, they are not rememberable as such; if they are not in typical human consciousness, they are not, strictly speaking, "real." But it is only in and through the trace of that non-event that the "experience" can be remembered. The moment can only be clothed in illusory form, but that illusory form gives it an "existence" that can then reach us in our waking lives. The form is the trace of the event that gives conscious existence to that event. The verse highlights this: "But only in time can the moment in the rose-garden . . . Be remembered; involved with past and future." The sudden existence of this moment in temporal consciousness is highlighted by the imposing "Be" at the beginning of the line. But this sense of existence is "involved with past and future," so that it signifies only a qualified being. Nevertheless, this qualified being is the kind of being that reaches us where we ordinarily live. The event takes conscious form as a memory and persists as a memory, an illusory, and yet potentially liberating, memory.

In fact, in that very same section, the mystical experience of the timeless moment is described, as Virkar-Yates crucially recognizes, in terms of Schopenhauer's aesthetics.[82] The soul in mystical experience is described as "surrounded / By a grace of sense, a white light still and moving, / *Erhebung* without motion, concentration / Without elimination."[83]

The state here is one of "concentration," of the mind gathered to itself, but not destroyed. The *erhebung*, the elevation, is itself "without motion." It provokes the self to a kind of stasis. The stasis, though, is the result of ec-stasis, a pulling of the self outside of itself. The stasis exists as one is "surrounded / By a grace of sense." Sensibility experiences this moment as one of grace, of something given, as something from outside the self gifting the self with an experience beyond temporal consciousness.

Schopenhauer's theory of the sublime is tortured but in general expresses a situation in which an aesthetic spectator contemplates both something that threatens the will and the will itself. It is this threatening element that enables the spectator, through conscious effort, to lift himself or herself above the will to pure, will-less knowing. Schopenhauer writes:

> But these very objects, whose significant forms invite us to a pure contemplation of them, may have a hostile relation to the human will in general, as manifested in its objectivity, the human body. They may be opposed to it; they may threaten it by their might that eliminates all resistance, or their immeasurable greatness may reduce it to nought. Nevertheless, the beholder may not direct his attention to this relation to his will which is so pressing and hostile, but, although he perceives and acknowledges it, he may consciously turn away from it, forcibly tear himself from his will and its relations, and, giving himself up entirely to knowledge, may quietly contemplate, as pure, will-less subject of knowing, those very objects so terrible to the will. He may comprehend only their Idea that is foreign to all relation, gladly linger over its contemplation, and consequently be elevated precisely in this way above himself, his person, his willing, and all willing. In that case, he is then filled with the feeling of the *sublime;* he is in the state of exaltation, and therefore the object that causes such a state is called *sublime.*[84]

Schopenhauer's sublime is different from beauty by involving consciousness. In beauty, the contemplation of an object spontaneously brings about pure, will-less knowing. With the sublime, on the other hand, the consciousness is involved as well. Consciousness elevates itself above the will and does in part contemplate the superior object in a pure way. Nevertheless, the self also continuously remembers the will, or rather, human willing in general.[85] The sublime then combines higher knowledge of an Idea with the remembrance of the will, and the self holds these two awarenesses together simultaneously.[86] The "elevation" here is the self-elevation of consciousness above the will, enabled by the contemplation of that which threatens it.

In Eliot's poetry, this elevation also represents a double vision that in the moment of reality is "understood / In the completion of its partial ecstasy, / The resolution of its partial horror."[87] The world is partially in ecstasy, partially in horror. It is partially being pulled out of itself and is partially enchained in its own suffering. Here, it is the timeless that threatens the will, but those moments of timelessness allow us to perceive the world as partially in ecstasy, partially in horror. As Virkar-Yates would assert, moments of atemporal Love cast the temporal will into relief.[88] But it is *only* through such experiences as these that completion and resolution can be "perceived." The moment provides a sense of perspective on the world of change and mutability. It makes it seem that the world's purpose is for ecstasy.

Unlike in Schopenhauer's theory, though, Eliot's moment provides the self with an eschatological orientation. The world is seen only in partial ecstasy. The experience of *erhebung* provides a temporal orientation to a final moment of stasis and an end to the partial ecstasy of the world.[89] When this moment becomes remembered and takes on temporal flesh, it provides a new orientation to that temporal experience, as something to be desired again. This is why Eliot's poetry moves to a final meditation on memory. The timeless moment may itself be beyond memory's capacity, but the remembering of those moments itself must occur in time. Two of these moments bear explicitly religious significance, those of the "draughty church" and the "rose-garden." This latter is specifically that which was represented earlier in the "lotos rose." Here the possibility is raised that the remembering of the timeless moment can be used in the overcoming of time itself. Schopenhauer's moment of elevation has become part of a temporal process in which memory takes on a key role. Tracing those memories requires an exploration of memory and allowing those memories to provoke the desire to reapproach the eternal. The poetry envisions a dialectic of timelessness and time, of engagement with form and a transcending of form, of selflessness and memory.

For the poet, this is a process of creating forms that point to the event that gave rise to it ("I can only say, there we have been: but I cannot say where"),[90] and the attempt to reapproach that event in ever newer forms.

234   DESIRE AND THE ASCETIC IDEAL

By "Little Gidding," these forms clearly include ritual and ascetic forms. For the reader, it means performing those forms in the hope that those forms themselves might provoke a similar experience of timeless love. The performance paradigm emerges in section V of "Burnt Norton," where the performance of artistic form becomes an incarnational event.

> Only by the form, the pattern,
> Can words or music reach
> The stillness, as a Chinese jar still
> Moves perpetually in its stillness.
> Not the stillness of the violin, while the note lasts,
> Not that only, but the co-existence,
> Or say that the end precedes the beginning,
> And the end and the beginning were always there
> Before the beginning and after the end.
> And all is always now.[91]

The stillness of the jar, the stillness of the form, suggests the eternal. The pattern or form does not strictly speaking change, though the spectator's perspective on it does. That changing perspective gives the feel of motion. Then, the poetry shifts to the musical metaphor, evoking the stillness of both the violin and the note that is lasting on it while it is being played. Here, you have a violin, which is a form designed to manifest acoustic reality, and a work of music, which is also a form. And then, the note, which is a naturally existing acoustical phenomenon made audible in performance. The poetry depicts a stillness involving the co-existence of instrument and note—and presumably the performer. The "end" of the musical performance was there prior to the building of the violin. The acoustical phenomenon pre-exists the building of the violin, and preexists the performance. From the perspective of aesthetics, it is beautiful significance that preexists the human being for whom it is intended. But we only know of the phenomenon through our experimentation in building forms. The beauty is implicit, but the form needs to be performed to give it flesh. Just as in the *Lotus Sutra*, the truth is known and made manifest in the performance of the text.

Eliot's poetry says nothing about experimentation here, but the point is implicit in what he writes. The note preexists the violin, in an odd way, but we only know about the note once the violin has been created. And that note can be rediscovered by other instruments as well and exist within other, larger artistic forms. The note "A" can be played by other instruments, and can also reoccur throughout a symphony or string quartet, and can be incorporated into other prolonged musical forms. But the thing that becomes "incarnated" in the violin is that which exists in the eternal "now" of the universe. There may very well be an allusion here to George Herbert's poem "Easter,"[92] in which Christ's crucifixion teaches the world to "tune" their strings. The wood of the cross becomes like a violin box, and Christ's suffering humanity becomes like a the string of the violin: "His stretched sinews taught all strings what key / Is best to celebrate this most high day."[93] Christ elevates humanity, and in that elevation reveals the perpetual "now" of God's eternity in and through the crucifixion and resurrection. The poetic speaker refers to Easter day as the only one in existence: "There is but one, and that one ever."[94] It is the resurrection that prompts us to know that God's power has become and can become incarnate in the world. It is God's performance in salvation that teaches the poet how to perform in writing his own poetry. God's performance enables ours.

The performance metaphor provokes the question of how artistic form can become one with that which it represents. But this is problematic when it comes to poetry. Music is different. Music is *one* with the violin that plays it. It does not stand for anything else but itself. Poetry *does* make evident reality, but through verbal representation, which is always already alienated from that which it signifies. But poetry retains something of the "musical" nature of beauty, and in that case can signal something that prose cannot. Poetry is the musical form of language. Further than that, though, poetry is language to be performed. When the language resonates within the memory of the reader, then the reader potentially reincarnates something of the music of the poem. A violin sounds a note; a poem sounds an idea, concept, image, that then takes life again within the memory and awareness of the reader. The signifier becomes absorbed into the memory of the reader, itself shaped by the reader's performances, in the hopes that from this encounter of illusion, an ecstasy may be gifted, or remembered, or at least invoked. Or as Moody has suggested, in *Four Quartets,* "Meaning itself . . . is merely instrumental: what matters is what the poem can do in the way of altering our values and redirecting our desires."[95]

It is significant then that the conclusion makes the leap, after a meditation on the difficulties of representation and interpretation, to mysticism

236 DESIRE AND THE ASCETIC IDEAL

and asceticism, though in the context of aesthetics. The poetry characterizes the mystical path as a figuration that necessarily embodies a paradox. In a reference to St. John of the Cross,[96] the poetry reads, "The detail of the pattern is movement, / As in the figure of the ten stairs."[97] Like the Chinese jar, John's text provides a pattern of the ascent to God, a pattern that clearly describes the approach of human desire to the divine. The "pattern" is in part the figuration of this approach, the metaphor of the "stairs." In a broader sense, "Only by the form, the pattern, / Can words or music reach the stillness,"[98] only by assuming a form can words and music approach the divine. The stillness of the pattern itself also becomes a metaphor for that which lies beyond the temporal experience of the art.[99] Finally, such forms themselves become part of a larger pattern when they are compared with other such texts of "ascent."

The pattern, that which signals the eternal, is couched in "detail." But there is more here than that. The pattern both moves and does not move. Or rather, it seems to move. The pattern is revealed in and through human formal activity. It is only revealed in and through the detail of the poetic form. In other words, the details of the form matter. The "figure" of the ten stairs is just that—a figure, a metaphor. It "details" movement: in and through its form, it describes a movement toward God that takes the soul through various stages. It is enabled by the presence of God in the life of the author, though the text may also "incarnate" meaning for the reader. For both, the experience seems like movement because of the engagement with temporal form. We human beings have the experience of moving closer to God through stages. God, as eternal love, does not move as we do. The paradox is that we move in order to be still. The process is, as Kearns declares in regard to Buddhist paths, "the deliberate, willed cultivation of . . . emptiness."[100]

This paradox is then described in greater detail through a series of enigmatic lines comparing the eternal nature of love and the time-bound process of desiring. This desiring, however, brings one to a stripping of the very conditions of time:

Desire itself is movement
Not in itself desirable;
Love is itself unmoving,
Only the cause and end of movement,
Timeless, and undesiring

Except in the aspect of time
Caught in the form of limitation
Between un-being and being.[101]

Desire is not in itself desirable. Desire receives validation as that which could be translated into its ultimate end, love. Love as the eternal does not move; love seems to move when it is "caught in the form of limitation." Love prompts desire; love is the end of desire meaning its telos, and also its ending or extinction. Desire and movement exist to come to rest in the still point.

Love is undesiring, "except in the aspect of time." Love can take on the form of desire, to move desire toward its own eradication. In other words, desire itself can be the "form of limitation." It is the union of love with desire that makes it seem as if love "moves." In reality, it is bringing desire to its own fulfillment. And what does Eliot mean by the "form of limitation between un-being and being"? The term "un-being" is crucial, it seems to me. The poetry deliberately avoids the term "non-being." "Un-being" means that something that was taken to be "being" is either found not to be or is stripped away. The term "un-being" implies a process of removing being. That which is termed the opposite of this removal is, paradoxically, being. We therefore stand in the middle, between the final state of a process of removal and that which is being removed. In this sense the passage might suggest that the state of liberation is a removal of what we consider being, a state of stripping our experience of being.[102] On the other hand, the relation could also be one of stripping away our understanding or experience of being in order to live in a more profound "being beyond being." Eliot's poetry resonates again with the dialectic of the temporal and the eternal, with that which must be removed, in and through the temporal, in order to merge into the alienated atemporal.

Ultimately the poetry is engaged in an explicitly theological way of thinking. If love alone is being, then love establishes a dialectic between time and the eternal, between the phenomenal world and love itself. The revelations of love establish this dialectic. Intrusions of the eternal into time marginalize time and show it to have an "Other." Love therefore is true being, and the world of time is "un-being." But human forms of limitation, including human desire, take themselves to be true being. The desire that "catches" love, though, is different. The more we try to "catch" it, the more our desire is "caught" by love in a process of transcending itself. In the language of John of the Cross, God enflames desire and sets one out on the pursuit of God. And the more you desire, the more God leads you on. Human life becomes a pattern of temporal stress and divine illumination, of suffering and stillness.

Eliot's ultimate vision here is of God making human beings into poems, by creating these patterns in life. Love's intrusions etch "details" into people's lives, initiating its own pursuit, prompting desire to a final, impersonal consummation. But also: the specter of suffering is here too. This is picked up in the next two *Quartets*. Human beings have these heightened moments of significance, but we also live in a world of suffering that seemingly tears us away from the timeless moments. But this existence of suffering is the precondition for having those experiences at all. They are concomitant with temporal, mutable experience. We therefore live ascetic lives, shaped from without by the poetic lines written into our flesh by suffering and love.

Conclusion

Four Quartets attempts to bracket the metaphysical for a phenomenology of time.[103] And from that phenomenology Eliot evokes time and its other. He then posits the different religious traditions as attempting to live in time while pointing to time's Other. For Eliot, this comes about through two fundamental experiences: of illumination and regret or alienation. In other words, Eliot brings the religious traditions together as ways of living in time, with a view of that which lies beyond time. These traditions name this limit differently, and sometimes in ways that are incommensurate. Eliot seeks to bring them into conversation poetically on temporal experience. Brooker has commented on the fact that Eliot believed there were "many truths": "Eliot did not believe there is no truth; on the contrary, he steadfastly maintained that there are many truths. He rechristened 'skepticism' as 'humility' and made it the cornerstone of his religious faith."[104] His allusions to the *upaya* doctrine in the *Lotus Sutra* were an attempt to think being doctrinally rooted and open to a plurality of truths simultaneously. In fact, as Kearns notes, Eliot drew the distinction between the truth of doctrine, which one might assent to or not, and that of wisdom, which is truth potentially shared across traditions.[105] When put together, then, Eliot envisages an analogical context for comparison, in which doctrinal differences are balanced by commonalities and resonance.

This is not, I think, the imposition of a universalizing Western philosophical construct onto Eastern materials. It is a phenomenology that, if anything, emerges *from* Eliot's restless engagement with the Eastern texts. The phenomenology of time is one that exists, for *Four Quartets,* at the interstices of these religious traditions. Eliot is really not comparing doctrines per se. He does seem to be saying that these traditions deal with universal human problems and experiences. And therefore they can be brought together and compared with how they express them and seek to solve them. This is the kind of comparison that poetry can make without certainty. This is what has led Cleo McNelly Kearns to assert that *Four Quartets* is "wisdom poetry."[106] But also, it depicts these traditions as ones that try to make sense of time, from within time by assessing the traces of memory and pursuing the Other in and through form. The *upaya* doctrine, especially as articulated in the *Lotus Sutra,* is especially useful to Eliot in providing him with the conception of a soteriological path in terms of performance, a performance enabled by the quasi-theological figure of the sutra's Buddha. Buddhism and Christianity in this context become not philosophical truths to be assented to, but paths of memory and desire to be performed. The violin, the example of an artistic form that incarnates a supersensual reality, also represents a symbol of tradition. Human beings perform texts, perform traditions, perform their life, and in doing so show something to be actual that is implicit in reality. The unheard is temporarily heard.

I don't think that this means that doctrinal truth is insignificant for *Four Quartets.* Performance requires thought and feeling in complex articulations. Even truth, though, as a cognitive state, exists to point to a being beyond being, a moment when the burning of rational desire becomes one with the atemporal reality that will bring it to rest. As with the *upaya* doctrine, then, Eliot can devise a kind of inclusivism in which traditions represent different capacities and measures of truth, and each existing to be performed. The intrusion of the eternal marginalizes all claims to truth. In naming the eternal love, Eliot clearly commits the poetry to Christian doctrine. Considered abstractly, this acknowledges such naming as the most relatively adequate naming of the atemporal. But, as with the Buddha in the *Lotus Sutra,* the eternal reaches human beings only in and through the specificities of form. And the eternal as such enables performance in and through those specificities. Love's skillful means provides Eliot with an overriding truth claim, and the suggestion that love reaches all in their specificity. Or as in Eliot's own translation of the epigraph from Heracleitos, "Although the Word (Logos) is common to all, most men live as though they had each a private wisdom of his own."[107]

NOTES

INTRODUCTION

1. Kearns, *T. S. Eliot and Indic Traditions*. I do not rehearse all of the sources to which Eliot had access. Kearns's work here is magisterial, and I would refer the reader to her thorough documentation. See esp. 21–29. For more on Eliot and India, see, for example,: Asher, "Silence, Sound and Eliot's Mystical Imagination"; Bruno, "Buddhist Conceptual Rhyming"; Caracciolo, "Buddhist Typologies"; Dustin, "Theravada Buddhist Influence"; Eakambaram, "Indian Reading"; Hart, "Fields of 'Dharma'"; Hauck, "Not One, Not Two"; Kearns, "T. S. Eliot, Buddhism"; Killingley, "Time, Action, Incarnation"; LeCarner, "T. S. Eliot, Dharma Bum"; McLeod, "Buddhism, T. S. Eliot"; Murata, "Buddhist Epistemology"; Shah, "Poetics of Appropriation"; Sharma, "Fade out the Buddha"; Amar Kumar Singh, *T. S. Eliot and Indian Philosophy*; Sri, "Dantean Rose"; Sri, *T. S. Eliot, Vedanta and Buddhism*; Sri, "Upanishadic Perceptions"; Harish Trivedi, "'Ganga Was Sunken.'" There is also quite a bit of scholarship on Eliot and non-Christian traditions written in Korean. I regret I do not have the language skills to read this.
2. Kearns, *T. S. Eliot and Indic Traditions*, 4.
3. Kearns, *T. S. Eliot and Indic Traditions*, 18–21.
4. Kearns, *T. S. Eliot and Indic Traditions*, 27–29.
5. Spurr, *Anglo-Catholic in Religion*.
6. Spurr, "Religions East and West," 56.
7. Leavis, *New Bearings in English Poetry*, 102.
8. The literature is vast and growing, and the following is not meant to be exhaustive. See, for example, Berman, *Modernist Commitments*; Boehmer, *Empire, the National, and the Postcolonial*; Boehmer, *Postcolonial Poetics*; C. Bush, *Ideographic Modernism*; Gandhi, *Affective Communities*; Gandhi, *Common Cause*; Gandhi, *Postcolonial Theory*; Hayot, *Chinese Dreams*; Patterson, *Race, American Literature*; Ramazani, *Hybrid Muse*; Ramazani, *Poetry in a Global Age*; Ramazani, *Transnational Poetics*; Van Der Veer, *Imperial Encounters*; Van Der Veer, *Modern Spirit of Asia*; Van Der Veer, *Value of Comparison*.
9. Ramazani, "Modernist Bricolage, Postcolonial Hybridity," 303–4.

242   NOTES TO PAGES 4–11

10. See the excerpt of a letter from Eliot to Egon Vietta, February 23, 1947, in Eliot, *Poems of T. S. Eliot,* 976.
11. Letter from Eliot to Vietta in Eliot, *Poems of T. S. Eliot,* 976.
12. Moody, "T. S. Eliot's Passage to India," 35.
13. I have in mind specifically the work of Francis X. Clooney and his colleagues. See esp. Clooney, *Theology after Vedānta,* 9–14.
14. Droit, *Cult of Nothingness,* 6.
15. Eliot, "Lecture VIII: The Nineteenth Century: Summary and Comparison," Clark Lectures, 746.
16. Kearns, *T. S. Eliot and Indic Traditions,* 16.
17. Kearns, *T. S. Eliot and Indic Traditions,* 209.
18. See esp. "Substitutes for Religion in the Early Poetry of T. S. Eliot" (123–39) and "F. H. Bradley's Doctrine of Experience in T. S. Eliot's *The Waste Land* and *Four Quartets*" (191–206) in Brooker, *Mastery and Escape.*
19. Brooker, *Mastery and Escape,* 124.
20. Eliot, "Dante" (II), 716.
21. For an intriguing parallel account, see Gadamer, *Truth and Method,* 81–169.
22. Kearns, *T. S. Eliot and Indic Traditions,* 45.
23. Ganeri, *Concealed Art,* 100.
24. Ganeri, *Concealed Art,* 97.
25. Ganeri, *Concealed Art,* 2.
26. Ganeri, *Concealed Art,* 41.
27. Jeffrey Perl and Andrew Tuck have also noted the importance of this "transformative" approach for the early Eliot. They traced this approach to the influence of the Indian thinker Nagarjuna on Eliot. They write, "For him [Nagarjuna], the goal is never a logically demonstrated theoretical proposition; rather it is a complex of subtle and dramatic psychological changes, changes that result in seeing the world fresh." See Perl and Tuck, "Hidden Advantage of Tradition," 118. They also acknowledge the importance of ritual and practice in the Indian traditions: "Part of the reason may be that, in much of Asian thought, and particularly in the Buddhist schools which Eliot studied, value is placed more on daily behavior and ritual practice . . . than on philosophical meaning, which, in any case, the philosophers themselves attempt to devalue" (125). While I think that the relationship between Eliot and Nagarjuna's thought should continue to be investigated, I believe that the concept of *upaya* itself explains many of Nagarjuna's concerns. This book then seeks to approach these same concerns from a different, though not wholly detached, perspective.
28. Taylor, *Secular Age,* 2–3.

NOTES TO PAGES 11–17   243

29. Schuchard, *Eliot's Dark Angel*.
30. Schuchard, *Eliot's Dark Angel*, 52.
31. Schuchard, *Eliot's Dark Angel*, 27–28.
32. Schuchard, *Eliot's Dark Angel*, 60.
33. Schuchard, *Eliot's Dark Angel*, 62.
34. Schuchard, *Eliot's Dark Angel*, 68.
35. Childs, *T. S. Eliot*, 13. Childs is referring to the account in Gordon, *T. S. Eliot*, 23–28.
36. Jain, *T. S. Eliot*, 114–33.
37. Brooker, *Mastery and Escape*, 136.
38. Craig Woelfel and Jayme Stayer have noted that narrow definitions of religion such as this are "tied to an anachronistic and Eurocentric notion of Christianity." See Woelfel and Stayer, "Introduction," 5. Their project, with which I am in deep sympathy, is to "find modernist art a critical liminal space for exploring new modes of religious experience in complex and resonant ways" (5–6). Perhaps more striking for my purposes is Woelfel's complementary formulation in *Varieties of Aesthetic Experience*, where he pushes us to consider the modernist work as "a liminal site of cross-pressured religious engagement, a space used to critique, simultaneously, traditional or orthodox religious belief and, simultaneously, entirely immanent or rational accounts of life, knowledge, and experience." See Woelfel, *Varieties of Aesthetic Experience*, 13. I believe Woelfel's idea of "cross-pressures" is a compelling way to think about Eliot's hybrid negotiations of different religious traditions. Where I differ, however, is in thinking about Eliot's project against the modern divorce of theory and practice in the understanding of the concept of religion.
39. Eliot, "Tradition and the Individual Talent," 112.
40. Levenson, *Modernism*, 14.
41. Levenson, *Modernism*, 14.
42. Aristotle, *Categories*.
43. Richards, *T. S. Eliot's Ascetic Ideal*, 14.
44. Eliot, "Preface to the 1928 Edition of *The Sacred Wood*," 414–15.
45. Brooker, *T. S. Eliot's Dialectical Imagination*, 77.
46. J. Z. Smith, "Religion, Religions, Religious," 271.
47. Halbfass, *India and Europe*, 156–57.
48. Halbfass, *India and Europe*, 269.
49. Halbfass, *India and Europe*, 272.
50. Said, *Orientalism*, 40.
51. King, *Orientalism and Religion*, 33.
52. King, *Orientalism and Religion*, 19.

244 NOTES TO PAGES 17–22

53. King, *Orientalism and Religion*, 24.
54. See Asad, *Genealogies of Religion*. He writes: "Thus, what appears to anthropologists today to be self-evident, namely that religion is essentially a matter of symbolic meanings linked to ideas of general order (expressed through either or both rite and doctrine), that it has generic functions/ features, and that it must not be confused with any of its particular historical or cultural forms, is in fact a view that has a specific Christian history. From being a concrete set of practical rules attached to specific processes of power and knowledge, religion has come to be abstracted and universalized" (42–43).
55. Brooker, *Mastery and Escape*, 124.
56. Brooker, *Mastery and Escape*, 124.
57. Eliot, "Dante" (I), 232–33.
58. Richards, *T. S. Eliot's Ascetic Ideal*, 1.
59. Richards, *T. S. Eliot's Ascetic Ideal*, 11–12.
60. Schuchard, *Eliot's Dark Angel*, 61.
61. Schuchard, *Eliot's Dark Angel*, 60.
62. Eliot, "Modern Dilemma," 813–14.
63. Richards, *T. S. Eliot's Ascetic Ideal*, 79.
64. Eliot, "Lecture VI: Crashaw," Clark Lectures, 707–8.
65. Eliot, "Lecture III: Donne and the Trecento," Clark Lectures, 653.
66. See Brooker, *T. S. Eliot's Dialectical Imagination*, 3. There, she writes that Eliot's intellectual development begins with a focus on "feeling and self-consciousness," then moves to a preoccupation with "analysis and detachment," and concludes with "the unification of flesh and spirit in the Incarnation." Crucially, she depicts this development as dialectic, as a process in which the previous stage is not lost but continues in a different form. Thus, a subsumption of feeling into intellect, and both gathered into a vision of God.
67. Eliot, *Letters of T. S. Eliot*, 4:432–33.
68. Flood, *Ascetic Self*, 122.
69. Flood, *Ascetic Self*, 813–14.
70. Flood, *Ascetic Self*, 2–3.
71. Flood, *Ascetic Self*, 15. Eliot too refers to the paradox of the end of the contemplative, ascetic path in his 1920 essay on Dante. He writes that "the true mystic is not satisfied merely by feeling, he must pretend at least that he *sees*, and the absorption into the divine is only the necessary, if paradoxical, limit of this contemplation." See Eliot, "Dante" (I), 233. In other words, the desire to see, and feel, the Divine, to attain the *visio Dei*, is also the paradoxical desire to eradicate ordinary vision.

72. Berman, *Modernist Commitments*, 10. She writes that "the text need not be explicitly preoccupied with themes of dislocation, hybridity, or transculturation, nor the author an exile or itinerant, for a narrative to function transnationally."

73. Eliot, "Dante" (I), 233.

74. Eliot, "Metaphysical Poets," 376.

75. Eliot, "Metaphysical Poets," 380.

76. Eliot, "Metaphysical Poets," 381.

77. Patterson, *Race, American Literature*, 7.

78. Patterson, *Race, American Literature*, 6.

79. Jahan Ramazani draws attention to this point made by Raymond Williams. He writes, "Whether these migrant writers left home compelled by politics or lured by economics, whether in search of cultural traditions or freedom from the burden of such traditions, whether for publishing opportunities, educational advancement, or new cultural horizons, they produced works that cannot always be read as emblematic of single national cultures. 'The most important general element of the innovations in form,' as Raymond Williams says of the modernists, 'is the fact of immigration to the metropolis, and it cannot too often be emphasized how many of the major innovators were, in this precise sense, immigrants.'" Ramazani, *Transnational Poetics*, 25.

80. Ramazani, *Transnational Poetics*, 7.

81. Eliot, *After Strange Gods*, 25–26.

82. Eliot, *After Strange Gods*, 24.

83. Eliot, *After Strange Gods*, 51–52n23.

84. More, "Cleft Eliot," 217. More relates the story of an encounter with a student that is worth sharing in full: "I once asked a young student of very advanced ideas about art and life how he, as an admirer of Mr. Eliot, reconciled *The Waste Land* with the program of classicism and royalism (i.e., the divine right of kings) and Anglo-Catholicism announced in a recent preface. His reply was quick and decisive: 'I don't reconcile them; I take the one and leave the other.' And to this rebuke I had nothing to say, since it pointed to a cleft in Mr. Eliot's career to which I am myself sensitive, though my young friend's order of values is the reverse of my own" (216).

85. More, "Cleft Eliot," 216.

86. Eliot, *After Strange Gods*, 25.

87. Eliot, *After Strange Gods*, 31.

88. Eliot, *After Strange Gods*, 31–32.

89. Eliot, *After Strange Gods*, 32.

90. Eliot, *After Strange Gods*, 32.

246   NOTES TO PAGES 29-38

91. Eliot, *After Strange Gods*, 32.

92. Perloff, *Poetics of Indeterminacy*, 17–18. For the formulation of the "other tradition," see 42.

93. Patterson, *Race, American Literature*, 6.

94. For the importance of Confucianism and Chinese culture for Pound, see C. Bush, *Ideographic Modernism*, and Hayot, *Chinese Dreams*.

95. Said, *Orientalism*, 40.

96. Said, *Orientalism*, 326.

97. Said, *Orientalism*, 339.

98. Patterson, *Race, American Literature*, 54–55.

99. Eliot, "Music of Poetry," 312–13.

100. Eliot, "Music of Poetry," 314.

101. Bakhtin, *Dialogic Imagination*, 279. Bakhtin writes, "the internal dialogism of the word (which occurs in a monologic utterance as well as in rejoinder), the dialogism that penetrates the entire structure, all its semantic and expressive layers . . . cannot be isolated as an independent act, separate from the word's ability to form a concept . . . of its object—it is precisely this internal dialogism that has such enormous power to shape style. . . . The word is born in a dialogue as a living rejoinder within it; the word is shaped in dialogic interaction with an alien word that is already in the object. A word forms a concept of its own object in a dialogic way" (279).

102. Eliot, "Music of Poetry," 316.

103. Patterson, *Race, American Literature*, 40.

104. Eliot, *Knowledge and Experience*, 362.

1. SKILLFUL MEANS AND ASCETICISM IN T. S. ELIOT'S CRITIQUE OF SCHOPENHAUER

1. Eliot, *After Strange Gods*, 32.

2. Kearns, *T. S. Eliot and Indic Traditions*, 67.

3. See also Kearns, *T. S. Eliot and Indic Traditions*, 95.

4. Eliot, "Lecture VIII," *Clark Lectures*, 746.

5. Jain, *T. S. Eliot*, 109.

6. Eliot to Vietta in Eliot, *Poems of T. S. Eliot*, 976.

7. Kearns, *T. S. Eliot and Indic Traditions*, 69.

8. Compare Eliot's comments to Herbert Read, in a letter of December 11, 1925: "Modern psychology is tiresome, misleading and full of humbug; but you cannot push it aside; you have to get straight through it somehow: for it has called into existence a thousand new questions which are potential in the humblest mind today, and which indefinitely complicate—to take one group of phenomena alone—any problem of religious belief.

Meanwhile—to make possible the required patience, attentiveness and anonymity—one needs of course some tentative scheme which shall simply go far enough to make action possible, and give to action a kind of moral and liturgical dignity." See Eliot, *Letters of T. S. Eliot*, 2:797.

9. Schwab, *Oriental Renaissance*, 370.
10. Tweed, *American Encounter with Buddhism*, 93.
11. Tweed, *American Encounter with Buddhism*, 93.
12. Welbon, *Buddhist Nirvāna*, 63.
13. On the reaction of Buddhism against the Vedic tradition, see Doniger, *The Hindus*, 180–81.
14. Schwab, *Oriental Renaissance*, 254.
15. Tweed, *American Encounter with Buddhism*, 1.
16. Almond, *British Discovery of Buddhism*, 114–15.
17. Almond, *British Discovery of Buddhism*, 50.
18. Donald Lopez Jr. points particularly to the Indian mutiny of 1857 as a galvanizing event in this regard. See Lopez, introduction to *Curators of the Buddha*, 2. Lopez also notes there the drastically changed environment for discussion of India in the latter half of the nineteenth century. On the Mutiny or Rebellion of 1857, see Doniger, *The Hindus*, 585–88.
19. See Schwab, *Oriental Renaissance*; Halbfass, *India and Europe*; Welbon, *Buddhist Nirvāna*; Droit, *Cult of Nothingness*.
20. Halbfass, *India and Europe*, 56.
21. Halbfass, *India and Europe*, 114.
22. Halbfass, *India and Europe*, 156–57; see also 114.
23. Halbfass, *India and Europe*, 120.
24. Moira Nicholls has usefully catalogued the wealth of Orientalist sources upon which Schopenhauer drew, including Anquetil-Duperron's *Oupnek'hat*, the *Asiatic Researches* of the Asiatic Society in Calcutta, the translation of the *Gita* by A. G. Schlegel, and numerous scholarly treatments of Buddhism, especially that of Burnouf. See Nicholls, "Influences of Eastern Thought," 177–79. Her complete catalogue is found on 197–204.
25. See Welbon, *Buddhist Nirvāna*, 171–92 and Halbfass, *India and Europe*, 123–28. Welbon notes (171) that Wagner had planned an opera on the life of the Buddha entitled *Die Sieger* (The Conquerors), itself modeled on material found in Burnouf's book.
26. Schwab, *Oriental Renaissance*, 428.
27. Droit, *Cult of Nothingness*, 96.
28. Burrows, *Crisis of Reason*. Burrows sees the political turmoil of the 1840s as partially to credit for this surprising resurgence (28–29).

248 NOTES TO PAGES 41–45

29. It was also, incidentally, a time period that witnessed the publication of an edition of the works of Meister Eckhart, who himself called for the "annihilation" of the will (1857). See Schwab, *Oriental Renaissance*, 428. On Eckhart's doctrine of annihilation, see Hollywood, *Soul as Virgin Wife*, 173–76.

30. See Halbfass, *India and Europe*, 110; Welbon, *Buddhist Nirvāna*, 162; Nicholls, "Influences of Eastern Thought," 183.

31. Schopenhauer, *World as Will*, 1:419.

32. See Halbfass, *India and Europe*, 110; Welbon, *Buddhist Nirvāna*, 162; Nicholls, "Influences of Eastern Thought," 183.

33. Schopenhauer writes: "Eternal becoming, endless flux, belong to the revelation of the essential nature of the will. Finally, the same thing is also seen in human endeavors and desires that buoy us up with the vain hope that their fulfillment is always the final goal of willing. But as soon as they are attained, they no longer look the same, and so are soon forgotten, become antiquated, and are really, although not admittedly, always laid aside as vanished illusions. It is fortunate enough when something to desire and to strive for still remains, so that the game may be kept up of the constant transition from desire to satisfaction, and from that to a fresh desire, the rapid course of which is called happiness, the slow course sorrow, and so that this game may not come to a standstill, showing itself as a fearful, life-destroying boredom, a lifeless longing without a definite object, a deadening languor." See Schopenhauer, *World as Will*, 1:164.

34. Welbon, *Buddhist Nirvāna*, 62.

35. Welbon, *Buddhist Nirvāna*, 168. See also Nicholls, "Influences of Eastern Thought," 189.

36. Welbon, *Buddhist Nirvāna*, 165.

37. Welbon, *Buddhist Nirvāna*, 165.

38. See Halbfass, *India and Europe*, 119 and Nicholls, "Influences of Eastern Thought," 189.

39. See Halbfass, *India and Europe*, 110; Welbon, *Buddhist Nirvāna*, 168; Nicholls, "Influences of Eastern Thought," 190.

40. Halbfass, *India and Europe*, 118.

41. Janaway, *Schopenhauer*, 92–93. See Schopenhauer, *World as Will*, 1:396.

42. Schopenhauer, *World as Will*, 1:370.

43. Schopenhauer, *World as Will*, 1:368–69.

44. Jain, *T. S. Eliot*, 106.

45. Eliot to Vietta in Eliot, *Poems of T. S. Eliot*, 976.

46. Jain, *T. S. Eliot*, 103.

47. *Official Register of Harvard University*, 9:17.

48. *Official Register of Harvard University*, 7:20–21.

49. Isomae, "Discursive Position of Religious Studies," 23.

50. Isomae, "Discursive Position of Religious Studies," 27.

51. Eliot, "Notes on Eastern Philosophy," T. S. Eliot Collection, Houghton Library, Harvard University.

52. Williams, *Mahāyāna Buddhism*, 173.

53. Williams, *Mahāyāna Buddhism*, 174.

54. See Lopez and Stone, *Two Buddhas Seated*, 185.

55. Eliot, "Notes on Eastern Philosophy," T. S. Eliot Collection.

56. Ziporyn, *Emptiness and Omnipresence*, 89.

57. Kearns, *T. S. Eliot and Indic Traditions*, 77.

58. Quotes from the Anesaki text are taken from the pamphlet's appearance in the *Encyclopaedia*. In later versions of the book, the text was edited slightly. See Anesaki, "Ethics and Morality (Buddhist)," 449.

59. Droit, *Cult of Nothingness*, 20.

60. Kearns notes that Anesaki's monistic metaphysics were most likely not appealing to the early Eliot. See Kearns, *T. S. Eliot and Indic Traditions*, 78.

61. Anesaki., "Ethics and Morality," 447.

62. Anesaki, "Ethics and Morality," 454.

63. Anesaki, "Ethics and Morality," 454.

64. Anesaki, "Ethics and Morality," 454n2.

65. Anesaki, "Ethics and Morality," 454.

66. Anesaki, "Ethics and Morality," 454.

67. For more on *upaya*, see esp. Gombrich, *How Buddhism Began*; Pye, *Skilful Means*; Bond, "Gradual Path"; and Ganeri, *Concealed Art*.

68. Anesaki, "Syllabus of Philosophy 24A," T. S. Eliot Collection.

69. Eliot, "Notes on Eastern Philosophy," T. S. Eliot Collection.

70. Eliot, "Notes on Eastern Philosophy," T. S. Eliot Collection.

71. Eliot, "Notes on Eastern Philosophy," T. S. Eliot Collection.

72. *Lotus Sutra*, 34.

73. *Lotus Sutra*, 34.

74. Williams, *Mahāyāna Buddhism*, 147.

75. *Lotus Sutra*, 36.

76. Eliot, "Lecture VIII," Clark Lectures, 746.

77. Eliot's consideration of Indian traditions solely in terms of Western mysticism is problematic. However, this particular issue is beyond the scope of the current study. For more on the characterization of Indian traditions as "mystical," see especially King, *Orientalism and Religion*.

78. Eliot's relationship to Schopenhauer is complex. M. A. R. Habib acknowledges that Eliot viewed Schopenhauer as a "romantic," as did Babbitt and Santayana. See Habib, *Early T. S. Eliot*, 64. Nevertheless, Habib argues

250 NOTES TO PAGES 56–59

that Eliot's very notion of irony, influenced as it is by Laforgue, is actually derived from Schopenhauer's own theory of humor (65–70). Ultimately Habib suggests that similarities between Eliot and Schopenhauer arise from the fact that Schopenhauer formed an especially powerful "'hetero-logical' tradition" to counter Hegel's Enlightenment synthesis, and that this tradition included such diverse writers as Laforgue, Nietzsche, Kierkeg-aard, Baudelaire, and Bergson (62–63).

79. Eliot, "Lecture I: Introduction," Clark Lectures, 613.

80. Eliot, "Lecture I," Clark Lectures, 614.

81. Eliot, "Lecture II: Donne and the Middle Ages," Clark Lectures, 637.

82. Eliot, "Lecture II," Clark Lectures, 635.

83. Eliot, "Lecture II," Clark Lectures, 637.

84. Eliot, "Lecture III," Clark Lectures, 651.

85. Eliot, "Lecture III," Clark Lectures, 651.

86. Schuchard, Eliot's Dark Angel, 60–61.

87. Eliot, "Lecture III," Clark Lectures, 651.

88. It should be noted that Eliot's depiction of Bergson here does not perfectly reflect someone like Schopenhauer. This becomes important below in El-iot's discussion of Laforgue. Schopenhauer does not glorify the "plunging into the flow of immediate experience." Eliot is taking Bergson as an ex-ample of a larger trend of psychological analysis. From Eliot's perspective, what Bergson and Schopenhauer would share is a turning away ultimately from the "apparatus of distinction and analysis" and a "turning back on the path of thought" (Eliot, "Lecture III," Clark Lectures, 651). For Schopen-hauer, the height of realization is the sudden annihilation of the self and the awareness of nothingness. It might be argued that Buddhism too holds a loss of the self as a preeminent goal. This is true, but this loss of self only emerges after the imagination and the "apparatus of distinction and analy-sis" have been engaged and transcended. It is this that allies them with the "classical" forms of mysticism described in Varieties. At any rate, Habib observes that Eliot was not alone in considering Schopenhauer a "roman-tic," as this was also held by Babbitt and Santayana (Habib, Early T. S. Eliot, 64). Habib makes the interesting claim that Schopenhauer's aesthetics are similar to Bergson's and were held to be so by T. E. Hulme (66).

89. As quoted in a note by Cuda and Schuchard in Eliot, "Lecture III," Clark Lectures, 663n9.

90. Eliot, "Lecture III," Clark Lectures, 653.

91. Eliot, "Lecture III," Clark Lectures, 652.

92. Eliot, "Lecture III," Clark Lectures, 652.

93. Eliot, "Lecture III," Clark Lectures, 664n16.

NOTES TO PAGES 59–63   251

94. Eliot, "Lecture III," Clark Lectures, 653.

95. For more on Laforgue's orientalism, see Schwab, *Oriental Renaissance,* 418–24.

96. Habib acknowledges that Laforgue's irony is indebted to Schopenhauer (Habib, *Early T. S. Eliot,* 65). He notes that Schopenhauer approaches irony through an analysis of humor, writing, "It is, maintains Schopenhauer, this very incongruity between 'abstract' and 'sensuous' knowledge, between thought and perception, which is the cause of laughter. According to Schopenhauer, the pleasure in laughter derives from the triumph of perception over the abstract concept" (65). Thus, "humour itself is structured irony, embracing the 'accommodation' of at least two viewpoints within subjectivity itself" (66). Habib traces this notion of irony to Eliot's analysis of Laforgue in the Clark Lectures, describing as he does Eliot's disjunction of "ideas" and "feelings" (64). This, ironically, suggests that Eliot's own interpretation of irony here also owes a partial debt to Schopenhauer. If Habib is right, Eliot is involved in a complicated form of negotiation with Schopenhauer's thought, embracing elements of his theory of humor and irony while distancing himself from his mysticism.

97. Eliot, "Lecture VIII," Clark Lectures, 743–44.

98. Eliot, "Lecture VIII," Clark Lectures, 745.

99. Eliot, "Lecture VIII," Clark Lectures, 745 (translated by the editors).

100. Eliot, "Lecture III," Clark Lectures, 746.

101. Kearns, *T. S. Eliot and Indic Traditions,* 145. Kearns indeed notes that Babbitt "wished to instate the notion of a disciplined and purified will," and that Buddhism offered a practical way with which to conceptualize this (145). She also notes that Eliot parts company with Babbitt by holding the importance of "myth, legend, and devotional practice" within the tradition (146). In general, according to Kearns, Eliot reacts against the humanism of Babbitt by emphasizing the necessity of giving oneself over to a particular tradition, along with all its cultural nuances (147). In other words, Babbitt's humanistic Buddhism could not take into account and validate the entirety of Buddhist practice. Kearns's entire discussion of Babbitt (143–52) is insightful and informative.

102. See especially Kearns, *T. S. Eliot and Indic Traditions,* 21–29.

2. T. S. ELIOT'S *Ars Religiosa*

1. Schuchard, *Eliot's Dark Angel.*

2. Schuchard, *Eliot's Dark Angel,* 52.

3. On Indian religious traditions, see Kearns. *T. S. Eliot and Indic Traditions.*

4. Brooker, *Mastery and Escape,* 124.

250 NOTES TO PAGES 63–68

5. Eliot's dissertation was published as a book in 1964. In an edited form, it is included in volume 1 of *The Complete Prose of T. S. Eliot,* edited by Jewel Spears Brooker and Ronald Shuchard. All references are taken from *The Complete Prose.*

6. Brooker, *Mastery and Escape,* 136. Habib concurs. See Habib, *Early T. S. Eliot,* 132–33.

7. See esp. Kearns, *T. S. Eliot and Indic Traditions,* 21–29.

8. Kearns, *T. S. Eliot and Indic Traditions,* 130. Kearns offers several Indic texts that might provide parallels to Eliot's project in the dissertation, including the work of Shankara and Patanjali (130).

9. See Moody, *Thomas Stearns Eliot,* 73. Kearns also builds on Moody's suggestion. See esp. Kearns, *T. S. Eliot and Indic Traditions,* 117–30.

10. Kearns, *T. S. Eliot and Indic Traditions,* 129.

11. Schuchard, *Eliot's Dark Angel,* 68. Schuchard observes that the decisive influence on Eliot's religiosity at this time was his exposure to the writings of T. E. Hulme. Schuchard believes Eliot's engagement with Hulme's work began as early as 1915 (57). This engagement with Hulme's religiosity roughly coincides with Eliot's concluding work on the dissertation. Schuchard argues that the period of 1915–16 is a turning point in Eliot's life, one that represents a transition in a "three-year philosophical-spiritual journey" that leads to an ultimate embrace of a "Christian humanism" (68).

12. Eliot, *Knowledge and Experience,* 376.

13. Eliot, *Knowledge and Experience,* 377.

14. Eliot, *Knowledge and Experience,* 375.

15. Eliot, *Knowledge and Experience,* 246. Brooker also notes Eliot's acceptance of a concept of feeling as immediate experience. See Brooker, "Eliot's Philosophical Studies," 183.

16. Eliot, *Knowledge and Experience,* 249.

17. Eliot, *Knowledge and Experience,* 245.

18. Habib notes that it is the abiding presence of feeling that casts the self into an ironic posture. Until the final approach to the Absolute, the self will always be enabled to objectify itself in an ironic manner. See Habib, *Early T. S. Eliot,* 136–37.

19. Brooker, *Mastery and Escape,* 136.

20. Brooker, *Mastery and Escape,* 187.

21. Eliot, *Knowledge and Experience,* 256.

22. Brooker, "Apprentice Years," xlvii–xliii. See also Levenson, *Genealogy of Modernism,* 181–86.

23. Kearns, *T. S. Eliot and Indic Traditions,* 125.

24. Kearns, *T. S. Eliot and Indic Traditions,* 125.

NOTES TO PAGES 68–70   253

25. Kearns, *T. S. Eliot and Indic Traditions,* 371. Brooker explains this as follows: "The idea that there are degrees of reality means that the line between the illusory and the real is not absolute, and thus Eliot claims that nothing is totally illusory, and that anything that can be a 'point of attention,' including thoughts, hallucinations, and falsehoods, is to some extent real." See Brooker, "Apprentice Years," xxxvi.

26. Eliot, *Knowledge and Experience,* 260–61.

27. Brooker reminds us that strictly speaking a "finite center" is not a self: "A finite center is not a self, or a knower, for immediate experience is prior to such distinctions. It is a *center* of being and feeling in one; it is *finite* because it breaks up into relational consciousness." See Brooker, *Mastery and Escape,* 198. See also Kearns, *T. S. Eliot and Indic Traditions,* 122.

28. Eliot, *Knowledge and Experience,* 373. Kearns notes that Eliot is in actuality making aesthetic experience paradigmatic for all experience. See Kearns, *T. S. Eliot and Indic Traditions,* 120–21.

29. For Eliot, a "point of view" is a system of relations between objects in the world. James Longenbach has described a point of view as "a unity that mingles the emotional, intellectual, and sensual aspects of the individual." See Longenbach, *Modernist Poetics of History,* 167. Longenbach is especially good at explaining how this notion of "system" informs Eliot's later literary criticism (see esp. 173–76). See also Levenson, *Genealogy of Modernism,* 196–202.

30. Eliot, *Knowledge and Experience,* 375.

31. Brooker notes that Eliot broadly claims that any philosophical system, then, would have to be based on nothing but faith, insofar as any philosophy is based on the objects that appear to the philosopher. See Brooker, "Apprentice Years," xlv.

32. See chapter 1, as well as Kearns, *T. S. Eliot and Indic Traditions,* 76–84.

33. For more on *upaya,* see esp. Gombrich, *How Buddhism Began;* Pye, *Skilful Means;* Bond, "Gradual Path"; Ganeri, *Concealed Art.*

34. Kearns, *T. S. Eliot and Indic Traditions,* 79.

35. Kearns also points the reader to the work of Jeffrey Perl and Andrew Tuck, who undertook a study of Eliot's notebooks on Indic thought. Perl and Tuck observe that the Buddhist tradition provides for a path that incorporates various voices and levels of truth on the path toward *nirvana.* Because of this, however, the context in which certain teachings are promoted or practices embraced is all-important. The truth of a statement will depend on which level of the path it is uttered, and to whom it is being uttered. See Perl and Tuck, "Hidden Advantage of Tradition," 124. The two point to Anesaki's introduction to Nagarjuna as the source of Eliot's embrace of

254 NOTES TO PAGES 71–78

relative levels of truth to the soteriological path. In his notebooks, Eliot writes: "A view is false in one sense, true in another. This kind of synthesis is characteristic of Buddhism from its very beginning under the name of middle path. . . . Life is neither pain nor pleasure. The views that the world exists or not, both are false, the truth lies in the middle, transcending both views." See Perl and Tuck, "Hidden Advantage of Tradition," 121.

36. Spurr, "Anglo-Catholic in Religion," 40.

37. Pye, *Skilful Means,* 122.

38. Gombrich, *How Buddhism Began,* 65.

39. Pye, *Skilful Means,* 131–32.

40. George Bond suggests that Theravada classifications of different types of suttas claimed that each higher stage of sutta was meant to "counteract the stage which precedes it" (Bond, *Gradual Path,* 38).

41. Buddhism contains an analogous term to faith, *shraddha,* which means "'confidence' born out of conviction" as well as "devotion to the Buddha, the *Dhamma* . . . and the *Sangha.*" Rahula, *What the Buddha Taught,* 8.

42. Eliot, *Knowledge and Experience,* 163.

43. Heb. 11:1 (NRSV).

44. Eliot's main concern in his dissertation is with Bradley's *Appearance and Reality.* I do not mean to imply that *Ethical Studies* is more important to Eliot than *Appearance and Reality,* either in general or in *Knowledge and Experience.* Rather, I am trying to trace the origin of Eliot's use of "leap" language at the conclusion of his text. Since Eliot's reading of Kierkegaard does not come until much later in his life, the reference remains puzzling. In *Ethical Studies,* Bradley specifically uses this term in his implied criticism of religion. Moreover, he does so in context of rejecting the very elements of religious practice that Eliot would come to embrace. When considered in context of Eliot's argument, along with the reference to transmigration, the allusion becomes much more clear.

45. Bradley, *Ethical Studies,* 280.

46. Bradley, *Ethical Studies,* 291.

47. Bradley, *Ethical Studies,* 293.

48. Bradley, *Ethical Studies,* 294–95.

49. Bradley, *Ethical Studies,* 293.

50. Bradley, *Ethical Studies,* 294.

51. Bradley, *Ethical Studies,* 297.

52. Bradley, *Ethical Studies,* 301.

53. T.S. Eliot, *Knowledge and Experience,* 381.

54. Ganeri, *Concealed Art,* 100.

55. Brooker, *Mastery and Escape,* 124.

NOTES TO PAGES 78–82   255

56. Brooker, *Mastery and Escape*, 124.

57. Eliot to Herbert Read, December 1925, in Eliot, *Letters of T. S. Eliot*, 2:797.

58. Eliot, "Lecture III," Clark Lectures, 653.

3. INDIA AMONG THE FRAGMENTS

1. Gish, *The Waste Land*, 14–16. See also Brooker and Bentley, *Reading "The Waste Land*," 14–16. Gish's account of early scholarly approaches to the poem is still extremely helpful and informs my approach. See esp. 9–17. In more recent scholarship, Anthony Cuda provides further resources to flesh out the more recent critical history. See Cuda, "CODA," 194–210.

2. "Eliot seized on images and impressions that had struck his imagination and did not belabor their moral significance. Beginning with 'The Fire Sermon,' he drew on memories of London formed during the preceding summer, when his attention was sharpened to visionary intensity by the presence of his mother; on scenes from his own life, particularly from his life with Vivien; and on the horrible noises and the disagreeable neighbors he complained of to John Quinn. Through all of these, like wine through water, ran the nightmarish emotional change of Eliot's vague but intensely acute horror and apprehension of the 'unknown terror and mystery in which our life is passed.' As Eliot said about Jonson's plays, that was enough to give the fragments a 'dominant tone,' a 'unity of inspiration that radiates into plot and personages alike.' What he had sensed at the very bottom of Jonson's constructions became the primary—almost the only—unity of his own poem." R. Bush, *T. S. Eliot*, 57.

3. Davidson, *T. S. Eliot and Hermeneutics*, 2.

4. Davidson, *T. S. Eliot and Hermeneutics*, 11.

5. Davidson, *T. S. Eliot and Hermeneutics*, 125.

6. "What connects them [i.e., the poem's 'vignettes'] is precisely what connects the disparate segments of our most distressing dreams . . . when the dream censor is able to agitate and then shatter a fantasy that gets too close to some forbidden truth, the forces that initiated the fantasy start the whole struggle again. In each segment, the same impulses reappear veiled in different objects or personae, unifying them from below." See R. Bush, *T. S. Eliot*, 63. In Bush's analysis, therefore, there is a subtle meta-narrative implicit in the poem's movements, a repeated approach to the reality of death, and a retreat from it (63). Further, the poem suddenly has a center, the scene in the Hyacinth Garden (64).

7. Gish, *The Waste Land*, 16; Cuda, "CODA," 204.

8. "Put out from ecstasy and longing to escape its actual state, it [i.e., the conscious mind] must operate in the realm of the imperfect, the confused, the

256 NOTES TO PAGES 82–83

contradictory, the failed or the unfulfilled. Contemplating this actuality, it must feel it as the negative of what it would be. To develop and intensify these feelings may be the only form in which the poet can maintain his passional life. The negation is a way of maintaining, in a dissociated and contradictory existence, the impulse toward the pursuit of beauty." Moody, *Thomas Stearns Eliot*, 83.

9. "The speaker thus traces to the experience of 'nothing' in the hyacinth garden his first intimation of the void at the centre of human relationships—the void by which arises for him the opportunity to glimpse a 'simple, terrible and unknown' something beyond it." Childs, *T. S. Eliot*, 127.

10. "If we think of *The Waste Land* as the thoughts, memories, overheard conversations, and remembered quotations of a single consciousness, the closing passage reveals most directly the narrator's way of approaching and comprehending experience. What begins in private fears and dreams takes on significance and universal meaning through the recognition and appropriation of other voices, not only the contemporary voices of London society but those of all human culture. It is as if all stories, legends, poems, songs, attest to the centrality of the narrator's opening lament and the urgency of his questions. The many voices converge into the voice of one who seeks to understand the 'riddle of existence' and 'the doctrine for the cessation of misery,' and who finds in the voices of prophecy and divine interpretation at least tentative ways of knowing. If the primary theme of the poem is that riddle, it reaches no absolute solution but only repeated assurances of some insight." Gish, *The Waste Land*, 102–3.

11. Bedient, *He Do the Police*. I discuss this text more fully below.

12. "Tiresias perceives the contemporary world in the poem from a perspective outside space and time altogether. He is thus not only one side of a binary perspective; he is also the suggestion that the reader must try to imagine that *The Waste Land* is a phenomenon to be viewed from the perspective of the Absolute, or at least from a more comprehensive perspective." Brooker and Bentley, *Reading "The Waste Land,"* 54. It should be noted that though Brooker and Bentley think of this point as that toward which the poem strives, they also think that the poem fails at achieving such a mythic perspective.

13. Leavis, *New Bearings in English Poetry*, 95.

14. Kearns, *T. S. Eliot and Indic Traditions*, 195–96.

15. Bedient, *He Do the Police*, x–xi.

16. Bedient, *He Do the Police*, xi.

17. Bedient, *He Do the Police*, 37.

18. Gish, *The Waste Land*, 37.

NOTES TO PAGES 83–88   257

19. See Eliot, *The Waste Land: A Facsimile,* 5.
20. Bedient, *He Do the Police,* 73.
21. Bedient, *He Do the Police,* 73.
22. See Bedient, *He Do the Police,* 79. Also cf. Gish, *The Waste Land,* 38.
23. Bedient, *He Do the Police,* 79.
24. Bedient, *He Do the Police,* 79.
25. Richards, *T. S. Eliot's Ascetic Ideal,* 68.
26. Brooks, "*The Waste Land,*" 137.
27. Eliot, *The Waste Land,* ll. 1–9. All references to *The Waste Land* are from *The Poems of T. S. Eliot,* vol. 1. References are to line numbers. I have also made great use of Lawrence Rainey's annotations to the poem, as becomes clear as we proceed. See Rainey, "Editor's Annotations." Rainey no doubt builds on the work of two other significant texts from which I have also profited, the classic set of annotations found in Southam, *Guide to the Selected Poems,* and the exhaustive research in Grover Smith, *T. S. Eliot's Poetry and Plays.*
28. See Rainey, "Editor's Annotations," 76; Southam, *Guide to the Selected Poems,* 72.
29. Chaucer, *Canterbury Tales,* l.1. The familiar prologue runs as follows: "Whan that Aprill with his shoures soote / The droghte of March hath perced to the roote, / And bathed every veine in swich licour / Of which vertu engendred is the flour, / Whan Zephirus eek with his sweete breeth / Inspired hath in every holt and heath / The tendre croppes, and the yonge sonne / Hath in the Ram his halve cours yronne, / And smale foweles maken melodye, / That slepen al the night with open eye— / So priketh hem nature in hir corages— / Than longen folk to goon on pilgrimages, / And palmers for to seken straunge strondes, / To ferne halwes, kouthe in sondry londes; / And specially from every shires ende / Of Engelond to Caunterbury they wende, / The holy blisful martyr for to seke / That hem hath holpen whan they they were seeke" (ll. 1–18).
30. Lilacs are also a charged image in American poetry, as Eliot well knew; they evoke Whitman's use of the imagery in "When Lilacs Last in the Dooryard Bloomed." (This is, incidentally, a reference both Rainey and Southam miss). There, the lilacs embodied death and brought to the poet's mind the memory of the dead beloved, in that poem President Lincoln: "Ever-returning spring, trinity sure to me you bring, / Lilac blooming perennial and drooping star in the west, / And thought of him I love." Here lilacs emerge out of the "dead land" and embody the "mixing" of memory and desire. James Miller sees references to the Whitman poem in section V of the poem. See Miller, *T. S. Eliot's Personal Waste Land,* 119–20.
31. Schopenhauer, *World as Will,* 1:164.

258   NOTES TO PAGES 88–92

32. All references to Indian texts in this chapter are taken from texts to which Eliot had access. The edition of the *Brhadaranyaka Upanishad* is in fact the text given by Eliot himself in his endnotes to *The Waste Land*, that of Paul Deussen (though I have used the English translation by V. M. Bedekar and G. B. Palsule). The references later to Patanjali's *Yoga Sutras* are from the translation by James Haughton Woods, one of Eliot's teachers at Harvard and later one of his friends and correspondents. Eliot read the Patanjali text in Sanskrit with Woods during his graduate studies.

33. Deussen, *Sixty Upaniṣads*, 6.2.15, 528.

34. Deussen, *Sixty Upaniṣads*, 6.2.9–14, 527–28.

35. Deussen, *Sixty Upaniṣads*, 6.2.15, 528.

36. Deussen, *Sixty Upaniṣads*, 6.2.15, 528.

37. Olivelle, *Upaniṣads*, 325.

38. Deussen, *Sixty Upaniṣads*, 6.2.16, 528–29.

39. Collins, *Selfless Persons*, 201.

40. Kearns, *T. S. Eliot and Indic Traditions*, 201.

41. Kearns, *T. S. Eliot and Indic Traditions*, 201. Kearns also sees the influence of Patanjali in "Tradition and the Individual Talent" (62).

42. Patañjali, *Yoga System*, ii.12–14, xxxiv.

43. Patañjali, *Yoga System*, ii.3, xxxiii.

44. Kearns, *T. S. Eliot and Indic Traditions*, 201.

45. Patañjali, *Yoga System*, iii.50, xxxix.

46. Kearns, *T. S. Eliot and Indic Traditions*, 201.

47. Patañjali, *Yoga System*, i.12, xxx. Patanjali writes: "i.12 The restriction of them, is by [means] of practice and passionlessness. i.13 Practice is [repeated] exertion to the end that [the mind-stuff] shall have permanence in this [restricted state.]." Later, he notes the "abstentions" and "observances" that can lead to a more profound discrimination: "ii.29 Abstentions and observances and postures and regulations-of-the-breath and withdrawal of senses and fixed-attention and contemplation and concentration . . . ii.32 Cleanliness and contentment and self-castigation and study and devotion to Ishvara are the observances" (xxxv).

48. Patañjali, *Yoga System*, iii.8, xxxvii.

49. Patañjali, *Yoga System*, iv.29, xli. See also Kearns, *T. S. Eliot and Indic Traditions*, 202.

50. Patañjali, *Yoga System*, iv.30, xli.

51. Cf. Schopenhauer, *World as Will*, 1:313–15: "Now absolutely every human life continues to flow on between willing and attainment. Of its nature the wish is pain; attainment quickly begets satiety. The goal was only apparent; possession takes away its charm. The wish, the need, appears again

on the scene under a new form; if it does not, then dreariness, emptiness, and boredom follow, the struggle against which is just as painful as is that against want. . . . The ceaseless efforts to banish suffering achieve nothing more than a change in its form. This is essentially want, lack, care for the maintenance of life. If, which is very difficult, we have succeeded in removing pain in this form, it at once appears on the scene in a thousand others, varying according to age and circumstances, such as sexual impulse, passionate love, jealousy, envy, hatred, anxiety, ambition, avarice, sickness, and so on. Finally, if it cannot find entry in any other shape, it comes in the sad, grey garment of weariness, satiety, and boredom, against which many different attempts are made. Even if we ultimately succeed in driving these away, it will hardly be done without letting pain in again in one of the previous forms, and thus starting the dance once more at the beginning; for every human life is tossed backwards and forwards between pain and boredom."

52. Arthur Schopenhauer, "Additional Remarks," 287.
53. Schopenhauer, "Additional Remarks," 290. The italics are Schopenhauer's.
54. I refer to the woman in the first section of part II as "Cleopatra," with the full awareness that she cannot be reduced to a single character reference. She combines many different character allusions. Further, within the context of the poem she hearkens back to the hyacinth girl and forward to the typist and Queen Elizabeth. The naming is meant to be a pragmatic tag only.
55. Eliot, *The Waste Land,* 73.
56. Eliot, *The Waste Land,* ll. 77–93.
57. Shakespeare, *Antony and Cleopatra,* 2.2.191–92.
58. Shakespeare, *Antony and Cleopatra,* 2.2.206–7.
59. Shakespeare, *Antony and Cleopatra,* 2.2.228–32.
60. G. Smith, *Eliot's Poetry and Plays,* 80. The description of the ark can be found in Exodus 25:10–22, and that of the candelabrum at Exodus 25:31–40.
61. Eliot, *The Waste Land,* l. 76.
62. Eliot, *The Waste Land,* l. 202.
63. Shakespeare, *Antony and Cleopatra,* 2.2.217–20.
64. Eliot, *The Waste Land,* ll. 88–89.
65. Rainey, "Editor's Annotations," 88.
66. Rainey, "Editor's Annotations," 89.
67. *The Oxford-English Dictionary* online, https://dictionary.oed.com, s.v. "coffer (*v*)."
68. *OED* online, s.v. "coffer (*n*)."
69. *OED* online, s.v. "coffer (*n*)."

260 NOTES TO PAGES 97–102

70. *OED* online, s.v. "coffer (*n*)."

71. Brooker and Bentley, *Reading "The Waste Land,"* 101–2.

72. Brooker and Bentley, *Reading "The Waste Land,"* 105.

73. Brooker and Bentley, *Reading "The Waste Land,"* 96. See Eliot, *The Waste Land: A Facsimile,* 11.

74. *OED* online, s.v. "coffer (*n*)."

75. *OED* online, s.v. "coffer (*n*)."

76. Shakespeare, *Antony and Cleopatra,* 2.2.204.

77. Shakespeare, *Antony and Cleopatra,* 2.2.222–24.

78. Eliot, *The Waste Land,* ll. 97–106.

79. Eliot, *The Waste Land,* 73.

80. Eliot, *The Waste Land,* 75.

81. Ovid, *Metamorphoses,* 144.

82. Ovid, *Metamorphoses,* 148.

83. Childs, *T. S. Eliot,* 118. It is because of this focus on the violations of male desire that Grover Smith is, I believe, egregiously wrong in claiming that it is the protagonist, his "Tiresias," who is really the victim of violation. See G. Smith, *Eliot's Poetry and Plays,* 80.

84. Eliot, *The Waste Land,* ll. 108–10.

85. Moody, *Thomas Stearns Eliot,* 86. Moody argues that this moment in the poem is meant to reflect certain seventeenth- and eighteenth-century verse styles and therefore the type of verse that exacerbated for Eliot the "dissociation of sensibility." The quickening of the verse at the mention of Philomela shows, for Moody, an alternative form of art, one that is responsive to "the experience of romantic passion" (85).

86. Cf. the passage from "East Coker": "The knowledge imposes a pattern, and falsifies, / For the pattern is new in every moment / And every moment is a new and shocking / Valuation of all we have been." Eliot, *Four Quartets,* "East Coker," 2.34–37.

87. Warren, *Buddhist Reader,* 352.

88. Brooks expressed the dynamics of this section in terms of love and lust: "Love is the aesthetic of sex; lust is the science. Love implies a deferring of the satisfaction of the desire; it implies a certain asceticism and a ritual. Lust drives forward urgently and scientifically to the immediate extirpation of desire. Our contemporary waste land is in large part the result of our scientific attitude—of our complete secularization." See Brooks, *"The Waste Land,"* 147–48. I do believe that such a mechanical view of love and of life in general lies at the heart of *The Waste Land.* I also think that a criticism of secularization is also perhaps lurking in the background of the poem as well. But if there is such a critique, it is a critique undertaken

in the context of the separation of thought and feeling. The scientific attitude isolates thought, making it supreme and beyond somatic experience. Thus Eliot's "asceticism" here is an engagement and rechanneling of such experience.

89. One reading that has emerged in the criticism is the identification of the woman in the dialogue specifically with the hyacinth girl. See Moody, *Thomas Stearns Eliot*, 85; Gish, *The Waste Land*, 59; Bedient, *He Do the Police*, 79–80. Eliot's endnotes and the facsimile edition of the poem are to blame for this. In the facsimile, as Bedient notes, at lines 49–50, Eliot had originally had the man respond, "I remember / The hyacinth garden. Those are pearls that were his eyes." See Eliot, *The Waste Land: A Facsimile*, 13. When Eliot wrote his endnotes, and after he had edited out the lines, he added in references back to the hyacinth episode. He connects line 126 in section II with lines 37 and 48 of section I, the first of which directs the reader to the hyacinth garden, the second to Madame Sosostris. Bedient and others take this to mean that the protagonist has married the hyacinth girl (Bedient, *He Do the Police*, 79). However, this is not necessarily the case, especially if there is a single protagonist, as Bedient suggests. The glance back toward the hyacinth garden could be a glance of nostalgia, of opportunities missed. It need not look back to a moment of monumental mistake, nor does the original poetic context suggest this.

90. Gish, *The Waste Land*, 58.

91. Cf. G. Smith, *Eliot's Poetry and Plays*, 81.

92. Eliot, *The Waste Land*, ll. 119–26.

93. See also Brooker and Bentley, *Reading "The Waste Land,"* 106.

94. Bedient interprets this line as demonstrating that the man in the dialogue is closer to enlightenment than is the female; at least he has attained a clearer vision of the truth. He writes, "he has all but reached the limit of nothingness . . . and already has knowledge . . . that there is fullness upon fullness on the other side." See Bedient, *He Do the Police*, 97. Also cf. Brooks, *"The Waste Land,"* 149; Davidson, *Eliot and Hermeneutics*, 119. I agree that there are intimations of transcendence here, intimations that will be reinvoked in the "Song of the Thames-daughters," but I also would argue that the context is overwhelmingly pessimistic. The poem itself can hint at transcendence, even if the current speaker does not fully recognize this. The speaker at the moment shows no signs of realizing the potential of his words. Death has become not an escape for him, but rather an alienating thought: "I think we are in rats' alley / Where the dead men lost their bones" (Eliot, *The Waste Land*, ll. 115–16).

95. Eliot, *The Waste Land*, ll. 47–48.

NOTES TO PAGES 104–115

96. Eliot, *The Waste Land,* l. 128. For more on the influence of the music hall on Eliot, see Schuchard, *Eliot's Dark Angel,* chapter 5, "In the Music Halls," 102–18.
97. Eliot, *The Waste Land,* ll. 135–38.
98. Southam, *Guide to the Selected Poems,* 78, Rainey, "Editor's Annotations," 88.
99. G. Smith, *Eliot's Poetry and Plays,* 81.
100. Brooks, "*The Waste Land,*" 150.
101. Brooks, "*The Waste Land,*" 81.
102. G. Smith, *Eliot's Poetry and Plays,* 81.
103. Shakespeare, *The Tempest,* 5.1.174–75.
104. Shakespeare, *The Tempest,* 5.1.174n.
105. Shakespeare, *The Tempest,* 5.1.171–72n. Orgel draws on the analysis of Anne Barton. See 5.1.174–75n.
106. Brooker and Bentley, *Reading "The Waste Land,"* 115.

4. LANGUAGE AND THE CULTIVATION OF DESIRE IN "THE FIRE SERMON"

1. Kearns, *T. S. Eliot and Indic Traditions,* 76.
2. Eliot, "Preacher as Artist," 166. See also Kearns, *T. S. Eliot and Indic Traditions,* 75–76.
3. Warren, *Buddhist Reader,* 352.
4. Ganeri, *Concealed Art,* 100.
5. Eliot writes, "The contemplation of the horrid or sordid or disgusting, by an artist, is the necessary and negative aspect of the impulse toward the pursuit of beauty." See Eliot, "Dante" (I), 232.
6. Eliot, "Baudelaire," 158.
7. Eliot, "Baudelaire," 159–60.
8. Kearns, *T. S. Eliot and Indic Traditions,* 209.
9. Theravada Buddhism splits its canon into three *pitakas* or "baskets": the *Sutta Pitaka,* the *Vinaya Pitaka,* and the *Abhidhamma Pitaka.* The *Sutta Pitaka* contains discourses and dialogues of the Buddha, birth narratives, mythological narratives, etc. The *Abhidhamma Pitaka,* the "higher teaching," contains higher-level conceptual analysis of the human person and the constituents of existence. The *Vinaya Pitaka,* however, contains narratives and sets of rules aimed at prescribing the behavior of the Sangha, the community of monks. See Gethin, *Foundations of Buddhism,* 202. Gethin's chapter on *Abhidharma* is a good overall introduction to the ontological analyses of the texts of this "basket" of the canon.
10. Warren, *Buddhist Reader,* 352–53. This publication is merely a reprinting of *Buddhism in Translations,* originally released in the Harvard Oriental Series, vol. 3, in 1896.

NOTES TO PAGES 115–120   263

11. Collins, *Nirvana*, 217.
12. Olivelle, introduction to *Upaniṣads*, xlii.
13. Gombrich, *How Buddhism Began*, 66.
14. Collins, *Nirvana*, 216.
15. Collins, *Nirvana*, 217.
16. Early Buddhism recognizes six *ayatanas*, which consist of the six senses along with their proper objects. The senses, or "bases . . . of mental processes," are the usual five physical senses plus consciousness, or the "mind base." See Nyanatiloka, *Buddhist Dictionary*, 28.
17. Gombrich, *How Buddhism Began*, 67.
18. Nyanatiloka, *Buddhist Dictionary*, 82.
19. Nyanatiloka, *Buddhist Dictionary*, 185–86.
20. Nyanatiloka, *Buddhist Dictionary*, 185.
21. Gombrich, *How Buddhism Began*, 67.
22. Gombrich, *How Buddhism Began*, 67.
23. For this part of the narrative of the Buddha's enlightenment, see Warren, *Buddhist Reader*, 81–83.
24. Warren, *Buddhist Reader*, 166.
25. Warren, *Buddhist Reader*, 115.
26. Dependent origination is explained in Warren, *Buddhist Reader*, 165–70. For slightly less mystifying explanations, see chapter 6 of Gethin, *Foundations of Buddhism*, 133–62; and Collins, *Selfless Persons*, 103–10.
27. The Four Noble Truths are given in Warren, *Buddhist Reader*, 368. The term *dukkha*, here translated as "misery," is usually translated as "suffering": "the truth concerning misery . . . the truth concerning the origin of misery . . . the truth concerning the cessation of misery . . . the truth concerning the path leading to the cessation of misery."
28. Goldman, "Karma, Guilt, and Buried Memories," 414.
29. For a thorough treatment of the Buddhist reinterpretation and ethicization of the ancient Indian karmic metaphysics, see Obeyesekere, *Imagining Karma*, esp. chapters 3 and 4.
30. Nyanatiloka, *Buddhist Dictionary*, 39.
31. Keown, *Nature of Buddhist Ethics*, 213.
32. Nyanatiloka, *Buddhist Dictionary*, 79.
33. Collins, *Selfless Persons*, 202.
34. Collins, *Selfless Persons*, 220. The Buddhist tradition walks a tightrope here, arguing consistently that such attachments are not absolutely determinative; the individual always has the capacity to change direction, respond to the *Dhamma*, and begin to undertake positive activity on the eightfold path (Jayatilleke, *Early Buddhist Theory*, 445). Such a freedom

NOTES TO PAGES 120–128

from absolute determination would seem to be a prerequisite to the activity of the person on the path; if all activity were simply determined by previous desires, the individual would be bound in a never-ending circle. The Buddha's own enlightenment would indeed seem to presuppose such a personal agency. Nonetheless, without the intervention of the *Dhamma*, it would at least be difficult for a sentient being to escape from the round of suffering.

35. Collins, *Selfless Persons*, 191. Also compare Gombrich, *How Buddhism Began*, 33.

36. Nyanatiloka, *Buddhist Dictionary*, 54.

37. Collins, *Selfless Persons*, 192.

38. Collins, *Selfless Persons*, 247. See also Gombrich, *How Buddhism Began*, 4: "The Buddha claimed not to be a philosopher; but the implications of all his teachings were so clearly nominalist that for over a thousand years Buddhist philosophy maintained the tradition that things as we conceive of them and talk about them are mere conceptualizations, mere labels—*prajñapti-mātra*. This has sometimes been interpreted to mean that early Buddhism, like the much later *Yogācāra* school, was idealistic; but that is a mistake: the ontology of the Pali canon is realistic and pluralistic; it does not deny that there is a world 'out there.'"

39. Nyanatiloka defines *nama/rupa* as "'Mind-and-body', mentality and corporeality" (see *Buddhist Dictionary*, 103). In general, name and form designate the body/mind relationship, but also the relationship between the mind and forms in the world in general. Gombrich, referring to the work of S. B. Hamilton, declares that the nama/rupa duality "refers to all individual existence: form is physical (not necessarily visible) identity, name conceptual identity" (*How Buddhism Began*, 44).

40. Jayatilleke, *Early Buddhist Theory*, 434.

41. Warren, *Buddhist Reader*, 165–66.

42. Warren, *Buddhist Reader*, 169–70.

43. Jayatilleke, *Early Buddhist Theory*, 450–51.

44. Warren, *Buddhist Reader*, 133–34.

45. Collins, *Selfless Persons*, 105.

46. Jayatilleke, *Early Buddhist Theory*, 316–17.

47. See Spiro, *Buddhism and Society*, 11–14.

48. Gethin, *Foundations of Buddhism*, has a brief summary on 110–11. See also Collins, *Selfless Persons*, 16–19 and 153–56. The distinction is found in many discussions of the Buddhist path, though most scholars criticize Spiro on envisioning too much of a hard distinction between the two different types. The Path is meant to unite them seamlessly.

49. Further, in one of the appendixes of the Warren volume, we find charts of the five *khandas* and their constituents, as defined by the early Buddhist scholastic tradition. Of the five, it is unsurprising that the consciousness group looms the largest, with 89 constituent states of consciousness. Constituents 1–21 are forms of good karma, while 22–33 are bad (Warren, *Buddhist Reader,* 373).
50. Warren, *Buddhist Reader,* 487–91.
51. Warren, *Buddhist Reader,* 333.
52. Warren, *Buddhist Reader,* 333.
53. Collins, *Nirvana,* 186.
54. Gethin, *Foundations of Buddhism,* 167.
55. Collins, *Nirvana,* 208–9.
56. See Warren, *Buddhist Reader,* 269–74.
57. Warren, *Buddhist Reader,* 271.
58. Warren, *Buddhist Reader,* 272.
59. Gombrich, *How Buddhism Began,* 21.
60. Pye, *Skilful Means,* 123. See also Gombrich, *How Buddhism Began,* 17.
61. Cited in Gombrich, *How Buddhism Began,* 17. The passage is from Rhys Davids, *Dialogues of the Buddha,* 206–7.
62. Pye, *Skilful Means,* 123. He continues: "Buddhism does not reject other thought systems but associates with them, with a view to realizing the intention of the Buddhist system. The striking thing is that this mode of correlation may involve a paradoxical, provisionally positive acceptance of ideas which are quite different from and even contradictory to the central intention or meaning of Buddhism itself."
63. Pye, *Skilful Means,* 123.
64. Gombrich, *How Buddhism Began,*65.
65. Lamotte, "Assessment of Textual Interpretation," 13.
66. Edgerton, *Beginnings of Indian Philosophy,* 25–26.
67. Gombrich, *How Buddhism Began,* 22.
68. Lopez, introduction to *Buddhist Hermeneutics,* 5.
69. Lopez, introduction to *Buddhist Hermeneutics,* 7.
70. Pye, *Skilful Means,* 131–32.
71. George Bond suggests that Theravada classifications of different types of suttas claimed that each higher stage of sutta was meant to "counteract the stage which precedes it" (Bond, "Gradual Path," 38).
72. Gombrich, *How Buddhism Began,* 21.
73. Gombrich, *How Buddhism Began,* 66.
74. Gombrich, *How Buddhism Began,* 65.
75. Pye, *Skilful Means,* 120.

266   NOTES TO PAGES 137–141

76. Another version of this story, as found in the *Majjhima-Nikaya,* is presented by Warren, *Buddhist Reader,* 338–41.

77. *Mahāvagga,* 85.

78. *Mahāvagga,* 87–88.

79. Gombrich, *How Buddhism Began,* 21.

80. Olivelle, *Upaniṣads,* lvi.

81. Olivelle, *Upaniṣads,* xlii.

82. Gombrich, *How Buddhism Began,* 21.

83. Gombrich, *How Buddhism Began,* 21. Also see 71: "But if one takes the point of view of the compiler of the text, the whole story is ancillary to the Fire Sermon, which has to come as its climax."

84. *Mahāvagga,* 113.

85. *Mahāvagga,* 119.

86. *Mahāvagga,* 119.

87. *Mahāvagga,* 121–22.

88. Gombrich, *How Buddhism Began,* 70.

89. Gombrich, *How Buddhism Began,* 71–72.

90. Gombrich, *How Buddhism Began,* 71.

91. Gombrich, *How Buddhism Began,* 70–71.

92. Eliot, *The Waste Land,* 75.

93. Bedient, *He Do the Police,* 151.

94. Eliot, *The Waste Land,* l. 295. Dante's Pia has repented her sins at the last moment of her life and now works her way up Mount Purgatory. She asks Dante to remember her when he returns to the world. His literary representations could inspire others to pray for her: "'Ah, when you are returned to the world and are rested from the long journey,' a third spirit continued after the second, 'remember me: I am Pia; Siena made me, Maremma unmade me: he knows it within himself who earlier, wedding me, had given me his ring and gem." See Dante Alighieri, *Divine Comedy,* vol. 2, *Purgatorio,* V.130–36. Eliot's lines are as follows: "'Trams and dusty trees. / Highbury bore me. Richmond and Kew / Undid me. By Richmond I raised my knees / Supine on the floor of a narrow canoe" (*The Waste Land,* ll. 292–95).

95. Eliot, *The Waste Land,* l. 299.

96. Cf. Brooker and Bentley, *Reading "The Waste Land,"* 145. They also place the problem of the Thames daughters as the loss of an ultimate value for which to live. However, they see the basic problem of ennui as reaching its high point at the end of section III. My reading differs with theirs here. I disagree with their assertion that "no directions of significant motion are imaginable now." As I argue, the song of the Thames daughters, sandwiched between

the Magnus Martyr fragment and the ascetic fragments of the end of the section, shows the mind in the process of attempting to formulate such a motion, given the pessimistic problematics of the poem.

97. Eliot, *The Waste Land*, ll. 301–2, 304–5.

98. Moody, *Thomas Stearns Eliot*, 94.

99. Childs, *T. S. Eliot*, 119, 121.

100. Gish, *The Waste Land*, 80.

101. Kearns, *T. S. Eliot and Indic Traditions*, 208. Childs also agrees with Kearns on the possible positive valence of these lines (see 120–21). He recognizes that the "desire to escape desire" expressed in the song of the Thames daughters leads right into the references to the ascetic texts of the Buddha and Augustine. However, because he does not take into consideration the echoes of the Buddha's skillful means, I believe that Childs too easily pits sensuality against asceticism. Indeed, he quotes a letter from Eliot to Paul Elmore More claiming that Eliot depicted himself as oscillating between the two options (121). Childs takes that letter as a warrant to support a distinction between the two in *The Waste Land*, without asking whether the poem could be attempting to imagine a path in which these two were not absolutely distinct.

102. Eliot, *The Waste Land*, 75.

103. Eliot, *The Waste Land*, ll. 307–11.

104. Augustine, *Confessions*, 3.1, 32–33. All citations to *Confessions* are to the Pusey translation.

105. Simpson, *Cassell's New Latin Dictionary*, s.v. "sartago (n)."

106. Simpson, *Cassell's New Latin Dictionary*, s.v. "circumstrepo (v)": "to make a noise round, shout clamorously around."

107. Damien Keown, in his analysis of Buddhist ethics, provides a robust, broad interpretation of Buddhist *chetana* but fails to acknowledge the similarly complex portrait Augustine paints of the will. He therefore misses the opportunity for a richer comparison. Such a comparison *is* undertaken, however, by David Clairemont, in "Moral Motivation and Comparative Ethics: Bonaventure, Buddhaghosa, and the Problem of Material Simplicity" (PhD diss., University of Chicago, 2005). Clairemont observes: "As V. J. Bourke puts it, 'will (voluntas) means the whole soul as active. . . . The Augustinian will is not a faculty but the soul itself as loving: indeed, will is but love in its strongest form.' So the idea of the will as separate faculty, as opposed to a unity of personality that acts in a directed way, had not yet emerged in Christian discourse, but the larger question of moral motivation could no longer be answered solely as a failure of practical rationality but rather was expended to include the entire orientation of one's desires

268   NOTES TO PAGES 146–156

and commitments" (105). In discussing Augustine's thoughts on the will in *The City of God,* Clairemont expands this view, observing: "For Augustine, willing is an activity of focusing on that to which one is drawn rather than, strictly speaking, a faculty that is exercised and thereby acts. It involves the rational dimension of the person insofar as the intellect has the ability to perceive the good to which one is drawn. It involves the affective dimension because willing is a form of desiring." Clairemont's work is a useful supplement to Keown's curiously incomplete view on this subject. See especially his account of the development of the concept of "the will" (88–110).

108. Augustine, *Confessions,* 10.53, 237–38.

109. Augustine, *Confessions,* footnote: 10.53, 237.

110. Pusey's translation of "cunning" has a more negative connotation than the term *artificiosas* seems ordinarily to have. It simply means "skillful, accomplished." See Simpson, *Cassell's New Latin Dictionary,* s.v. "artificiosus (*adj*)."

111. Augustine, *Confessions,* 5.23–24, 91–92.

112. Eliot, *The Waste Land,* ll. 309–10.

113. Kearns, *T. S. Eliot and Indic Traditions,* 210.

5. TRANSCENDENCE REVISITED

1. Bedient, *He Do the Police,* 5.

2. Bedient, *He Do the Police,* 5–6.

3. Bedient, *He Do the Police,* 176.

4. Ganeri, *Concealed Art,* 3–4.

5. Ganeri, *Concealed Art,* 4

6. Ganeri, *Concealed Art,* 19.

7. Ganeri, *Concealed Art,* 35.

8. Ganeri, *Concealed Art,* 1.

9. Eliot, *Knowledge and Experience,* 362.

10. Eliot, "Baudelaire," 160.

11. Eliot, "Baudelaire," 162.

12. Eliot, "Baudelaire," 158. "Such suffering as Baudelaire's implies the possibility of a positive state of beatitude. Indeed, in his way of suffering is already a kind of presence of the supernatural and of the superhuman. He rejects always the purely natural and the purely human. . . . His *ennui* may of course be explained, as everything can be explained in psychological or pathological terms; but it is also, from the opposite point of view, a true form of *acedia,* arising from the unsuccessful struggle towards the spiritual life."

13. Eliot, *The Waste Land,* ll. 328–29. See also the Ricks and McCue commentary on these lines, 688.

14. Eliot, *The Waste Land,* l. 327.

NOTES TO PAGES 156–160   269

15. Bedient, *He Do the Police,* 176. Brooker and Bentley also depict this moment in the poem as a "hallucination," the dreaming of that which will satisfy a lack, though as such actually beginning with the water dripping song, in the imagining of the sound of water dripping. Brooker and Bentley, *Reading "The Waste Land,"* 178. Moody concurs, writing: "As it may do in dreams, the mind has imaged what it desires in a form which remains true to the actual deprivation. This is not to satisfy desire with delusions. But it does sustain patience." See Moody, *Thomas Stearns Eliot,* 99. Also cf. R. Bush, *T. S. Eliot,* 75.

16. Eliot, *The Waste Land,* ll. 359–65.

17. Eliot, *The Waste Land,* 76.

18. Cited in Rainey, "Editor's Annotations," 118; cf. Southam, *Guide to the Selected Poems,* 89.

19. Luke 24:16; cf. Rainey, "Editor's Annotations," 116–17.

20. Luke 24:26–27.

21. Luke 24:31.

22. Luke 24:32.

23. Kearns sees the "third" as possibly a reference to the Christ of Josiah Royce's *The Problem of Christianity:* "This ghostly figure, half perceived, may be the projection of a communal interpretation or may be the sign of a real presence. In either case, it draws together the 'I' and the 'you' of the text and begins to overcome their solipsism and isolation, to draw them into community." See Kearns, *T. S. Eliot and Indic Traditions,* 214.

24. Bedient has a different interpretation here. He interprets the "second" as the "spiritual part of the protagonist himself." See Bedient, *He Do the Police,* 78.

25. Eliot, *The Waste Land,* l. 384.

26. Eliot, *The Waste Land,* l. 388.

27. Eliot, *The Waste Land,* l. 390.

28. It is because the poem does not end at the chapel that I cannot agree with Harriet Davidson's observation that the allusions to Weston represent a constant wandering activity, a continuous deferral: "no answers are necessary, because none are available." See Davidson, *T. S. Eliot and Hermeneutics,* 113. Davidson's argument neglects the ascetic portion of Eliot's poem. Eliot's poem prompts the reader to ask the question of whether there is an end to the quest for meaning. The references to the BU represent the moment when the poem's consciousness imagines an end to such wandering. The end of the poem leaves it to the reader to decide whether in death there is an encounter with meaning or merely a physical death. But Davidson's observation takes into account only one half of this dual vision.

NOTES TO PAGES 160–164

29. Eliot, *The Waste Land*, ll. 395–409.

30. Deussen, *Sixty Upaniṣads*, 5.2.1–3, 508–9.

31. Such linguistic wordplay is common in the Upanishads as the authors create hidden connections between disparate phenomena through occasionally dubious linguistic derivations. In this case, it is important to note that the dubious nature of the derivation belongs to the BU itself, not to Eliot, though he sees fit to play along.

32. Kearns, *T. S. Eliot and Indic Traditions*, 221.

33. Kearns, *T. S. Eliot and Indic Traditions*, 220.

34. Deussen, *Sixty Upaniṣads*, 5.3.1, 509.

35. Eliot, *The Waste Land*, ll. 400–402.

36. Bedient, *He Do the Police*, 196. In fact, I would emphatically argue, in agreement with Bedient here, against the reading of Brooker and Bentley, whose interpretation becomes less convincing in its closing stages. The characterization of the *Datta* commentary as existentialist, for example, is inadequate (Brooker and Bentley, *Reading "The Waste Land,"* 191). There is a clear theological element to the passage, and if it is existentialist, it is more Kierkegaard than Sartre. There may be "choice" involved, but it is an ambiguous choice that has as its counterpart a surrender. This surrender is not first and foremost to a way of life, but to an imperative from outside the self. It is also the case that I fundamentally disagree with them on interpretation in the final section. The thunder passage does not highlight necessarily the inadequacy of interpretation (197), but rather a relative adequacy of a variety of interpretations. Indeed, this is my argument in general; a knowledge of the Indian sources highlights a perspective that insists on the utility of various linguistic formulations in the cultivation of the self. It also is not the case that the poem shows the "mythic" position not to exist. Rather, I believe that it shows that moments of transcendence are the necessary precondition for any linguistic innovation. To the extent that fragments are able to be recombined at all, this process is enabled by the influence of sources external to the self that interrupt the self's understandings and allow the self to "dislocate language into meaning." Thus I strongly differ with Brooker and Bentley in their interpretation of this final section.

37. Gish, *The Waste Land*, 98, 93.

38. Eliot, *The Waste Land*, ll. 402–4.

39. Moody sees this moment as a reference back to the "surrender" in the Hyacinth Garden (*Thomas Stearns Eliot*, 102). I would agree with Moody, with the observation that in the Hyacinth Garden, it was the other human being who incited the surrender, and insofar as she did this, was a "divine" figure.

NOTES TO PAGES 164–175   271

40. Eliot, *The Waste Land*, ll. 405–9.
41. Deussen, *Sixty Upaniṣads*, 2.1.16–20, 428–29.
42. Deussen, *Sixty Upaniṣads*, 2.1.18, 428.
43. Deussen, *Sixty Upaniṣads*, 4.3.21, 489–90.
44. Deussen, *Sixty Upaniṣads*, 4.3.32, 491.
45. Patañjali, *Yoga System*, iv.29, xli.
46. Kearns, *T. S. Eliot and Indic Traditions*, 37.
47. Eliot, *The Waste Land*, 76.
48. Eliot, *The Waste Land*, ll. 410–16.
49. Eliot, *The Waste Land*, 702.
50. Lawrence Rainey notes that Eliot actually misremembers the passage from Dante: "Eliot's adaptation of these lines is based on a minor mistake. Because the word for 'key' in modern Italian is *chiave*, he assumes that the verb *chiavar* in the passage by Dante means 'to lock' or 'to turn the key.' But the word *chiavi* in medieval Italian meant 'a nail,' and what Ugolino heard, in the English translation of John Sinclair, was 'the door of the terrible tower nailed up'" ("Editor's Annotations," 120).
51. Eliot, *The Waste Land*, 77.
52. *OED* online, s.v. "sympathy (*n*)."
53. Shakespeare, *Coriolanus*, 5.3.173–77.
54. Shakespeare, *Coriolanus*, 5.3.183.
55. Eliot, *The Waste Land*, ll. 417–22.
56. See also Bedient, *He Do the Police*, 200.
57. Kenner, *Invisible Poet*, 152. He also notes, however, the regret of the "would have": this relationship did not happen.
58. Deussen, *Sixty Upaniṣads*, 2.1.20, 429.
59. Eliot, *The Waste Land*, l. 422.
60. Eliot, *The Waste Land*, 77.
61. Kearns, *T. S. Eliot and Indic Traditions*, 225.
62. Kearns, *T. S. Eliot and Indic Traditions*, 228.
63. Kearns believes that the end could represent the silence of the reader/ quester who has failed to ask the appropriate question of the fisher king. Thus the ending would be open-ended; it would leave open to the reader whether the land would be saved in the silence or whether its sterility would continue. See Kearns, *T. S. Eliot and Indic Traditions*, 226–27.
64. It is true that Eliot added his infamous endnotes after the initial composition of the poem. However, once the endnotes were included in the poem, they became fair game for interpretation. Eliot was one of the most meticulous poets in the language, and he wrote deliberately, even when his aim was to fill space. I therefore think we are justified in seeing Eliot's notes as

272 NOTES TO PAGES 176–182

an expansion of the poem proper. It is appropriate to interpret Eliot's final "revision."

65. Eliot, "Dante" (II), 711.

66. I am in agreement with Moody on this point: "To end 'What the Thunder Said' with the Sanskrit invocation is to imply that it has been a form of Upanishad; and to imply also that it has been aspiring to the state of final blessedness in which the individual being is consumed within the All." See Moody, *Thomas Stearns Eliot,* 106.

67. It is for this reason that I cannot agree with Kenner when he argues that the activity of the protagonist ends at line 394. See Kenner, *Invisible Poet,* 150. A focus on the allusions of the poem and the movement through translations can easily show the Indian references at the end to be a part of that movement of the poem.

68. Gish, *The Waste Land,* 103. She argues that such narratives represent, for the poem, "tentative ways of knowing."

69. Eliot, "Tradition and the Individual Talent." Eliot writes: "No poet, no artist of any art, has his complete meaning alone. His significance, his appreciation is the appreciation of his relation to the dead poets and artists. . . . The existing monuments form an ideal order among themselves, which is modified by the introduction of the new (the really new) work of art among them. The existing order is complete before the new work arrives; for order to persist after the supervention of novelty, the *whole* existing order must be, if ever so slightly, altered; and so the relations, proportions, values of each work of art toward the whole are readjusted; and this is conformity between the old and the new. Whoever has approved this idea of order, of the form of European, of English literature will not find it preposterous that the past should be altered by the present as much as the present is directed by the past" (106–7).

6. LANGUAGE IN THE MIDDLE WAY

1. Kearns, *T. S. Eliot and Indic Traditions,* 81.

2. Kearns, *T. S. Eliot and Indic Traditions,* 76.

3. Kearns, *T. S. Eliot and Indic Traditions,* 78.

4. Tuck, *Comparative Philosophy,* 33.

5. Perl and Tuck, "Foreign Metaphysics," 82.

6. Perl and Tuck, "Foreign Metaphysics," 84.

7. Perl and Tuck, "Foreign Metaphysics," 83.

8. Perl and Tuck, "Foreign Metaphysics," 84.

9. Perl and Tuck, "Foreign Metaphysics," 82.

10. Kearns, *T. S. Eliot and Indic Traditions,* 81.

NOTES TO PAGES 183–187   273

11. Kearns, *T. S. Eliot and Indic Traditions*, 81.

12. Eliot, *Four Quartets*, "East Coker," 1.33–34. All references to *Four Quartets* are taken from the Ricks and McCue volume.

13. Indeed, a reference to the Buddhist notion of *samsara*, the round of rebirth, is strongly implied. Further, the fire here, as so often in the *Quartets*, symbolizes human desire and attachment, here with a particularly sexual valence. One is reminded of the Buddha's Fire Sermon, to which Eliot specifically referred in *The Waste Land*.

14. Eliot, *Four Quartets*, "East Coker," 1.44–46.

15. Eliot, *Four Quartets*, "East Coker," 2.31–43.

16. Eliot, *Four Quartets*, "East Coker," 2.39; Dante Alighieri, *Divine Comedy*, vol. 1, *Inferno*,: "Nel mezzo del cammin di nostra vita / mi ritrovai per una selva oscura / che le diritta via era smarrita" (1.1–3). All citations of the *Commedia* are taken from the Durling translation.

17. Dante Alighieri, *Inferno*, 1.10–12.

18. Dante Alighieri, *Inferno*, 1.30.

19. Some have suggested that the beasts are allegorical representations for sensual indulgence, wrath, and avarice, respectively. I am indebted to Michael Murrin for this interpretation of the beasts in *Inferno* (oral communication, November 10, 2009). According to Martinez and Durling, any ascription of allegory here has to be conjecture (in Dante Alighieri, *Inferno*, 1.32n). Murrin's interpretation differs somewhat from Charles Singleton's interpretation in *Commentary*, part 2, of Dante Alighieri, *The Divine Comedy*, vol. 2, *Inferno*. He suggests that the she-wolf represents "concupiscentia" or "cupiditas" (10) and that the lion "with raging hunger" (1.47) represents a desire for consumption threatening to tear the pilgrim off the path before him. He does not have a suggestion for the leopard, though he sums up Dante's passage with the general observation that, at the very least, the three animals represent "sinful dispositions" (10).

20. Eliot, *Four Quartets*, "East Coker," 2.42.

21. Eliot, *Four Quartets*, "East Coker," 2.20–21.

22. Eliot, *Four Quartets*, "East Coker," 2.34–35.

23. Eliot, *Four Quartets*, "East Coker," 2.37–38.

24. Nietzsche, "Truth and Falsity," 636.

25. Eliot, *Four Quartets*, "East Coker," 2.20–21.

26. Eliot, *Four Quartets*, "East Coker," 2.10–15.

27. Eliot, *Four Quartets*, "East Coker," 2.18.

28. This kind of poetic wrestling has, in fact, already been described earlier. Recall the passage from "Burnt Norton" similar to this one: "Words strain, / Crack and sometimes break, under the burden, / Under the tension,

274   NOTES TO PAGES 187–196

slip, slide, perish, / Decay with imprecision, will not stay in place, / Will not stay still" (Eliot, *Four Quartets,* "Burnt Norton," 5.13–17).

29. Eliot, *Four Quartets,* "East Coker," 3.38–43.
30. Eliot, *Four Quartets,* "East Coker," 4.1–2.
31. Eliot, *Four Quartets,* "East Coker," 4.4.
32. Eliot, *Four Quartets,* "East Coker," 4.10.
33. Eliot, *Four Quartets,* "East Coker," 4.21–25.
34. *OED* online, s.v. "sound (*adj*)."
35. Eliot, *Four Quartets,* "East Coker," 5.1–11.
36. Eliot, "Tradition and the Individual Talent," 109.
37. Eliot, "Tradition and the Individual Talent," 109.
38. Eliot, "Tradition and the Individual Talent," 108.
39. Eliot, "Tradition and the Individual Talent," 109.
40. Eliot, "Tradition and the Individual Talent," 109.
41. Eliot, "Tradition and the Individual Talent," 106.
42. Eliot, "Tradition and the Individual Talent," 106.
43. Eliot, *Four Quartets,* "East Coker," 5.186–87.
44. Eliot, *Four Quartets,* "East Coker," 5.183.
45. Eliot, *Four Quartets,* "East Coker," 5.184.
46. Garfield, *Fundamental Wisdom.* Garfield's translation and commentary in turn owe much to the Tibetan Geluk-pa tradition, both to its classical commentaries (by such figures as Candrakirti and Tsong Khapa) and to its contemporary Tibetan expositors (such as Geshe Yeshes Thap-Khas and Gen Lobzang Gyatso) (see especially 97–98, where Garfield acknowledges these debts). Garfield's translation and his analytical essays on the Madhyamaka have reignited debates on Nagarjuna, challenging some prominent readings of his texts influenced by deconstruction and Wittgenstein. For a history of the interpretation of Nagarjuna in the West, see Tuck, *Comparative Philosophy.* For further elucidations of Garfield's reading of Nagarjuna, see his essays collected in Garfield, *Empty Words.*
47. Eliot, "Notes on Eastern Philosophy," T. S. Eliot Collection.
48. Eliot, "Notes on Eastern Philosophy," T. S. Eliot Collection.
49. Eliot, "Notes on Eastern Philosophy," T. S. Eliot Collection.
50. Eliot, "Notes on Eastern Philosophy," T. S. Eliot Collection.
51. Garfield, *Fundamental Wisdom,* 111.
52. Collins, *Selfless Persons,* 104–5. Collins's references are from the *Samyutta Nikaya,* II.13–14, II.62.
53. Collins, *Selfless Persons,* 105.
54. Warren, *Buddhist Reader,* 133–34.

NOTES TO PAGES 196–202   275

55. Collins, *Selfless Persons,* 156. See also Gethin, *Foundations of Buddhism,* 145–46. Jonardon Ganeri has traced various Indian teachings of multiple levels of truth from the Upanishads and early Buddhist texts to later, more systematic accounts. See Ganeri, *Concealed Art.*

56. Garfield, *Fundamental Wisdom,* 1.1, 1.6. All references to Nagarjuna's text are taken from Garfield's translation.

57. Garfield, *Fundamental Wisdom,* 106.

58. Garfield, *Fundamental Wisdom,* 111.

59. Garfield, *Fundamental Wisdom,* 9.5.

60. Garfield, *Fundamental Wisdom,* 185.

61. Garfield, *Fundamental Wisdom,* 18.4–5.

62. Garfield, *Fundamental Wisdom,* 182.

63. Garfield, *Fundamental Wisdom,* 248.

64. Garfield, *Fundamental Wisdom,* 18.7.

65. Garfield admits as much, at 185n59: "Though subject and object as well as internal and external objects are, for Nāgārjuna, all ultimately empty and, in important senses, interdependent, they are not identical. Physical objects are, as Kant would emphasize, empirically external to the mind in a way that pains are not; and the conventional perceiver is not one with the perceived. When I see an elephant, it is not, thereby, the case that I have a trunk!"

66. Garfield, *Fundamental Wisdom,* 305.

67. Garfield, *Fundamental Wisdom,* 305.

68. Garfield, *Fundamental Wisdom,* 18.8, 18.10.

69. Arnold, "Mapping the Middle Way," 80.

70. Garfield, *Fundamental Wisdom,* 211.

71. Garfield, *Fundamental Wisdom,* 212.

72. Garfield, *Fundamental Wisdom,* 316.

73. Paul Williams, in his important book *Mahāyāna Buddhism,* is by and large in agreement with this interpretation. He describes "emptiness" as "in a sense, an abstraction. It is the absence of inherent existence and is seen through *prajñā,* analytic understanding in its various forms. . . . It is the absence of inherent existence itself related to the object which is being critically examined in order to find out if it has inherent existence" (62). In other words, emptiness is posited of entities once one has analytically and contemplatively searched for essence and not found one. Once essence is not found, the phenomenon itself can be said to be empty, though still conventionally existent.

74. Garfield, *Fundamental Wisdom,* 332. Alternately, Williams has deftly summed this up, stating, "We should not think that this world is empty but nirvāṇa is some really existing alternative realm or world. Nirvāṇa is

276   NOTES TO PAGES 203–205

attainable here and now through the correct understanding of the here and now" (*Mahayana Buddhism*, 69).

75. Garfield, *Fundamental Wisdom*, 310.

76. This becomes Nagarjuna's defense of the Buddhist path, with all of its intentional activities. Collins has remarked on the distinction that he, following M. E. Spiro, makes between *kammic* and *nibbanic* Buddhism. *Kammic* Buddhism is the process of undertaking the right kinds of actions in order to obtain better rebirths, while *nibbanic* Buddhism is the rarefied practice undertaken by monks intent on attaining the ultimate soteriological release (Collins, *Selfless Persons*, 16). Collins makes this distinction to explain how Buddhism could provide for participation by both villagers and religious monastic virtuosos, but I believe the same model can hold for the Buddhist Path as a whole and in other contexts. This distinction allows the element of cultivation, *bhavana*, into Buddhism. In order to attain *nirvana*, one must undergo a cultivation of the self that begins with the proper actions and continues through the proper meditation techniques. Indeed, the Buddhists added their own particular brand of meditative technique, *vipassana* meditation, to the more broadly practiced *samadhi* meditation. This meditation passed through the "one-pointedness" of *samadhi* to a reinsertion of Buddhist analysis within this conceptual meditative tranquility (111). Thus, even in the most extensive stages of meditation, some sense of mental cultivation is at work. It is through this combination of calm abiding and intentional analysis that an impossible transformation takes place: the desires of the self are finally arrested and cease, and the monk is able to see things truly. In the Madhyamaka, this means attaining great creative powers: "When he arises from his meditation he still sees inherent existence, but he knows that this is not how things are, and he is like a magician viewing his own creations" (Williams, *Mahāyāna Buddhism*, 73). The end result, then, is the world viewed differently, as a soteriological laboratory that the newly awakened meditator can manipulate in order to bring others to the same enlightenment.

77. Kearns, *T. S. Eliot and Indic Traditions*, 109.

78. Garfield, *Fundamental Wisdom*, 24.23, 24.25.

79. Garfield, *Fundamental Wisdom*, 310.

80. Eliot, *Four Quartets*, "East Coker," 2.34–35.

81. Eliot, *Four Quartets*, "East Coker," 2.36–37.

82. Eliot, *Four Quartets*, "East Coker," 2.47–48.

83. Eliot, *Four Quartets*, "East Coker," 5.1.

84. Eliot, *Four Quartets*, "East Coker," 5.15–16.

85. Eliot, *Four Quartets*, "The Dry Salvages," 1.17–18.

NOTES TO PAGES 205–216   277

86. Eliot, *Four Quartets*, "The Dry Salvages," 2.37–48.

87. Eliot, *Four Quartets*, "The Dry Salvages," 2.50–51.

88. Eliot, *Four Quartets*, "The Dry Salvages," 2.56–60; 67.

89. Eliot, *Four Quartets*, "East Coker," 4.11–12.

90. Eliot, *Four Quartets*, "Burnt Norton," 5.30–32.

91. Eliot, *Four Quartets*, "The Dry Salvages," 2.70.

92. Eliot, *Four Quartets*, "The Dry Salvages," 2.73–75.

93. Eliot, "Lecture III," Clark Lectures, 651.

94. Eliot, *Four Quartets*, "East Coker," 5.18.

7. PERFORMING THE DIVINE ILLUSION

1. Virkar-Yates, "Absolute Music."

2. Virkar-Yates, "Absolute Music," 88.

3. Virkar-Yates, "Absolute Music," 89.

4. Eliot, *Four Quartets*, "Burnt Norton," 1.1–3.

5. Eliot, *Four Quartets*, "Burnt Norton," 1.4–5.

6. Eliot, *Four Quartets*, "Burnt Norton," 1.6.

7. Eliot, *Four Quartets*, "Burnt Norton," 1.9–14.

8. Hart, "Eliot's Rose Garden," 256.

9. Hart, introduction to *Counter-Experiences*, 38. See also Hart, "Experience of Nonexperience."

10. Eliot, *Four Quartets*, "Burnt Norton," 1.6–10.

11. Hart, "Eliot's Rose Garden," 254.

12. Steve Ellis also remarks on the Eden narrative and the sense of exile evoked in this opening. See Ellis, "*Four Quartets*," 104.

13. Brooker, *Mastery and Escape*, 136.

14. Ricoeur, *Time and Narrative*, 26.

15. Eliot, *Four Quartets*, "Little Gidding," 3.13–14.

16. Eliot, *Four Quartets*, "Burnt Norton," 1.36.

17. Eliot, *Four Quartets*, "Burnt Norton," 2.43.

18. Eliot, *Four Quartets*, "Burnt Norton," 1.11–15.

19. Eliot, *Four Quartets*, "Burnt Norton," 1.15–17.

20. Hart also sees this journey as one within the garden of memory, though he primarily discusses the footfalls in terms of "profiles of the past" in the mind of the speaker that exist only in terms of an "empty intention" for the reader. See Hart, "Eliot's Rose Garden," 248–49.

21. Eliot, *Four Quartets*, "Burnt Norton," 1.17–22.

22. As Joshua Richards describes it, the rose here represents "the divine fullness." Richards, *T. S. Eliot's Ascetic Ideal*, 151. See also Hart, "Eliot's Rose Garden," 254.

NOTES TO PAGES 217–221

23. I believe the references to John of the Cross and later the *Lotus Sutra* reinforce the idea that the remembered experience in the rose garden is a "mystical" or, as Ellis would have it, "visionary" experience. See Ellis, "Four Quartets," 104. Kearns is also in agreement. See Kearns, *T. S. Eliot and Indic Traditions*, 234. I therefore cannot completely agree with Brooker's assertion that the experience was one completely within time and given over to simple self-deception. See Brooker, *T. S. Eliot's Dialectical Imagination*, 153. Brooker is right that this experience does not represent the fulfillment that the speaker will eventually find in immediate experience. However, I believe her criticism of Ellis misses the nature of the dialectic of memory and desire that Eliot invokes here. Brooker does insist that the garden is created of memory and desire (153). However, if the memory sets off a search for a deeper fulfillment, it must be representing a touch of the divine. John of the Cross insists that human beings pursue God only when their love is awakened by an encounter with the divine presence (see John of the Cross, *Spiritual Canticle*, 484). It is the memory of the heightened experience that sets the speaker off again on a search to reach a higher fulfillment, one that might not be expressed fully until later in the *Quartets*.
24. Brooker, *T. S. Eliot's Dialectical Imagination*, 155.
25. Kearns, *T. S. Eliot and Indic Traditions*, 9.
26. Eliot, *Four Quartets*, "Burnt Norton," 1.28–33.
27. Hart, "Eliot's Rose Garden," 251.
28. Hart, "Eliot's Rose Garden," 252.
29. John of the Cross, *Spiritual Canticle*, 497.
30. Kearns, *T. S. Eliot and Indic Traditions*, 234.
31. Kearns, *T. S. Eliot and Indic Traditions*, 234.
32. Brooker also sees Bradley's philosophy at work in "Burnt Norton." See Brooker, *Mastery and Escape*, 205.
33. Eliot, *Four Quartets*, "Burnt Norton," 1.34–39.
34. Eliot, *Four Quartets*, "Burnt Norton," 1.35.
35. Eliot, *Four Quartets*, "Burnt Norton," 1.36.
36. Hart, "Eliot's Rose Garden," 254. Hart picks up both on the juxtaposition of these two flowers and the important reference to Dante (254).
37. P. S. Sri, in a thoughtful reading, sees the garden scene as constructed like a mandala, with the lotus in the middle. I don't think we have enough warrant, either in the poem or in Eliot's philosophical materials, to make this claim, but I think it is a very fascinating idea, and it surely draws our attention to the contemplative nature of this vision. See Sri, *T. S. Eliot*, 103–5.
38. Eliot, *Four Quartets*, "Burnt Norton," 1.39–43.
39. Kearns, *T. S. Eliot and Indic Traditions*, 79.

NOTES TO PAGES 221–227   279

40. See Lopez, *Lotus Sutra*, 122–56. Lopez, along with Katia Buffetrille, is the translator for Burnouf, *Introduction to the History*.
41. Lopez, *Lotus Sutra*, 135.
42. Lopez, *Lotus Sutra*, 163.
43. On Kern, see Lopez, "*Lotus Sutra*," 169. Kearns agrees that Eliot most likely would have read Kern's English translation. See Kearns, *T. S. Eliot and Indic Traditions*, 77–78.
44. Kearns, *T. S. Eliot and Indic Traditions*, 84.
45. Eliot, "Notes on Eastern Philosophy," T. S. Eliot Collection.
46. Lopez and Stone, *Two Buddhas Seated*, 187.
47. Lopez and Stone, *Two Buddhas Seated*, 187.
48. Lopez and Stone, *Two Buddhas Seated*, 187.
49. Lopez and Stone, *Two Buddhas Seated*, 187.
50. Lopez and Stone, *Two Buddhas Seated*, 49.
51. Leighton, "Dōgen's Appropriation of *Lotus Sutra*," 89.
52. *Lotus Sutra*, 22.
53. Ziporyn, *Emptiness and Omnipresence*, 87.
54. Ziporyn, *Emptiness and Omnipresence*, 87.
55. Ziporyn, *Emptiness and Omnipresence*, 97.
56. Ziporyn, *Emptiness and Omnipresence*, 90.
57. Lopez and Stone, *Two Buddhas Seated*, 37.
58. Though most interpreters see this position as inclusivist, some have interpreted a more intolerant view. See especially Matsumoto, "*Lotus Sutra* and Japanese Culture." Matsumoto writes in an attempt to come to terms with the sutra's role in the development of Japanese nationalism in the twentieth century, of which Anesaki was a part. The sutra's interpretation has thus become a flashpoint in assessing that past, as one can see throughout the Hubbard and Swanson volume. Yo Hamada in fact notes that Anesaki's own project was allied with an attempt to see all competing religious factions in Japan as ultimately metaphysically united: "He [Anesaki] regarded religion as an aspect of consciousness that is inherent in all humans. As a result, differences among denominations have no essential meaning." See Hamada, "Japanese Religiosity," 266. Hamada sees Anesaki's project as suggesting that the government could use this realization for its own unifying purposes (266).
59. *Lotus Sutra*, 23.
60. *Lotus Sutra*, 24.
61. *Lotus Sutra*, 62.
62. Cattoi, "Transformation or Rediscovery?," 73.
63. *Lotus Sutra*, 137.

64. Paul Griffiths also sees this text as always under erasure: "It is as though the speaking of the Lotus is constantly deferred, constantly pointed to by the words of the text we have, but never given." Griffiths, "Lotus Sutra as Good News," 15.

65. *Lotus Sutra*, 138.

66. *Lotus Sutra*, 138.

67. *Lotus Sutra*, 139.

68. Ziporyn, *Emptiness and Omnipresence*, 84.

69. *Lotus Sutra*, 139–40.

70. *Lotus Sutra*, 139.

71. Ziporyn, *Emptiness and Omnipresence*, 108.

72. To be sure, the extent to which the Buddha resembles divinity is very controversial in contemporary scholarship, as it probably was when composed. Lopez and Stone suggest the Buddha is "ever present" and "perpetually active" though not strictly speaking eternal in the same way as a monotheistic God (*Two Buddhas Seated*, 184). Paul Williams is largely in agreement, claiming that the Buddha in the sutra has an enormously long life, but still a "finite" one (see *Mahāyāna Buddhism*, 151). Ziporyn thinks the Buddha's "eternal life" resides in all "sentient beings" on the way to full Buddhahood (*Emptiness and Omnipresence*, 110). Leo D. Lefebure maximally refers to the Buddha in the sutra as "cosmic reality" (see "*Lotus Sutra* and Christian Wisdom," 116). Cattoi likewise describes him as "ground of the whole of the universe and thus the very essence of all sentient beings" ("Transformation or Rediscovery?," 74). Lopez and Stone acknowledge that the Buddha's status in the sutra has been a source of debate from early in the Tiantai tradition (*Two Buddhas Seated*, 184–85). I simply observe that, regardless of the Buddha's ultimate metaphysical status, it would be difficult to conceive of the Buddha as being more powerful, efficacious, and omnipresent than he is in this text.

73. *Lotus Sutra*, 140.

74. *Lotus Sutra*, 142.

75. *Lotus Sutra*, 143.

76. *Lotus Sutra*, 140.

77. Ziporyn explains this compellingly: "His absence is a mode of his presence, his effectiveness in the world, his being here with his children . . . it is his absence that makes them search for him, feeling his effect that much more deeply. In fact, both being there and not being there are alternate modes of being there, of doing the Buddha work in the world. For really, as the Buddha says, nothing is either simply there or not there, either present or absent, either thus or otherwise. It is both; it is neither. Being there is a

NOTES TO PAGES 230–237   281

way of being gone; being gone is a way of being there. It is the alternation, the interaction, the skillful deployment of presence and absence that is the true presence. Here the *Lotus Sutra* offers us yet another new Middle Way: between being and nonbeing, between presence and absence" (*Emptiness and Omnipresence*, 111).

78. *Lotus Sutra*, 142.

79. Eliot, *Four Quartets*, "Burnt Norton," 2.43.

80. Hart, "Eliot's Rose Garden," 256.

81. Eliot, *Four Quartets*, "Burnt Norton," 2.37–43.

82. Virkar-Yates, "Absolute Music," 89.

83. Eliot, *Four Quartets*, "Burnt Norton," 2.26–29.

84. Schopenhauer, *World as Will*, 1:201–2.

85. See also Virkar-Yates, "Absolute Music," 89.

86. Schopenhauer, *World as Will*, 1:202.

87. Eliot, *Four Quartets*, "Burnt Norton," 2.3–32.

88. Virkar-Yates, "Absolute Music," 88.

89. Virkar-Yates, "Absolute Music," 89.

90. Eliot, *Four Quartets*, "Burnt Norton," 2.22.

91. Eliot, *Four Quartets*, "Burnt Norton," 5.4–13.

92. Ronald Schuchard has shown that Herbert's influence can be seen throughout *Four Quartets*. See *Eliot's Dark Angel*, 183–97. He argues that Herbert became, for Eliot, a model of the "contemplative poet," which was a "tradition that he wished to revive" (183). Schuchard notes that Eliot described this model as one in which the poet would try "'to explain to himself his intenser human feelings in terms of the divine goal'" (183).

93. Herbert, "Easter," in *Complete English Poems*, ll. 11–12.

94. Herbert, "Easter," l. 30.

95. Moody, "*Four Quartets*," 142.

96. Hart, "Eliot's Rose Garden," 257.

97. Eliot, *Four Quartets*, "Burnt Norton," 5.23–24.

98. Eliot, *Four Quartets*, "Burnt Norton," 5.4–6.

99. Or, as Ellis puts it, "art and its permanence gestures towards the eternal 'now.'" See Ellis, "*Four Quartets*," 111.

100. Kearns, *T. S. Eliot and Indic Traditions*, 239.

101. Eliot, *Four Quartets*, "Burnt Norton," 5.25–32.

102. Moody observes that in the *Quartets*, "the only significant moments are those of holy dying, so that the whole of an individual's life can be condensed and refined to just those moments in which the destructive fire is consciously known and accepted as Love." See Moody, "*Four Quartets*," 154.

103. Hart uses the term "phenomenology" in a far more technical sense than I do. See, for example, "Eliot's Rose Garden," 260.
104. Brooker, *Mastery and Escape*, 210.
105. Kearns, *T. S. Eliot and Indic Traditions*, 251.
106. Kearns, *T. S. Eliot and Indic Traditions*, 231.
107. Eliot, *Poems of T. S. Eliot*, 905–6.

BIBLIOGRAPHY

Alighieri, Dante. *The Divine Comedy of Dante Alighieri.* Vol. 1, *Inferno.* Translated by Robert M. Durling. Introduction and notes by Ronald L. Martinez and Robert M. Durling. New York: Oxford University Press, 1996.

———. *The Divine Comedy of Dante Alighieri*, Vol. 2, *Purgatorio.* Translated by Robert M. Durling. Intro. and notes by Ronald L. Martinez and Robert M. Durling. New York: Oxford University Press, 2003.

Almond, Philip C. *The British Discovery of Buddhism.* New York: Cambridge University Press, 1988.

Anesaki, Masaharu. "Buddhist Ethics and Morality." T. S. Eliot Collection. Houghton Library, MS Am 1691.14 (12). Harvard University.

———. "Ethics and Morality (Buddhist)." *Encyclopaedia of Religion and Ethics,* vol. 5, edited by James Hastings, 447–55. New York: Charles Scribner's Sons, 1951.

———. "Syllabus of Philosophy 24A." T. S. Eliot Collection. Houghton Library, MS Am 1691.14 (12). Harvard University.

Aristotle. *Categories.* Translated by E. M. Edghill. Internet Classics Library. https://classics.mit.edu//Aristotle/categories.html.

Arnold, Daniel. "Mapping the Middle Way: Thoughts on a Buddhist Contribution to a Feminist Discussion." *Journal of Feminist Studies in Religion* 14, no. 1 (Spring 1998): 63–84.

Asad, Talal. *Genealogies of Religion: Discipline and Reasons of Power in Christianity and Islam.* Baltimore: Johns Hopkins University Press, 1993.

Asher, Curt. "Silence, Sound and Eliot's Mystical Imagination." *Yeats Eliot Review* 19, no. 3 (2002): 27–31.

Augustine, *Confessions.* Translated by E. B. Pusey. London: J. M. Dent & Sons, 1907.

Bakhtin, Mikhail. *The Dialogic Imagination: Four Essays.* Translated by Caryl Emerson and Michael Holquist. Edited by Michael Holquist. Austin: University of Texas Press, 1981.

Baudelaire, Charles. *The Flowers of Evil.* Translated by James McGowen. New York: Oxford University Press, 1993.

Bedient, Calvin. *He Do the Police in Different Voices: "The Waste Land" and Its Protagonist.* Chicago: University of Chicago Press, 1986.

284   BIBLIOGRAPHY

Berman, Jessica. *Modernist Commitments: Ethics, Politics, and Transnational Modernism.* New York: Columbia University Press, 2011.

Boehmer, Elleke. *Empire, The National, and the Postcolonial, 1890–1920: Resistance in Interaction.* New York: Oxford University Press, 2002.

———. *Postcolonial Poetics: 21st-Century Critical Readings.* New York: Palgrave Macmillan, 2018.

Bond, George. "The Gradual Path as a Hermeneutical Approach to the Dhamma." In *Buddhist Hermeneutics,* edited by Donald Lopez Jr., 29–46. Studies in East Asian Buddhism 6. Honolulu: University of Hawai'i Press, 1988.

Bradley, F. H. *Ethical Studies.* New York: G. E. Stechert, 1927.

Brooker, Jewel Spears. "Apprentice Years, 1905–1918: Introduction." In *The Complete Prose of T. S. Eliot: The Critical Edition.* Vol. 1, *Apprentice Years, 1905–1918,* edited by Jewel Spears Brooker and Ronald Schuchard, xxvii–lxii. Baltimore: Johns Hopkins University Press, 2014. https://muse.jhu.edu/primary/eliot/volume1#this_volume?

———. "Eliot's Philosophical Studies: Bergson, Frazer, Bradley." In *The New Cambridge Companion to T. S. Eliot,* edited by Jason Harding, 175–86. New York: Cambridge University Press, 2017.

———. *Mastery and Escape: T. S. Eliot and the Dialectic of Modernism.* Amherst: University of Massachusetts Press, 1994.

———. *T. S. Eliot's Dialectical Imagination.* Baltimore: Johns Hopkins University Press, 2018.

Brooker, Jewel Spears, and Joseph Bentley. *Reading "The Waste Land:" Modernism and the Limits of Interpretation.* Amherst: University of Massachusetts Press, 1990.

Brooks, Cleanth. "*The Waste Land:* Critique of the Myth." In *Modern Poetry & the Tradition,* 136–72. Chapel Hill: University of North Carolina Press, 1939.

Bruno, Tim. "Buddhist Conceptual Rhyming and T. S. Eliot's Crisis of Connection in *The Waste Land* and 'Burnt Norton.'" *Asian Philosophy* 23, no. 4 (2013): 365–78.

Burnouf, Eugène. *Introduction to the History of Indian Buddhism.* Translated by Katia Buffetrille and Donald S. Lopez Jr. Chicago: University of Chicago Press, 2010.

Burrows, J. W. *The Crisis of Reason: European Thought, 1848–1914.* New Haven: Yale University Press, 2000.

Bush, Christopher. *Ideographic Modernism: China, Writing, Media.* New York: Oxford University Press, 2010.

Bush, Ronald. *T. S. Eliot: A Study in Character and Style.* New York: Oxford University Press, 1983.

Caracciolo, Peter. "Buddhist Typologies in *Heart of Darkness* and *Victory* and Their Contribution to the Modernism of Jacob Epstein, Wyndham Lewis and T. S. Eliot." *The Conradian* 14, no. 1/2 (December 1989).

Cattoi, Thomas. "Transformation or Rediscovery? Soteriological and Cosmological Themes in the *Lotus Sutra* and the Philokalic Tradition." *Buddhist-Christian Studies* 40 (2020): 63–78. Project MUSE, https://doi.org/10.1353/bcs.2020.0004.

Chaucer, Geoffrey. *The Canterbury Tales*. Ed. Jill Mann. New York: Penguin Books, 2005.

Childs, Donald. *T. S. Eliot: Mystic, Son and Lover*. New York: St. Martin's Press, 1997.

Clairemont, David. "Moral Motivation and Comparative Ethics: Bonaventure, Buddhaghosa, and the Problem of Material Simplicity." PhD diss., University of Chicago, 2005.

Clooney, Francis X. *Theology after Vedānta: An Experiment in Comparative Theology*. Albany: State University of New York Press, 1993.

Collins, Steven. *Nirvana and Other Buddhist Felicities: Utopias of the Pali Imaginaire*. Cambridge Studies in Religious Traditions 12. New York: Cambridge University Press, 1998.

———. *Selfless Persons: Imagery and Thought in "Theravāda" Buddhism*. New York: Cambridge University Press, 1982.

Copleston, Frederick. *Arthur Schopenhauer: Philosopher of Pessimism*. London: Search Press, 1975.

Cuda, Anthony. "CODA: *The Waste Land's* Afterlife: The Poem's Reception in the Twentieth Century and Beyond." In *The Cambridge Companion to "The Waste Land,"* edited by Gabrielle McIntire, 194–210. New York: Cambridge University Press, 2015.

Davidson, Harriet. *T. S. Eliot and Hermeneutics: Absence and Interpretation in "The Waste Land."* Baton Rouge: Louisiana State University Press, 1985.

Deussen, Paul. *The Philosophy of the Upanishads*. Translated by A. S. Geden. New York: Dover, 1966.

———. *Sixty Upaniṣads of the Veda*. Translated from German by V. M. Bedekar and G. B. Palsule. Delhi: Motilal Banarsidass, 1980.

Doniger, Wendy. *The Hindus: An Alternative History*. New York: Penguin Books, 2009.

———. *The Rig Veda: An Anthology*. New York: Penguin Books, 1981.

Doniger O'Flaherty, Wendy. *Textual Sources for the Study of Hinduism*. Translated by Wendy Doniger O'Flaherty, with Daniel Gold, David Haberman, and David Shulman. Chicago: University of Chicago Press, 1988.

BIBLIOGRAPHY

Droit, Roger-Pol. *The Cult of Nothingness: The Philosophers and the Buddha.* Translated by David Streight and Pamela Vohnson. Chapel Hill: University of North Carolina Press, 2003.

Dustin, Lheisa. "Theravada Buddhist Influence in *The Waste Land?*" *Notes and Queries* 56, no. 3 (September 2009): 417–20.

Eakambaram, N. "An Indian Reading of *Murder in the Cathedral.*" *Comparative Literature Studies* 29, no. 2 (1992): 172–82.

Edgerton, Franklin. *The Beginnings of Indian Philosophy.* Cambridge, MA: Harvard University Press, 1965.

Eliot, Thomas Stearns. *After Strange Gods: A Primer of Modern Heresy.* In *The Complete Prose of T. S. Eliot: The Critical Edition.* Vol. 5, *Tradition and Orthodoxy, 1934–1939,* edited by Iman Javadi, Ronald Schuchard, and Jayme Stayer, 25–26. Baltimore: Johns Hopkins University Press, 2017. Project MUSE, https://muse.jhu.edu/primary/eliot/volume5#this_volume.

———. "Baudelaire." In *The Complete Prose of T. S. Eliot: The Critical Edition.* Vol. 4, *English Lion, 1930–1933,* edited by Jason Harding and Ronald Schuchard, 155–67. Baltimore: Johns Hopkins University Press, 2015. Project MUSE, https://muse.jhu.edu/primary/eliot/volume4#this_volume.

———. The Clark Lectures. In *The Complete Prose of T. S. Eliot: The Critical Edition.* Vol. 2, *The Perfect Critic, 1919–1926,* edited by Anthony Cuda and Ronald Schuchard, 609–761. Baltimore: Johns Hopkins University Press; London: Faber & Faber, 2014. Project MUSE, https://muse.jhu.edu/primary/eliot/volume2#this_volume.

———. "Dante" (I). In *The Complete Prose of T. S. Eliot: The Critical Edition.* Vol. 2, *The Perfect Critic, 1919–1926,* edited by Anthony Cuda and Ronald Schuchard, 226–37. Baltimore: Johns Hopkins University Press, 2014. Project MUSE, https://muse.jhu.edu/primary/eliot/volume2#this_volume.

———. "Dante" (II). In *The Complete Prose of T. S. Eliot: The Critical Edition.* Vol. 3, *Literature, Politics, Belief, 1927–1929,* edited by Frances Dickey and Ronald Schuchard, 700–745. Baltimore: Johns Hopkins University Press, 2015. Project MUSE, https://muse.jhu.edu/primary/eliot/volume3#this__volume.

———. *Four Quartets.* In *The Poems of T. S. Eliot.* Vol. 1, *Collected and Uncollected Poems,* edited by Christopher Ricks and Jim McCue, 177–209. Baltimore: Johns Hopkins University Press, 2015.

———. *Knowledge and Experience in the Philosophy of F. H. Bradley.* In *The Complete Prose of T. S. Eliot: The Critical Edition.* Vol. 1, *Apprentice Years, 1905–1918,* edited by Jewel Spears Brooker and Ronald Schuchard, 238–386. Baltimore: Johns Hopkins University Press, 2014. Project MUSE, https://muse.jhu.edu/primary/eliot/volume1#this_volume.

———. *The Letters of T. S. Eliot.* Vol. 2, *1923–1925,* edited by Valerie Eliot and Hugh Haughton. London: Faber and Faber, 2009.

———. *The Letters of T. S. Eliot.* Vol. 4, *1928–1929,* edited by Valerie Eliot and Hugh Haughton. New Haven: Yale University Press, 2013.

———. "The Life of Prayer: An Unsigned Review of *Prayer and Intelligence,* by Jacques and Raissa Maritain, trans. Algar Thorold." In *The Complete Prose of T. S. Eliot: The Critical Edition.* Vol. 3, *Literature, Politics, Belief, 1927–1929,* edited by Frances Dickey, Jennifer Formichelli, and Ronald Schuchard, 446–48. Baltimore: Johns Hopkins University Press, 2015. Project MUSE, https://muse.jhu.edu/primary/eliot/volume3#this_volume.

———. "The Metaphysical Poets." In *The Complete Prose of T. S. Eliot: The Critical Edition.* Vol. 2, *The Perfect Critic, 1919–1926,* edited by Anthony Cuda and Ronald Schuchard, 375–85. Baltimore: Johns Hopkins University Press, 2014. Project MUSE, https://muse.jhu.edu/primary/eliot/volume2#this _volume.

———. "The Modern Dilemma." In *The Complete Prose of T. S. Eliot: The Critical Edition.* Vol. 4, *English Lion, 1930–1933,* edited by Jason Harding and Ronald Schuchard, 810–16. Baltimore: Johns Hopkins University Press, 2015. Project MUSE, https://muse.jhu.edu/primary/eliot/volume4#this _volume.

———. "The Music of Poetry." In *The Complete Prose of T. S. Eliot: The Critical Edition.* Vol. 6, *The War Years, 1940–1946,* edited by David Chinitz and Ronald Schuchard, 310–25. Baltimore: Johns Hopkins University Press, 2017. Project MUSE, https://muse.jhu.edu/primary/eliot/volume6#this_volume.

———. "Notes on Eastern Philosophy." T. S. Eliot Collection. Houghton Library, MS Am 1691.14 (12). Harvard University.

———. *The Poems of T. S. Eliot.* Vol. 1, *Collected and Uncollected Poems,* edited by Christopher Ricks and Jim McCue. Baltimore: Johns Hopkins University Press, 2015.

———. "The Preacher as Artist: A Review of *Donne's Sermons: Selected Passages.*" In *The Complete Prose of T. S. Eliot: The Critical Edition.* Vol. 2, *The Perfect Critic, 1919–1926,* edited by Anthony Cuda and Ronald Schuchard, 165–69. Baltimore: Johns Hopkins University Press, 2014. Project MUSE, https:// muse.jhu.edu/primary/eliot/volume2#this_volume.

———. "Preface to the 1928 Edition of *The Sacred Wood: Essays on Poetry and Criticism.*" In *The Complete Prose of T. S. Eliot: The Critical Edition.* Vol. 3, *Literature, Politics, Belief, 1927–1929,* edited by Frances Dickey, Jennifer Formichelli, and Ronald Schuchard, 413–15. Baltimore: Johns Hopkins University Press, 2015. Project MUSE, https://muse.jhu.edu/primary/eliot/volume3 #this_volume.

———. "The Search for Moral Sanction." In *The Complete Prose of T. S. Eliot: The Critical Edition*. Vol. 4, *English Lion, 1930–1933*, edited by Jason Harding and Ronald Schuchard, 446–55. Baltimore: Johns Hopkins University Press, 2015. Project MUSE, https://muse.jhu.edu/primary/eliot/volume4#this_volume.

———. "Tradition and the Individual Talent." In *The Complete Prose of T. S. Eliot: The Critical Edition*. Vol. 2, *The Perfect Critic, 1919–1926*, edited by Anthony Cuda and Ronald Schuchard, 105–14. Baltimore: Johns Hopkins University Press, 2014. Project MUSE, https://muse.jhu.edu/primary/eliot/volume2#this_volume.

———. T. S. Eliot Collection, Houghton Library, Harvard University.

———. *The Waste Land*. In *The Poems of T. S. Eliot*. Vol. 1, *Collected and Uncollected Poems*, edited by Christopher Ricks and Jim McCue, 53–77. Baltimore: Johns Hopkins University Press, 2015.

———. *The Waste Land: A Facsimile and Transcript of the Original Drafts Including the Annotations of Ezra Pound*. Edited by Valerie Eliot. San Diego: Harcourt, 1971.

Ellis, Steve. "*Four Quartets*." In *The New Cambridge Companion to T. S. Eliot*, edited by Jason Harding, 103–15. New York: Cambridge University Press, 2017.

Euripides. *Euripides: The Bacchae and Other Plays*. Translated by John Davie. New York: Penguin Books, 2005.

Flood, Gavin. *The Ascetic Self: Subjectivity, Memory and Tradition*. New York: Cambridge University Press, 2004.

Freccero, John. *Dante: The Poetics of Conversion*. Edited by Rachel Jacoff. Cambridge, MA: Harvard University Press, 1986.

Gadamer, Hans-Georg. *Truth and Method*. 2nd rev. ed. Translated by Joel Weinsheimer and Donald G. Marshall. New York: Continuum, 1989.

Gandhi, Leela. *Affective Communities: Anticolonial Thought, Fin-de-Siècle Radicalism, and the Politics of Friendship*. Durham, NC: Duke University Press, 2006.

———. *The Common Cause: Postcolonial Ethics and the Practice of Democracy, 1900–1955*. Chicago: University of Chicago Press, 2014.

———. *Postcolonial Theory: A Critical Introduction*. New York: Columbia University Press, 1998.

Ganeri, Jonardan. *The Concealed Art of the Soul: Theories of Self and Practices of Truth in Indian Ethics and Epistemology*. New York: Oxford University Press, 2012.

Garfield, Jay L. *Empty Words: Buddhist Philosophy and Cross-Cultural Interpretation*. New York: Oxford University Press, 2002.

———, trans. *The Fundamental Wisdom of the Middle Way: Nāgārjuna's "Mūlamadhyamakakārikā."* New York: Oxford University Press, 1995.

Gethin, Rupert. *The Foundations of Buddhism.* New York: Oxford University Press, 1998.

Gish, Nancy. *The Waste Land: A Poem of Memory and Desire.* Boston: Twayne, 1988.

Goldman, Robert P. "Karma, Guilt, and Buried Memories: Public Fantasy and Private Reality in Traditional India." *Journal of the American Oriental Society* 105, no. 3 (1985): 413–25.

Gombrich, Richard F. *How Buddhism Began: The Conditioned Genesis of the Early Teachings.* New Delhi: Munshiram Manoharlal, 1996.

Gordon, Lyndall. *T. S. Eliot: An Imperfect Life.* New York: W. W. Norton, 1998.

Griffiths, Paul. "The *Lotus Sutra* as Good News: A Christian Reading." *Buddhist-Christian Studies* 19 (1999): 3–17.

Habib, M. A. R. *The Early T. S. Eliot and Western Philosophy.* New York: Cambridge University Press, 1999.

Halbfass, Wilhelm. *India and Europe: An Essay in Understanding.* Albany: State University of New York Press, 1988.

Hallisey, Charles. "Roads Taken and Not Taken in the Study of Theravāda Buddhism." In *Curators of the Buddha: The Study of Buddhism under Colonialism,* edited by Donald S. Lopez Jr., 31–61. Chicago: University of Chicago Press, 1995.

Hamada, Yo. "Japanese Religiosity amid the Changing Chaos of Several Forms of Nationalism." In *A New Japan for the Twenty-First Century: An Inside Overview of Current Fundamental Changes and Problems,* edited by Rien T. Segers, 219–33. New York: Routledge, 2008.

Hart, Kevin. "Eliot's Rose Garden: Some Phenomenology and Theology in 'Burnt Norton.'" *Christianity and Literature* 64, no. 3 (June 2015): 243–65. Project MUSE, https://muse.jhu.edu/article/738720/summary.256.

———. "The Experience of Nonexperience." In *Mystics: Presence and Aporia,* edited by Michael Kessler and Christian Sheppard, 188–206. Chicago: University of Chicago Press, 2003.

———. "Fields of 'Dharma': On T. S. Eliot and Robert Gray." *Literature and Theology* 27, no. 3 (September 2013): 267–84.

———. Introduction to *Counter-Experiences: Reading Jean-Luc Marion,* edited by Kevin Hart, 1–54. Notre Dame, IN: University of Notre Dame Press, 2007.

Hauck, Christina. "Not One, Not Two: Eliot and Buddhism." In *A Companion to T. S. Eliot,* edited by David E. Chinitz, 40–52. Chichester, UK: Wiley-Blackwell, 2009.

Hayot, Eric. *Chinese Dreams: Pound, Brecht, "Tel Quel."* Ann Arbor: University of Michigan Press, 2012.

Herbert, George. *The Complete English Poems*. Edited by John Tobin. New York: Penguin Books, 1991.

Hollywood, Amy. *The Soul as Virgin Wife: Mechthild of Magdeburg, Marguerite Porete, and Meister Eckhart*. Notre Dame, IN: University of Notre Dame Press, 1995.

Holy Bible: The New Revised Standard Version with Apocrypha. New York: Oxford University Press, 1989.

Holy Bible, Containing the Old and New Testaments: Translated out of the Original Tongues and with the Former Translations Diligently Compared and Revised, by His Majesty's Special Command [King James Version]. New York: Thomas Nelson, 1938.

Homer. *The Odyssey of Homer*. Translated by Richmond Lattimore. New York: Harper & Row, 1965.

Inden, Ronald. *Imagining India*. Bloomington: Indiana University Press, 2000.

———. "Orientalist Constructions of India." *Modern Asian Studies* 20, no. 3 (1986): 401–46.

Isomae, Jun'Ichi. "The Discursive Position of Religious Studies in Japan: Masaharu Anesaki and the Origins of Religious Studies." *Method and Theory in the Study of Religion* 14 (2002): 21–46.

Jain, Manju. *T. S. Eliot and American Philosophy: The Harvard Years*. New York: Cambridge University Press, 1992.

Janaway, Christopher. *Schopenhauer*. New York: Oxford University Press, 1994.

Jayatilleke, K. N. *Early Buddhist Theory of Knowledge*. Delhi: Motilal Banarsidass, 1963.

John of the Cross. *The Spiritual Canticle*. In *The Collected Works of St. John of the Cross*, 3rd ed., translated by Kieran Kavanaugh, OCD, and Otilio Rodriguez, OCD, 461–630. Washington, DC: ICS, 2017.

Kearns, Cleo McNelly. *T. S. Eliot and Indic Traditions: A Study in Poetry and Belief*. New York: Cambridge University Press, 1987.

———. "T. S. Eliot, Buddhism, and the Point of No Return." In *The Placing of T. S. Eliot*, edited by Jewel Spears Brooker, 128–35. Columbia: University of Missouri Press, 1991.

Kenner, Hugh. *The Invisible Poet: T. S. Eliot*. London: Methuen, 1959.

Keown, Damien. *The Nature of Buddhist Ethics*. New York: St. Martin's Press, 1992.

Killingley, Siew-Yue. "Time, Action, Incarnation: Shades of the Bhagavad Gītā in the Poetry of T. S. Eliot." *Literature and Theology* 4, no. 1 (March 1990): 50–71.

King, Richard. *Orientalism and Religion: Postcolonial Theory, India, and "The Mystic East."* New York: Routledge, 1999.

Lamotte, Etienne. "The Assessment of Textual Interpretation in Buddhism." In *Buddhist Hermeneutics*, edited by Donald Lopez Jr., 11–27. Studies in East Asian Buddhism 6. Honolulu: University of Hawai'i Press, 1988.

Leavis, F. R. *New Bearings in English Poetry: A Study of the Contemporary Situation*. London: Chatto & Windus, 1955.

LeCarner, Thomas Michael. "T. S. Eliot, Dharma Bum: Buddhist Lessons in *The Waste Land*." *Philosophy and Literature* 33, no. 2 (2009): 402–16.

Lefebure, Leo D. "The *Lotus Sutra* and Christian Wisdom: Mutual Illumination in Interreligious Dialogue." *Buddhist-Christian Studies* 40 (2020): 105–23. Project MUSE, https://doi.org/10.1353/bcs.2020.0006.

Leighton, Taigen Dan. "Dōgen's Appropriation of *Lotus Sutra* Ground and Space." *Japanese Journal of Religious Studies* 32, no. 1 (2005): 85–105.

Levenson, Michael. *A Genealogy of Modernism: A Study of English Literary Doctrine, 1908–1922*. New York: Cambridge University Press, 1984.

———. *Modernism*. New Haven: Yale University Press, 2011.

Lincoln, Bruce. *Theorizing Myth: Narrative, Ideology, and Scholarship*. Chicago: University of Chicago Press, 2000.

Longenbach, James. *Modernist Poetics of History: Pound, Eliot, and the Sense of the Past*. Princeton: Princeton University Press, 1987.

Lopez, Donald S., Jr. Introduction to *Buddhist Hermeneutics*. Studies in East Asian Buddhism 6. Honolulu: University of Hawai'i Press, 1988.

———. Introduction to *Curators of the Buddha: The Study of Buddhism under Colonialism*, 1–29. Chicago: University of Chicago Press, 1995.

———. *The "Lotus Sutra": A Biography*. Princeton: Princeton University Press, 2016.

Lopez, Donald S., Jr., and Jacqueline Stone. *Two Buddhas Seated Side by Side: A Guide to the "Lotus Sutra."* Princeton: Princeton University Press, 2019.

The Lotus Sutra, Saddharma-pundarîka: or, The Lotus of the True Law. Translated by H. Kern. Sacred Books of the East, vol. 21. Oxford: Clarendon Press, 1884. Coppell, TX: eclassics, 2020.

Magee, Bryan. *The Philosophy of Schopenhauer*. Oxford: Clarendon Press, 1983.

The Mahāvagga: Vinaya Texts, Part I. Translated by T. W. Rhys Davids and Hermann Oldenberg. Sacred Books of the East, vol. 13. Edited by F. Max Müller. Delhi: Motilal Banarsidass, 1966. www.sacred-texts.com/bud/sbe13/sbe1312.htm.

Matsumoto, Shiro. "The *Lotus Sutra* and Japanese Culture." In *Pruning the Bodhi Tree: The Storm over Critical Buddhism*, edited by Jamie Hubbard and Paul L. Swanson, 388–403. Honolulu: University of Hawai'i Press, 1997.

Matthiessen, F. O. *The Achievement of T. S. Eliot: An Essay on the Nature of Poetry*. Boston: Houghton Mifflin, 1935.

McLeod, Beryl Rosay. "Buddhism, T. S. Eliot and the Four Quartets." *Journal for the Study of Religion* 5, no. 1 (March 1992): 3–16.

McGinn, Bernard. *The Foundations of Mysticism: Origins to the Fifth Century.* The Presence of God: A History of Western Christian Mysticism, vol. 1. New York: Crossroad, 1991.

———. *The Growth of Mysticism: Gregory the Great through the 12th Century.* The Presence of God: A History of Western Christian Mysticism, vol. 2. New York: Crossroad, 1994.

Miller, James E., Jr. *T. S. Eliot's Personal Waste Land: Exorcism of the Demons.* University Park: Pennsylvania State University Press, 1977.

Moody, A. David. "*Four Quartets:* Music, Word, Meaning and Value." In *The Cambridge Companion to T. S. Eliot,* edited by A. David Moody, 142–57. New York: Cambridge University Press, 1994.

———. *Thomas Stearns Eliot: Poet.* 2nd ed. Cambridge: Cambridge University Press, 1994.

———. "T. S. Eliot's Passage to India." In *The Fire and the Rose: New Essays on T. S. Eliot,* edited by Vinod Sena and Rajiva Verma, 25–43. Delhi: Oxford University Press, 1992.

More, Paul Elmore. "The Cleft Eliot." In *T. S. Eliot: The Contemporary Reviews,* edited by Jewel Spears Brooker, 214–17. New York: Cambridge University Press, 2004.

Murata, Tatsuo, "Buddhist Epistemology in T. S. Eliot's Theory of Poetry." In *T. S. Eliot and Our Turning World,* edited by Jewel Spears Brooker, 80–88. New York: Macmillan, 2001.

Nicholls, Moira. "The Influences of Eastern Thought on Schopenhauer's Doctrine of the Thing-in-Itself." In *The Cambridge Companion to Schopenhauer,* edited by Christopher Janaway, 171–212. New York: Cambridge University Press, 1999.

Nietzsche, Friedrich. "Truth and Falsity in an Ultramoral Sense." Translated by Mazemilia A. Mügge. In *Critical Theory since Plato,* rev. ed., edited by Hazard Adams, 634–39. Fort Worth, TX: Harcourt Brace Jovanovich, 1992.

Nyanatiloka, Bhikkhu. *Buddhist Dictionary: Manual of Buddhist Terms and Doctrines.* Edited by Nyanaponika. Colombo, Sri Lanka: Frewin, 1972.

Obeyesekere, Gananath. *Imagining Karma: Ethical Transformation in Amerindian, Buddhist, and Greek Rebirth.* Berkeley: University of California Press, 2002.

Official Register of Harvard University. Vol. 7, no. 14, May 12, 1910. Harvard University Archives.

Official Register of Harvard University. Vol. 9, no. 22, June 15, 1912. Harvard University Archives.

Olivelle, Patrick. Introduction to *Upaniṣads,* translated by Patrick Olivelle, xxiii–lvi. New York: Oxford University Press, 1996.

Ovid. *Metamorphoses*. Translated by Rolfe Humphries. Bloomington: Indiana University Press, 1955.

Oxford English Dictionary. Oxford: Oxford University Press, 2009. https://dictionary.oed.com.

Patañjali. *The Yoga System of Patañjali; or, The Ancient Hindu Doctrine of Concentration of Mind Embracing the Mnemonic Rules, Called Yoga-Sūtras, of Patañjali and the Comment, Called Yoga-Bhāshya, Attributed to Veda-Vyāsa and the Explanation, Called Tattva-Vāiçāradī, of Vāchaspati-Miçra*. Translated by James Haughton Woods. Delhi: Motilal Banarsidass, 1914.

Patterson, Anita. *Race, American Literature, and Transnational Modernisms*. New York: Cambridge University Press, 2008. Kindle.

Perl, Jeffrey M. "The Language of Theory and the Language of Poetry: The Significance of T. S. Eliot's Philosophical Notebooks, Part Two." *Southern Review* 21, no. 3 (Autumn 1985): 1012–23.

———. *Skepticism and Modern Enmity: Before and after Eliot*. Baltimore: Johns Hopkins University Press, 1989.

Perl, Jeffrey M., and Andrew P. Tuck. "Foreign Metaphysics: The Significance of T. S. Eliot's Philosophical Notebooks, Part One." *Southern Review* 21, no. 1 (January 1985): 79–88.

———. "The Hidden Advantage of Tradition: On the Significance of T. S. Eliot's Indic Studies." *Philosophy East and West* 35, no. 2 (April 1985): 115–31.

Perloff, Marjory. *The Poetics of Indeterminacy: Rimbaud to Cage*. Evanston, IL: Northwestern University Press, 1983.

Pye, Michael. *Skilful Means: A Concept in Mahayana Buddhism*. 2nd ed. New York: Routledge, 2003.

Rahula, Walpola. *What the Buddha Taught*. New York: Grove Press, 1974.

Rainey, Lawrence. "Editor's Annotations to *The Wasteland*." In *The Annotated Waste Land with Eliot's Contemporary Prose*, 75–126, edited by Lawrence Rainey. New Haven: Yale University Press, 2005.

Ramazani, Jahan. *The Hybrid Muse: Postcolonial Poetry in English*. Chicago: University of Chicago Press, 2001.

———. "Modernist Bricolage, Postcolonial Hybridity." In *Modernism and Colonialism: British and Irish Literature, 1899–1939*, edited by Richard Begam and Michael Valdez Moses, 288–313. Durham, NC: Duke University Press, 2007.

———. *Poetry in a Global Age*. Chicago: University of Chicago Press, 2020.

———. *A Transnational Poetics*. Chicago: University of Chicago Press, 2009.

Rhys Davids, T. W. *Dialogues of the Buddha: Part I, Sacred Books of the Buddhists*. Edited by F. Max Müller. London: Pali Text Society, 1899.

Richards, Joshua. *T. S. Eliot's Ascetic Ideal*. Boston: Brill Rodopi, 2020.

Ricoeur, Paul. *Time and Narrative*. Vol. 1. Translated by Kathleen McLaughlin and David Pellauer. Chicago: University of Chicago Press, 1984.

Said, Edward. *Orientalism*. New York: Vintage Books, 1978.

Schopenhauer, Arthur. "Additional Remarks on the Doctrine of the Vanity of Existence." *Parerga and Paralipomena: Short Philosophical Essays*. 2 vols. Translated by E. F. J. Payne. New York: Oxford University Press, 1974.

———. *The World as Will and Representation*. 2 vols. Translated by E. F. J. Payne. New York: Dover, 1969.

Schuchard, Ronald. *Eliot's Dark Angel: Intersections of Life and Art*. New York: Oxford University Press, 1999.

Schwab, Raymond. *The Oriental Renaissance: Europe's Rediscovery of India and the East, 1680–1880*. Translated by Gene Patterson-Black and Victor Reinking. New York: Columbia University Press, 1984.

Shah, Ramesh Chandra. "Poetics of Appropriation: A Comparatist Perspective." *Literary Criterion* 24, no. 3–4 (1989): 96–107.

Shakespeare, William. *Coriolanus*. Edited by Philip Brockbank. Arden Edition of the Works of William Shakespeare. London: Methuen, 1976.

———. *The Tempest*. Edited by Stephen Orgel. The Oxford Shakespeare. New York: Oxford University Press, 1987.

———. *The Tragedy of Antony and Cleopatra*. Edited by Barbara Everett. New York: Signet, 1998.

Sharma, Jitender Kumar. "Fade out the Buddha, Fade in Lord Krishna: Comparative Observations on T. S. Eliot and Hermann Hesse." In *Influence of Bhagavadgita on Literature Written in English: In Honour of Ramesh Mohan*, 214–20. Meerut, India: Shalabh, 1988.

Simpson, D. P. *Cassell's New Latin Dictionary*. New York: Funk & Wagnall, 1960.

Singh, Amar Kumar. *T. S. Eliot and Indian Philosophy*. New Delhi: Sterling, 1990.

Singleton, Charles. *Commentary*. Vol. 2 of *Dante Alighieri, The Divine Comedy: Inferno*. Bollingen Series 80. Princeton: Princeton University Press, 1970.

Smith, Grover. *T. S. Eliot's Poetry and Plays: A Study in Sources and Meaning*. Chicago: University of Chicago Press, 1974.

Smith, Jonathan Z. "Religion, Religions, Religious." In *Critical Terms for Religious Studies*, edited by Mark C. Taylor, 269–84. Chicago: University of Chicago Press, 1998.

Sophocles. *Oedipus the King*. In *The Three Theban Plays*. Translated by Robert Fagles. New York: Penguin Books, 1984.

Southam, B. C. *A Guide to the Selected Poems of T. S. Eliot*. New York: Harcourt, Brace & World, 1968.

Spiro, Melford E. *Buddhism and Society: A Great Tradition and Its Burmese Vicissitudes*. New York: Harper Paperbacks, 1970.

Spurr, Barry. *"Anglo-Catholic in Religion": T. S. Eliot and Christianity*. Cambridge: Lutterworth Press, 2010.

——. "Religions East and West in *The Waste Land*." In *The Cambridge Companion to "The Waste Land*," edited by Gabrielle McIntire, 54–68. New York: Cambridge University Press, 2015.

Sri, P. S. "The Dantean Rose and the Hindu-Buddhist Lotus in the Poetry of T. S. Eliot." In *T. S. Eliot, Dante, and the Idea of Europe*, edited by Paul Douglass, 39–52. Newcastle upon Tyne, UK: Cambridge Scholars, 2011.

——. *T. S. Eliot: Vedanta and Buddhism*. Vancouver: University of British Columbia Press, 1985.

——. "Upanishadic Perceptions in T. S. Eliot's Poetry and Drama." *Rocky Mountain Review* 62, no. 2 (Fall 2008): 34–49.

Taylor, Charles. *A Secular Age*. Cambridge, MA: Harvard University Press, 2007.

Trivedi, Harish. "'Ganga Was Sunken . . .': T. S. Eliot's Use of India." In *The Fire and the Rose: New Essays on T. S. Eliot*, edited by Vinod Sena and Rajiva Verma, 44–62. Delhi: Oxford University Press, 1992.

Tuck, Andrew P. *Comparative Philosophy and the Philosophy of Scholarship: On the Western Interpretation of Nāgārjuna*. New York: Oxford University Press, 1990.

Tweed, Thomas. *The American Encounter with Buddhism, 1844–1912: Victorian Culture and the Limits of Dissent*. Chapel Hill: University of North Carolina Press, 1970.

Upaniṣads. Translated by Patrick Olivelle. New York: Oxford University Press, 1996.

Van der Veer, Peter. *Imperial Encounters: Religion and Modernity in India and Britain*. Princeton: Princeton University Press, 2001.

——. *The Modern Spirit of Asia: The Spiritual and the Secular in China and India*. Princeton: Princeton University Press, 2013.

——. *The Value of Comparison*. Durham, NC: Duke University Press, 2016.

Virkar-Yates, Aakanksha. "Absolute Music and the Death of Desire: Beethoven, Schopenhauer, Wagner and Eliot's *Four Quartets*." *Journal of Modern Literature* 40, no. 2 (Winter 2017): 79–93. https://doi.org/10.2979/jmodelite.40 .2.05.

Wagner, Richard. *Tristan und Isolde*. Translated by Lionel Salter. Chor und Orchester der Bayreuther Festspiele, Karl Böhm. 1966; Deutsche Gramophon, 1966.

——. *Wagner's "Ring of the Nibelung": A Companion*. Trans. Stewart Spencer. New York: Thames and Hudson, 1993.

Warren, Henry Clarke, ed. and trans. *A Buddhist Reader: Selections from the Sacred Books*. Mineola, NY: Dover, 2004.

Welbon, Guy Richard. *The Buddhist Nirvāna and Its Western Interpreters.* Chicago: University of Chicago Press, 1968.

Williams, Paul. *Mahāyāna Buddhism: The Doctrinal Foundations.* New York: Routledge, 1989.

Woelfel, Craig Bradshaw. *Varieties of Aesthetic Experience: Literary Modernism and the Dissociation of Belief.* Columbia: University of South Carolina Press, 2018.

Woefel, Craig, and Jayme Stayer. "Introduction: Modernism and the Turn to Religion." *Renascence* 73, no. 1 (Winter 2021): 3–11.

Ziporyn, Brook A. *Emptiness and Omnipresence: An Essential Introduction to Tiantai Buddhism.* Bloomington: Indiana University Press, 2016.

INDEX

Abhidhamma, 127

Absolute, the: and faith, 64–65; as formal limit to knowing, 68–69, 72; and God, 211; and Mahayana Buddhism, 211; and memory, 174; as ultimate metaphysical unity, 68, 74–75; and *The Waste Land*, 82, 152, 174

acedia, 109

Aeneid (Virgil), 96

After Strange Gods (Eliot): and anti-Semitism, 25; Babbitt criticized in, 27–28; on challenges of undertaking rites and customs of another place, 29–30, 35; on Eliot's study of Indic texts, 28, 35; and insistence on cultural homogeneity, 23–25, 27–29, 31; on orthodoxy and tradition, 25–26

Agni (Vedic fire god of sacrifice), 136, 140–41

Agni priests: and fire sacrifices, 140; "The Fire Sermon" and the conversion of, 6, 113–15, 118, 136, 139; and the *Maha-vagga*, 115, 132, 136; and *upaya*, 148

ahavaniya ("the offertorial fire"), 115

Almond, Philip C., 40

Ambrose, 147–48

Anesaki, Masaharu: on aesthetic training for enlightenment, 51, 55; and *bodhi-chitta*, 50–51; and the Buddha nature, 47, 50, 193–94; Eliot as student of, 4, 37, 45–47, 52, 70, 181–82, 193–94, 222; on Four Noble Truths of Buddhism, 49–50; on Hinduism's influence on Buddhism, 50; and the *Lotus Sutra*, 52, 70, 221–23; and Mahayana Buddhism, 37–38, 46, 211; and Nagarjuna, 180–81,

193–94; on *nirvana*, 48–49, 62; on religious praxis and moral activity, 50, 56; and Schopenhauer, 37–38, 45–48, 55, 62, 193; and Tiantai Buddhism, 45, 47; and *upaya*, 37, 51, 55, 110

Angirasa, 140–41

Anglicanism, 39

Anglo-Catholicism. *See under* Eliot, T. S.

Antony and Cleopatra (Shakespeare), 94–95, 98

Appearance and Reality (Bradley), 169

Aquinas, Thomas, 1, 4, 57–59

arhats (enlightened monks), 54, 132

Aristotle: on boundaries and knowledge, 14; and mysticism, 57–58; and *phrone-sis*, 26; and scholasticism, 1, 4. See also *Nicomachean Ethics* (Aristotle)

Arnold, Daniel, 201

Asad, Talal, 18, 244n14

asceticism: and the *Brhadaranyaka Upanishad*, 154, 172; and Christianity, 19, 23; and the *Confessions*, 5, 166–67; and desire, 8, 18–19, 22, 31; and *Four Quartets*, 21, 235–36, 238; and memory, 22; and the "middle way," 21, 37, 130, 195; and poetry, 22–23; and Schopenhauer, 44, 84; and sin, 2, 19; and subjectivity, 21–22; and suffering, 8; and transcendence, 9–10, 22, 56; and *upaya*, 21, 23, 166–67; and *The Waste Land*, 5, 8, 21, 84, 105–6, 111, 143, 153–55, 175

atman (the individual self): and *brahman*, 138; and cognition, 123; and fire, 116; and karma, 125–26; and Schopen-hauer, 7, 42; spider analogy for, 166;

298 INDEX

atman (the individual self) (*continued*)
and the Upanishads, 42, 116, 123,
125–26, 138; and the will, 42
Augustine. See *Confessions* (Augustine)
avidya (ignorance), 90

Babbitt, Irving, 18, 25, 27–28, 30, 61
Bakhtin, Mikhail, 33, 82, 246n101
Baudelaire, Charles, 9, 108–10, 155–56,
268n12. See also *Ennui* (Baudelaire)
Bedient, Calvin, 82–84, 152, 164, 261n94,
270n36
Benjamin Major (Richard of St. Victor),
58–59
Bentley, Joseph, 82, 97, 105, 266n96,
269n15
Bergson, Henri, 57–58, 250n88
Berman, Jessica, 23
bhavana (mental cultivation), 48
bodhichitta (the Buddha's awakening
mind), 50–51
bodhisattva (person on the path to Buddhahood), 56, 225–27
boredom: and desire, 87–88, 91–93, 108;
and hopelessness, 9; and nothingness,
92–93; and Schopenhauer, 85, 87–88,
92–93, 102; and vanity, 93; and *The
Waste Land*, 9, 85, 93, 103, 108
Bradley, F. H.: the Absolute as ultimate
metaphysical unity for, 68, 74–75; on
Christian devotional practices, 75–76;
Eliot's engagement with the writings
of, 12, 63–64, 74–76, 213, 254n44;
faith in the writings of, 73–76; and
idealism, 15, 169, 171; and transmigration, 64–65. See also *Appearance
and Reality* (Bradley); *Ethical Studies*
(Bradley)
brahman (ultimate reality behind phenomenal world): and *atman*, 138; and
the *Brhadaranyaka Upanishad*, 88–89,
163; and dreams, 167–68, 173; and fire,
116; and nothingness, 42; and Prajapati, 163; and Schopenhauer, 7, 42;

and the Upanishads, 42, 116, 138; and
the Vedas, 138; and the will, 42
Brahmanas, 116
Brhadaranyaka Upanishad: and asceticism, 154, 172; and *atman*, 166; and
brahman, 88–89, 163; and compassion
toward otherness, 168–69; Deussen's
translation of, 161–63, 177; and dreams,
165–68, 172–74; faith and truth in, 89;
and flame imagery, 90; and memory,
153; and Prajatapi, 161–63, 177; and
rebirth, 88; spider imagery in, 165–66,
168, 173; and thunder, 97, 161–63, 173,
177; and *The Waste Land*, 6, 88, 97, 123,
153–54, 160, 162–63, 175, 177; water
and rain in, 160, 167, 172
Brooker, Jewel Spears: on Bradley's
influence on Eliot, 12, 15, 63–64, 213;
on Cleopatra in *The Waste Land*, 97;
on Eliot's belief in "many truths," 238,
253n25; on Eliot's dialectical imagination, 34; on Eliot's practically oriented
early approach to religion, 9, 18, 63, 78;
on mysticism in *The Waste Land*, 82;
on quasi-religious element of Bradley's
philosophy, 67–68; on sexual reification in *The Waste Land*, 105
Brooks, Cleanth, 85, 260n88
Buddha: and Angirasa, 140–41; and
bodhichitta, 50–51; and *Dhamma*,
137–39; and *dharmakaya*, 46–47,
52–53; and divinity, 229; the Naga's
battle with, 139–40; and Nanda, 131;
upaya and the teachings of, 37, 51–53,
62, 70–71, 101, 106, 110, 132–33, 135,
150. *See also* Buddhism
Buddhaghosa, 125–26, 196
Buddhism: and desire, 4, 22, 62, 101,
130, 146, 229–30; distinction between
"spirit" and "letter" of a text in, 134,
139; Eliot's Christianity influenced by,
6, 23, 193; hermeneutics of, 134–36,
139; Hinduism's influences on, 50, 115;
khandhas of, 116–17; and language,

111–12, 150; Madhyamaka Buddhism, 180–82, 193–95, 197, 209; Mahasanghika Buddhism, 71, 133; Mahayana Buddhism, 5, 37–38, 52, 70–71, 111, 132, 221; and the "middle way," 21, 37, 127, 180, 182, 193, 195–97, 201–2; and mysticism, 40; Nikaya Buddhism, 10; and nothingness, 42–43, 236; Pali as language of scriptures in, 1, 36, 45, 117, 132–33; protreptic nature of, 10, 108; realism and empiricism in, 121–22; Romantics' engagement with, 38–40; and Schopenhauer, 41–43, 46, 55–56, 61–62; the self's nonessential nature in, 21, 40, 46, 189, 196, 211, 220; and suffering, 110, 122, 145; Theravada Buddhism, 37, 71–72, 110, 121–22, 133, 145, 183, 221; Tiantai Buddhism, 37, 45, 47, 193–94, 222–23; translations into different languages of, 133

Burnouf, Eugène, 39, 181, 221

"Burnt Norton" (Eliot). See under *Four Quartets* (Eliot)

Bush, Ronald, 81, 255n2, 255n6

Calvin, John, 16

Canterbury Tales, The (Chaucer), 86, 257n29

Chandogya Upanishad, 153–54

Chaucer, Geoffrey, 86, 257n29

chetana (intention or volition), 119, 130, 145

Childs, Donald, 12, 82, 100, 142, 256n9, 267n101

chitta (mind), 47

Chittamatra texts, 47

Clairemont, David, 267n107

Clark Lectures (Eliot, 1926): on human love *versus* divine love, 20; and Laforgue, 59–61; on metaphysical poetry, 56; and mysticism, 57–59, 79, 209; on Schopenhauer and Buddhism, 7, 36, 56, 61

Cleopatra: *Antony and Cleopatra*, 94–95, 98; barge of, 94–95, 98; beauty of, 94; burial imagery, 97; fire imagery, 100, 102; perfumes of, 94–97; Punic Wars, 96; as quasi-divine figure, 95; as silenced sexualized Other, 85, 93, 98–100, 103; and Venus, 94

Collins, Steven: on Buddhism and fire, 115; on existence and verbal form, 127; on fire in the Vedas, 136; on "middle way" in Buddhism, 195; on *nirvana* and suffering, 121, 130; on realism and empiricism in Theravada Buddhism, 121–22; on "two truths" in Buddhism, 196; on vegetation imagery and model of cyclical existence, 90

colonialism, 3–4

Commedia (Dante), 57, 65, 220

Confessions (Augustine): and asceticism, 5, 166–67; and beauty, 147–50; conversion in, 147–48; and desire, 144–46, 148–49; flame imagery in, 144; and language, 150; and memory, 149; Neoplatonism in, 150; on praise as sacrifice, 147; and sin, 145–47; temporal tension in, 214; and theodicy, 150; wandering in, 143–44; and *The Waste Land*, 111–12, 143, 145, 149–50, 152

Confucianism, 27–30

Coriolanus (Shakespeare), 171

dakshinagni ("southern fire"), 115

Dante: human love and divine love differentiated by, 20; metaphysical system of, 23–24; and the "middle way," 185–87, 208–9; and mysticism, 8, 10, 13, 18, 57–59, 79; and Purgatory, 9, 20, 141, 266n94; rose of paradise of, 213, 216, 220, 230; and Ugolino della Gherardesca, 169. *See also specific works*

Davidson, Harriet, 81, 269n28

Descartes, René, 57

desire: and asceticism, 8, 18–19, 22, 31; and attachment, 111, 118, 146, 203; and boredom, 87–88, 91–93, 108;

300   INDEX

desire (*continued*)
and Buddhism, 4, 22, 62, 101, 130, 146, 229–30; and "The Fire Sermon," 5, 108, 114–15, 118, 120, 136, 149; and *Four Quartets*, 184, 188, 236–37; and karma, 91, 128; and language, 112; and love, 237; and the *Majjhima-Nikaya*, 129–30; and memory, 8, 90–91, 111–12, 149, 152, 156, 168, 172, 174; and Nanda, 131; and *nirvana*, 129–30, 132, 149; and *samsara*, 43, 122–23, 149, 160, 172, 174, 195; Schopenhauer's interpretation of, 4, 38, 43, 85, 87–88, 91–93; and sin, 111, 145–46, 189; and suffering, 110, 112, 120–22, 129, 195; and transience, 184; and *upaya*, 22; and *The Waste Land*, 5, 8, 85–87, 91, 93, 102, 108, 111, 145, 152, 155–56, 168

Deussen, Paul: *Brhadaranyaka Upanishad* translated by, 161–63, 177; Eliot on his interest in, 1, 29, 35, 45; and Schopenhauer, 45; and the Upanishads, 36; and Vedanta, 9

Dewey, John, 29

Dhamma (knowledge gained through direct experience), 137–39

dharmakaya (higher reality of Buddha), 46–47, 52–53

dharmata (emptiness), 46

dhatu (environment), 47

Dickens, Charles, 83

Digha-Nikaya, 129

Divine Comedy (Dante), 57, 65, 220

Droit, Roger-Pol, 40

"Dry Salvages, The" (Eliot). See under *Four Quartets* (Eliot)

dukkha (suffering), 120

Durkheim, Émile, 12

"East Coker" (Eliot). See under *Four Quartets* (Eliot)

"Easter" (Herbert), 235

Eckhardt, Meister, 58

Edgerton, Franklin, 134

Eliot, T. S.: and Anesaki, 4, 37, 45–47, 52, 70, 181–82, 193–94, 222; and Anglo-Catholicism, 2–4, 12, 26, 63, 70, 189; anti-Semitism of, 25; colonialism endorsed by, 3; as Harvard University student, 1, 11–12, 36–37, 44–47, 52, 63, 70, 180–82, 193–94, 222; and hybridity, 3–5, 24–25, 30, 34, 78, 178, 211; Romanticism rejected by, 11, 37, 56; on shock and terror in poetry, 176–77. *See also specific works*

Enlightenment, 15, 18, 31, 40

Ennui (Baudelaire), 9, 109

erhebung (exaltation), 210, 231–33

Eternalism, 126–27, 195

Ethical Studies (Bradley), 64, 73, 254n44

Eucharist, 188–89, 204

"Fire Sermon, The" (The Buddha): Aditta-pariyaya as Pali language title of, 136; and attachment, 113–18, 120–21; and aversion, 108, 114–15; coffer box in, 101–2; and desire, 5, 108, 114–15, 118, 120, 136, 149; fire and burning imagery in, 53, 90, 111, 114–17, 120, 125, 149; and ignorance, 118; and karma, 121; and language, 128; and the *Mahavagga*, 111–13, 136–38; and the "middle way," 123, 125, 127; monastic and repetitive nature of, 113; and *nirvana*, 149; priests of Agni converted and liberated in, 6, 113–15, 118, 136; and *samsara*, 113, 115, 149; and suffering, 107, 121; and transcendence, 110; and *upaya*, 6, 107, 111–12, 132, 136, 140; and the Vedas, 115; and *The Waste Land*, 101, 107, 111, 112–13, 152

Flood, Gavin, 21–22

Foucault, Michel, 18

Four Noble Truths (Buddha), 49–50, 118, 130

Four Quartets (Eliot): and asceticism, 21, 235–36, 238; and "Burnt Norton,"

210–21, 230–31, 234–37; and Dante's *Inferno*, 185, 204; and desire, 184, 188, 236–37; and "The Dry Salvages," 183, 205–9; and "East Coker," 183, 185, 192–93, 204, 206–9, 260n86; and emptiness, 219–21; and the Garden of Eden, 213–14, 216; God's gaze in, 218–19; and human knowledge, 188, 190–91; interreligious comparison and theological inclusivism in, 30, 31, 34; and Jesus, 187–88, 204, 207–8; and John of the Cross, 236, 278n23; and language, 184–87, 190, 194, 204–9; and "Little Gidding," 214, 234; "lotos rose" in, 214, 220–21, 230, 233; and the *Lotus Sutra*, 6, 221; and love, 237–40; and Mahayana Buddhism, 221; and memory, 214–16, 218–19, 230–31, 233; and metaphysics, 211; and the "middle way," 123, 180–81, 183–90, 192–93, 204; and mysticism, 235–36; and Nagarjuna, 183; and redemption, 212–13; and soteriology, 212; and subjectivity, 204; and suffering, 206–8, 238; and transience, 184; and un-being, 237; and *upaya*, 6, 21; and world wars, 190

"Game of Chess, A" (Eliot), 94
Ganeri, Jonardon, 10–11, 76, 108, 153–54
Garden of Eden, 213–14, 216
Garfield, Jay, 193–95, 198–203, 274n46, 275n65
garhapatya ("householder's fire"), 115
Gatilas (Vedic ascetics), 139–40
Gethin, Rupert, 130
Gish, Nancy: on *Brhadaranyaka Upanishad* and *The Waste Land*, 177; on critical theory and *The Waste Land*, 80; on mysticism in *The Waste Land*, 82; and single protagonist theory regarding *The Waste Land*, 83; on The Thames Daughters in *The Waste Land*, 142; on thunder in *The Waste Land*, 164

God: the Absolute, 211; and beauty, 149; and desire, 238; gaze of, 218–19; and love, 148, 216–17; theodicy, 150
Goldman, Robert, 118–19
Gombrich, Richard: on Buddha and philosophy, 264n38; on fire in the Vedas, 115, 136; on "The Fire Sermon" in the *Mahavagga*, 111, 132, 136–38, 140–41; on flame imagery in the *Mahavagga*, 116; on *upadana*, 117; on *upaya*, 132, 141
Gordon, Lyndall, 83

Halbfass, Wilhelm, 16–17, 40–41
Hale, Emily, 213
Hart, Kevin, 212, 218
Hartmann, Eduard von, 29, 35–36, 46, 60–61
Hebrews, Letter to, 73
Heracleitos, 240
Herbert, George, 235
Hinduism: Buddhism influenced by, 50, 115; and desire, 62; Romantics' engagement with, 39; and Schopenhauer, 42. *See also* Upanishads; Vedas
Hulme, T. E., 11, 18–19, 57, 63

Ignatius of Loyola, 58
Inferno (Dante), 20, 169, 185, 204
Introduction à l'histoire du Buddhisme indien (Burnouf), 39

Jain, Manju, 12, 36
Jayatilleke, K. N., 122–23, 125–27
Jesus: appearance on road to Emmaus of, 158; crucifixion and self-sacrifice of, 158, 188–89, 235; and the Eucharist, 188–89, 204; and *Four Quartets*, 187–88, 204, 207–8; and the Letter to the Hebrews, 73; as surgeon, 188, 204, 208; and *The Waste Land*, 158
John of the Cross, 57–58, 217–18, 236, 238, 278n23

302 INDEX

Kant, Immanuel, 27–28, 42

karma (*kamma*): and *atman*, 125–26; and attachment, 115–16; and *chetana*, 119; and consciousness, 117; and desire, 91, 128; and the *Digha-Nikaya*, 129; and "The Fire Sermon," 121; and language, 128; and Providence, 40; and retribution, 118–19; and *samsara*, 118–19, 126; and Schopenhauer, 43; seeds and fruit of, 125; and soteriology, 195–96; and suffering, 120; and transmigration, 119; and the Upanishads, 118–19, 126; water imagery, 88, 91; and the *Yoga Sutra*, 90

Kassapas (Gaya, Nadi, Uruvela), 139–40

Kaushitaki Upanishad, 122

Kearns, Cleo McNelly: on asceticism and *The Waste Land*, 84; on *Brhadaranyaka Upanishad* and dreams, 168; on *Brhadaranyaka Upanishad* and *The Waste Land*, 162–63; on Buddhism and the cultivation of emptiness, 236; on the *Confessions* and *The Waste Land*, 149; on Deussen, 9; on Eliot and *Yoga Sutras*, 90; on Eliot and mysticism, 2, 8, 82; on Eliot and Nagarjuna, 182–83; on Eliot and Theravadan Buddhism, 37–38; on Eliot's distinction between truth of doctrine and wisdom, 238; on Eliot's introduction to Madhyamaka Buddhism, 181; and Eliot's use of Indic sources, 2, 8, 62, 64; on the ending of *The Waste Land*, 175; on "The Fire Sermon," 107, 110; on *kleshas*, 91; on *Knowledge and Experience*, 65; on lotus imagery in Buddhism, 221; on mythical tropes in the *Lotus Sutra*, 70; on *nirvana* and *samsara*, 203; on *shunyata*, 219; on surrender and recovery in Eliot's works, 217; on The Thames Daughters in *The Waste Land*, 142; on Tientai Buddhism and the *Lotus Sutra*, 222

Kenner, Hugh, 172

Keown, Damien, 119, 267n107

Kern, Hendrik, 222

khandhas (five elements of existence in Buddhism), 116–17

Kierkegaard, Søren, 11, 73, 212

King, Richard, 17

kleshas (vestiges of attachment), 91

Knowledge and Experience (Eliot): and the Absolute, 68; and asceticism, 6; and Buddhism, 69–73; and faith, 65–67, 72–73, 76–77; and feeling, 67; and hallucination, 155; religion as a scheme for action in, 66; religious influences on, 64; on theory and the test of praxis, 69; and transmigration, 64–66, 68–70, 72, 119

Lacan, Jacques, 81

Laforgue, Jules, 7–8, 36, 59–61

Lamotte, Etienne, 134

Lanman, Charles, 28, 35

Lawrence, D. H., 58

Leavis, F. R., 3, 82

Levenson, Michael, 13–14

"Little Gidding" (Eliot). See under *Four Quartets* (Eliot)

Lopez, Donald S., 221, 225

Lotus Sutra: and Anesaki, 52, 70, 221–23; and *bodhisattvas*, 56, 225–27; and the Buddha nature, 194, 221; Buddha's project for enlightenment described in, 223–24; burning imagery in, 53; Burnouf as translator of, 221–22; and *Four Quartets*, 6, 221; and ignorance, 223–25, 228; Kern as translator of, 222; mythical tropes in, 70; and *nirvana*, 224–28; parables in, 53–54; and *samsara*, 225; and the Tathagata, 226–29; and Tiantai Buddhism, 222; and *upaya*, 6, 46, 52–53, 70–71, 133, 210, 221, 223, 225, 229, 238–39

Luther, Martin, 16

Madhyamaka Buddhism: and essence, 195; and *Four Quartets*, 193; and the "middle way," 180, 182, 193; and Nagarjuna, 180–82, 184; soteriology, 209; tetralemma in, 197

Mahasanghika Buddhism, 71, 133

Mahavagga: and beauty, 148; Brahma's pleading in, 137–38; fire imagery in, 116; and "The Fire Sermon," 111–13, 136–38; and Müller's *Sacred Books of the East* series, 136; priests of Agni in, 115, 132, 136; Rhys Davids' translation of, 111; and *upaya*, 112, 136–37, 148; and the Vedas, 148–49; and *The Waste Land*, 111

Mahayana Buddhism: and the Absolute, 211; and Anesaki, 37–38, 46, 211; distinction between conventional and ultimate truth in, 196; flexibility of, 71–72, 133; and *Four Quartets*, 221; and the "middle way," 180; and *upaya*, 5, 52, 70, 111, 132. *See also* Madhyamaka Buddhism

Majjhima-Nikaya, 129–30

Maurras, Charles, 18

maya (illusion), 7, 42

memory: and the Absolute, 174; and asceticism, 22; and the *Confessions*, 149; consciousness, 231; and deception, 217, 231; and desire, 8, 90–91, 111–12, 149, 152, 156, 168, 172, 174; and dreams, 173; and *Four Quartets*, 214–16, 218–19, 230–31, 233; and suffering, 110, 112; and *The Waste Land*, 86–87, 103–4, 111, 152, 154, 156, 168, 174

Metamorphoses (Ovid), 99

"Metaphysical Poets, The" (Eliot), 24

Middleton, Thomas, 104

"middle way": between asceticism and hedonism, 21, 37, 130, 195; and Buddhism, 21, 37, 127, 180, 182, 193, 195–97, 201–2; and Dante, 185–87, 208–9; between eternalism and annihilationism, 195; and "The Fire Sermon," 123, 125, 127; and *Four Quartets*, 123, 180–81, 183–90, 192–93,

204; and Madhyamaka Buddhism, 180, 182, 193; and Nagarjuna, 180–82, 193, 196–97, 201–2; between nihilism and essentialism, 181; and *paticcasamuppada*, 197; and poetic creation, 192; and transience, 184; and *upaya*, 37; and the *Visuddhimagga*, 125; and *The Waste Land*, 123

"Modern Dilemma, The" (Eliot), 2, 18–19

modernism, 13, 30

Moody, A. David, 2, 6, 65, 82, 100, 141–42, 235, 269n15, 281n102

More, Paul Elmer, 71, 245n84

Mulamadhyamakakarika (Nagarjuna), 180–82, 193, 198–99

Müller, Max, 12, 136

"Music of Poetry, The" (Eliot), 31–33

mysticism: and absorption into the divine, 24, 59; and Buddhism, 40; classical mysticism, 57–58, 79; and Dante, 8, 10, 13, 18, 57–59, 79; and divine love, 216–17; and *Four Quartets*, 235–36; and intuition, 44; and metaphysics, 14; and modernity, 17; romantic mysticism, 56–58; and Schopenhauer, 44; and "Tradition and the Individual Talent," 12–13; and *The Waste Land*, 82

Nagarjuna: and Anesaki, 180–81, 193–94; and the Buddha nature, 193–94; and dependence (*paticcasamuppada*), 195, 197–98, 200–202, 206–7; and emptiness, 201–2, 219, 221; and *Four Quartets*, 183; and language, 181, 183, 194, 198–202, 206; and Madhyamaka Buddhism, 180–82, 184; and the "middle way," 180–82, 193, 196–97, 201–2; and *Mulamadhyamakakarika*, 180–82, 193, 198–99; on *nirvana* and *samsara*, 182, 219; and soteriology, 203; and subjectivity, 198–99, 201; and suffering, 203, 207–8; and Theravada Buddhism, 183

Nanda, 130–31

Neoplatonism, 150
nibbana. See *nirvana* (nibbana)
Nichts. See nothingness
Nicomachean Ethics (Aristotle), 26
Nietzsche, Friedrich, 41, 183–86, 204, 208–9
Nikaya Buddhism, 10
nirvana (nibbana): and consciousness, 146; and desire, 129–30, 132, 149; and emptiness, 198, 202–3; and enlightenment, 125; and fire, 115; and "The Fire Sermon," 149; and the *Lotus Sutra*, 224–28; and nothingness, 39, 48, 102; and *samsara*, 182, 202–3, 219, 225; and Schopenhauer, 7, 43; and soteriology, 202; and suffering, 110, 121; and *upaya*, 54, 70; and the will, 43
nothingness: and boredom, 92–93; and *brahman*, 42; and *nirvana*, 39, 48, 102; and Schopenhauer, 7, 9, 41–43, 46–48, 85, 93, 102, 193, 250n88; and *The Waste Land*, 93, 103–4, 141–42
Nyanatiloka, Bhikkhu, 118–19

Olivelle, Patrick, 89
"On the Vanity of Existence" (Schopenhauer), 92
Orientalism: cultural "other" described in nonrational terms under, 40; postcolonial scholars, 3; and Pound, 30; and Said, 17, 30–31; and Schopenhauer, 36–38, 56, 128; and *The Waste Land*, 3, 85
Original Sin, 11–12
orthodoxy, 25–26, 38
Our Mutual Friend (Dickens), 83
Ovid, 99

Page-Barbour lectures (Eliot, 1933), 35. See also *After Strange Gods* (Eliot)
Pali, Buddhist scriptures in, 1, 36, 45, 117, 132–33
Paradiso (Dante), 20, 213, 216
Patanjali, 28, 35, 90–91, 120, 167, 258n47

paticcasamuppada (doctrine of dependent origination), 117, 124–26, 195, 197
Patterson, Anita, 24, 30–31, 33
Perl, Jeffrey, 180–83, 242n27, 253n35
Perloff, Marjory, 30
Philosophical Fragments (Kierkegaard), 212
phronesis (interplay between habit and intellect), 26
Pound, Ezra, 25, 27, 30
Prajapati, 153–54, 161–63, 177
prajnaparamita texts, 46
prakrti (realm of all matter), 90
Protestant Christianity, 15, 27
Puranas, 42
Purgatorio (Dante), 9, 20, 141, 266n94
purusha (inner transcendent consciousness), 90
Pusey, E. B., 144, 147
Pye, Michael, 71–72, 132–33

"Questions for King Milinda," 126–27

Rainey, Lawrence, 86, 96, 104, 157
Ramazani, Jahan, 3–4, 245n79
Reformation, 15–16
Rhys Davids, T. W., 111, 132
Richard of St. Victor, 58–59
Richards, Joshua, 14, 18–20, 84
Ricoeur, Paul, 214, 216
Rig Veda (Vedic text), 134
Rimbaud, Arthur, 30
Romanticism, 11–12, 37–41
Rousseau, Jean-Jacques, 57
Royce, Josiah, 12
Rta (cosmic order), 115

Sacred Wood, The (Eliot), 12, 14
Said, Edward, 3, 17, 30
samkhara (constructions of consciousness), 47, 120
samsara (rebirth): and attachment, 120, 198–99; and *avidya*, 90; and desire, 43, 122–23, 149, 160, 172, 174, 195;

and "The Fire Sermon," 113, 115, 149; and karma, 118–19, 126; and *nirvana*, 182, 202–3, 219, 225; and *paticcasamuppada*, 195; and rain imagery, 160; renunciation of ritual activity as way of transcending, 90; and suffering, 43, 122, 195

Samyutta Nikaya (Buddhist scriptural collection), 123–25

Sanskrit, 1, 28, 35–36, 45, 133

Santayana, George, 56

Scholasticism, 1, 4

Schopenhauer, Arthur: and Anesaki, 37–38, 45–48, 55, 62, 193; and asceticism, 44, 84; and *atman*, 7, 42; and boredom, 85, 87–88, 92–93, 102; and *brahman*, 7, 42; and Buddhism, 41–43, 46, 55–56, 61–62; and Chittamatra texts, 47; and desire, 4, 38, 43, 85, 87–88, 91–93; on dogma, 44; Eliot's engagement with works of, 1, 4, 7, 29, 35–37, 45, 56, 61–62, 110; and Hinduism, 42; Indic religious texts interpreted by, 4, 7, 36, 38–41, 61, 110; and Kant, 42; and karma, 43; and Laforgue, 60–61; and mysticism, 44; and *nirvana*, 7, 43; and nothingness, 7, 9, 41–43, 46–48, 85, 93, 102, 193, 250n88; and Orientalism, 36–38, 56, 128; and sexual reification, 102; theory of the sublime of, 210, 232–33; and the Upanishads, 45; and the Vedas, 42; and *The Waste Land*, 91–92, 102; on the will, 7–8, 38, 41–44, 47, 87–88, 93, 248n33

Schuchard, Ronald, 11–13, 18, 63, 65, 252n11, 281n92

Schwab, Raymond, 38, 40–41

"Search for Moral Sanction, The" (Eliot), 1

secularism, 11

Shackleton, Ernest, 157–58

Shakespeare, William: *Antony and Cleopatra*, 94–95, 98; *Coriolanus*, 171; *The Tempest*, 104–5

shunyata (emptiness), 46, 219

sin: and alienation, 18, 146–47; and asceticism, 2, 19; and desire, 111, 145–46, 189; and language, 145; Original Sin, 11–12; and Purgatory, 9; and the self, 189; and soteriology, 212

Smith, Grover, 104

Smith, Jonathan Z., 15–16

Southam, B. C., 86, 104

Spiritual Canticle (John of the Cross), 217–18

Spiro, M. E., 128

Spurr, Barry, 3, 5, 70–71

Stayer, Jayme, 243n18

Stone, Jacqueline, 225

suffering: and asceticism, 8; and attachment, 116, 121–22; and Baudelaire, 109, 268n12; and Buddhism, 110, 122, 145; and dependence, 202–3; and desire, 110, 112, 120–22, 129, 195; and "The Fire Sermon," 107, 121; and *Four Quartets*, 206–8, 238; and hope, 9; and karma, 120; and liberation, 8; and memory, 110, 112; and Nagarjuna, 203, 207–8; and *nirvana*, 110, 121; and *samsara*, 43, 122, 195; and soteriology, 203, 207; and the supernatural, 109; and Theravada Buddhism, 145

Tathagata, 124, 226–29

Taylor, Charles, 11

Tempest, The (Shakespeare), 104–5

Teresa of Ávila, 57–58

Theravada Buddhism: Eliot's engagement with, 37–38, 110, 221; flexibility of, 71–72, 133; and the "middle way," 180; and Nagarjuna, 183; realism and empiricism of, 121–22; and suffering, 145

Tiantai Buddhism, 37, 45, 47, 193–94, 222–23

"Tradition and the Individual Talent" (Eliot), 12–14, 25, 178, 191–92, 209, 272n69

transmigration. See under *Knowledge and Experience* (Eliot)
Tristan und Isolde (Wagner), 60
Tuck, Andrew, 180–83, 242n27, 253n35
Tweed, Thomas, 38–40

Ugolino della Gherardesca, 169
Underhill, Evelyn, 12, 14
upadana ("clinging"), 116–17
Upanishads: and *atman*, 42, 116, 123, 125–26, 138; and attention, 122; and *brahman*, 42, 116, 138; and Deussen, 36; dream passages in, 154; and empiricism, 122; and Eternalism, 126–27, 195; fragmentary nature of, 178; and karma, 118–19, 126; and Schopenhauer, 45; and transcendence, 110; and transformation in the mind of the listener, 10; and *upaya*, 153; and *The Waste Land*, 150, 152–54. See also *Brhadaranyaka Upanishad; Chandogya Upanishad*
upaya (skillful means): and asceticism, 21, 23, 166–67; the Buddha's teaching through, 37, 51–53, 62, 70–71, 101, 106, 110, 132–33, 135, 150; and desire, 22; and "The Fire Sermon," 6, 107, 111–12, 132, 136, 140; and *Four Quartets*, 6, 21; and hermeneutics, 135; higher truth reached through, 5, 10, 22, 54–55, 62, 64, 70, 83, 106; and language, 112; and the *Lotus Sutra*, 6, 46, 52–53, 70–71, 133, 210, 221, 223, 225, 229, 238–39; and the *Mahavagga*, 112, 136–37, 148; and Mahayana Buddhism, 5, 52, 70, 111, 132; and the "middle way," 37; and *nirvana*, 54, 70; and transmigration, 70; and the Upanishads, 153; and the Vedas, 148; and *The Waste Land*, 6, 21, 152–53

Vedanta, 9, 21, 45
Vedas: and *brahman*, 138; and the *Brhadaranyaka Upanishad*, 162; and fire, 90,

115, 136; and "The Fire Sermon," 115; and the *Mahavagga*, 148–49; and Romanticism, 39; and Sanskrit, 133; and Schopenhauer, 42; and *upaya*, 148
Vietta, Egon, 1
Vijnanavada, 121
Vinaya Pitaka, 113
Virgil, 9, 96
Virkar-Yates, Aakanksha, 210, 231, 233
Visuddhimagga, 125

Wagner, Richard, 41, 60
Warren, Henry Clarke: and Buddhaghosa, 198; and desire, 118; and the *Digha-Nikaya*, 129; and "The Fire Sermon," 111, 113, 128, 136; and the *Majjhima-Nikaya*, 129; and the Middle Doctrine, 117–18; and "Questions for King Milinda," 126; and the *Samyutta Nikaya*, 123–24; and Theravada Buddhism texts, 37–38; and *upaya*, 132; and the *Visuddhimagga*, 125
Waste Land, The (Eliot): and the Absolute, 82, 152, 174; and *Antony and Cleopatra*, 94; "April," 86–87; and asceticism, 5, 8, 21, 84, 105–6, 111, 143, 153–55, 175; and boredom, 9, 85, 93, 103, 108; and the *Brhadaranyaka Upanishad*, 6, 88, 97, 123, 153–54, 160, 162–63, 175, 177; burial imagery in, 97; and *The Canterbury Tales*, 86; circular structure of, 175; Cleopatra, 85, 93–103, 105; coffers and coffered ceiling in, 94–98, 100–101, 105; and the *Confessions*, 111–12, 143, 145, 149–50, 152; and critical theory, 80; and desire, 5, 8, 85–87, 91, 93, 102, 108, 111, 145, 152, 155–56, 168; domination of others in, 178; ending lines of, 175, 177; endnotes in, 175, 271n64; and "The Fire Sermon," 101, 107, 111, 112–13, 152; fragmentary nature of, 80–81, 83–84; and "A Game of Chess," 94; Indic sources, 3, 31, 84–85; and Jesus Christ, 158; "laquearia," 94,

96; Magnus Martyr Church fragment in, 87; and the *Mahavagga*, 111; and memory, 86–87, 103–4, 111, 152, 154, 156, 168, 174; and metamorphosis, 101–2; and the "middle way," 123; and mysticism, 82; and nothingness, 93, 103–4, 141–42; and Orientalism, 3, 85; and pessimism, 84–85; Philomela's rape in, 98–102, 104; and Schopenhauer, 91–92, 102; and sexual reification, 102–3, 105; single protagonist thesis regarding, 82–84; spider imagery in, 164, 167–68; and syncretism, 78; and telos, 157; and *The Tempest,* 104–5; Thames daughters in, 99, 141–42; and thirst, 156; and thunder, 97, 156, 161, 163–64, 174; and the Upanishads, 150, 152–54; and *upaya,* 6, 21, 152–53; visions and hallucinations in, 155–59, 174, 176; water and rain imagery in, 86, 88, 91, 156, 160–61, 174

Welbon, Guy, 40, 43

Williams, Paul, 275nn73–74

Williams, Raymond, 245n79

Woelfel, Craig, 243n18

Women Beware Women (Middleton), 94, 104

Woods, James, 28, 35, 37, 45, 47–48, 90

World as Will and Representation, The (Schopenhauer), 41, 45–46, 87–88

Yoga Sutras (Patanjali), 90

Ziporyn, Brook A., 224, 280n77

RECENT BOOKS IN THE SERIES
STUDIES IN RELIGION AND CULTURE

Spirit Deep: Recovering the Sacred in Black Women's Travel
Tisha M. Brooks

In Search of Justice in Thailand's Deep South: Malay Muslim and Thai Buddhist Women's Narratives
Edited by John C. Holt, compiled by Soraya Jamjuree, and translated by Hara Shintaro

Precarious Balance: Sinhala Buddhism and the Forces of Pluralism
Bardwell L. Smith

Words Made Flesh: Formations of the Postsecular in British Romanticism
Sean Dempsey

A Language of Things: Emanuel Swedenborg and the American Environmental Imagination
Devin P. Zuber

The Pragmatist Turn: Religion, the Enlightenment, and the Formation of American Literature
Giles Gunn

Rethinking Sincerity and Authenticity: The Ethics of Theatricality in Kant, Kierkegaard, and Levinas
Howard Pickett

The Newark Earthworks: Enduring Monuments, Contested Meanings
Lindsay Jones and Richard D. Shiels, editors

Ideas to Live For: Toward a Global Ethics
Giles Gunn

The Pagan Writes Back: When World Religion Meets World Literature
Zhange Ni

Freud and Augustine in Dialogue: Psychoanalysis, Mysticism, and the Culture of Modern Spirituality
William B. Parsons

Vigilant Faith: Passionate Agnosticism in a Secular World
Daniel Boscaljon

Postmodernism and the Revolution in Religious Theory: Toward a Semiotics of the Event
Carl Raschke

Textual Intimacy: Autobiography and Religious Identities
Wesley A. Kort

When the Sun Danced: Myth, Miracles, and Modernity in Early Twentieth-Century Portugal
Jeffrey S. Bennett

Encountering the Secular: Philosophical Endeavors in Religion and Culture
J. Heath Atchley

Religion after Postmodernism: Retheorizing Myth and Literature
Victor E. Taylor

Mourning Religion
William B. Parsons, Diane Jonte-Pace, and Susan E. Henking, editors

Praise of the Secular
Gabriel Vahanian

Doing Justice to Mercy: Religion, Law, and Criminal Justice
Jonathan Rothchild, Matthew Myer Boulton, and Kevin Jung, editors

Bewildered Travel: The Sacred Quest for Confusion
Frederick J. Ruf

Sacred Claims: Repatriation and Living Tradition
Greg Johnson

Religion and Violence in a Secular World: Toward a New Political Theology
Clayton Crockett, editor

John Ruskin and the Ethics of Consumption
David M. Craig

Pontius Pilate
Roger Caillois

The Value of Solitude: The Ethics and Spirituality of Aloneness in Autobiography
John D. Barbour

Meditation and the Martial Arts
Michael L. Raposa

Between Faith and Thought: An Essay on the Ontotheological Condition
Jeffrey W. Robbins